PITTSBURGH
An Urban Portrait

Franklin Toker

PITTSBURGH

An Urban Portrait

THE PENNSYLVANIA STATE UNIVERSITY PRESS
UNIVERSITY PARK AND LONDON

Library of Congress Cataloging-in-Publication Data

Toker, Franklin
Pittsburgh : an urban portrait.
Includes bibliography and index.
1. Pittsburgh (Pa.)—Description—Tours.
2. Pittsburgh (Pa.)—Buildings, structures, etc.—
Guide-books.   3. Pittsburgh Region (Pa.)—
Description and travel—Tours.   4. Architecture—
Pennsylvania—Pittsburgh—Guide-books.   I. Title.
F159.P63T65   1986   917.48′860443   85-71786
ISBN 0-271-00415-0

Maps drawn by Marlene Boyle

Overleaf: Pittsburgh, from Mt. Washington /*Courtesy University of Pittsburgh*
(Norman Schumm)

For three small Pittsburghers:
Sarah Augusta, Maxwell, and Jeffrey

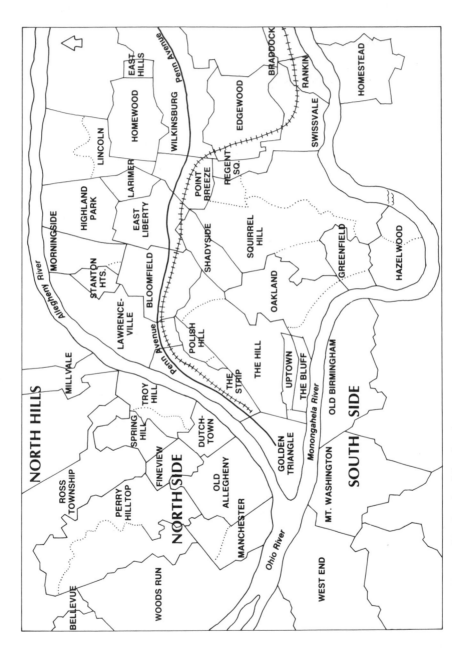

Map 1. The neighborhoods of Pittsburgh.

Contents

A hillside neighborhood: Spring Hill, on the North Side /*Clyde Hare*

Introduction

The chief distinction of Pittsburgh is not smoke, and it never was. There has been no major smoke in Pittsburgh for thirty years, and even when smoke hung thick over the city for a century it was accepted stoically and almost affectionately as the life-sign of its prosperity. Instead, the chief distinction of Pittsburgh is work. As surely as Paris represents glamor, Dallas wealth, and Rome the *dolce vita*, so Pittsburgh stands for industry and production. Always fairly small (its current population is about 400,000, with a metropolitan region of 2.4 million), Pittsburgh is the classic overachiever among American cities. It was a dominant force in world industry for a hundred years through such individual and corporate giants as Carnegie, Frick, Westinghouse, Heinz, the Mellons, Rockwell, Gulf, Alcoa, and PPG. It was Pittsburgh that gave, or rather sold, the world its first mass-produced oil, steel, aluminum, and glass, and it perfected two other techniques that were even more critical to modern life. In Pittsburgh Heinz created the world's first hygienically packaged food and Westinghouse supplied AC electricity to supplement Edison's DC in every corner of the globe. But what Pittsburgh produced went beyond industry. The list of notables in science and the arts who were born here or did some of their best work while living here includes Stephen Foster, John Augustus Roebling, Mary Cassatt, Gertrude Stein, Mary Roberts Rinehart, George S. Kaufman, Rachel Carson, Willa Cather, Martha Graham, Gene Kelly, Jonas Salk, "Mister Rogers," and Andy Warhol.

Justly or not, the staggering productivity that has come out of Pittsburgh is not generally associated with it. Like Andrew Carnegie's several thousand public libraries around the world, Jonas Salk's polio vaccine, George Ferris's carnival wheels, Stephen Foster's songs, Heinz ketchup, or the Rockwell space shuttle, what was produced here belongs no longer to Pittsburgh but to the world.[1] There is a widespread impression also that so much creativity came out of the city that nothing is left but its grimy, worn-out shell—a myth that must puzzle anyone who has visited Pittsburgh in the last twenty years. What visitors find today is one of the delightful cities of America, with a setting of three rivers and a score of hills that rivals the topography of San Francisco. Like its West Coast counterpart, Pittsburgh has a distinctive civic identity. It is a city that speaks its own language: "redd up" for clean, "yuns" for you-all, "gumbands" for elastics, "anymore" for nowadays, "needs fixed," and a hundred other peculiarities of usage and accent (note how Mister Rogers says *umbrella* on television).

Pittsburgh is a cohesive town, and it has always been marked by the gift of synergism. Its early farmers distilled their corn into whiskey in order to transport it to markets over the Alleghenies. Making whiskey required the manufacture of glass bottles, using the local coal; the steel barons later used the same coal (as coke) to fire their blast furnaces. Heinz used Pittsburgh's glass and steel to package his foods, while Westinghouse applied the compressed air of the blast furnaces to power his railroad brakes and switches.

Cohesiveness is the key to Pittsburgh's social life as well as its economic endeavors. The city has one of the highest rates of owner-occupied homes in the nation, a conservative work ethic and a still more conservative family life, a low crime rate, and a passion for sports. The richness of Pittsburgh's social

---

1. This is literally true in the case of Pittsburgh's fabled collections of art, seven of which have left the city. Andrew Mellon's Renaissance canvases and Paul Mellon's modern paintings went to the National Gallery in Washington, Duncan Phillips' exquisite Post-Impressionist art to the same city, Henry Frick's Old Masters to New York, Paul Mellon's British works to Yale, and Louise and Walter Arensberg's Dada and Cubist art to Philadelphia, while G. David Thompson's early modern collection was scattered at auction to museums worldwide. Pittsburgh does, however, retain Andrew Carnegie's matchless collection of dinosaur fossils.

fabric can be seen and not merely read in statistics. Sitting astride its hills and snuggled in its valleys are a chain of ethnic neighborhoods created and preserved by the streams and gullies (Pittsburgh calls them "runs" and "hollows") that form their natural boundaries. There is a substantial Arab community in Oakland. Slavs, Ukrainians, and Russians still predominate on the South Side; Italians on Mt. Washington, in Bloomfield, and in Junction Hollow; blacks on The Hill, in Homewood, and in Manchester; Germans on Troy Hill and Spring Hill; the Polish on Polish Hill; Jews and Episcopalians in Squirrel Hill; and the founding Scotch-Irish in the heavily forested suburbs of Fox Chapel and Sewickley Heights.[2] Pittsburgh uses 720 bridges to bind together districts that are separated by rivers and hills; 1,000 more bridges link

2. Prepositions attach themselves irregularly to the various Pittsburgh hills. One lives *in* Squirrel Hill but *on* Troy Hill and The Hill (part of the city that has definitized its article, along with The Strip, The Hump, The Point, and The Bluff); *in* Mt. Lebanon and Mt. Oliver but *on* Mt. Washington.

The Allegheny County Courthouse /*Clyde Hare*

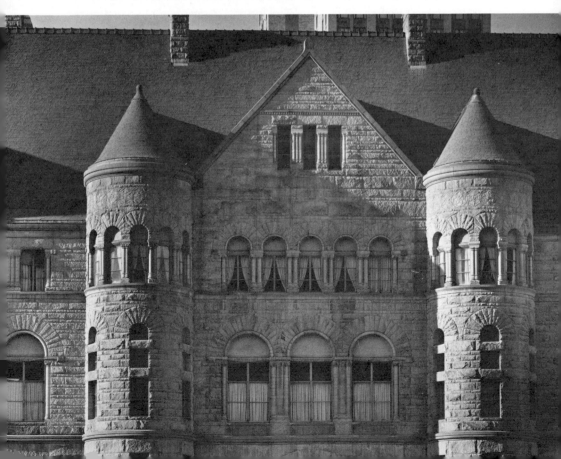

the other 130 communities of Allegheny County that surround the city. The hills and valleys can be inconvenient—the airport, for example, had to be built fifteen miles from the Golden Triangle to secure enough flat land—but they also make Pittsburgh a vibrantly green city, since one-third of it is too steep to be built on and is covered with trees instead.

Pittsburgh's setting is the gift of Nature, but to it are grafted three quantities that are man-made: its industry, its architecture, and the deep affection Pittsburghers have for their city. Pittsburgh industry has always been heroic in scale and complexity, whether producing steel, robots, or spacecraft. Pittsburgh fabricated the steel for Chicago's skyscrapers and engineered the St. Louis Gateway Arch, trained the genius of the Brooklyn Bridge, and helped produce new copper sheets when the Statue of Liberty grew old. A cauldron of smoke by day and of fire by night, the industrial setting left an indelible mark on the native and outside architects who came to build in Pittsburgh. On April 27, 1886, the master architect of America rose from his deathbed and said: "If they honor me for the pigmy things I have already done, what will they say when they see Pittsburgh finished?" The architect was Henry Hobson Richardson, and by "Pittsburgh" he meant his Allegheny County Courthouse and Jail, then as today acclaimed as the outstanding American building of the nineteenth century. Frank Lloyd Wright also built his masterpiece, Fallingwater, near Pittsburgh. Richardson and Wright are just two of several dozen masters whose buildings stand in or near Pittsburgh, together with those of a distinguished local school.

The environment of Pittsburgh is popularly supposed to be raw and masculine, and it does spawn fine quarterbacks—Namath, Unitas, Montana, and Marino come immediately to mind. But it is an environment that nurtures artists in still greater numbers. The region is unusually rich in musicians, painters, photographers, filmmakers, and writers. Among musicians, not only Stephen Foster but Oscar Levant, Lena Horne, Henry Mancini, Billy Eckstine, Errol Garner, Art Blakey, Perry Como, Byron Janis, and Lorin Maazel were born or trained here. George Romero uses the city, affectionately, as the background for most of his horror movies, and the *Pietà* painted in 1933 by John Kane (now in Carnegie Institute) placed the lamentation over the body of Christ in the middle of Pittsburgh's Oakland district. Such unself-conscious identification between an artist and a city parallels the love the medieval painters Duccio and Giotto bore for their hometowns of Siena and Florence, which they too substituted in their paintings for Christ's Jerusalem. Not all Pittsburghers express their urban attachment as artistically as Romero or Kane, but the bond between the city and its citizens is passionate and fierce.

A Note on This Book

It is a sizable gap in American scholarship that this remarkable city—probably the most intensively industrialized spot on earth—has gone largely unstudied. Until recently there was only one book on the buildings of Pittsburgh, while research on other aspects of the city is even more meager. The last comprehensive history of Pittsburgh appeared in 1906, and no full-scale economic, industrial, or social history of the region has ever been issued. In the realm of wider readership Pittsburgh fares no better: the most often cited descriptive book on the city was published in 1964, and its most recent guidebook carries the date of 1916. It is not surprising that the nation and the world still think of Pittsburgh, *if* they think of Pittsburgh, as it was half a century ago.

I began to write this book in 1983 as an urban history of Pittsburgh, but it became apparent at once that a traditional urban history, such as Richard Krautheimer produced on medieval Rome or Harold Mayer and Richard Wade for Chicago, could not be attempted until other studies had filled in the many gaps in our knowledge of Pittsburgh over the past 200 years. What was possible, and perhaps more urgently needed than a study of old Pittsburgh, was a portrait of contemporary Pittsburgh that would paint the broad outlines of how the city developed in the past and fill in details of its urban life today. I took as my models Mary McCarthy's penetrating studies of Florence and Venice, although the paucity of information on Pittsburgh obliged me to research and publish far more detail in my portrait than McCarthy needed for hers.

Like any portrait, this urban portrait can only show what Pittsburgh looks like on the outside, although I have tried to use the outside to reveal much of the inner social and economic life of the city as well. The focus is on existing neighborhoods, streets, and buildings to the exclusion of buildings and complexes no longer standing, but where fragments of old Pittsburgh are still viable, especially in street patterns and neighborhood boundaries, I have tried to trace them back to their origins. The result could be termed a history of the present, rather than a history of the past.

To catch the rhythms of Pittsburgh most closely, I have used the format of a guidebook, with specific itineraries, detailed maps, and new (rather than historical) photographs. I hope some readers will use this as a literal guidebook to Pittsburgh, but I imagine most will use it as a figurative guide. Literal or figurative, my objective is to show how one of America's most notable cities was born and shaped, and how it is reshaping itself today.

I am happy to acknowledge several debts I incurred in conducting research for this book, beginning with one to my students at Carnegie-Mellon University and the University of Pittsburgh (particularly those in a 1984 undergraduate honors seminar there), with whom I developed some of the ideas that appear here. I am indebted to my typist, Genevieve Davidson, and my assistant, Mary Barbour, for their excellent work during the last stages of writing, and to Marlene Boyle for her fine vari-scale maps. I also thank the photographers who are listed in the photographic credits, particularly Maurice Tierney and Pamela Bryan, for their cooperation in providing nearly half the illustrations, along with my own views of the city. Avon Books kindly gave me permission to quote from John Edgar Wideman's *Sent for You Yesterday* (1983).

For their aid in my research I am indebted to the staffs of the Historical Society of Western Pennsylvania, the Pennsylvania Division of Carnegie Library, and the Pittsburgh History and Landmarks Foundation. The last-named kindly gave me access to its recent survey of historic architecture in Allegheny County. For the final version of this book I owe thanks to the Institute for Advanced Study at Princeton, New Jersey, where I completed the revisions; to my publisher, Chris Kentera, and his excellent staff; to David Wilkins, Helen Wilson, and Raymond Gindroz for their close reading of an earlier draft; and to my wife, Ellen, for her constant support. The authors (often anonymous) of thousands of newspaper and magazine articles have helped me create this portrait of Pittsburgh: I trust they will be pleased to recognize their contributions and will regard that as the acknowledgment it would be impossible to give them separately. Pittsburgh itself has been the main supporter of this work through its stimulating environment and the encouragement of friends in a book club, a study group, and my department at Frick Fine Arts. I came to Pittsburgh after directing archaeological excavations for five years in Florence, and it has enriched my life fully as much as that other fabled town. I can only hope that readers who discover Pittsburgh through this book will somehow be enriched as well.

Readers are encouraged to send corrections or emendations to the text to The Pennsylvania State University Press, 215 Wagner Building, University Park PA 16802.

The Triangle and the three rivers /*Courtesy Department of City Planning, City of Pittsburgh (Aerial Data Reduction Associates)*

The Making of Pittsburgh

In the beginning was the land. This, Nature's first and richest gift to Pittsburgh, required 500 million years to prepare. What would one day be Pittsburgh was the highest of a series of stone terraces created from sediment and the fossilized remains of plant life that grew and decayed in the various shifts of the Atlantic Ocean, when periodically the Pittsburgh district would be dry and periodically flooded in a vast swamp that extended throughout the Midwest. Between the layers of sandstone, limestone, and shales, Nature stored away natural gas, some of the world's purest oil, and coal in greater abundance than anywhere on earth. Finally, and almost by caprice, Nature pushed up the Allegheny Mountains about 120 million years ago to ensure that Pittsburgh would mature by self-reliance in isolation from Philadelphia and the East Coast. Fortunately, Pittsburghers knew how to use the land, first growing crops on it, later exploiting the fossil deposits and minerals of western Pennsylvania to fuel its industries. Today, Pittsburgh takes from the land on a worldwide scale: bauxite to make its aluminum, uranium for its nuclear reactors, chromium for its aerospace vehicles.

After the land, Nature gave Pittsburgh the gift of water. Its location at the confluence of the Allegheny, the Monongahela, and the Ohio rivers made it the most central city in North America, with access through the Great Lakes and the St. Lawrence, Ohio, and Mississippi rivers to every part of the continent east of the Rockies. In making these fine waterways for Pittsburgh, Nature moved with uncharacteristic speed. During the last of the ice ages, from about 100,000 to 25,000 years ago, glaciers crept to within forty miles north of Pittsburgh and blocked the flow of a prehistoric form of the Monongahela River, splitting it into the three separate rivers we see today. For thousands of years the Monongahela coursed outside its original banks. Before retreating to its old bed, it eroded a broad plain through what are now the Pittsburgh districts of Braddock, Rankin, Point Breeze, Homewood, East Liberty, Shadyside, Bloomfield, and The Strip. This unique plain cutting through the center of a hilly town prepared an ideal track bed for the Pennsylvania Railroad when it reached Pittsburgh in 1852. The railroad, in turn, transformed the quiet neighborhoods along its path into focal points of settlement for the factories, the workers, and the millionaires of post–Civil War Pittsburgh.

The combination of a rich land and swift-flowing water advanced industry in other ways, too. The Pittsburgh coal seam lay just below the surface of the land, where it was soon exposed by the erosive action of the three rivers. Early industrialists needed only to build chutes into the side of Mt. Washington ("Coal Hill" until 1851) in order to funnel the coal to their glass and iron furnaces at its base. Had the hills met the rivers in steep banks, these industrial installations could have found no room to build in Pittsburgh. Fortunately, each of the rivers eroded broad flatlands or "bottoms" at their banks, almost as though created to the specifications of a modern industrial packager. The Monongahela flatlands became industrialized first, in the mid-nineteenth century: Jones on the south bank, Laughlin on the north. The bottoms on the east and west banks of the Ohio became the industrial centers of Manchester and McKees Rocks. The flatlands on the south banks of the Allegheny became The Strip, tailormade at first for iron foundries and strip mills, and later for the blocks-long fruit and vegetable markets that stand there today. Opposite The Strip, the bottoms along the Allegheny's north bank provided a level site for David Redick in 1788 when he laid out Allegheny City (now the North Side).

A generation earlier, in 1753, a young George Washington had stood at the flatlands of The Point, where the three rivers meet, and exclaimed at discovering the ideal site for a fort that would allow the British to outwit the French in the struggle for control of North America. On that military note, Pittsburgh's recorded history began.

There was considerable interest in the Land at the Forks of the Ohio long before Europeans began to write about it. University of Pittsburgh anthropologists working near Avella, forty-seven miles southwest of Pittsburgh, have determined that paleo-Indians camped at the Meadowcroft rock shelter there for 17,000 years—the longest-known sequence of habitation in the eastern half of North America. We have even more dramatic evidence of building, or at least earth-moving, nearer to our site. Around 1,500 years ago, prehistoric Indians created a huge burial mound over a natural formation at McKees Rocks, just down the Ohio River from Pittsburgh, while the top of Grant's Hill in the Golden Triangle seems to have been used for the same purpose.

The history of Pittsburgh is thus a long one, although it is short in terms of records. The first written accounts of the area came from French, English, and Dutch explorers who made contact with the Delaware, Shawnee, Seneca, and Iroquois tribes who lived here. They, and later Washington, could not have explored western Pennsylvania without the sophisticated network of trails created by the Indians, and these trails still serve today as the basis for nearly all the important highways of the district. But the Indians had left The Point by 1754, when Virginia constructed Fort Prince George at the western apex of what is now the Golden Triangle. The French demolished the little stockade four months later and replaced it with le Fort DuQuesne "under the title of the Assumption of the Blessed Virgin at the Beautiful River." France intended to make its settlement here the nerve center and possibly the capital of an empire that stretched from Montreal to New Orleans. This dream vanished when the British took the little fort in 1758 and replaced it with Fort Pitt, the largest, most costly, and most elaborate fortress constructed by England in the New World. Around it, similarly in honor of England's prime minister, was designated the garrison town of Pitts-borough, or Pittsburgh.

At first the city did not fare as well as the elegant fort. For a quarter of a century it was just a collection of huts and log houses, but in 1784 it was given a proper street plan. By 1786 it had a newspaper (today the Pittsburgh Post-Gazette), and by 1787 it had the beginnings of the University of Pittsburgh. The growth of Pittsburgh produced a flowering of architecture in four main periods: 1790 to 1840, 1840 to 1875, 1875 to 1930, and (following twenty years of relative stagnation) 1950 to today. From 1790 to about 1820 the city's wealth derived primarily from agricultural marketing and the victualing of hundreds of thousands of settlers on their way west. The growth of the city in its mercantile phase was steady but unspectacular: its population at mid-century stood at just over 45,000. Despite widespread destruction in the

Golden Triangle in the Great Fire of 1845 and the obliteration of nearly everything else by later industrial plants, more of early Pittsburgh survives than one might suspect. The restored Fort Pitt and its original Blockhouse of 1764, an 1814 building at the Allegheny Arsenal in Lawrenceville, the Beulah Presbyterian Church in Churchill, and the Burke Building on Fourth Avenue are excellent examples of the late Georgian, Federal, and Greek Revival styles in public architecture. Private architecture survives in even greater numbers: the Martin and Neill log houses in Squirrel Hill, from the 1760s and 1780s; a dozen wood and fieldstone houses in the South Hills and the North Hills; and the two outstanding plantation houses of Woodville (1785), immediately southwest of Pittsburgh, and the Meason House at Mt. Braddock (1802) near Uniontown, about forty miles to the south.

It was in the next period, 1840 to 1875, that Pittsburgh showed a decisive switch from a commercial to an industrial base both in its economy and its architecture. By the 1870s Pittsburgh was the acknowledged "Forge of the Universe," turning out half the glass, half the iron, and much of the oil in the United States. In 1868 the Boston journalist James Parton reported finding 50 glass factories, 16 potteries, 46 foundries, 31 rolling mills, 33 machinery works, and 53 oil refineries in the city—some 500 centers of production in all. Parton gave Pittsburgh its metaphorical title of "Hell with the Lid Taken Off," not to condemn the city (as Lincoln Steffens later used it in his *Shame of the Cities* of 1904) but in amazement at its scale and energy. It was this period also that altered the ethnic composition of the city from predominantly Scotch-Irish with an admixture of German, to the beginnings of the great waves of immigration from Central and Eastern Europe. By 1870 the population was over 85,000.

At mid-century the Pittsburgh architectural idiom switched from the manly and optimistic Greek Revival style to the more fantastic and escapist Gothic Revival, almost as though the convulsive growth and industrialization of those years had induced some inner doubts in the managerial class. Different personal interpretations of Gothic Revival style survive in Trinity Cathedral in the Golden Triangle, in John Notman's St. Peter's Church in Oakland, in Frank Furness's suburban railroad station in Edgewood, and in the four villas inspired by Andrew Jackson Downing at Evergreen Hamlet. In the 1880s Pittsburgh's taste was weaned from Gothic to Romanesque Revival through the impact of Richardson's Allegheny County Courthouse and Jail and his Emmanuel Episcopal Church on the North Side.

But the vital structures of Pittsburgh were its factories, not its elegant churches and public monuments. Here academic architects were pushed aside by builders and engineers who were familiar with the iron and glass that Pittsburgh supplied more copiously than any town on earth. A visitor to Pittsburgh in 1852 commented: "There is a perfect mania here for improvements. Every day somebody commences to tear down an old house and put up a new one with an iron front." In aesthetic and social terms, the industrializa-tion of Pittsburgh was certainly not a change for the better. The recurring cholera epidemics of the 1830s and the Great Fire of 1845 were the results of overcrowding and the placing of living quarters and factories right next to each other. In 1852 Pittsburgh lost Liberty Avenue, its widest and most elegant street, to the tracks of the Pennsylvania Railroad; they remained there until 1906. The unlovely aspect of Pittsburgh was not lost on the writer Willard Glazier, who described Pittsburgh in 1883 much more harshly than Parton had just fifteen years earlier: "Pittsburg is a smoky, dismal city, at her best. At her worst, nothing darker, dingier or more dispiriting can be imagined. The city is in the heart of the soft coal region; and the smoke from her dwellings, stores, factories, foundries and steamboats, uniting, settles in a cloud over the narrow valley in which she is built, until the very sun looks coppery through the sooty haze."

Glazier saw Pittsburgh at the beginning of its third and most notorious age, which ended with the deaths of its two most representative figures, Andrew Carnegie and Henry Clay Frick, in 1919. This was the period of the gigantic manufacturing complexes, which began with Carnegie's Edgar Thomson Steel Works in the Pittsburgh suburb of Braddock in 1873. That mill was emulated by all the major industries, whose factories began to exceed in scale even the immense installations of England and Germany. H. J. Heinz centralized his food-processing operations in seventeen buildings alongside the Allegheny on the North Side, and Alcoa created the world's first complex for the production of aluminum farther up the Allegheny at New Kensington, while the huge glass plants of PPG stood on the opposite side of the river at Creighton.

Westinghouse Air-Brake Works, Wilmerding /*Franklin Toker*

Music Hall Foyer at Carnegie Institute, Oakland /*Courtesy Carnegie Institute*

George Westinghouse commissioned factories of astonishing bulk for his electric works at Turtle Creek, for his air-brake plant at Wilmerding, and for his signaling works at Swissvale.

Around the turn of the twentieth century, the age of heroic industry reached a peak with the building of two spectacular plants: George Mesta created the world's most versatile machinery works at his mile-long plant in West Homestead, and Jones & Laughlin produced a seven-mile-long steelworks downstream on the Ohio at Aliquippa, with a meticulously crafted company town to boot. The heroic era reached a peak in financial terms as well, as the various private cartels transformed themselves into publicly held corporations. In 1901, in an age that knew neither income tax nor severe inflation, Andrew Carnegie sold his steelmaking operations to U.S. Steel for $492,000,000, the equivalent of several billion dollars today. The same transaction made instant millionaires of eighty-nine of his top managers. Even more astute were the brothers A. W. and R. B. Mellon, the prime shareholders in Koppers, Carborundum, and Alcoa, and the virtual owners of Mellon Bank and Gulf, one of the early oil combines.

The first years of the twentieth century were the best and worst of times for Pittsburgh. The city had engorged itself demographically at the same rate that it had engorged financially, greeting the year 1900 with a population of

321,000, or nearly quadruple what it had been thirty years earlier. Thousands of immigrants poured into the region, often recruited directly in the villages of Eastern Europe by agents representing Carnegie and Frick. The city was burgeoning in all its districts: the steelmaking neighborhoods of the South Side, Hazelwood, Lawrenceville, and The Strip were appallingly crowded; the company-run boroughs of Homestead, Braddock, Turtle Creek, McKeesport, and McKees Rocks were little better. Pittsburgh was a black town, particularly in winter. The streetlights were kept burning twenty-four hours a day, and businessmen took two or three clean shirts to the office every morning. It was also a tired town, dispirited with the bloody labor clashes in The Strip in 1877 and Homestead in 1892 and embarrassed by the scathing indictment of social conditions in the Russell Sage Foundation's six-volume *Pittsburgh Survey* of 1909–14. The rates for typhoid fever and industrial accidents in Allegheny County were regarded as the highest in the world. H. L. Mencken later said of Pittsburgh:

> Here was the very heart of industrial America, the center of its most lucrative and characteristic activity, the boast and pride of the richest and grandest nation ever seen on earth—and here was a scene so dreadfully hideous, so intolerably bleak and forlorn that it reduced the whole aspiration of man to a macabre and depressing joke. Here was wealth beyond computation, almost beyond imagination—and here were human habitations so abominable that they would have disgraced a race of alley cats. I am not speaking of mere filth. One expects steel towns to be dirty. What I allude to is the unbroken and agonizing ugliness, the sheer revolting monstrousness, of every house in sight.

It would take half a century for Pittsburgh to reform itself, although some steps were taken around 1900. For the most part, the industrialists and civic leaders at the turn of the century engaged in cosmetic urbanism, commissioning buildings of such splendor that they diverted attention from the real problems of the city. Carnegie led the way by funding an immense library and museum in the Oakland district in 1890. Within two decades Oakland had developed into one of the best City Beautiful complexes in the country, with a huge flower conservatory, two fine university campuses, and a score of public halls and churches. In the same years the business elite built itself five palatial railroad stations—one was by Furness, another by Burnham—and a dozen of America's early skyscrapers. Pittsburghers enjoyed their buildings so much that their favorite deck of cards in 1912 carried the images of fifty-two of them, plus jokers.

Fortunately, the industrialists had an excellent eye for architecture. As a result, Pittsburgh today displays the works of more distinguished architects than any other city in the United States. The list begins with Benjamin Henry Latrobe, the main architect of the Capitol and much of the White House in

Washington, with one building still standing here (others, by Robert Mills, William Strickland, and John Haviland, are lost). It continues with the three most eminent American Victorian architects: John Notman, Frank Furness, and Richardson. From the gilded age of the Beaux Arts style, Pittsburgh preserves buildings by George Post, Ernest Flagg, Peabody & Stearns, Daniel Burnham, Bertram Grosvenor Goodhue, Ralph Adams Cram, and John Russell Pope. Among the distinguished modern architects whose works stand in or near Pittsburgh are Albert Kahn, Frank Lloyd Wright, Walter Gropius, Marcel Breuer, Ludwig Mies van der Rohe, William Lescaze, Harrison & Abramovitz, Skidmore, Owings & Merrill, I. M. Pei, Edward Larabee Barnes, Hugh Stubbins, and The Architects Collaborative. The post-Modern school is represented here in buildings by Robert Venturi, Richard Meier, Johnson & Burgee, and Kohn Pedersen Fox. There are also two extraordinary works—one is a boat—by the master beyond school, Louis Kahn. A few architectural stars are missing from this list, above all Stanford White, Louis Sullivan, and Eero Saarinen, but overall no American city can cite so many designers of prominence.

Along with the imported architects, Pittsburgh has consistently produced its own capable school of designers. Carnegie and Frick, the Kaufmanns and the Mellons, gave their largest commissions to such Pittsburgh-based architects as Henry Hornbostel, Frederick Osterling, Alden & Harlow, Rutan & Russell, and Benno Janssen. All appeared regularly in national architectural magazines, as did the house and apartment designer Frederick Scheibler. Today, several hundred architects make their home in Pittsburgh. Among the firms that enjoy a national

LTV coke works, Hazelwood, with the University of Pittsburgh's Cathedral of Learning in the distance /*Pamela Bryan*

Downtown Pittsburgh, from Oxford Centre /*Maurice Tierney*

reputation are Bohlin Powell Larkin Cywinski, Burt Hill Kosar Rittelmann, Deeter Ritchey Sippel, The Design Alliance, IKM/SGE, Tasso Katselas, Arthur Lubetz, Leonard Perfido, UDA Architects, and Williams Trebilcock Whitehead.

A romantic spirit, often inclined to playfulness, is a prime ingredient of Pittsburgh architecture, whether by local or imported designers, but its two key manifestations are scale and exuberance. The scale derives both from the daunting topography and from the colossal aspect of industry in the Pittsburgh region. George Richardson's 1932 Westinghouse Bridge, with its record-breaking concrete arches, matches the heroic proportions both of the Turtle Creek valley and the miles-long Westinghouse electric works nestled below. A taste for the colossal and exuberant certainly inspired Charles Klauder's 535-foot-high Gothic Cathedral of Learning at the University of Pittsburgh and Benno Janssen's Mellon Institute next door. (At the Mellon, each of the sixty-two columns is a single monolith of Indiana limestone weighing sixty tons. Their weight was so great that steel plates had to be set over the roadway manholes each time a column was brought to Oakland from the East Liberty railroad station.) Colossality and exuberance were the main effects sought and obtained by H. H. Richardson in his courthouse of 1884–88, and they were central to Henry Hornbostel's 1907 project to erect a 700-foot tower on top of the courthouse, so that Richardson's original tower would have served as no more than a crutch to the new building.

While only one building of such mad ambition was erected in Pittsburgh after World War II—the Civic Arena, with its retractable dome—the city's taste for the colossal was evident in the reconstruction work of the Pittsburgh Renaissance. After setting all-time production records during World War II, Pittsburgh in 1945 was an exhausted city, a sure candidate for the slag heap of history. Instead, it reversed its decline the very next year, throwing itself into planning for smoke and flood control, for the first urban redevelopment authority in the nation, for Gateway Center, Mellon Square, a new airport, and a parkway linking the city with the new Pennsylvania Turnpike. Encompassing a score of new skyscrapers and culminating in the U.S. Steel Building of 1971, the Pittsburgh Renaissance spent a half-billion dollars in what still ranks as the most intensive peacetime reconstruction of any city center in history.

Today Pittsburgh is undergoing a transformation still more profound than its postwar renaissance. Its population is much smaller than its 1950 peak of 700,000, and its economy has a wholly different configuration. Thirty years ago Pittsburgh depended on heavy manufacturing. Today only one in five Pittsburgh workers is in manufacturing, and only 5 percent—down from 40 percent—are in steel or other metals. Research and development is Pittsburgh's third largest industry, and several hundred thousand jobs have been added to the local economy in medicine, biotechnology, information and financial services, the arts, and education. Pittsburgh has tightened its grip on third place as a corporate headquarters city for the *Fortune* 500, after New York and Chicago, but many of the corporations have been radically transformed. Westinghouse is a national force in broadcasting and a world leader in nuclear power. U.S. Steel is today primarily an energy and real-estate holdings company. National Intergroup has added banking and pharmaceuticals to its holdings in steel, and Allegheny International has left steel altogether for high-technology and consumer goods. Many firms have entered fields not traditionally associated with Pittsburgh: USAir, the General Nutrition Corporation, Papercraft, and the Hillman Company enjoy leading or dominant industry positions in airlines, vitamins, gift wrappings, and venture capital. A host of new companies compete in high-tech, including one that sells robots to Japan. Pittsburgh looks and feels like a different city, as blue collars give way to white. Stranger still, after a century of vilification, Pittsburgh is now receiving praise: the 1985 Rand-McNally *Places Rated Almanac* listed it as the most livable city in the United States.[1]

In adjusting to new realities, Pittsburgh is carrying out its traditional role as an urban pioneer to the nation. It industrialized first, it became obsolescent first, and it overcame obsolescence first. Pittsburgh was yesterday what Atlanta and Dallas are today: they will be Pittsburgh tomorrow. The critical choice facing postindustrial Pittsburgh is not survival, which it has capably and even brilliantly achieved, but a new meaning for itself. The strength of the old Pittsburgh lay precisely in the fact that it did not care what the rest of the nation thought of it. If, now, Pittsburgh seeks national acceptance, it may be at

---

1. Still, old attitudes die hard. The heading announcing the Rand-McNally findings in the *Washington Post* read: "Pittsburgh? No. 1? Gimme a break!" On television, Johnny Carson said: "Pittsburgh is kind of like Newark without the cultural advantages."

the price of its own remarkable heritage. The old Pittsburgh had terrible economic disparities, but it forged itself by its great labor into one of the most distinctive of world cities. It was a production center, and production (unlike services or the information industry) is tied to a place. The old Pittsburgh *was* a place, and it showed its confidence of place in a hundred ways, including its food, its speech, and its architecture. Whether the new Pittsburgh will be so distinctive is not yet clear, but so long as it is committed to work, its star must continue to rise.

The Golden Triangle

No one recalls who first likened downtown Pittsburgh to a Golden Triangle, but when the term received national publicity in the *Saturday Evening Post* in 1914 it was already long established locally, perhaps for generations. Certainly the 255 acres bounded by Grant Street and the Allegheny and Monongahela rivers are among the most golden in the United States. The Triangle constitutes a city in itself, with its two retail strips on Wood and Smithfield streets, a government center on Grant, a sacred grove of two churches and the Duquesne Club on Sixth Avenue, and even a token sin strip among the cast-iron fronts and Romanesque Revival loft buildings on Liberty Avenue. The compactness of the Golden Triangle is a marvel in its own right. While the rest of Pittsburgh glorifies in bigness, the Triangle takes pride in its miniaturization: no two points in it are more than a fifteen-minute walk away. While it has significantly invigorated the Triangle, the new subway from Grant Street to Gateway Center is so short that its entire route is hardly longer than the subway platform beneath Times Square in New York.

Being so small, downtown Pittsburgh is the preserve of pedestrians and not of cars. In winter, pedestrians tend to stay indoors by using the subway and the tunnels, atriums, and interior streets of the new buildings. During the other seasons pedestrians move outdoors and enjoy Point State Park and the four squares. Of the four, Market Square dates from 1784, but the others are new: PPG Place (1984) is a sort of Place Vendôme, all brittle and classically finished; Heinz Hall Plaza (1982) conveys a touch of the Trevi Fountain in Rome; and Mellon Square is a fashionable period piece from the early 1950s, when "organic" and "modern" were words architects could still use without stumbling. With a half-dozen shopping complexes and four department stores in an area of about fifteen blocks, the Triangle has become one of the liveliest retail centers in the country. "Where else," asks one city planner, "would a W. T. Grant be replaced by a Saks Fifth Avenue?"

Opposite: The Golden Triangle, with the reconstructed Fort Pitt in Point State Park
/Courtesy Greater Pittsburgh Convention & Visitors Bureau (Walter Eiseman)

The Triangle has always been strategic, whether in terms of military, retail, or corporate prestige. The early town of shanties and log huts outside Fort Pitt was deliberately burned by the British commandant to lift an Indian siege in 1763 in the first of many instances of Pittsburgh's urban improvement by fiat. The next year John Campbell (a trader and surveyor who later planned Louisville) created the nucleus of an urban pattern in Pittsburgh in four blocks along the Monongahela riverfront. But there could be no city until the three parties that claimed ownership of Pittsburgh were satisfied: the Delaware Indians in 1768, the Commonwealth of Virginia in 1779, and the heirs of William Penn in 1784. In order to sell their land, the Penns ordered Pittsburgh to be laid out in haste by the surveyor George Woods and his assistant Thomas Vickroy in the early weeks of June 1784. The project was beset with problems: one was the odd shape of the land, with its sudden rise of eighty feet at Grant's Hill, where the Courthouse now stands; a second was the surveyor's chain, allegedly one inch too long in every ten feet; and a third was the squatters, who used their muskets to persuade Woods to lay streets around rather than through the houses they had illegally put up. Woods compromised by creating a triangular town, with one street grid parallel to the Allegheny, another parallel to the Monongahela, and an urban hemorrhage where the two clash on Liberty Avenue. The plan had its faults, but its tight, neoclassical geometry has kept the Triangle dense and lively for 200 years, and it saved downtown Pittsburgh from the sprawl common to many American cities.[1]

The Woods plan is the sacred cow of Pittsburgh. Since 1784 its only significant deviations have been the suppression of three streets at Gateway Center and of two short blocks at Oliver Plaza and PPG Place. Although the plan of the Golden Triangle remained static, its building coverage changed with every generation. The Triangle comprised almost the whole of Pittsburgh until the 1830s, but during the next half-century newer districts grew up around it, and it lost its industrial plants, its housing, and its main churches to them, while it took on its present character as the corporate center of Pittsburgh. Around 1890 there was a brief rivalry between the Triangle and the Oakland district, with Andrew Carnegie favoring the latter, but fortune returned to the Triangle with the flood of cash unleashed on Pittsburgh by the

---

1. It is ironic that the region that epitomized *laissez-faire* in America had such enthusiasm for the planning of cities. Pittsburgh was laid out six years before Washington and was followed by Allegheny City (1788), the Utopian communities of the Harmony Society at Harmony (1805) and Economy (1824), John Augustus Roebling's nearby Saxonburg (1832), America's first romantic suburb at Evergreen Hamlet (1851), and the industrial towns of Natrona (1850), George Westinghouse's Wilmerding (1890), Frederick Law Olmsted's Vandergrift (1896), and Jones and Laughlin's steel town of Aliquippa (1907–12). On a smaller scale but no less remarkable were Clarence Stein's world-famed Chatham Village on Mt. Washington (1932) and Walter Gropius's Aluminum City Terrace at New Kensington (1941). The creation of these towns suggests that Pittsburgh's leaders had nothing against planning so long as they were in charge of it.

creation of U.S. Steel in 1901. What might be termed the real-estate War of the Three Henrys followed: Carnegie's partner Henry Frick erected four skyscrapers on Grant Street; a second partner, Henry Oliver (and his estate), developed a block of holdings along Sixth and Oliver avenues; while a third partner, Henry Phipps, created five more buildings near the intersection of Sixth Street and the Allegheny riverfront. The Mellons, who owned more of the Golden Triangle than any of the steel tycoons, followed with a half-dozen buildings of their own: Mellon Bank (1924), skyscrapers for Koppers and Gulf around 1930, and two buildings on Mellon Square in the early 1950s. No Renaissance pope could have carved up Rome more effectively.

While the Golden Triangle developed itself internally, it also extended its dominance over the rest of the Pittsburgh metropolitan district by making itself the focus of all the roads in Allegheny County. This octopus configuration began to take shape with the arrival of the railroad in 1852, but its real impetus came in the first years of the motorcar, around 1900. The head of city planning, Edward Manning Bigelow, created Schenley and Highland parks and four elegant carriage roads (Schenley Drive and Bigelow, Beechwood, and Washington boulevards), which made the residential districts of Oakland, Squirrel Hill, Shadyside, Point Breeze, and Highland Park into organic extensions of the Triangle.

Around 1910 Frederick Law Olmsted, Jr., designed a fifth road—built in 1922–27 as the Boulevard of the Allies—to show off the glory of the Monongahela Valley as Bigelow Boulevard had earlier highlighted the Allegheny. It was followed by the Liberty Bridge and Liberty Tunnels to the new suburbs south of the Monongahela River and two other commuter roads to the suburbs of the Ohio and Allegheny river valleys. The final tentacle to the octopus (how many commuters must see it that way!) was the Penn-Lincoln Parkway of the 1950s, which connected Pittsburgh to the Pennsylvania Turnpike on the east and the new airport on the west. The Parkway, the Crosstown Expressway, and the rehabilitation of The Point had all been articulated in a 1939 master plan drawn up by New York's Robert Moses. The expansion of the high-tech industrial parks along the expressways in the 1970s and 1980s has altered but not overthrown the hegemony of the Golden Triangle over the city and the county.

The remaking of the Triangle during the Pittsburgh Renaissance of the 1950s was a closely held process, guided by Richard King Mellon and Mayor David Lawrence with a largely self-taught staff under Park Martin, Wallace Richards, and John Robin. The third upgrading of the Triangle in the 1980s (the so-called Renaissance II) has, by contrast, been a technocratic rather than an autocratic process, with Mayor Richard Caliguiri, the Allegheny Conference on Community Development, and the Urban Redevelopment Authority acting as godfathers instead of gods. The results are nevertheless extraordinary by any measure: the subway, the rebuilding of Grant Street, the

Lawrence Convention Center, Liberty Center, Oxford Centre, Mellon Bank Center, PPG Place, Chatham Center II, Fifth Avenue Place, and the Consolidated Natural Gas tower in the Triangle, with spin-off developments in The Strip, Firstside, the South Side, and the North Side—in all about five times as much building as in the original renaissance of a quarter of a century ago. The Triangle's current state of health is excellent: where it leads, the rest of Pittsburgh is sure to follow.

The Point and Gateway Center

On that low point of land, fringed now with steamboats and covered with grimy houses, scarcely visible in the November fog and smoke, modern history began.

So wrote James Parton in his astute observations on Pittsburgh in the 1868 *Atlantic Monthly*. The case can be made that the three events that took place at **Point State Park** and **Gateway Center** were as crucial to history as the events in Boston harbor, Independence Hall, or the Capitol at Williamsburg, for what happened at The Point was not merely of national but of world importance. Here North America was secured for the British and not the French; here, a century later, the industrial might of the world was secured for the United States and not Europe; and here began the most dramatic urban rebirth of any industrial city in history. The Point shows it all today. On the fifty-nine acres bounded by Stanwix Street and the Allegheny and Monongahela riverbanks stand twelve office and residential towers, four bridges over land and water, two military strongholds, and one of the world's tallest fountains. The views across the water west, north, and south of The Point capture the spirit of the Industrial Revolution at Pittsburgh, while east of The Point stands Gateway Center, which in 1950 gave birth to the modern history of Pittsburgh. Indeed, without Gateway Center the city might not have had a modern history at all.

Fort Pitt and the Blockhouse

Fort Pitt was intended to be the Gibraltar of the New World, and its construction became the first great thing Pittsburgh did. When the military engineer Captain Harry Gordon devised it in 1759, he had the benefit of three centuries of expertise on fortifications, going back to Renaissance Italy. The principle was clear: create as many pointed bastions as possible in order to deflect cannon fire from direct broadside hits on the long sides, and extend the bastions far enough to pin down enemy snipers should they approach too close to the curtain walls. Gordon's solution was elegant and grandiose: a pentagon half a mile in perimeter, with bastions at each angle. Inside, a parade

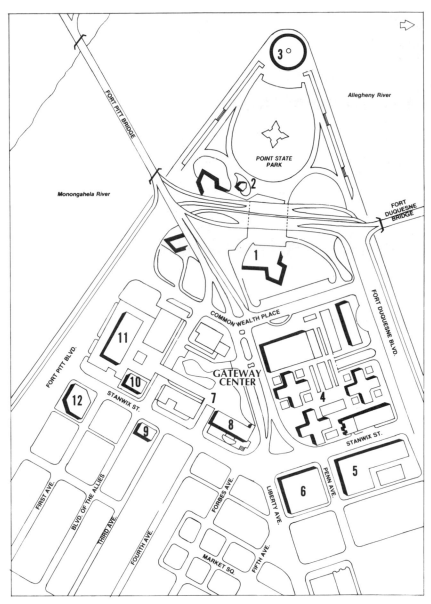

Map 2. The Golden Triangle: The Point and Gateway Center

1 Fort Pitt
2 The Blockhouse
3 Point State Park Fountain
4 Gateway Plaza

5 Horne's
6 Fifth Avenue Place
7 Equitable Plaza
8 Four Gateway

9 St. Mary of Mercy Church
10 United Steelworkers
11 Westinghouse
12 Riverfront Center

The Fort Pitt Blockhouse
/Franklin Toker

ground with casemates, magazines, and housing for 1,000 men; outside, a moat with a drawbridge and an earthen embankment. The walls were nearly fifteen feet high and seven and a half feet thick, of solid stone faced with 1,244,160 bricks. The bricks were made locally, the stone was quarried locally, and the timber was planed at a stream in Pittsburgh's West End that is still known as Saw Mill Run.

Luckily, the greatest fort England ever built in the Western Hemisphere was put to the test only once, in Pontiac's War of 1763, for despite its elegance it had major problems: its two river-oriented bastions were only earthworks and eroded badly in the spring floods, and none of the bastions was effective against snipers. Dismayed by this poor performance, Colonel Henry Bouquet constructed three blockhouses in 1764—one remains—as redoubts to catch snipers in a deadly crossfire. When the French threat diminished, however, the fort was allowed to tumble into ruins within a generation. When architect Charles Stotz rebuilt two bastions of Fort Pitt in the 1950s, he used archaeological observations for the plan and all details of his reconstruction, but he wisely avoided earthworks. Inside, he created the **Fort Pitt Museum** (1972), with a set of dioramas on both the military and early industrial history of Pittsburgh. The pentagonal **Blockhouse,** many times modified, still stands opposite the fort, with its original sandstone base, a complete rim of wooden girders, and coursed, common-bond brick walls. Iron cranking plates in the walls support the upper floor, and the diminutive building bears a (modern) pyramidal roof of wooden shingles. This glimpse into American colonial history is the oldest structure in Pittsburgh.

The Point Fountain and Bridges

By 1836 so much of Fort Pitt had been vandalized that even the last vestiges of its earthen ramparts were gone. A few voices were raised to suggest that The Point could be laid out as a fine park for a city that had none, but the fate of the site was sealed in 1854, when the Pennsylvania Railroad built a freight depot over it. It was not until nearly a century later, in 1946, that the city and state agreed to redevelop The Point for joint use as a historic park and an office complex. Frank Lloyd Wright (commissioned by department store owner Edgar J. Kaufmann) made a breathtaking proposal for a circular mega-structure thirteen levels high and one-fifth of a mile in diameter, with a helical auto ramp four and a half miles long. Pittsburgh shied away from this vision of the future, but it did adopt Wright's ideas for a colossal fountain at The Point and for twin bridges crossing the rivers close by. George Richardson, who engineered the **Fort Pitt Bridge** over the Monongahela (1959) and the **Fort Duquesne Bridge** over the Allegheny (1968), was a world master of bridge design during his forty-year reign in Pittsburgh. He and his partner, Ben Gordon, in collaboration with Charles Stotz and Ralph Griswold, the architect and landscape architect of Point State Park, transformed the potentially ugly overpass connecting the two bridges into a luminous portal of three paper-thin stretched barrel vaults. The tensioning of the prestressed reinforcing rods in the concrete vaults was so complex that final calculations were personally overseen by the celebrated Swiss bridge builder Eugène Freyssinet just before his death in 1962.

The eye-catching element in Point State Park turned out not to be its restored fort but its **fountain.** All the planners who had eyed The Point for a hundred years imagined some culminating element here: Wright saw it as a fountain, but for Robert Moses it was a shining beacon, and for other visionaries it was a colossal steelworker, or the legendary Joe Magarac, or an allegorical Meeting of the Waters.[2] What emerged in 1974 (designed by Stotz, Hess, MacLachlan & Fosner, with GWSM, Inc., as landscape architects) was an enormous man-made geyser that normally jets about 150 feet high but can rise to challenge all aquatic records at over 300 feet. It spews 6,000 gallons of water a minute from a 100,000-gallon hidden reservoir that is fed in turn by a glacial formation fifty-six feet below ground (the so-called fourth river, beloved of Pittsburgh trivia quizzes). The fountain was not the only way to accentuate The Point, but since the old Pittsburgh had its columns of fire and smoke, there is some appropriateness to its beguiling play of waters as the symbol and beacon for the cleaned-up city of today.

2. Legend has it that Magarac (Slovak for "jackass") was the strongest steelworker in Pittsburgh. He would measure the consistency of a ladle of molten steel by tasting it, and he ended his life by leaping into a blast furnace to upgrade the quality of its iron ore.

Gateway Center

Gateway Center (consisting of **Gateway Plaza,** 1950–53, and **Equitable Plaza,** 1955–68) was more than a postwar investment by the Equitable Life Assurance Society. It was a leap of faith in the future of Pittsburgh, and, in a way no longer imaginable, it was an electrifying demonstration of the healing power of modern architecture. It was particularly a leap of faith for such Pittsburgh corporations as J&L Steel, PPG Industries, People's Gas, and Westinghouse, who signed leases at Gateway Center without so much as a picture of the buildings they were promising to move into. Conceived in 1947, **One, Two,** and **Three Gateway** were among the world's most talked-about buildings following World War II. The architects were Otto Eggers and Daniel Higgins, with Irwin Clavan; Clarke & Rapuano were the landscape architects. The design of these cruciform towers represented a tug-of-war between the traditionalists Eggers and Higgins, former partners of John Russell Pope (Eggers was also a major force in building the Pentagon), and the more progressive Clavan, who in the same years designed cruciform-tower housing estates in New York on the model of Le Corbusier's 1922 towers-in-the-park scheme for Paris. Between seven and fifteen cruciform towers were originally projected, in traditional brick and limestone. At the last minute the designs were respecified for stainless steel, but scarcities during the Korean War required that chrome-alloyed steel be substituted.

When building resumed across Liberty Avenue at Equitable Plaza, the landscape architects Simonds & Simonds used more informal site planning, although a continuous podium makes it more difficult to enter from the adjoining streets. Every June, the Three Rivers Arts Festival takes over its checkerboard terrace and vine-covered arbors for a fortnight of exhibits and performances that attract more than half a million participants. The Bell Telephone Building and the Pennsylvania State Office Building on the plaza are dull office slabs, but the bold shape of the long glass tower and the stainless-steel service core of **Four Gateway** (Harrison & Abramovitz, 1960) are fine expressions of the abstract style of the 1950s. Four Gateway was Harrison & Abramovitz's third and best-received office building in Pittsburgh. After it opened they were rewarded with another half-dozen commissions in the city and became its semi-official court architects.

Fifth Avenue Place and the Joseph Horne Company

Gateway Center had only Rockefeller Center and a few other precedents in large-scale commercial site planning. One of the criticisms that was made of it (in Jane Jacobs's *The Death and Life of Great American Cities* and elsewhere) is the way it turned its back on the larger city. **Fifth Avenue Place** (Stanwix St.,

Left: Gateway Center: Four Gateway on the right /Maurice Tierney ▪ Right: Fifth Avenue Place (Hugh Stubbins, architect), with the Joseph Horne Company store at left /Courtesy Jenkins-Empire Associates

Penn, Fifth, & Liberty Aves.; The Stubbins Associates, with Williams Trebilcock Whitehead, 1985–87) will become the first building in thirty-five years to create a visual link to the Gateway complex, rather than shy away from it, as PPG and Riverfront Center do. The building will be the headquarters of the Hillman Company, which finances high-style construction across the continent. In keeping with that corporate image, Fifth Avenue Place will be a distinctive and colorful entrance portal to the city from the airport. Its luxuriously appointed shopping arcade will be part of that same image, as well as a commemoration of the Jenkins Arcade that long stood on this site in the homespun dress of the old Pittsburgh.

Opposite Fifth Avenue Place stands one of the best remnants of old Pittsburgh—the **Joseph Horne department store** (NE corner Stanwix & Liberty; W. S. Fraser, 1892; Peabody & Stearns, 1902 and 1922). The exterior is handsome in a conventional Beaux Arts way, while the interior is truly fine. The high Tuscan Doric columns with gilded bead-and-reel and egg-and-dart moldings are beautifully articulated and fitted into the ceiling module. The effect is a cross between Versailles and a parking garage, big and airy enough to make it into a genuine social meeting place. The elaborate brass window surrounds at ground level are not there just for show: Horne's was devastated by the St. Patrick's Day Flood that struck Pittsburgh in 1936 and afterward created these fittings so that enormous brass plates can be shut over the windows to create a vacuum and keep the Allegheny out, should it ever rise again.

United Steelworkers, Westinghouse, and Riverfront Center

The United Steelworkers Building (formerly IBM; SW corner Allies & Stanwix; Curtis & Davis, 1964) is the main monument to organized labor in Pittsburgh, which is the city of its birth in the United States. (The Iron & Steel Workers Union of 1876 founded the predecessor to the American Federation of Labor here in 1881.) It is also a landmark in skyscraper architecture. From its birth in Chicago in the 1880s, the dogma of skyscraper construction was that the exterior walls supported nothing. This dogma held fast for three-quarters of a century until shattered by this Gateway building, which was rented for a decade by IBM and is now owned by the United Steelworkers. U.S. Steel, as supplier and fabricator of the steel, and the design firm of Curtis & Davis of New Orleans knew that they were making structural history here, and they confidently publicized it during construction by painting the three different types of steel in the outside walls red, white, or blue to designate their different structural roles in the bearing wall. The thirteen-story diamond-faceted walls covered in stainless steel have a floating quality, particularly at night, when the structure appears to hover over its heavy concrete base.

Stanwix Street: St. Mary of Mercy and the United Steelworkers Building
/Franklin Toker

The Steelworkers Building faces the brick **St. Mary of Mercy** church (William Hutchins, 1936) on the diagonally opposite corner of Allies and Stanwix. Behind it is a renovated older building shared by the *Pittsburgh Press* and the *Pittsburgh Post-Gazette*, and toward the Monongahela shore stands the **Westinghouse Electric Corporation** world headquarters (NW corner Stanwix & Fort Pitt Blvd.; Harrison & Abramovitz, 1968), a trial run for the same architects' U.S. Steel Building a few years later. This dark gray anodized aluminum slab is less remarkable in design than the exemplary research centers the company built in the 1950s and 1960s in the Pittsburgh suburbs of Churchill and Monroeville, but it is technically distinguished by its pioneer integration of the lighting, heating, and air-conditioning systems, and by having the world's first talking elevators—by Westinghouse, of course.

Skidmore, Owings & Merrill took a more informal approach to corporate architecture in its **Riverfront Center** for National Intergroup (SE corner Stanwix & Fort Pitt Blvd.; 1983), which is a skewed hexagon wrapped in sunscreens of Italian travertine. The appearance of sunscreens in Pittsburgh marks the final confirmation of the efficacy of its stringent pollution controls: in the old Pittsburgh few people worried about overexposure to the sun.

Market Square and Central Downtown

The **Market Square** district consists of some twenty blocks in the heart of the Golden Triangle. Market Square was once the center of Pittsburgh, and it remains an intriguing relic of the old city, together with the High Victorian Gothic storefronts along its neighboring streets. But the history of Pittsburgh is written out in other parts of the central downtown, too: in PPG Place; Firstside, with its cast-iron and Romanesque Revival depots along the Monongahela; and the eclectic skyscrapers on Fourth Avenue that speak of Pittsburgh's immense wealth at the turn of the century.

Market Square, the only open space in the 1784 plan of Pittsburgh, was the setting for a courthouse, a city hall, and a sequence of market buildings until 1961. Historically, the square (Pittsburghers called it the diamond) was always meant to be paved and built on, not green and open as it appears in its present pseudo-restoration. Its perimeter buildings summarize Pittsburgh's architectural history and include Gallagher's Pub and Ryan's Ale House (2 & 3 Market Place) from the Civil War era, a fragment of Philip Johnson's glassy PPG Place, and a Tudor Revival Burger King. Two of the better citizens of the square are **Nicholas Coffee** and the **1902 Landmark Tavern** (23 & 24 Market Place; restoration by UDA Architects, 1982). The former displays a tall Chippendale front crowned by a neon coffee cup with aroma wafting out: this joking reference to Philip Johnson's Chippendale-topped AT&T Building in New

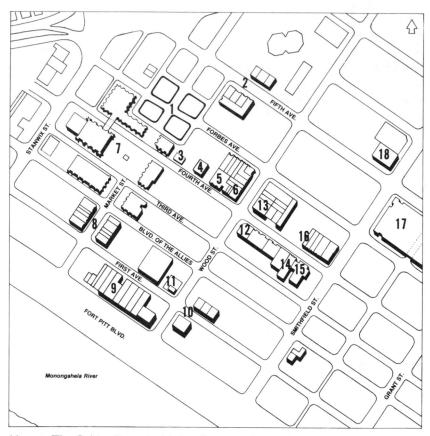

Map 3. The Golden Triangle: Market Square and central downtown

1 Market Square
2 Victorian buildings, Fifth Ave.
3 Burke Bldg.
4 Benedum-Trees
5 Investment Bldg.
6 Arrott Bldg.

7 PPG Place
8 Storefronts on Market St.
9 Cast-iron buildings, Ft. Pitt Blvd.
10 Beaux Arts buildings, First Ave.
11 Watson-Standard Bldg.
12 Union National Bank

13 The Bank Center
14 Magee Bldg.
15 Dollar Bank
16 Industrial Bank
17 Kaufmann's
18 Park Bldg.

Left: Market Square: Nicholas Coffee and the 1902 Landmark Tavern /*Courtesy UDA Associates* ▪ *Right:* 214–218 Fifth Avenue and the Buhl Building /*Franklin Toker*

York serves also as an efficient device to give height to the facade and thus monumentality to an urban gathering place that needs it.

If the architectural fare is somewhat timid on Market Square, it is decidedly eccentric in the storefronts densely packed on Fifth Avenue to the north. Two particularly good examples of retail and office blocks from the early twentieth century are the **Buhl Building** (205 Fifth Ave.; Janssen & Abbott, 1913), decked out in ebullient blue and cream terra-cotta plaques, and the **100 Fifth Avenue Building** (originally the Diamond Savings Bank Building; SE corner Fifth & Liberty; MacClure & Spahr, 1904). Twelve stories high and topped by the finest surviving Beaux Arts copper cornice in the city, this handsome block bends backward from its central entrance to fit one of the small triangular lots of the 1784 city plan. The block adjoining the Buhl Building to the east represents an earlier generation of buildings constructed during or just after the Civil War. The double-unit commercial structure at **214–218 Fifth Avenue** is an Italianate cast-iron front from the 1860s or 1870s, with large glass panes and floral interlace designs stamped out by the iron molds. Diagonally opposite, at 213 Fifth Avenue, stands the **Floyd Building,** a handsome Ruskinian Gothic concoction topped by parti-colored brick and sandstone trefoil arches. Complementing this pyrotechnical display of High Victorian style is a delightful storefront in the Art Deco mode of the 1930s at **221–225 Fifth Avenue.** Its ground floor has been modernized, but the original stainless-steel mullions above make a fine contrast with the spandrel zones of porcelain tiles laced with floral ornament.

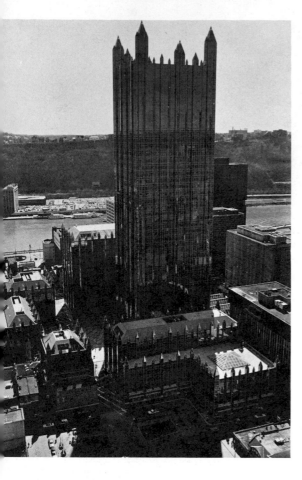

PPG Place and Market Square /*Courtesy*
Pittsburgh Post-Gazette (*Mark Murphy*)

PPG Place

The construction of a world headquarters for PPG Industries in 1979–84
between Third and Fourth avenues, south of Market Square, was so important
to the architecture and urbanism of downtown Pittsburgh that one tends to
think of the history of this area as either pre- or post-PPG. **PPG Place**
occupies five and a half acres in a complex of eight elements and six city
blocks. The central element is a half-acre open plaza, with a forty-story glass
tower in front of it and five uniformly detailed low-rise structures around it.
Between the tower and the Gateway complex on Stanwix Street lies the three-
story Wintergarden hall, while an atrium below Two PPG Place is home to a
score of restaurants and specialty shops. Everything is sheathed in uniform
mirror glass—20,000 pieces of silver PPG Solarban in the tower alone.

Pittsburgh Plate Glass was founded in 1883, just half a block from where it
is today, and it is now the largest producer of glass in the world, as well as a

giant in paints, plastics, and chemicals. When the company cast its eye on Market Street in 1979 with a view to building a headquarters tower at its place of birth, it knew that it would be relatively easy but profitless to buy the single half-acre that it required for its own needs. It wanted to upgrade the whole district in the manner of Rockefeller Center and so purchased an area ten times larger in order to create not just a tower but a small universe. The creation of PPG Place was an act of outstanding generosity by an American corporation toward its home city. It was also a daring move, both in the financial and the political risks involved in securing such a large amount of land, and for the unconventional choice of a post-Modern Gothic design. This was only the second time (Johnson's AT&T headquarters was the first) that an American corporation had chosen fantasy over International School sobriety for its public image, although in the end it got both.

The main precedent for Philip Johnson and John Burgee's design was the Victoria Tower at the Houses of Parliament in London, which reaches to half of PPG's height of 635 feet, but there is also a specific local precedent in Charles Klauder's Cathedral of Learning at the University of Pittsburgh. Johnson's tower is a brilliant apparition when seen from outside the Triangle—for example, from West Park on the North Side—but unlike Klauder's tower, which has a rich variety of surface and texture, PPG cannot escape being monotonous at close range. The interior, with its towering lobby and repetitive arches, is particularly unyielding, although handsome in its deep red glass paneling. Despite these blemishes, PPG Place is the best contribution to the Pittsburgh skyline since Richardson and Klauder. Those few who are truly unhappy with Johnson's glass tower should not throw stones, and certainly not inside the lobby, where closed-circuit television cameras watch from behind one-way glass.

Firstside

Just a few steps south of PPG Place, across the Boulevard of the Allies, lies **Firstside,** an old and finely scaled district of ten blocks along the Monongahela waterfront. Here, between Stanwix and Market streets, are the four oldest blocks in Pittsburgh, the survivors of John Campbell's provisional town plan of 1764. The character of Firstside was shaped by the Great Fire of 1845, which leveled most of it, and by the 1922 aggrandizement of Second Avenue into the Boulevard of the Allies. The resulting traffic flow cut Firstside off from the rest of downtown and so, paradoxically, preserved it.

The oldest and architecturally the most consistent block left in the Golden Triangle is the **100 block of Market Street,** between the Boulevard of the Allies and First Avenue. The block begins with the former **St. Clair Hotel** (1870) in Second Empire style, complete with turret and mansard roof, at the southwest corner of Market and Boulevard of the Allies. Behind it are two dense rows of commercial structures, with residential lofts on the top floors. These buildings are mid- and late nineteenth-century substitutes for those lost in the fire of 1845, but their Greek Revival idiom and the density of this short block produce the illusion of a streetscape from the earliest days of town.

Whatever fate held in store for Pittsburgh in 1784, George Woods was sure it would be linked to the Monongahela, and so he drew most of the downtown lot lines as narrow strips on the numbered avenues parallel to the Monongahela shore. In consequence, scores of buildings, particularly in Firstside, have double facades because they stretch from one avenue to another. This is the case in the **200 block of Fort Pitt Boulevard,** between Market and Wood, where a dozen of the best old commercial buildings in town front on both the Monongahela shoreline and on First Avenue. Here, until 1955, stretched a broad wharf, where hundreds of steamboats once picked up and disgorged passengers and freight. (The steamboat and barge trade was so voluminous at Pittsburgh that for a century the city claimed to be the world's busiest inland port; in some quarters it still does.) The **Conestoga Building** (NW corner Fort Pitt Blvd. & Wood St.; Longfellow, Alden & Harlow, 1890) got its name because the westward pioneers bought their covered wagons in the Conestoga

The Monongahela waterfront, with the Wood-Allies Garage /*Maurice Tierney*

district of Lancaster County and rode them across the Alleghenies to Pittsburgh, where they embarked by boat for the West.

Most of the structures on the shorefront predate the Conestoga by a generation, and several feature cast-iron fronts. Two good examples from the mid-1870s, **235–237** and **239 Fort Pitt,** mix Italianate and High Victorian Gothic detailing in their facades, which were bolted to the traditional brick and wood structures behind them. West of this pair, at **229,** is a beautifully restored Italianate brick and stone facade. In 1984 Louis D. Astorino Associates transformed a nondescript three-story warehouse at **227** into a four-story, post-Modern evocation of the oriel fronts that were common on Pittsburgh's streets a century ago.

Wood Street

Wood Street unfolds its architectural character block by block from the Monongahela shoreline to Liberty Avenue, giving the archaeological stratigraphy of post-fire Pittsburgh in miniature. One block inland from the river, at the corner of Wood and First Avenue, stand four Beaux Arts skyscrapers: the **West Penn Building** (14 Wood St.; Charles Bickel, 1907); **100 Wood Street,** in the style of Louis Sullivan's disciples Purcell and Elmslie; and **311** and **321 First Avenue,** with matching facades on the Boulevard of the Allies. All four buildings, as well as the earlier and less astute Conestoga, typify the Pittsburgh spirit as the city that saw itself as the halfway point and the synthesis of Chicago and New York, with the power of the first tempered by the urbanity of the second.

At the northwest corner of Wood and First stands what may be the oldest of Pittsburgh's dozen cast-iron fronts, the **Watson-Standard Building** of around 1860. Despite its over-restoration in 1983, the Gothic facade of Watson-Standard was the partial inspiration for the design of its immediate neighbor, the **Wood-Allies Garage** (224 Blvd. of the Allies; Burt Hill Kosar Rittelmann Associates, 1984), a nine-level steel-deck cage that begins with a red neo-Romanesque brick base and ends as a parody of the fake-Gothic pinnacles of PPG behind it.

After two blocks that are predominantly Beaux Arts in character, Wood Street switches its architectural code at the Boulevard of the Allies to the Art Deco of **Point Park College** (Janssen & Cocken, 1929), a twenty-one-story failed athletic club and failed hotel that is now a leading college for the performing arts. The predominant style switches again at Third Avenue, to the International School lines of the **YWCA** (Skidmore, Owings & Merrill, 1963), and again at Fourth Avenue for the mid-Victorian storefronts at 409, 411, 413–415, and 417 Wood Street. The orange metal-clad McDonald's closing the sequence of these five blocks at the corner of Forbes Avenue makes one appreciate the solid value of Wood Street's architecture all the more.

Left: The Burke Building and PPG Place /*Franklin Toker* ▪ *Right:* Fourth Avenue: the Investment, Arrott, and People's Savings Bank buildings /*Franklin Toker*

Fourth Avenue

The two-block stretch of Fourth Avenue from Market to Smithfield, intersected at mid-point by Wood Street, was once the gathering place for the dozen banks in which Pittsburgh stored its enormous profits in oil, iron, glass, and steel in the years when it was second only to New York in terms of amassed capital. Today Pittsburgh still has important banks, and it ranks fourth among the financial centers of the United States, but only two of its banks are headquartered on Fourth Avenue, and the oil and stock exchanges that once animated the street were torn down years ago. Most of the old buildings are still standing, however, and Pittsburghers use them for dining, shopping, and dancing; one of the old bank vaults now specializes in the storage of computer tapes.

As the oldest commercial building and the only unmutilated Greek Revival structure downtown, the **Burke Building** (209 Fourth Ave.; John Chislett, 1836) has seen it all. It stood for a decade before the Great Fire skirted it by a few feet in 1845. The patrons were the Irish-born lawyers Robert and Andrew Burke; the architect, John Chislett, had been born in England in 1800 and was trained in the neoclassical tradition in Bath. He came to Pittsburgh around 1833 and reigned as the dominant architect in the early Victorian city. His concept for the Burke Building was more domestic than commercial: a brick structure faced in sandstone, Doric columns *in antis* by the door, and a four-square plan with fireplaces and a central stair hall. With windows elongated almost to doors in the manner popularized by Jefferson and Bulfinch, it is uncompromisingly elegant.

The sight of the Benedum-Trees, Investment, and Arrott buildings eyeing each other on the short block of Fourth Avenue below Wood calls to mind the fortified towers of medieval Bologna or San Gimignano, but in formal terms the effect is syncretic, not antagonistic. The basic rhythm for the group was set by Frederick Osterling in his **Arrott Building** (1902), at the northwest corner of Fourth and Wood. Osterling (1865–1934) was a prolific, quarrelsome, and sometimes brilliant designer for nearly half a century in Pittsburgh. His range of styles included Richardsonian Romanesque, Classical Revival, and Modern Gothic. His design for the Arrott insurance magnates demonstrates the usual academic sequence of a large-scale base intended for retail purposes, a "shaft" of office floors in rusticated brick patterning, and a cap of four stories with tall arched windows and an exuberant copper cornice. The lobby inside is a superb mix of marble, mosaic, and brass.

Three years after Osterling, Thomas H. Scott designed the Machesney Tower at 221 Fourth Avenue, later renamed the **Benedum-Trees Building** for the two oilmen who bought it. Besides Osterling's tower, Scott had to contend with two powerful neighbors across the street in Frank Furness's long-destroyed Farmers' Deposit National Bank of 1884 and George Post's Bank of Pittsburgh. (Constructed in 1896, Post's bank fell in the 1940s, but its front columns were resurrected in a cemetery in Pleasant Hills.) At nineteen stories, Benedum-Trees was only slightly lower than the Arrott, and it clearly responded both to the Arrott and to the Bank of Pittsburgh in its dramatic base of Corinthian columns and oriel windows, the aggressively vertical terra-cotta shaft, and its enormous overhanging entablature complete with lions and florid curved brackets.

John Donn's **Investment Building** (formerly the Insurance Exchange; 239 Fourth Ave.; 1927), the middle skyscraper of the group, is a generation younger than the towers left and right of it. Its brick shaft is a total abstraction without ornament, but at the top the corners are sliced away to reveal a set of elegant obelisks, powerful enough to catch the eye of Philip Johnson when he designed a neoclassical obelisk for the PPG plaza just down the block.

The Bank Center (414 Wood, 317 Fourth & 314–318 Forbes Ave.) is a recycling of a recycling. These six buildings were sewn together once in 1902, again in 1926, and a third time in 1976. The oldest of the six are the **Freehold Building** (93–95 Fourth), a Chicago School product of 1893 in brick and brownstone, and the **Real Estate Trust Company,** with only the surviving trace of a Palladian arch, at 311–315 Fourth Avenue. These were joined in 1901 by Alden & Harlow's **People's Savings Bank** (now a branch of Pittsburgh National Bank; 307 Fourth, NE corner Fourth & Wood), a fifteen-story tower that competes with and mirrors Osterling's Arrott tower across the

Stairwell in the People's Savings (Pittsburgh National) Bank /*Maurice Tierney*

street. Like the Arrott, it breaks down into an imposing granite base of three stories, a ten-story brick shaft, and a two-story cap. The structure would be competent rather than remarkable except for a brilliantly handled semicircular stairwell inside and raised brick panels that are scattered in random distribution outside, giving the building the appearance of a decaying Roman ruin.

In 1902 Frederick Osterling cut sideways through the block to create a fourth building, the **Colonial Trust Company,** with twin Albertian facades on Fourth and Forbes avenues and (allegedly) the world's longest bank lobby in between. Osterling stretched the duo into a trio in 1926, when the lobby was extended as a T shape with a severe Ionic facade at 414 Wood. The sixth and last piece of the puzzle fell into place the next year, when Press C. Dowler created a link on Wood Street between the People's Bank tower and the Colonial Trust facade. The Bank Center was born in 1976 as a project to create a shopping mall out of these six buildings. The Argentinian-born designer Rodolfo Machado, then working for the IKM Partnership and teaching at Carnegie-Mellon University, created a cool minimalist scheme that was widely praised but underfunded, and what we see today is a later, mediocre recycling. While the original old buildings still have the power to fascinate, the 1970s renovation is already old hat.

Banking on Fourth Avenue

The south side of the 300 block of Fourth Avenue from Wood to Smithfield

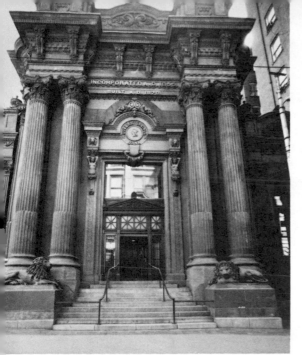

Left: Dollar Bank /Courtesy Dollar Bank ▪ Right: The former Industrial Bank and Union Trust /Franklin Toker

streets was built up as a sequence of four banks and a newspaper office, and it survives today as a fine parade of bankers' clothing. The three banks at the southern end of the block are the **Union National Bank** (306 Fourth Ave.; MacClure & Spahr, 1906), the **Commonwealth Trust** (312 Fourth; Frederick Osterling, 1907), and the **Keystone Bank** (324 Fourth; MacClure & Spahr, 1903), all of which are now amalgamated as the Union National Bank headquarters. They are predictably sober except for the beautifully articulated Keystone Bank, where a light court was recessed in the facade and garlanded above by a bridgelike arch. The upper end of the block is, by contrast, anything but sober. It speaks volumes about American social and business attitudes to compare the efflorescence of the Dollar Bank of 1871 at the top of the block to the straitlaced Union National at the bottom.

Dollar Bank (348 Fourth Ave., SW corner Smithfield; Isaac Hobbs & Sons, 1871; wings, 1906) is the ultimate in public-relations architecture: a building that is all doorway. The red sandstone facade features a sumptuous pair of double columns guarding the door with the help of two dozing lions. Isaac Hobbs, the designer, was a fashionable Philadelphia architect and architectural publisher whose conception of the bank shows at once what was both splendid and hopeless in Victorian architecture. The ornament is vigorous, learned, and delightful, but the essential lines of the facade are drowned by the Baroque and Italianate details that are heaped on in the manner of a Victorian tea service. This imbalance of the part and the whole would be the problem to occupy H. H. Richardson, who was just beginning his architectural career as this bank went up. Osterling, Richardson's pupil-from-afar, captured the simplifying ability of his "master" reasonably well next to Dollar Bank in the **Magee Building** (346 Fourth; 1890) for the *Pittsburgh Times*, with a facade enlivened by fine grotesque carvings.

The solid line of buildings on the north side of the 300 block of Fourth Avenue has been broken by a parking lot, but even so it neatly demonstrates how distinctive structures can flourish within the wider unity of a city block. The flagship of the upper block is the **Standard Life Building** (originally the Pittsburgh Bank for Savings; 345 Fourth; 1903), which Alden & Harlow were building at the same time as their People's Bank tower at the lower corner of the block. They dressed this one as they had the other, in deep red Roman bricks and terra-cotta plaques, and further encouraged the two skyscrapers to "talk" to each other by exaggerating the detail in the upper floors, particularly the elephantine voussoirs over the top windows. To the left of Standard Life is the much lower Richardsonian Romanesque facade of the **Fidelity Trust Building** (341 Fourth; 1889) by James Steen. The earliest building of the group, the Fidelity Trust begins well with a base of two massive arched doors and a dwarf mezzanine of three rectangular openings with colonettes, but in the upper floors the facade changes rhythm at almost every level, as though slices of six different buildings had been inexplicably piled together.

A decade after the construction of the Fidelity Trust, in 1898, Daniel Burnham came to Pittsburgh at the behest of Henry Clay Frick to build the small **Union Trust Company** next door, at 337 Fourth. This was the first of some twenty projects Burnham started in Pittsburgh (seventeen were realized—more than he created for any city except his native Chicago). It is a conventional Greek temple front, with a podium of deeply channeled blocks and severe Doric columns above.

Next door to Burnham's monument, the Pittsburgh architect Charles M. Bartberger built the more accomplished **Industrial Bank** (333 Fourth; now a bar) in 1903. Bartberger was the German-trained son of the prolific German-born Charles S. Bartberger (or Barthberger), who was Pittsburgh's major architect from around 1853 to 1880. His bank appears to synthesize three great monuments of neoclassicism that were popular models for Beaux Arts architects in America around 1900: Nicholas Hawksmoor's St. Mary Woolnoth in London (1716–24), Claude-Nicolas Ledoux's salt storehouse at Chaux (1783), and Peter Speeth's Women's Prison in Würzburg (1810). For dramatic effect, Bartberger capriciously overscaled such elements as the penultimate triglyphs, which suddenly and irrationally droop down onto the masonry surface. Every element of the facade "speaks" as well as looks the part it was meant to play: the public banking hall below is marked by the two-story sweep of the entrance arch, and the boardroom above is denoted by the incisive punctuation of its fat colonettes. Finally, Bartberger was subtle and

112 and 110 Smithfield Street
/*Franklin Toker*

amusing in his contextual references. The single perky acroterion on his
pediment mimics the five that Burnham used with dour seriousness next door,
while the combination of arch below and dwarf mezzanine above is a tribute
to the same feature in Steen's Fidelity Trust two doors away. The Industrial
Bank design was Bartberger's finest hour. Perhaps he knew it. At any rate, when
the opportunity came, he seized it.

Smithfield Street was born as a cross-street like Wood, but when it received
its bridge connection to the South Side in 1818 it became richer and larger
scaled, and its small old buildings were cannibalized into larger new ones.
There are, nonetheless, some worthy survivors. One is Edward B. Lee's elegant
Adam-style **Americus Club** (now the Pitt Building; NW corner Blvd. of the
Allies & Smithfield). Built in 1918, the clubhouse was amputated on its left side
four years later in the construction of the Boulevard of the Allies. Two more
lively survivors stand at **110** and **112 Smithfield:** the first is an 1881 High
Victorian Gothic commercial block with all the pugnacity of a particularly
revolting piece of Eastlake furniture, but it is marvelous in the sparkle of its
blue, red, and light brown tiles; the second is the L-shaped former home of
Engine Company No. 2. This ex-firehouse is three stories tall, with a
bleached white granite base and two stories of beautifully dressed sandstone.
Its authorship is unknown, but it seems to have been built at the same time as
its neighbor and refaced in 1901 with a set of Art Nouveau arches.

Kaufmann's Department Store /*Courtesy Kaufmann's*

Kaufmann's Department Store and the Park Building

The intersection of Smithfield Street and Fifth Avenue, the busiest in town, is also among the more handsome, with **Kaufmann's Department Store** and the old Mellon Bank headquarters on the east corners, and the Park Building and the classicizing Swindall-Rust headquarters (the old Frank & Seder department store) on the west. The key building of the four is Kaufmann's, both for its social importance and as a prime recollection of three remarkable figures: Edgar Kaufmann, Benno Janssen, and Frank Lloyd Wright. Morris, Henry, Jacob, and Isaac Kaufmann arrived in Pittsburgh from Germany around 1860, and by 1871 they had a flourishing trade on the South Side. In 1885, the year Morris's son Edgar was born, they built the "Big Store" at the corner of Smithfield and Fifth. The corner of the store now standing at Smithfield and Forbes was built in 1898 by Charles Bickel, and it purloins motifs from the Romanesque and Classical revivals, as well as from the Chicago School of Louis Henry Sullivan and his colleagues. In 1913 Edgar Kaufmann took charge of the firm and had Benno Janssen design a new terra-cotta block to replace the 1885 store at the corner of Smithfield and Fifth. That same year Kaufmann purchased the first of 1,500 acres for a country retreat near Pittsburgh that is now world-famous as Fallingwater. An extension by Janssen on Forbes Avenue at Cherry Way followed a few years later, then in 1930 Janssen lavishly modernized the whole ground-floor interior in Art Deco style, with piers of

Park Building (George Post, architect): the telemones /*Courtesy* Pittsburgh Post-Gazette (*Harry Coughanour*)

black Carrara glass and murals by Boardman Robinson. Critics regarded it as the most beautiful store in America—as well as the most profitable.[3]

The glass and murals are gone now, and so too is the office that Wright built for Kaufmann in 1936 and 1937 (the same years as Fallingwater) on the store's tenth floor. Wright designed the furniture and paneling for this sumptuous suite, including a cypress plywood mural, and he selected the wall fabrics himself. The office served Kaufmann for twenty years, until his death in 1955, when it was dismantled. After another twenty years of temporary installation in Pittsburgh, it was donated to the Victoria and Albert Museum in London.

3. Janssen (1874–1964) is undeservedly forgotten today. He was born to a German-American family in St. Louis, enrolled at the Ecole des Beaux-Arts in Paris in 1902, and soon after came to work in Pittsburgh. Janssen was the best academicist Pittsburgh ever produced, on a par with or superior to Carrère & Hastings, Trumbauer, Adler, Pratt, and the host of others who took care of America's very rich before and after World War I. Kaufmann and the Mellons were his best clients: Kaufmann gave him nearly a dozen commissions and even lived in Janssen's own home in Squirrel Hill before ordering a new house from him in Fox Chapel.

Edgar Kaufmann is also undeservedly neglected today as a patron of architecture. He commissioned buildings from Janssen, Wright, Richard Neutra (a winter house in Palm Springs, California), Joseph Urban (a swimming pool at the Irene Kaufmann Settlement on The Hill), and the important Pittsburgh architect Dahlen Ritchey (the Civic Arena on the Lower Hill). After Janssen retired in the 1930s, Kaufmann switched his architectural allegiance to Wright, who he knew through the involvement of his son Edgar, Jr., with the Taliesin Fellowship. Together Wright and Kaufmann planned Fallingwater in 1935–37.

Overall, Kaufmann was Wright's outstanding patron. Their partnership lasted twenty years and yielded nearly a dozen uncompleted projects in addition to the two that were realized. These included Wright's Broadacre City models, which were exhibited at Kaufmann's store, his extensive sketches for a megastructure at The Point, a Rhododendron Chapel near Fallingwater, Kaufmann's winter house (next to the one built by Neutra), a hillside apartment for Mt. Washington, a Pittsburgh planetarium, and a parking garage next to the Kaufmann store on Smithfield Street. Although disappointingly little came of it, the partnership of Wright and Kaufmann was one of the most intense collaborations of artist and patron in architectural history.

George Post's **Park Building** has stood as a Pittsburgh landmark diagonally opposite Kaufmann's for nearly a century. It was Pittsburgh's fourth steel-cage skyscraper, following the Conestoga and Carnegie buildings, and its neighbor at 335 Fifth Avenue (the Hamilton Building of 1889, now unrecognizable behind the crude aluminum facade of the Landmark Savings Association). Post's patrons were David and William Park, brothers who were steelmen and major investors in Pittsburgh. The site was appropriate: the Pittsburgh Iron Foundry was built here in 1805, and here were cast the cannons that Commodore Perry fired on Lake Erie and Andrew Jackson used at the Battle of New Orleans. For the Parks, Post basically recast his earlier Havemeyer Building in New York, but the Pittsburgh product was substantially more interesting. The base is simplified and strong, the shaft of nine identical middle floors is well articulated by the corner windows, and the two-story entablature of engaged Composite columns with the thirty telemones above could not be more effective. The telemones are cast in terra-cotta and originally were polychromed. Pittsburgh has always loved them, perhaps because these mythological creatures straining at their work monumentalize the hard physical labor that for so long characterized the city's work force.

The Sixth-Oliver and Penn-Liberty Corridors

There are two distinct corridors in the Golden Triangle: one along Sixth and Oliver avenues, connecting Mellon Square and Oliver Plaza; the other involving nine blocks of Penn and Liberty avenues, parallel to the Allegheny riverfront. The **Sixth-Oliver corridor** is august: it features the Mellons and the scarcely less prominent Olivers, the Duquesne Club, two of Pittsburgh's oldest churches, Brooks Brothers, Saks, and Gimbel's. The **Penn-Liberty corridor,** on the other hand, has always carried the slightly bawdy or at least the lively cast of a port, which for two centuries it was. In 1760 it became the western terminus of the Forbes Road to central Pennsylvania, and by 1820 it was the terminus of the new turnpike to Philadelphia—a competitor to the National Pike, which had bypassed Pittsburgh.

In 1829 the first barges reached Pittsburgh on the Pennsylvania Canal, which was Pittsburgh's answer both to the Erie Canal of 1825 and the B&O Railroad of 1829. (The canal was an enormously expensive and almost mad scheme to link Pittsburgh to the Atlantic Ocean through rivers, canals, and funicular railway portages over the Allegheny Mountains; the classic description of it is in Charles Dickens's *American Notes* of 1842.) Later, in 1852, Pittsburgh became the western terminus of the Pennsylvania Railroad. Until

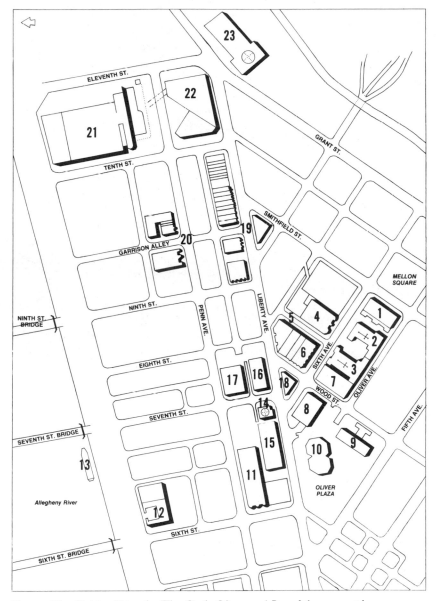

Map 4. The Golden Triangle: The Sixth-Oliver and Penn-Liberty corridors

1 Oliver Bldg.
2 Trinity Cathedral
3 First Presbyterian Church
4 Duquesne Club
5 Coffey Way
6 Granite Bldg.
7 300 Sixth Avenue
8 One Oliver Plaza
9 Pittsburgh National Bank
10 Two Oliver Plaza (Equibank)
11 Heinz Hall and Plaza
12 Fulton Bldg.
13 American Wind Symphony Barge
14 Keenan Bldg.
15 Consolidated Natural Gas
16 Clark Bldg.
17 Benedum Center
18 PAT headquarters (subway)
19 Victorian buildings, Liberty Ave.
20 Penn Ave. department stores
21 Lawrence Convention Center
22 Liberty Center
23 Penn Station

the railroads declined in the 1950s, the Penn-Liberty corridor was the dominant center of the hotel, entertainment, and wholesale trades in Pittsburgh.
After a generation of neglect, Penn-Liberty has come back to life, with
exhibitions at the Lawrence Convention Center and music and theater at
Heinz Hall, the Benedum Center, and the Fulton Theater.

Sixth Avenue

The **Sixth-Oliver corridor** is perfect in its symmetry, with Mellon Square to
the east and Oliver Plaza to the west, two Daniel Burnham skyscrapers at the
ends of the block, two venerable churches in the middle, and an Indian burial
ground on its central axis. The burial ground originated in a small hillock that
must have been one of the few dry spots in the Triangle when the Allegheny
River regularly flooded it each spring. The French, knowing the Indians had
used it, took it over for their own burials from 1754 to 1758. (Virgin Alley, a
name that caused such embarrassment in Pittsburgh that it was changed to
Oliver Avenue in 1917, was the sanctified way leading to the cemetery—the
Allée de la Vièrge.) The British and Americans added more graves still, so that by

Trinity Cathedral and graveyard, and
the Oliver Building /*Courtesy* Pittsburgh Post-Gazette (*Bill Levis*)

the time of the last burial in 1854, 4,000 recorded bodies and probably ten times that many unrecorded ones rested here. When the Penn heirs carved up the town in 1784, the sacredness already attached to Sixth Avenue made it the obvious choice for the three free lots they doled out to the Episcopal, Presbyterian, and German-Evangelist congregations. The Presbyterians and Episcopalians are still on the block 200 years later; the German and Evangelist congregations are only a few hundred feet away.

Henry Oliver, one of the Scotch-Irish managers who led Pittsburgh to dominance in the age of industry (he controlled the fabulous Mesabi iron-ore range), reaped millions from J. P. Morgan's buy-out of Carnegie Steel in 1901, and he proceeded to invest it downtown. Before he died in 1904, he commissioned Daniel Burnham to build a department store at the lower end of this block. Oliver's heirs commissioned the **Oliver Building** on Mellon Square from Burnham in 1908–10 as a memorial to the industrialist. Burnham produced a wider, deeper, taller version of his building for Henry Clay Frick of a few years earlier. Its base of grayish-pink granite Doric columns is well, if coldly, handled, while the main facade above is a mass of cream terra-cotta covering a full acre and a half on the Smithfield Street facade alone. The cap to the building consists of three stories of banded Corinthian pilasters and an exuberant cornice line 347 feet in the air. The interior decoration is carried out with similar élan: white marble with dark splashes of bronzework in the lobby and Honduras mahogany trim in the offices upstairs. The heirs were satisfied enough to ask Burnham for still more buildings, including a memorial bathhouse next to the Oliver ironworks on the South Side (still standing, but not by Burnham). These properties were later capitalized into the realty holding company that built Oliver Plaza sixty years later.

Trinity Cathedral and Graveyard, and First Presbyterian Church

Trinity Episcopal Cathedral and **First Presbyterian Church** are two Gothic Revival monuments with impeccable design pedigrees. Trinity's first and second churches of 1787 and 1805 were a block away; the third church (1824) was built on this site by the rector, John Henry Hopkins, who publicized it in his "Essay on Gothic Architecture" of 1836. The present Trinity Cathedral (1872) was designed by Gordon W. Lloyd, a Detroit architect who was English-born and English-trained, both in the older archaeological school of Pugin and in the newer, more rhetorical Gothic of Sir George Gilbert Scott. The influence of Scott would explain the bold massing of the octagonal spire over the Trinity tower, but the interior is decidedly American and assimilates several features of the late style of Richard Upjohn, to whom the church has occasionally been attributed. Trinity is a ravishingly austere building inside, with compound piers and archivolts of gray stone standing out against the cream white walls and a series of deep brown diaphragm arches soaring across the nave. If Gordon Lloyd was this good (and not even his obituary suggested that he was), all honor to him!

First Presbyterian, on the opposite side of Trinity's graveyard, is the successor church to one that was redesigned and expanded by Benjamin Henry Latrobe in 1812, and to a later Gothic Revival design by Charles S. Bartberger at mid-century. The architect of the present building, Theophilus P. Chandler, Jr., was a practiced Philadelphia architect with excellent social connections both there and in Boston. In Pittsburgh he was the favored architect of the Thaw family, and he was called to design three Presbyterian churches here. His challenge at First Presbyterian Church in 1905 was to make the church look good against the backdrop of Trinity and to uphold Presbyterianism in the most intensely Presbyterian city in the country. His response was a much more showy design than Trinity's, with double towers in front and a fantastic march of gables and pinnacles on the side aisle flanking the cemetery. The interior is distinguished by its rich and structurally daring woodwork and by fourteen stained-glass windows by Tiffany—outstanding even in a city that abounds in some of the best stained glass in the country.

There is a host of good architectural neighbors to the two congregations on Sixth Avenue. The open-air pulpit in front of First Presbyterian, an unusual medieval feature, points directly across the street at the most powerful of these, the **Duquesne Club** (325 Sixth Ave.; Longfellow, Alden & Harlow, 1889; Alden & Harlow, 1902; Janssen & Cocken, 1931). The club moved here in 1879, six years after its founding, and a decade later erected its present Richardsonian Romanesque brownstone facade (the segregated women's entrance on the right is now in disuse). Inside the Duquesne Club are scattered fifty-four dining rooms, mainly private suites maintained by the major Pittsburgh corporations.[4] Next door is the **Granite Building** (formerly the German Savings Bank; 301–313 Sixth Ave., NE corner Wood; Bickel & Brennan, 1890). The most sumptuously textured building in the city, this Romanesque Revival bank mimics H. H. Richardson's every stylism and becomes a fairly tedious catalogue of all the shapes and textures granite can come in.

The dank and unappealing **Coffey Way** alongside the Duquesne Club got its name from John Arbuckle's 1865 coffee-roasting works, among the first in

4. The role played by the club in the development of Pittsburgh since 1873 can be exaggerated, but not by much. One explanation offered for the peculiar bunching of skyscrapers in certain parts of the Triangle is that the corporate C.E.O.'s prefer not to build too far from the clubhouse on Sixth Avenue. In a study of civic leadership in Pittsburgh, Arnold J. Auerbach polled the Executive Committee of the Allegheny Conference on Community Development in 1958, with these results: twenty-four of the twenty-five members belonged to the Duquesne Club, nineteen to the Mellon-centered Rolling Rock Club at Ligonier, and thirteen to the Fox Chapel Golf Club. All, needless to say, were Republicans.

the world. When Arbuckle's building was torn down around 1936, workmen cemented a set of patriotic roundels from the old factory to a brick wall at the end of the alley on the left. They are Pittsburgh's oldest surviving public sculptures and represent Washington, Lincoln, and Liberty, plus one unidentified.

The **300 Sixth Avenue Building** (SE corner Wood; Daniel Burnham, 1904) completes the Sixth Avenue sequence as the counterpart terra-cotta slab to the Oliver Building. It served for a generation as McCreery's Department Store, then from the 1940s to the 1960s as the Spear & Company store. Not a particularly strong design to begin with, the building was further compromised by an unsympathetic rehabilitation. The new base did, however, include one superb feature: the electrically illuminated stained-glass mural of an ironworker (called *The Puddler,* by the Harrington Carved Glass Company of New York, 1942), which is one of the prime icons of the city.

The Sixth-Oliver corridor has three complementary Beaux Arts buildings in the adjoining block, between Oliver and Fifth avenues. One is the old **Third National Bank** (now Bell Savings; SE corner Oliver & Wood; Daniel Burnham, 1904), an exquisite small bank that is well maintained. Not so fortunate are the old **White Dog Café** at 308 Oliver Avenue, a charming Tudor vernacular restaurant by Alden & Harlow of around 1905, now badly mutilated as the

Left: The Duquesne Club, Granite Building, PAT headquarters, and Keenan Building /*Franklin Toker* ▪ *Right: The Puddler,* Wood Street at Sixth Avenue /*Franklin Toker*

Left: Oliver Plaza: Pittsburgh National Bank, Equibank, and One Oliver towers /*Courtesy Equibank* ▪ *Right*: Heinz Hall: the Grand Lobby /*Courtesy Heinz Hall for the Performing Arts*

Charles M. Schwab brokerage house; and Alden & Harlow's **Farmers' Deposit Bank** of 1903, at the northeast corner of Wood and Fifth, which is likewise almost unrecognizable in its modernization. Today, the bank tower that once was praised as one of the most handsome in America is called only by its address, 301 Fifth Avenue, as though no one wanted to own up to it.

Oliver Plaza

The closing of the tail end of Oliver Avenue from Wood to Liberty in the 1960s created a trapezoid block on which now rise three tall towers, whose tenants include such major Pittsburgh corporations as Pittsburgh National Bank, Equibank, Allegheny International, Copperweld, and Dravo. The first tower, William Lescaze's **One Oliver Plaza** (1968), is a thirty-eight-story glass and steel box standing on a base of dark granite. At the Fifth Avenue end of the block, the **Pittsburgh National Bank Building** (Welton Beckett Associates, 1972) replaced an Italian Renaissance tower that Daniel Burnham erected for a PNB predecessor, the First National Bank. Pittsburgh National was conceived as a glass slab, with an extruded service core that is clad in pearl-gray granite. It does its job well, but it makes one question architectural obsolescence to realize that PNB, at thirty stories, is merely three floors higher than the 1912 tower it replaced.

Two Oliver Plaza (Equibank), by Skidmore, Owings & Merrill, was squeezed between the two earlier towers in 1976. Although handicapped by weak linkage to the streets in front and behind it, Equibank is an elegant solution to its cramped site: two interlocking octagons of mirror glass. The geometry relates well to its low-rise neighbor at **606 Liberty Avenue** (the former Meyer and Jonasson department store; MacClure & Spahr, 1910), which, in turn, got its odd polygon shape because it conformed to the old course of Oliver Avenue before it was plugged at Wood Street. After Equibank, a fourth office tower was projected for this same block by the famed Argentinian-American designer Cesar Pelli, but it has yet to be built. The newest addition to Oliver Plaza is instead the bright but minuscule **TIX,** a ticket kiosk for cultural events that was designed by Albert Filoni of Mac-Lachlan, Cornelius & Filoni in 1984.

Sixth Street

Sixth Street is not to be confused with Sixth Avenue, but many people do. It is only two blocks long—half of it occupied by parking garages—but it is a lively street because it links Oliver Plaza and Liberty Avenue with the North Side area across the Allegheny. Its critical building is **Heinz Hall** (NW corner Sixth St. & Penn Ave.), whose rehabilitation first breathed life into the Penn-Liberty corridor after years of decline. Marcus Loew's sumptuous fake-Rococo Penn Theater (C. W. & G. L. Rapp, 1926) opened here in the glory years of vaudeville and the movies, but it lost its clientele and went dark in the mid-1960s. The restoration funded by the Howard Heinz Endowment and carried out by Stotz, Hess & MacLachlan in 1971 was a spark for the performing arts all over Pittsburgh. Under the careful tutelage of William Steinberg and André Previn and with the world's largest orchestra endowment—estimated at $60 million—the Pittsburgh Symphony joined the top rank of American orchestras.

Pittsburgh responded hungrily to its cultural and architectural offerings, and **Heinz Hall Plaza** (MacLachlan & Fosner, 1982) was created alongside as a second amenity a decade later. The restoration of Heinz Hall was not faultless, but it caught the right mix of Hollywood theatricality and contemporary performance needs. Ornamental terra-cotta was newly fabricated for the exterior, while inside one of the world's leading acousticians, Heinrich Keilholz, molded five tons of plaster into an acoustical reflector over the stage. Opera, ballet, and musicals were so well received that the Heinz-backed Pittsburgh Trust for Cultural Resources has embarked on the restoration of the nearby Fulton and Stanley theaters for the overflow.

The Sixth Street Bridge /*Joel DeGrand*

The link between Sixth Street and the North Side evidently fascinated Henry Phipps, who commissioned five office towers on or near the Allegheny shoreline between 1900 and 1930. Phipps was a poor North Side boy who grew rich with his neighbor Andrew Carnegie. In 1901 he abandoned Pittsburgh for New York after selling his Carnegie Steel shares to J. P. Morgan, but—rare for Gilded Age Pittsburgh—Phipps had a conscience. He built flower conservatories on the North Side and in Oakland, established a fine natatorium here in the Golden Triangle, commissioned a rent-subsidized model apartment block for his old North Side neighbors, and gave a fortune for tuberculosis research to Johns Hopkins University in Baltimore.

The pull of his old roots was surely Phipps's motive in constructing all his commercial investment buildings in full view of the North Side. (Old-timers swear that Phipps had in mind two more buildings for the north shore of the Allegheny, which would have cemented the whole district as his personal fief.) Phipps's Bessemer and Manufacturers' buildings, the latter incorporating the natatorium, have been lost to parking garages, but the **Fulton Building** (107 Sixth St.; Grosvenor Atterbury, 1906) still stands. The Fulton's open-mouth arch seven stories high (a restatement of the Dorilton Apartments facade in New York) is witty and perfect for a "portal" building into Pittsburgh; its shape undoubtedly influenced the open bracing of the Sixth Street Bridge when it was rebuilt in 1925. The Fulton is distinctive, too, in its obvious debt to Louis

Sullivan for its ornament and in the disarming luxury of its marble-clad, skylit lobby. The gloriousness of this space seems to have suggested the next move for Phipps and his clan: first Pittsburgh, next Manhattan, and then their greatest building coup, as kingpins in the Florida land boom of the 1920s.

Pittsburgh's "Three Sisters," the **Sixth, Seventh,** and **Ninth Street bridges** (Vernon Covell et al., engineers; Stanley Roush, architect; 1925–28) over the Allegheny form one of the lyrical sights of the city. The original Sixth Street Bridge dated from 1819; its replacement, by John Augustus Roebling, stood here from 1859 to 1892, after which there was a third bridge from 1892 to 1925.[5] Some fragments of the north abutment of Roebling's structure are still imbedded in the existing Sixth Street Bridge, which was rebuilt with its companions as part of a massive highway and bridge program that made

5. Roebling came from Germany to the Pittsburgh area in 1832 because he predicted that it was going to become the center of the industrial world. He created a communal settlement at Saxonburg, twenty-five miles to the northeast, but he was drawn to Pittsburgh by his invention of wire rope, which was first used on the portage railway portion of the Pennsylvania Canal, east of Pittsburgh. In 1845 Roebling used the wire rope again in Pittsburgh for the world's first suspension aqueduct bridge. He later tested both the wire rope and his engineering acumen in three other spectacular demonstrations in Pittsburgh: his Smithfield Street Bridge (1846), his Sixth Street Bridge (1859), and his cables for the Monongahela Incline on the South Side (1869). After these tests in Pittsburgh and elsewhere, Roebling was ready to build his great bridge in Brooklyn.

The American Wind Symphony Barge (Louis Kahn, architect) /*Courtesy American Wind Symphony (Herb Ferguson)*

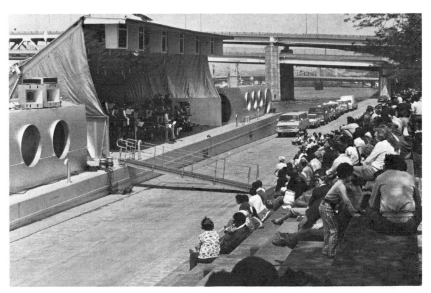

Pittsburgh the world center of bridge technology in the 1920s and early 1930s. The bridges are the best public sculptures in the city, with a palpable lightness that comes from their special quality as self-anchoring suspension structures. The parabolic curves of their cables seem to lift the bridges effortlessly over the broad river with the consummate grace of a pole-vaulter.

Pittsburgh is the only city with structures designed by both of the grand Kahns of American architecture, Albert and Louis. They are fairly close to each other on opposite banks of the Allegheny, but while Albert Kahn's Heinz factories stay put, Louis Kahn's **American Wind Symphony Barge** *Point-Counterpoint II* (1976) spends only three seasons of each year here, then floats down the Ohio and Mississippi rivers for concert tours in the summer. The story of the barge goes back to the early 1960s, when the Pittsburgh-based American Wind Symphony performed in England, and Kahn was asked to remodel an old barge on the Thames. A decade later, Kahn created a second AWS boat from scratch. It is clad in burnished steel, and with its huge portholes it looks like a silver flute gliding over water. Kahn's meticulous design accommodates a hydraulically lifted stage, a galley, and quarters for the crew and the conductor—who doubles as the boat's captain.[6]

Seventh Street

Seventh Street is no longer than other cross-streets in the Penn-Liberty district, but it has more elegant surviving buildings than most. Two of these rise quite dramatically near the river's edge: the **Homes Building** (121–123 Seventh; c. 1905), a bright, scrupulously maintained Chicago School commercial block; and the **Century Building** (130 Seventh; Rutan & Russell, 1907), a twelve-story reinforced concrete shaft ornamented with mullions of green jade terra-cotta and several dozen grimacing heads. The architectural king of Seventh Street was and is Colonel Thomas J. Keenan, founder in 1884 of the *Evening Penny*—today the *Pittsburgh Press*—and a major downtown developer. He placed the **Keenan Building** (today the Mid-Town Towers; NW corner Seventh & Liberty; Thomas Hannah, 1907) so adroitly that it dominates Seventh Street, Sixth Avenue, and the full extent of Liberty. It rises from a base with sculpted portraits of George Washington, William Penn, and Andrew Carnegie into a shaft of eighteen stories of cream terra-cotta, and it is topped

6. That Kahn's work should occasionally stray from Pittsburgh (the barge is generally moored in the Allegheny at The Point or near the Seventh Street Bridge) is not inappropriate, because he had a skittish relationship with the city. In the satellite town of Greensburg, he created the *Tribune-Review* printing plant, one of his seminal works of the early 1960s. But a period of illness later in the decade denied him the commission for the new galleries at Carnegie Institute, which went first to Charles Luckman and finally to Edward Larabee Barnes. What might have been Kahn's Pittsburgh museum ended up in Fort Worth, Texas.

Consolidated Natural Gas Building
/*Courtesy Cushman & Wakefield of Pennsylvania*

by the world's first poured-concrete dome. The bold angle and eccentric dome make the Keenan stand out all over downtown. The dome was Keenan's window on the world; he fitted it out as a luxurious penthouse and lived in it. Rumor was that he did not live there alone, however, and—true or not—a whole generation of Pittsburgh ladies crossed the street rather than come into contact with a scarlet building.

The **Consolidated Natural Gas Company Building** that is rising alongside the Keenan Building near the corner of Seventh and Liberty is a maverick in Pittsburgh for the corporation that began it and for the real-estate deal that gave it birth. It was started by Allegheny International, the new form of an old specialty steel company that reconstituted itself into a conglomerate of advanced-technology companies and such consumer-oriented firms as Sunbeam and Oster. Through some maneuvers that could only work in a closely held town like Pittsburgh, AI agreed to build in Penn-Liberty if the Stanley Theater across Seventh Avenue would upgrade its acts from rock to opera. Civic leaders were delighted to strike the bargain, and AI found a home. The building's name reflects not AI but Consolidated Natural Gas, a larger tenant. The design was entrusted to the most successful new architectural firm of the 1980s, Kohn Pedersen Fox, who came up with a retail arcade at ground floor and a 1920s setback shaft of thirty stories above, colored and ornamented in the best Michael Graves fashion. The design is lively and distinctive, upbeat but ultimately conservative. The project is masonry-clad rather than metal- or glass-skinned, in a contextual bow to its neighbors. Its height parallels Equibank across the street, while its cap reflects the Art Deco top of the Allegheny

General Hospital, clearly visible a mile away on the North Side. It also salutes the nearby Allegheny River, wrapping around its crown a curved-bridge sweatband such as the Chrysler Building might wear if it went out jogging.

The **Benedum Center for the Performing Arts** and the **Clark Building** (both by Hoffman & Henon, 1927) were constructed together at the west end of the block bounded by Penn, Seventh, and Liberty by Pittsburgh movie mogul James Bly Clark. The Clark Building, a 1920s update of the Frick and Oliver buildings, was created as a base for Clark's extensive movie operations—he owned large chunks of MGM, Warner Brothers, and Paramount—and to provide an exchange for the Pittsburgh jewelry trade. The Hollywood interests have moved out, but the jewelers are still there.

More in the public eye than the commercial block is the other half of Clark's complex: the attached Stanley Theater, now the Benedum Center. Its calm Adamesque exterior belies its considerable size (4,000 seats, now reduced by one-third) and lavish interior decoration. Typical of the 1920s, it had a gigantic Wurlitzer organ, frescoes in the stair halls, and a six-ton amber crystal chandelier that was assembled by eight men working in sixteen-hour shifts for a week. As the Stanley, it attracted all the popular music stars from Al Jolson to Frank Sinatra. As the Benedum, it will support a hectic schedule of musicals, the Pittsburgh Ballet Theater, and the city's premier cultural attraction of the 1980s: the Pittsburgh Opera.

Liberty Avenue

The five blocks of **Liberty Avenue** from Seventh to Tenth streets constitute a faithful record of late-Victorian commercial life. Among the heartiest survivors, though one of the newer structures in the sequence, is a small triangular building at the intersection of Wood, Liberty, and Sixth avenues. This is the headquarters of the **Port Authority of Allegheny County (PAT)**, but most Pittsburghers remember it as Azen's Furriers. It was built by Edward Stotz in 1928 as the Monongahela National Bank and was remodeled by Azen's in 1947 in last-gasp Art Deco. When PAT created its subway and eleven miles of suburban Light Rail Transit for half a billion dollars in 1985, it had IKM/SGE remodel Azen's into a headquarters and subway stop. It emerged from this second rehabilitation with slick, neo-neoclassical columns at ground level and a Sol LeWitt marble and slate mural on the mezzanine level below, so the money was well spent both on art and transportation.

Liberty Avenue displays a fine collection of cast-iron fronts from the third quarter of the nineteenth century, beginning with the double stores at **805–807** and **927–929 Liberty Avenue** from the 1860s. (One can read the foundry stamp on the first facade: Anderson & Phillips, #150 Water St., Pgh.) Other cast-irons follow at **951–953 Liberty,** with vases of flowers in low relief.

The Triangle Building, Liberty
Avenue /*Franklin Toker*

The heyday of cast iron was brief, and briefer in Pittsburgh than in other
cities because Pittsburgh knew best that cast-iron buildings were brittle and
volatile if subject to fire. They also tended to be monotonous, relieved only by
bits of Gothic or Italianate detail. For these reasons the city continued to ship
cast-iron prefabs all over the Midwest, but it built few for itself after 1875.
Pittsburgh's preferred commercial style in the 1870s was the elaborate High
Victorian Gothic, sometimes incorporating cast-iron mullions within a brick
or stone front, at other times only simulating the material for effect. Good
examples are the six-story loft at **811 Liberty;** a storefront of 1881 at **820
Liberty,** with segmental arches and exaggerated keystones in the manner of
Frank Furness; and a near twin, but not so bold, around the corner in the
Hefren-Tillotson Building (306–308 Seventh Ave.; c. 1875). Another master
of the genre is the **Triangle Building** by Andrew Peebles at the intersection of
Liberty, Smithfield, and Seventh Avenue, from 1884. We know Peebles only
from this work and his fine First Lutheran Church on Grant Street (he pulled
out of the courthouse competition against H. H. Richardson). Here he used
cast iron for the multitude of columns only; the walls combined brick and
stone trim for effects of texture that metal could never provide. Especially
effective is the sense of "live" masonry as the wall bevels out to meet its wider
base, and the stone lintels appear to split as they are forced upward by the
pressure of the mullions below them. As in the best work of Furness, we are
presented with a metaphorical picture of a structural system at work, and we
respond emotionally to it.

Liberty Avenue divides its late-Victorian building stock about equally be-tween Gothic and Romanesque. The latter style reigned in the 1880s and 1890s, even before Richardson conquered Pittsburgh and half of America with his Allegheny County Courthouse and Jail. The massive blocks and quieter designs of the Romanesque had greater appeal to this period than the earlier, fussy designs of the Gothic, and they lent themselves better to the wholesale loft buildings of seven to ten stories that were built in substantial numbers on Liberty in those years. A bold demonstration of commercial Romanesque Revival work is the sequence from 901 to 925 Liberty Avenue, which once constituted a continuous row of lofts (some of them Gothic and Italianate) broken only by a single alley. The sequence was later interrupted by a fire at 917–919, but it is still awesome in the effect of the massive sandstone blocks marching in step. Particularly striking are the **Maginnis Building** at 913–915, of 1891, and the **Ewart Building** by Charles Bickel of the same year, at 921–925.

Penn Avenue

The commercial work on Liberty had its echo one short block toward the river on **Penn Avenue,** particularly from Seventh to Tenth streets. The notable structures here were retail rather than wholesale buildings, and they attracted consumers who were dismayed by the hurly-burly on Liberty Avenue. Fine Beaux Arts high-rises line Eighth and Ninth streets in the manner of the Homes and Century buildings on Seventh Street. Among them are the **General Nutrition Building,** now housing the Pittsburgh-based world leader in vitamins but originally built as the Spear & Company department store (915–921 Penn; Charles Bickel, 1910); the **Arbuthnot Stephenson Building** (NE corner Penn & Garrison Alley; W. S. Fraser, 1890); and the **Eiben & Irr Building** (940 Penn Ave.; John Barr, 1888), with the radically remodeled twelve-story Convention Tower next door.

Liberty Center, Lawrence Convention Center, and Penn (Union) Station

Liberty Center (Burt Hill Kosar Rittelmann Associates and UDA Architects, with The Architects Collaborative, 1985–87), the David L. Lawrence Con-vention Center (Celli-Flynn Associates, 1981), and Penn Station (Daniel H. Burnham, 1901) all stand on land developed in 1829 for the Pittsburgh terminus of the Pennsylvania Canal. All three had to be designed to satisfy multiple viewpoints and to embody the "come-hither" look of a public trans-portation or social gathering place. Of the three complexes, Liberty Center

Liberty Center /*Courtesy Burt Hill Kosar Rittelmann Associates*

demanded the most ingenuity of its architects: at the station Burnham had to contend with just one main viewpoint, while at Liberty Center there are five (Liberty and Penn from both east and west, plus Grant Street). In addition, the program was far more complex: a 614-room hotel, a half-million square feet of office space, and a major retailing component. The designers responded with a straightforward plan of two towers of twenty-five and twenty-seven stories and several low structures that will give the rectangular plot the more dynamic feeling of a triangle. The elevations are no less straightforward: *echt* Pittsburgh materials of stainless steel, aluminum, and glass, and elevations that begin historicist at the base, where they mirror the Romanesque and academic revival facades facing them, then turn corporate high-tech where they sail over the surrounding buildings.

The **David L. Lawrence Convention Center** has a superb site as a link between the Golden Triangle and The Strip, with a fine view from its back rooms over the Allegheny River. The exterior is unexceptional, with the windowless walls typical of buildings with this function, but there is much creativity in the suspended roof system that allows for vast unimpeded spaces inside. In its short life the building has already made an impact on the Golden Triangle, which will magnify as the revitalization of both Penn-Liberty and The Strip continues.

Like every public building, **Penn Station** is part architecture and part politics. Pittsburgh had a strong dislike for the Pennsylvania Railroad, which it regarded as an eastern monopoly that bled Pittsburgh as it fattened Phila-

Penn Station: the rotunda /*Franklin Toker*

delphia. This vigorous and self-confident pile of brick and terra-cotta was designed to mollify such resentment, which had been fanned into a white heat in the Pittsburgh railroad riots of 1877. The architect in charge was Pittsburgh's favorite outsider, Daniel Burnham; the patron was the railroad's president, Alexander Cassatt. Cassatt, like his more famous sister, Mary, was a native of Pittsburgh, and so he would have understood local sentiments. Like Mary, again, Cassatt had an artistic bent, which he demonstrated by building three of the best railroad stations in the country: McKim, Mead & White's Pennsylvania Station in New York, Burnham's Union Station in Washington, and this one.

Burnham won the Penn Station commission in 1898 and responded with a low-lying structure with a rectangular cab stand in front. This concept he shelved—it surfaced later as the key to his Washington station—in favor of a twelve-story skyscraper with a fantastic domed rotunda that combined imperial Roman scale and a whiff of Art Nouveau in its surface decoration. The station is adequate, but the rotunda turned out to be one of the best things Burnham ever did, along with his Frick and Flatiron buildings of the same years. James Van Trump suggested that Burnham appropriated the design from the main gate of the Paris Exposition of 1900 by René Binet. It works perfectly as a gate here, beckoning travelers the whole length of Liberty Avenue with its bejeweled terra-cotta ornament and the voluptuousness of its supple curves.

Grant Street and Mellon Square

It has taken two centuries of urban doctoring to bring Grant Street to its present state of coherence. In 1829 the city filled in the tongue of Hogg's Pond that cut Grant Street at its mid-point (the earth came from the digging of the

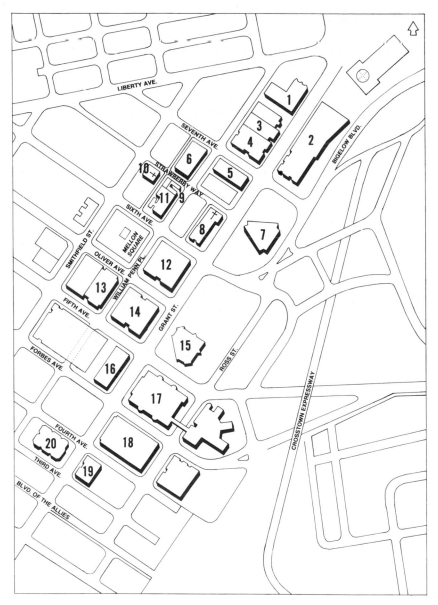

Map 5. The Golden Triangle: Grant Street and Mellon Square

1 Moorhead (Federal) Bldg.
2 Post Office & Federal Courts
3 Federal Reserve Bank
4 Gulf
5 Koppers
6 Bell Telephone
7 U.S. Steel

8 First Lutheran Church
9 Harvard-Yale-Princeton Club
10 Smithfield United Church
11 Alcoa Bldg.
12 Westin William Penn Hotel
13 Three Mellon Bank Center
14 Union Trust (2 Mellon Bank)

15 One Mellon Bank Center
16 Frick Bldg.
17 Allegheny Courthouse & Jail
18 City-County Bldg.
19 Grant Bldg.
20 One Oxford Centre

Pennsylvania Canal tunnel under Grant's Hill). In 1832, 1846, and 1912 Grant's Hill itself was leveled down to a manageable rump, and in 1927 the Pennsylvania Railroad freightyards were removed from the corner of Grant and Seventh Avenue. Only then could Grant Street blossom into a showcase of government and corporate architecture. Today, splendidly repaved in brick and granite, it is as handsome an architectural promenade as any street in the nation.

Occupying the northernmost block of Grant from Liberty to Seventh are several large but muted federal government buildings. It comes as no surprise to find the state and federal presence so slight in Pittsburgh: since the Whiskey Rebellion of Pittsburgh-area farmers in 1794, the city has tended to ignore both Harrisburg and Washington and controls its destiny through city and county government alone. The **William S. Moorhead (Federal) Building** (Altenhof & Brown, 1964) stands twenty stories tall at the intersection of Grant and Liberty and yet has no impact on the city whatever. Across the street, the **New Post Office and Federal Courts Building** (Trowbridge & Livingston, with J. A. Wetmore, 1932) occupies a full block from Liberty to Seventh with only a little more effect. A more winning federal presence is carried off by the **Federal Reserve Bank of Cleveland—Pittsburgh Branch** at 717 Grant, halfway through the block (Walker & Weeks, Henry Hornbostel & Eric F. Wood, 1931), which consists of an office tower and a banking hall with fine interior decoration in Aztec and Egyptian motifs. The exterior is clad in marble and aluminum and punctuated by imposing, if rather chilling, heraldic reliefs in slick Art Deco style.

Gulf and Koppers Buildings

Samuel Kier ran the world's first oil refinery at the southeast corner of Grant and Seventh in the 1850s, so it was appropriate that the **Gulf Building** (Trowbridge & Livingston, with E. P. Mellon) was built on the diagonally opposite corner in 1932. The construction of Gulf and the **Koppers Building** (Graham, Anderson, Probst & White, with E. P. Mellon, 1929) was a carefully controlled Mellon project: A. W. Mellon commissioned both buildings, E. P. Mellon helped design them, and the Mellon-Stuart firm built them. The green-roofed Koppers building, home to a giant construction-materials firm, is the lower of the two towers, a set-back Art Deco rendering of a U-shaped French château. The lobby inside is tinted in green, brown, and red marble with bronze metalwork. The mailbox is a miniaturized Koppers Building, with stylized pineapples and an exaggerated roof, while the pilaster strips take on elements of Greek, Egyptian, Aztec, and Mayan designs.

At nearly 600 feet, the Gulf Building was the tallest in Pittsburgh for almost half a century, but it makes an impression that is anything but domineering.

Left: Gulf (foreground) and Koppers buildings /*Courtesy Chevron Corporation* ▪ *Right:* U.S. Steel Building /*Courtesy Robert Geiger, John W. Galbreath & Co.*

The materials are pearl-gray and light gray granite, the form svelte and even playful. Its stepped-pyramid top is the third and most effective recall of the Mausoleum of Halicarnassus in Pittsburgh (after the Soldiers' and Sailors' Memorial Hall and Carnegie Institute in Oakland). Trowbridge & Livingston had employed the motif years before in their 1914 Bankers' Trust tower in Manhattan, but here it takes on a 1920s twist as it rises up in broad terraces (illuminated with banks of lights until the 1970s) to an electric weather beacon. The lobby is severely classical in motif, with the main corridor laid out in modular compartments of deep red and yellow posts and lintels, like a well-appointed Etruscan tomb. The building is no longer associated with oil: Gulf sold it in 1985 when it merged with Chevron.

The five-skyscraper complex of **Bell Telephone of Pennsylvania** diagonally opposite Gulf at 416–420 Seventh Avenue and on Grant Street has probably housed the telecommunications industry longer than any of its thousand-score buildings in the nation. The oldest component is Frederick Osterling's Romanesque Revival switching hall of 1890. (The architect's monogram is on the second pier to the right, following Richardson's practice at the Courthouse a few years before.) At seven stories, Osterling's building is high but not technically a skyscraper, since it contains no steel and is supported by its bulging thick walls. Alden & Harlow added an eleven-story skyscraper behind it in 1905 on Montour Way, and two more additions were created by the James T. Windrim firm of Philadelphia in 1908 and 1930 in the

Classical Revival and Art Deco styles. By the time Bell added its forgettable (but nuclear-bomb-resistant) box of 1969 on Grant Street, the style had changed to late International School.

U.S. Steel Building

U.S. Steel was founded in 1901 by J. P. Morgan as the first billion-dollar corporation in America. Today its profits come from so many fields apart from steel that observers expect it to take a new name. It was still "Big Steel" in 1971, however, when it erected the **U.S. Steel Building** at 600 Grant Street (Harrison & Abramovitz and Abbe). The Rockwell and Heinz world headquarters share the building with U.S. Steel today, but the structure remains an advertisement for steel. Architectural advertising is an old tradition in Pittsburgh, going back to 1892, when the Carnegie Building left its steel cage standing naked in the sky for six months so people could gape at it. Westinghouse is all-electric, PPG all-glass, Alcoa all-aluminum. But since exposed steel corrodes and is prohibited by fire codes, U.S. Steel had to be more ingenious. Cor-Ten, a steel invented in 1934, solved the corrosion problem, because its initial rust forms a protective coating around the steel. (And not only the steel: a good stretch of Grant Street has been covered in rust as well.) The fire liability of exposed steel was solved by filling the eighteen basic columns around the building with half a million gallons of water and antifreeze. If attacked by fire, the liquid solution would dissipate its heat by convection and so resist flames for four hours. Harrison & Abramovitz molded the building into a triangle with three rectangles of office space set in neoclassical harmony about the braced core. The building is large enough (11,000 windows; 64 stories, each with an acre of floor space) that the unprotected steel columns outside would be liable to expand and contract as much as nine inches. The solution was an innovative "hat" that clamps on the top two stories and tightens the exterior frame all the way to the base whenever it is buffeted by wind loads or erratic changes in temperature. Unfortunately the same imagination was not applied to the styling of the building, which looks more like a mechanical diagram than architecture. The only point at which the inner drama of the engineering becomes an architectural drama is in the two-story lobby, where cross-braced girders cut crazily through terrazzo walls. U.S. Steel is a building that commands respect for its engineering and sensitivity to urban design, but it is a hard building to love.

The **First English Evangelical Lutheran Church** (615 Grant St., SW corner Strawberry Way; Andrew Peebles, 1888) is one of three surviving branches of the German and Evangelical congregations that together received a land grant on Sixth Avenue from the Penns. It is an eccentric, handcrafted High Victorian Gothic design, with all the richness that is missing from U.S.

Steel across the street. I he tower begins as a squat shape in irregularly coursed brownstones, lifts up to a high lancet belfry with a dwarf arcade at the top, reaches a crescendo in four gables with clock faces, then soars in a slate-covered needle to 170 feet. The effect is lively and colorful, the color reinforced by pink mortar between the stones (a subliminal touch copied from Richardson's courthouse). The interior is less remarkable, though well conceived for a cramped site. The *Good Shepherd* window (by Frederick Wilson of the Tiffany Studios, 1898) bathes everything in the radiance of its opalescent glass, and Grant Street suddenly seems far away.

Beside First Lutheran, there are two other sanctuaries along Strawberry Way. The first is the **Harvard-Yale-Princeton Club** (617–619 William Penn Place, SW corner Strawberry Way), one of two plain brick rectangles that were built here in 1894 as worker housing, then remodeled in high-style Georgian in 1930 by the academic classicist Edward B. Lee. HYP uses only the right block as its clubhouse; neighboring Alcoa has offices in the left block. The end wall of the tiny court that separates the two blocks incorporates relics from the schools back East: two stone columns from the old Appleton Chapel at Harvard, six stones of uncertain ancestry from Princeton and Yale. Overhead is the fantastic sight of the rose window and aluminum spire of Smithfield United Church. Until women were admitted here in 1980, only two female guests had been officially entertained. One was the actress Cornelia Otis Skinner, the other Mae West. West remarked on the occasion: "It's rather difficult for me to think up things to say to Harvard-Yale-Princeton men collectively. Of course, I can think of plenty to say to men individually."

The **Smithfield United Church** (620 Smithfield St., SE corner Strawberry Way; Henry Hornbostel, 1926) is the sixth home of a congregation that has moved only a few hundred feet from its original site of 1787. It is significant as one of the three downtown works—another two dozen are in Oakland—by Pittsburgh's premier architect, Henry Hornbostel, and as an outstanding example of the modern inner-city church.[7] The contrast of spiritual and mundane values is the key to understanding Hornbostel's approach to the design. He placed the church hard against the sidewalk to integrate it uncompromisingly with the city, and he used standard industrial materials: steel, limestone, poured and cast cement. The main floor, right off the street, is not a sanctuary but a gym, complete with showers and locker rooms. The congrega-

7. Hornbostel (1867–1961) came to Pittsburgh in 1903 to build the campus of what is now Carnegie-Mellon University, and he stayed thirty years as a designer and sometime dean of the CMU architecture school. He had graduated from Columbia in 1891, spent four years at the Ecole des Beaux-Arts (where he was known as *l'homme perspectif* for his brilliant drawings), taught at Columbia, worked for Stanford White, and was runner-up to Bernard Maybeck in the competition for the campus design of the University of California at Berkeley. Although Pittsburgh was his main base, Hornbostel continued as an active architect in New York until World War I. The Hell Gate, Queensboro, and Manhattan bridges are his most prominent works there.

tion has used it for various purposes over the years, today as a day-care center for children and as a dormitory for the homeless at night. The sanctuary one floor up is rich in its wood trim, stained glass, and lavish plaster fan vaults. Higher still, on the roof, Hornbostel made history with the world's first structural use of aluminum, an unforgettable filigree spire that recalls the contemporary Watts Tower in Los Angeles.

Mellon Square

The creation of **Mellon Square** (Smithfield St., between Oliver & Sixth Aves.) was an inspired mix of altruism and self-interest. The Mellons had been here since Judge Thomas Mellon resigned from the bench in 1869 and opened a bank, saying that any man who could not get rich in Pittsburgh within ten years was a fool. The original bank was on the west edge of what is now Mellon Square, but its cast-iron replacement of 1873 and all successive buildings have been on the south edge. Banking, however, was just the visible tip of the Mellon money machine. Their investments in steel and its chemical byproducts, oil, aluminum, real estate, and transportation were even more lucrative. Today the Mellons of Pittsburgh are assumed to be the wealthiest family in the world. Their many business ventures were originally headquartered in the bank until they required their own buildings.

Two generations of aluminum: the spire of the Smithfield United Church and the Alcoa Building /Maurice Tierney

Opposite: Mellon Square, with Alcoa and the Westin William Penn Hotel /*Courtesy Greater Pittsburgh Convention & Visitors Bureau (George Hetrick)*

At the end of the 1920s Gulf and Koppers moved two blocks away, to Seventh Avenue. Alcoa tried to bolt from the family circle and build in New York after World War II, but Richard K. Mellon had not backed the Pittsburgh Renaissance only to find it scorned at home. He quashed the move to New York, and he and his cousin Paul Mellon conceived a grand complex that would house Alcoa and the expanded bank operations in twin towers facing each other across a lavish park. Construction of the park (Mitchell & Ritchey, with Simonds & Simonds, landscape architects, 1955) and its underground parking garage required demolition of a full city block, but it paid off handsomely in sight lines to all the surrounding buildings.[8] Apart from creating a place in which the perimeter buildings might preen, Mellon Square is a lively environment for its lunchtime users. The design in Venetian terrazzo appears today somewhat thin in the manner of the Eisenhower years (and also a little unsubtle with its scores of M's), but the trees and fountains have aged well, and Kenneth Snelson's *Forest Devil* sculpture in stainless-steel pipes is a welcome newcomer.

Of the newer structures encircling Mellon Square, the **Alcoa Building** (Harrison & Abramovitz, with Altenhof & Brown and Mitchell & Ritchey, 1953) is certainly the most prominent. Using aluminum wherever possible, Alcoa's thirty-story tower is radically lighter and more efficient than buildings of comparable size. Its curtain wall was not built up piece by piece but prefabricated in aluminum sheets that contained both windows and the floor zone. The windows swing open in special rubber gaskets, so that after three decades Alcoa has required minimal cleaning and maintenance on the exterior. Inside, the same spirit of radical innovation prevailed: aluminum furniture, aluminum piping and wiring, aluminum air-conditioning ducts, and an unusually airy and fanciful lobby. This list of distinctions should have propelled Alcoa to top rank among postwar skyscrapers, but the design community shunned it for thirty years until Richard Meier returned to the prefabricated aluminum skin as an ideal medium for the taut high-tech style of the 1980s.

On the south side of Mellon Square it is tradition and not innovation that stands paramount. **Three Mellon Bank Center** consists of a low banking hall (Trowbridge & Livingston, with E. P. Mellon) of 1924 and a forty-one-story

---

8. A dozen buildings ring Mellon Square. Clockwise from the south they are: the Mellon banking hall and tower; the Park Building and **Saks Fifth Avenue** (the old W. T. Grant's, effectively glass-fronted in 1977 by Robert Bridges Associates) on the southwest corner; Burnham's Oliver Building to the west; **Gimbel's** (the old Kaufmann & Baer store; Starrett & Van Vleck, 1914) to the northwest; the aluminum spire of Smithfield United Church and the Alcoa tower to the north; the classical **James H. Reed Building** (formerly Duquesne Light; MacClure & Spahr, 1902 and later) and the **Porter Building** (Harrison & Abramovitz, 1958) to the northeast; the Westin William Penn Hotel to the east; and the Union Trust to the southeast. All the perimeter buildings have architectural distinction except for the Porter Building, which, as the cliché goes, looks like the box that Alcoa was shipped in.

Mellon Bank, on Mellon Square
/Courtesy Mellon National Corporation
(Jeff Comella)

tower (Harrison & Abramovitz, with W. Y. Cocken) of 1952 that Mellon Bank
shared with U.S. Steel for twenty years. The tower is conservative, without
significant innovations beyond its prewar model of Rockefeller Center. More
exhilarating by far is the banking hall, with its ring of fifteen-ton Ionic
columns of imported Italian marble. The hall is a vast basilical space, 65 feet
tall and more than 200 feet long, its aisles coffered and painted deep blue with
speckles of gold leaf. Befitting its place as the heart of Mellon operations, the
hall commemorates A. W. and R. B. Mellon with portraits and inscriptions
right at its sacred center—on the walls of the vault.

   The building that derived the most benefit from the creation of Mellon
Square was the **Westin William Penn Hotel** (Janssen & Abbott, 1913; Janssen
& Cocken, with Joseph Urban, 1929). This was the last of four buildings
constructed in a row by Henry Clay Frick, who reserved the presidential suite
for himself when he was not living in his Victorian mansion in Point Breeze or
in Manhattan. Determined as always, Frick vowed that this would be the finest
hotel in the country. He stole the chef from the Plaza in New York, the *maître
d'hôtel* from the Savoy in London, and the chief clerk from the Bellevue
Stratford in Philadelphia. Benno Janssen rendered Frick's wishes into a sumptuous—and air-conditioned—Edwardian clubhouse, with lavish public rooms
below and a cafeteria, dormitory, and library on the top floors for the servants
who accompanied the guests in the early years of the hotel. When the original
block was doubled in size in 1929, Janssen called in his friend Joseph Urban,
the chief set designer for the Metropolitan Opera as well as for the Ziegfeld
Follies in the 1920s. The hall Urban created on the seventeenth floor (named
the **Urban Room** today) is awash with black Carrara glass, ceiling-height
windows draped in orange velour, and a frescoed ceiling. This Art Deco

masterpiece and the rest of the William Penn are now being restored to faultless elegance in a massive restructuring of the building that is also amalgamating its 1,650 rooms into 600. Recently brought to light in the rebuilding of the hotel is a relic of Americana that really belongs in the Smithsonian: the original bubble machine invented by Lawrence Welk when he played here in the 1940s.

Frick Building, Union Trust, and One Mellon Bank Center

The **Frick Building** (437 Grant St., Daniel Burnham & Co., 1901), the Union Trust, and One Mellon Bank Center occupy three corners of the intersection of Grant and Fifth, with Richardson's courthouse on the fourth. Frick purchased this site despite a major impediment: here stood John Notman's St. Peter's Church of 1852, which the congregation obliged Frick to rebuild stone by stone on a new site in Oakland. (Frick would later buy out St. Paul's Cathedral to build the Union Trust, as well as Third Presbyterian Church to put up the William Penn.) Frick was determined to get this particular land because by building his proud tower he would darken and humiliate Andrew Carnegie's headquarters in the Carnegie Building, which stood immediately behind it on Fifth Avenue (replaced in 1952 by the Kaufmann store annex). Frick liked the result so well that he hired Burnham again in 1906 to punish Carnegie a second time with the **Allegheny Building** around the corner at 429 Forbes Avenue, which deprived the Carnegie Building of light from the south after the first tower had cut it off from the east. Unfortunately in all this architectural mayhem the big loser was not Carnegie, who by 1901 permanently resided in Scotland, but Richardson's courthouse. That building had been conceived as the benevolent and protective tower for the whole of the Golden Triangle, and now just fifteen years later it was being dwarfed and emasculated by a massive high-rise right across the street.[9]

9. Frick battled Carnegie's architectural legacy at every chance: here on Grant Street; in Point Breeze, where Frick moved right between the estates owned by Carnegie and his brother Tom; on Forbes Avenue in Oakland, where Frick purchased the Cathedral of Learning site with the intent of overshadowing Carnegie's museum; and on Fifth Avenue in Manhattan, where their two homes still stand as the last word in opulence. Frick was born fourteen years after Carnegie, in 1849, in the village of West Overton, forty miles southeast of Pittsburgh. Nearby were the coalfields of Connellsville, which he eventually turned into the largest coking operation in the world. His 12,000 ovens reduced coal to coke to make it burn many times more fiercely when used at the blast furnaces in Pittsburgh. Frick's mastery of coke made him both Carnegie's most important partner and his most dangerous rival. In 1892 Carnegie left to Frick the task of crushing the strike at the Homestead works, which cost a dozen lives. From New York the anarchist Emma Goldman dispatched Alexander Berkman to assassinate Frick. Berkman gained entry to his office, shot Frick in the neck and back and stabbed him in the leg and hip, but Frick finished his day's work as he sat bleeding at his desk. At the end of his life Carnegie sought reconciliation with Frick, who replied: "Tell Mr. Carnegie that I'll see him in Hell."

Left: Union Trust Building (Two Mellon Bank Center) /*Courtesy Burt Hill Kosar Rittelmann Associates (Brud Bavera)* ▪ *Right:* Union Trust: the rotunda built for Henry Frick /*Courtesy Mellon National Corporation (Jeff Comella)*

Whatever the motives, Frick's tower is a fine building. It was one of Burnham's best works up to that time, the first skyscraper in which he overthrew the cumbersome base-shaft-cap formula for a sleek, almost totally unornamented tower of cold elegance. What Burnham learned here he used with profit one year later in the nearly identical elevation of the Flatiron Building in New York. The interior of the Frick Building is particularly fine. It has two lobbies: the lower was created out of a basement in 1912 when the city cut twelve feet off The Hump that remained of Grant's Hill, leaving the first lobby high in the air. The main lobby is introduced by two lions by Alexander Phimister Proctor—the prototypes for his famed lions at the New York Public Library—and dominated at the end by *Fortune and Her Wheel*, John La Farge's stained-glass window of a maiden gliding over rough waters. Below it is a bust of Frick in white marble that is covered by a black velvet hood at the end of each working day. A gold-plated gas jet in the form of a barebreasted nymph stands a few feet to the right, ready to light up cigars for Frick and his friends. To the left is a set of fine turn-of-the-century telephone booths rendered in brass and San Domingo mahogany. The offices upstairs are, or were, similarly lavish in their appointment, and none more so than Room 1926, Frick's personal suite, which for sixty years was home to his daughter Helen's eleemosynary trust.

For his **Union Trust Building** (535 Grant; originally the Union Arcade, and now Two Mellon Bank Center) of 1916, Frick made the somewhat surprising choice of Gothic over Classical style. Some have hypothesized that this was a nostalgic gesture to the Catholic cathedral that had stood on the site, but there were more practical reasons. The construction of the Woolworth tower in New York in 1914 had made Gothic fashionable again for commercial work, and the Arcade (a shopping mall originally) was probably dressed in Gothic to appeal to its female clientele. Burnham was dead, but Frick obtained excellent work locally from Frederick Osterling and Osterling's temporary draftsman Pierre Liesch, who came from Luxembourg and could skillfully concoct an approximation of a Flemish guildhall. (Osterling nonetheless was the true parent to the building and so proud of it that he reproduced it in miniature in his studio on Isabella Street on the North Side.) Like the Woolworth, the Union Trust is clad in white terra-cotta plaques, and it has the same efflorescence of trefoil hood molds projecting out as a cornice line. The building makes its own statement, however. The roofline is lively without being busy, and it culminates in a forest of dormers with two chapel-like elevator shafts poking out at top. Internally, the Union Trust is without question the most glamorous of Pittsburgh's downtown buildings. The four-story open shopping arcade was closed when business conditions no longer warranted it, but the stained-glass Cyclops eye still glowers from the top of the central light well, ten stories high.

One Mellon Bank Center (500 Grant St.; Welton Beckett Associates, 1983) is a fifty-four-story steel-clad tower that may have tried to be a good neighbor to too many buildings at once. It derives its color and mansard roofs from the Union Trust, its material from U.S. Steel, the plan of its tower from Richardson, and the tower elevation from the Frick Building. This technically capable building (the steel skin acts as a framed tube to withstand wind loads)

The Allegheny County Courthouse and Jail, with the Frick Building opposite /Clyde Hare

The Courthouse main stairway /*Courtesy Department of Works, County of Allegheny*

should look better when joined by the hotel and office towers that are planned for the same block, but for now its best appearance is at night, when huge lights turn the top of the tower into a medieval idyll.

Allegheny County Courthouse and Jail

He left to his country many monuments of art, foremost among them this temple of justice.

To many critics the **Allegheny County Courthouse and Jail** (1884–88) by Henry Hobson Richardson is the most distinguished American building of the nineteenth century. Some architects, Philip Johnson among them, go farther and call it flat out the best building in the United States. Certainly it gives the impression of being a near-perfect building: a perfect solution to a difficult design problem, perfect compliance with the allocated budget (Allegheny County was so pleased with this that it proclaimed the budget, to the penny, in massive brass plaques in the lobby), and a perfect tribute to the dead Richardson (quoted in part above) that is cut into the walls on the third floor. The Courthouse is unequivocally a *nineteenth*-century building in its eclectic style, its technology, and its structural system, but it is instructive in a way that transcends period. Its perfection is marred here and there: by the removal of its entrance stairs during the widening of Grant Street (one enters through the ex-basement today); by the dry interior carving detailed after Richardson died in 1886 by his pupils Shepley, Rutan & Coolidge; and by the poor care that generations of bureaucrats have given it. But it is hard to imagine a building

Left: The Courthouse interior courtyard and park /*Courtesy Department of Works, County of Allegheny* ▪ *Right:* The Jail, following an escape (1980) /*Courtesy* Pittsburgh Post-Gazette *(Harry Coughanour)* ▪ *Below:* City-County Building, Grant Street /*Courtesy Mayor's Office, City of Pittsburgh (Mike Rizzo)*

that corresponds more closely to what the client wanted from it and what the city and the nation needed of it as a symbol of justice in the turbulent days of America's coming of age as an industrial power after the Civil War.

The immediate demand on Richardson when he reluctantly entered the Courthouse competition in 1883 was to replace John Chislett's Greek Revival courthouse of 1842 on Grant's Hill. The specific requirements were complex: a welter of courtrooms, administrative offices, politicians' suites (some with secret stair access), and public counters where citizens could pay their taxes and record their properties, their passports, and their newborn babies. Three farsighted county commissioners laid out the main lines of the building in the competition program, and it was they, not Richardson, who insisted on the spacious courtyard at the center of the building and who designed the basic shape of 200 by 300 feet, with a jail on the trapezoid block behind. It was Richardson, however, who assembled the various components of the program in such masterly fashion. To the basic concept and shape of a Renaissance palace (on one of his preparatory sketches, now at Harvard, Richardson wrote: "Get Farnese"), he added details taken from nearly two dozen historical precedents.[10]

With all its learned precedents the Courthouse might have become a Victorian horror, but it emerged instead as a brilliantly organized office building with its functions horizontally layered in a complex programmatic sequence. The public offices are at ground level, the main courtrooms on the second floor, and the administrative offices on the top floor. Through this horizontal layering, Richardson ran a complex set of vertical conduits: a grand staircase in front, four elevator shafts, each with a dog-leg stair tower wrapped around them, and pneumatic tubes so paperwork could be passed quickly between the first and third floors. Richardson made the Grant Street tower 300 feet high because in it he placed the fresh-air intake for his ventilation system: foul air was expunged from the Courthouse by ducts in the two back towers. The offices and courtrooms were then arrayed around the courtyard so that no part of the building was deprived of natural illumination. There are other indications of Richardson's painstaking concern for functionality, too: the Courthouse is completely fireproof and was one of the first American buildings to use electricity. Richardson designed it as a three-story structure but

10. Among Richardson's precedents: the superposed arches of the courtyard elevation are taken directly from the Roman Pont du Gard; the two back towers are copies of the early Renaissance companile in Piazza San Marco in Venice; the front tower details are from the Romanesque collegial church in Torres, Spain; the jail, with its central octagon and extended arms, is a remake of the fifth-century monastery of Kalat Siman in Syria; the idea of the bridge to the jail is borrowed from the Bridge of Sighs in Venice, but the form is that of the Rialto Bridge; the acanthus-leaf cornice all around the building is taken from Notre-Dame in Paris. A multitude of other details stem from French, German, Italian, and Spanish Romanesque precedents.

provided for the insertion of two mezzanines if later needed. Today we see the building at its fully expanded state of five floors.

What is wonderful about the Courthouse is the way Richardson addressed both the physical and the metaphysical aspects of the problem. The double role of the front tower as both vent intake and symbolic guardian of the city is one instance of that. The *tourelles* on the long sides also have a dual purpose: in functional terms, they house the judges' chambers and the jury rooms set between the courtrooms; in symbolic terms, the tourelles and the gaping arches between them represent the city gates (Richardson probably got the concept from the Roman Porta Niger in Trier or the main gates of Rome), so that justice is seen as the guardian of the city gates. Finally, the Courthouse exemplifies the elusive attribute that every architect strives to achieve in his or her buildings: the expression of the place (what the Romans called *genius loci*). The Courthouse does not merely stand in Pittsburgh—it is *about* Pittsburgh. Richardson thrilled to the vitality of this city, which he captured perfectly in the abstract rhythms of the courtyard walls (these he turned inside out to make the Marshall Field Wholesale Store in Chicago two years later) and the Cyclopean scale of the granite blocks in the jail.

The genius of the Courthouse is the culminating genius of many traditions that Richardson saw as united in the Pittsburgh of the 1880s. His choice of stone exemplied his conception of the city as the mid-point of the country— Massachusetts granite outside, Indiana limestone inside. Technically too, the building is at a crucial mid-point: among the last of the great stone palaces that began with the Romans, and among the first of the modern office buildings of today. But its range as the culminating building of the nineteenth century goes even one step beyond. Functional and artistic, poetic and profound, the Courthouse complex represents the marriage of the classical and the romantic—the two fundamental wellsprings of Western civilization.

The **City-County Building** (414 Grant St.; Henry Hornbostel & Edward B. Lee, 1915) is both the city hall of Pittsburgh and an overflow for the county administrative and judicial offices that have left the Courthouse. (Other county functions take place in Frederick Osterling's turn-of-the-century **Morgue** and Stanley Roush's **County Office Building** of 1929, both on Ross Street.) Here Hornbostel solved a problem even more intractable than the one presented to Richardson a generation earlier, since not only the same confusing mix of justice, politics, and taxes had to be accommodated here but also the collective egos of both the city and the county governments. In addition, he had to contend with the fame of the Courthouse across Forbes Avenue. In his solution Hornbostel neither mirrored nor challenged Richardson but, instead, created a building totally amiable and elegant in its own language. The three huge portico arches and the three-story Doric colonnade above ensure that the City-County Building will be read externally as a public monument. Internally, the building also reads as grand and ceremonial through

One Oxford Centre /*Courtesy*
Oxford Development Corporation

Hornbostel's ingenious vaulted and skylit corridor, which reveals the full nine-story height of his central light-well. Hornbostel, like every Beaux Arts architect, sought to convey the inner essence of the institutions he worked for. In the noble and even inspiring chambers of the City-County Building, he lifts us from the indignity to the dignity of civic life.

Hornbostel seems to have known that his **Grant Building** (330 Grant; with Eric Fisher Wood, 1927) would be his swan song in Pittsburgh. In the prospectus brochure for it, he portrayed this structure looming above all his other Pittsburgh buildings, including his church and two synagogues, his campuses for Pitt and CMU, his bridges, hotels, and monuments. The old eclectic here assumed the last of his many styles in a lively, almost garish Art Deco, although this was tamed down considerably between conception and execution, and it became tamer still as some of the ornament was shaved off over the years. The present lobby (by The Space Design Group of New York, 1984), a replacement for Hornbostel's original, is a combination of architectural non sequiturs in the ironic grammar of ornament of a Graves or Venturi. Externally, the building is a powerful sight, with its dramatically proportioned setbacks in the manner of a giant's throne. Over it all, a rooftop beacon spells P-I-T-T-S-B-U-R-G-H in Morse code all night long.

The forty-six-story **One Oxford Centre** (301 Grant, SW corner Fourth Ave.; Hellmuth, Obata, Kassabaum, 1983), opposite the Grant Building, creates a rather successful duet with it because the architects here, too, understood the power of geometry in their elegant interlocking octagons of silver-painted aluminum and glass. Oxford serves as the headquarters for many professional firms and for the Duquesne Light and Joy Manufacturing corporations, but it also provides an atrium of high-fashion shops and an athletic center and clubhouse set over its parking garage. Neither structurally nor stylistically innovative, Oxford nevertheless has the self-confidence that makes for good contextual architecture. It demonstrates that new downtown buildings need not be, and perhaps should not be, definitive architectural statements. The Triangle is still in a state of development rather than completion, and its best years lie ahead rather than behind it.

Oakland, with the Cathedral of Learning and Carnegie Institute (foreground) /Courtesy University of Pittsburgh (Norman Schumm)

Oakland: The Second Founding of Pittsburgh

Like several Italian cities of Etruscan origin, Pittsburgh has not one but two sacred centers: besides the Golden Triangle there is Oakland, cradled on a high plateau three miles to the east. The nerve center of education and culture for western Pennsylvania, Oakland fills to overflowing a tight wedge of land a mile long and between a half and a quarter of a mile wide. It is sharply detached from the rest of Pittsburgh by the gullies of Junction and Panther hollows to the east, the flatlands of the Monongahela River to the south, and the steep slopes of The Hill to the north and west.

These crowded 700 acres are much more than a college neighborhood, although they are that, too. They represent an attempt at the turn of the century to create a second Pittsburgh at a moment when the old Pittsburgh had so decayed that it required a shimmering alter ego a goodly distance away. Only this can explain why Oakland was not throttled at its birth, as were all other attempts to challenge the supremacy of the Triangle. The golden years of Oakland lasted only two decades, from 1890 to 1910, but these were crucial decades for American cities: the decades of the City Beautiful movement in city planning, and of the Beaux Arts style in architecture. For Pittsburgh these were also years of judgment, if not years of atonement, as both the muckraker Lincoln Steffens and the publications of the *Pittsburgh Survey* targeted Pittsburgh as the most corrupt and socially repressive city in the United States. The creation of Oakland, one of the best pieces of cosmetic urbanism in the country, was a direct response by the civic leaders of Pittsburgh to these attacks.

The limestone terraces that form the Oakland plateau were settled in successive waves. The first settlement began with the sale of the Manor of Pittsburgh by the Penns in the 1780s and 1790s. A generation later the healthful climate of this farmland district became a refuge for a score of wealthy families who were distressed by the cholera epidemics that regularly swept the Golden Triangle in the 1830s. More of the gentry abandoned the downtown after the Great Fire of 1845, but industrialization followed them to Oakland with the inauguration of the J&L mills in south Oakland in 1859; annexation to Pittsburgh followed a decade later.

Oakland would have become one of the crowded but colorful worker neighborhoods of Pittsburgh, comparable to Bloomfield or Lawrenceville, had it not been for a woman who clung to its past and four men who boldly fashioned its future. The woman was Mary Schenley; the men were Andrew Carnegie, Franklin Nicola, Henry Hornbostel, and John Bowman. Born in 1825, Mary Elizabeth Croghan Schenley was barely out of her teens when she inherited a thousand acres of choice land in central Pittsburgh from the holdings, a hundred times larger, that had been amassed by her grandfather James O'Hara before and after the revolutionary war. Although she owned so much of it, Mary Schenley did not choose to live in Pittsburgh. At fifteen she eloped with a captain in the British army who was twice-widowed and three times her age. She lived the remaining sixty-two years of her life in England and France, and when she died in 1903 she had not set foot in Pittsburgh for forty years. Still, she remained loyal to her city, and in 1889 she gave 400 acres to create Schenley Park as the eastern border of Oakland. The decisive move in the creation of Beaux Arts Oakland was made the next year, when Andrew Carnegie weaned away twenty acres of Schenley Park for construction of a huge library, museum, and music hall. Carnegie quadrupled his complex in size in 1907, and the Scaifes, Mellons, and Heinzes enlarged it again with the addition or restoration of an elaborate group of art galleries in 1974.

Carnegie's patronage of Oakland was the sign to other industrial leaders to endow the area with buildings of such magnificence that it might create a new Pittsburgh free from the stigma of the old. In one failed scheme, even the city hall of Pittsburgh was to move from the Triangle to Oakland. No planning document survives for the reshaping of Oakland, and probably none was ever drawn up, but the general intent seems to have been to make Oakland into a permanent re-creation of the six-month World Columbian Exposition held in Chicago in 1893. The fair took America by storm in its lavishness, its bold scale of planning, and the grandeur of its look-alike Imperial Roman buildings. Carnegie published an essay on the value of the fair for America, and he surely intended his own Carnegie Institute to act as a perpetual fair for art and natural history. Carnegie's partner Henry Phipps created a huge flower conservatory in 1893 that was not only the obvious successor to Horticultural Hall at the world's fair but actually sheltered many of the plants that had been on view in Chicago (some are still alive there today). The new campus of the Carnegie Technical Schools (now Carnegie-Mellon University) was built by Henry Hornbostel in the years 1903 to 1922 in the general shape of the Chicago fair's midway. Thus, the buildings and the streets of Oakland concretized the vision of a more glorious America that had been fleetingly raised in Chicago.

The man who effected the actual transformation of Mary Schenley's cow-fields into Pittsburgh's City Beautiful was Franklin Nicola. A wealthy Ohioan, Nicola had acquired some Schenley land while the heiress was still alive. His Schenley Hotel of 1898 was a stock venture that included Carnegie, Frick, A. W. Mellon, Westinghouse, and Heinz among its principal shareholders. It survives in superb condition, recently renovated as the University of Pittsburgh's student union. In 1905 Nicola's Schenley Land Company bought the remainder of the Schenley estate in the heart of Oakland and planned it as a model city with a separate character to each of its four quarters. The residential quarter (Schenley Farms) accommodated ninety-six houses, with another thirty-nine on a terrace above; the educational quarter took shape in 1908 as a vast Acropolis for the University of Pittsburgh. The monumental quarter eventually housed the Soldiers' and Sailors' Memorial Hall, the Masonic Temple, and other civic institutions, and in the social quarter a half-dozen private clubs still flourish.

With the exception of the Cathedral of Learning at the University of Pittsburgh, monumental Oakland was essentially complete, at least on paper, by 1910. It is best represented by the twelve blocks along the central spine of

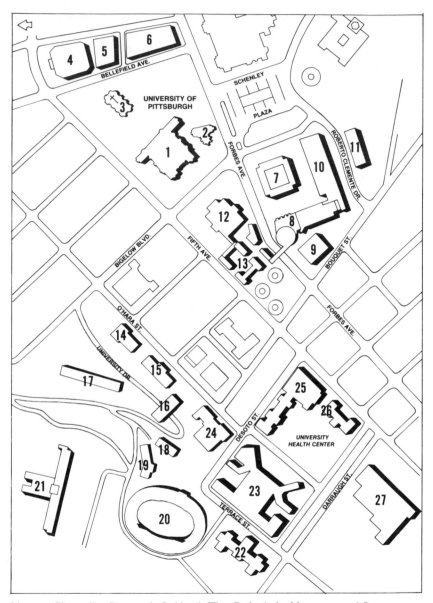

Map 6. Chancellor Bowman's Oakland: The Cathedral of Learning and Pitt

Fifth Avenue from the eastern outpost of Henry Hornbostel's Rodef Shalom Temple, past St. Paul's Cathedral, Benno Janssen's megalithic columns at Mellon Institute, and concluding with the Cathedral of Learning, Hornbostel's Soldiers' and Sailors' Memorial and his Schenley Apartments (now university dormitories). Since the time of Hornbostel and Nicola, the famed baseball sanctuary of Forbes Field has been demolished, several dozen hospital and educational buildings have been constructed, and there has been substantial rehabilitation of the houses in the shopping and entertainment area around Craig Street. The four founding fathers and the mother of Oakland would be surprised and at times dismayed to see what it is today, but in its general lines it has become what they envisioned: one of the great civic centers in the nation.

Chancellor Bowman's Oakland: The Cathedral of Learning and Pitt

To most Pittsburghers, Oakland is a college town in the midst of the city. Carnegie-Mellon University and Carlow College mark the eastern and western borders of this town, but at its heart are encamped the 50,000 students and employees of the University of Pittsburgh and its six affiliated hospitals. Pitt (the football nickname is by now inescapable) was born downtown in 1787 as the Pittsburgh Academy. After several changes of names and sites, it settled in 1908 on the forty-three acres that Franklin Nicola had reserved for it in Oakland a few years earlier. Along the way Pitt took care to educate Thomas Mellon and his sons, Andrew and Richard, who would later reward it with major funding for the Cathedral of Learning. Today, the university operates 52 buildings on 125 acres of land in Oakland. It is noted for strong departments in the humanities and the natural and social sciences, and it has made such contributions as daylight saving time, heavier-than-air aircraft before the Wright Brothers, the Salk polio vaccine, synthetic insulin, and pioneer work in heart and liver transplants.

The Cathedral of Learning

The university built only a few of the scores of Greco-Roman buildings that were to have crowned the eastern brow of The Hill in Henry Hornbostel's competition-winning scheme of 1908. The Acropolis concept was dropped when John Bowman (appointed university chancellor in 1920) decided to create the most extravagant college building in the world. A native of Nebras-

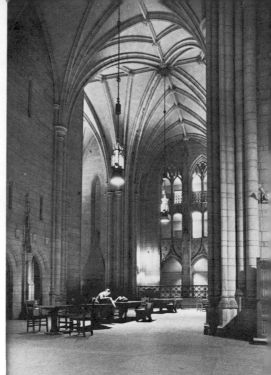

Left: The Cathedral of Learning, with Carnegie Institute's bronze statue of Johann Sebastian Bach /*Maurice Tierney* ▪ *Right:* The Commons Room, Cathedral of Learning /*Maurice Tierney*

ka, Bowman came to Pittsburgh in the same year that Bertram Grosvenor Goodhue began to build the Nebraska State Capitol in Lincoln as a towering beacon rising 400 feet over midwestern cornfields. Bowman needed a building of comparable brilliance to raise the importance of Pitt over an industrial landscape that had little use for education. (Prophetically, the decline of steel in Pittsburgh has done just that: Pitt is now the city's largest employer.) He found it in the **Cathedral of Learning.** Projected to rise fifty-five stories, the Cathedral would have been by far the tallest building in Pittsburgh and the second-tallest skyscraper in the world, after Manhattan's Woolworth Building.

To realize his astonishing vision, Bowman needed a site and an architect. The Mellons provided the former—fourteen acres that had been owned by H. C. Frick. The choice of designer fell on Charles Klauder, a Philadelphian who had assisted James Gamble Rogers in the Gothic dormitories at Yale and then worked independently for Princeton. (Bowman's memoirs record that he passed over Ralph Adams Cram because he was too fussy and Goodhue because he was dying. E. P. Mellon seems to have served briefly as his architect until they had a falling out.) There had never been such a tall education building before, although the Université de Montréal later came close, and Stalin's Moscow University topped it. Klauder was obliged to choose his prototypes from a disparate lot. What the Beaux Arts architects called the *parti* (the basic building image) developed from the Harkness Tower at Yale, on which he had assisted Rogers. To this he added elements from the plan and elevation of Goodhue's Nebraska State Capitol and from the first- and second-place winners in the *Chicago Tribune* competition of 1922. Undoubtedly influential too was Cass Gilbert's Woolworth Building, for its deft handling of scale, its "modern Gothic" style, and even its nickname as the "Cathedral of Commerce." By 1925 Art Deco had arrived from Paris, and this new style also left a strong impress on Klauder's design, particularly in the aluminum spandrel strips between the windows. (Aluminum was always a good thing to include in a Mellon-financed building—R. B. even had a model of the Cathedral cast in it.)

Chancellor Bowman unveiled his spectacular progeny in 1925 as a "Tower of Learning," but John McMahon, a Scots-born draftsman in Klauder's studio, muttered instead that it was a "Cadral of Larnin'," and the name stuck. The steel framework was begun in 1926 and work continued until October 21, 1929, eight days before the Stock Market Crash. To ensure that the building would not be truncated in the Depression, Bowman ordered the four floors of the base left bare of stonework until the full height of the building was reached. Some 17,000 adult Pittsburghers and 97,000 school children contributed to the project, which came to completion inside and out in 1937.

Frank Lloyd Wright was partially accurate when he scorned the Cathedral as "the world's largest keep-off-the-grass sign." In functional terms it never worked well, and increasingly the upper floors have been turned into administrative offices. Urbanistically, however, it is a sure triumph. The forty-story elevation can be monotonous when seen head-on, despite the setbacks and Gothic tracery, but when it is seen obliquely on Fifth or Forbes avenues from the east—precisely the routes A. W. and R. B. Mellon would take from their homes in Squirrel Hill—the composition sparkles with corner pinnacles that bud, bloom, and vanish into thin air. But aesthetic success was only secondary to Bowman, whose objective in building the Cathedral was to dominate everything in Pittsburgh physically and psychologically. Here it succeeded. For half a century his tower has blazed as the most brilliant structure in the city, and for a million working-class parents in western Pennsylvania, education means getting their children into the Cathedral at Pitt.

Klauder's natural aptitude for the extravagant was unleashed even more inside than outside the Cathedral, and in the **Commons Room** he concocted one of the most evocative architectural fantasies of the twentieth century. This immense room, 100 feet wide and 200 feet long, looks and acts like a cavern in a coal mine, calling Pittsburghers back to their bituminous or anthracitic origins. It is technically Gothic in construction, since the stone shafts and the rib-vaulting sixty feet above the floor are self-supporting, but the massive central piers are in fact screens for the main structural steel of the tower above.

The style is fifteenth-century English Perpendicular. The room is kept quiet despite its use by thousands of students every day because the stones between the ribs are actually Guastavino acoustical tiles. The carving is a botany lesson in indigenous western Pennsylvania plant life by the local carver Joseph Gattoni; the gates were fashioned in wrought iron by Samuel Yellin of Philadelphia. The Cathedral interior is remarkably intimate in feeling, from the warm green Vermont marble floors to the Gothic tracery that appears unexpectedly every few floors. The public rooms on the seventeenth floor offer excellent lookouts over Oakland, and the windows of the thirty-sixth floor provide still better views over the whole of Pittsburgh.

In the midst of its Gothic reverie, the Cathedral preserves on its ground floor an odd classical reminiscence of the "Mother of Oakland," Mary Schenley, and twenty rooms that record the contributions of Pittsburgh's ethnic communities to the city. Schenley is remembered by a gilt-stucco ballroom and an oval antechamber from her demolished family home "Pic-nic" in the Stanton Heights district. The rooms were created in 1835 by the Philadelphia carver Mordecai Van Horn, and they are among the most lavish Greek Revival designs in America. The other special designs are the twenty **Nationality Rooms** that were conceived in the 1920s by sociologist Ruth Crawford Mitchell as a means of linking the university with the immigrant cultures of the steelworking families. Guided tours at noonday and on weekends give a fascinating, if occasionally fantastic, view of twenty different architectural styles. Each room is a reproduction of a specific or synthetic environment, from fifth-century B.C. Athens through eighth-century A.D. China, Renaissance Italy, and Napoleonic France (bending the rules a little, since the rooms are supposed to predate the university's founding in 1787). While all the rooms are interesting, particularly enchanting are the Syria-Lebanon Room (the library of an eighteenth-century Damascus villa) and the Greek, Swedish, and Irish rooms. In the Irish Room, Pitt students and faculty read the whole of James Joyce's *Ulysses* every Bloomsday, June 16.

The grounds around the Cathedral were intended to carry a thicket of Oxford-style quadrangles, but in the end they were left luxuriously green except for memorial buildings to two quite different sons of Pittsburgh: Stephen Foster and H. J. Heinz. Klauder's **Stephen Foster Memorial** was completed in 1937, right in the shadow of the Cathedral. It is a combination theater (the popular Three Rivers Shakespeare Festival plays here each summer), social hall, research library, and dodecagonal shrine to the memory of Pittsburgh's rakish composer.

Heinz Memorial Chapel (1938) stands in isolation east of the Cathedral, where it seems to jump bolt-upright 253 feet from its flat plain to the top of its copper flèche. In setting, detailing, and emotional impact it more than holds it own against the better-known college chapels at Harvard, Duke, Princeton, and the University of Chicago. The chapel shows Klauder as a master at

Heinz Chapel /*Franklin Toker*

mixing sources of inspiration: the way the chapel leaps up as a miniature mountain is surely a rerun of the architectural darling of his generation, the island abbey of Mont-St.-Michel. The dimensions of the chapel and the general concept of the building as a bejeweled vessel could only stem from King Louis IX's Sainte-Chapelle in Paris. Klauder used a third model, St.-Maclou at Rouen, as precedent for the entrance-apse. Inside, the predominant note is the richness of the stone and wood carving and the luminescence of the stained glass. The doublet windows in the transept are claimed to be the highest anywhere, at seventy-three feet, and the quality and iconographic inventiveness of the glass throughout the chapel are probably without equal in the United States. Their fabricator was Charles Connick of Pittsburgh and Boston, who learned his trade in the glasshouses here and was a leader in the rediscovery of the principles of Gothic stained glass. This prodigious show of glass (about a quarter of a million separate pieces) would have particularly pleased H. J. Heinz, who loved stained glass and did much to promote its rebirth in Pittsburgh. It recalls Heinz in another way as well: his tremendous success in food processing came from his scrupulous quality control and his flair for advertising. Both these traits he combined in his decision to market his products in clear rather than frosted glass bottles, so customers could see how pure his foods were. The cornerstone of his empire was horseradish, but its prosperity was truly built on glass.

Mellon Institute, Carnegie-Mellon University /*Franklin Toker*

Mellon Institute

The **Mellon Institute** (4400 Fifth Ave., NW corner Bellefield; Janssen & Cocken, 1931–37), the former YMHA at 315 S. Bellefield, and the Board of Education are among the best of the dozen handsome buildings that ring the Cathedral grounds. The Institute, a division of Carnegie-Mellon University, is an astonishing performance in scale and architectural fantasy, almost equal to the Cathedral itself. It was one of four huge buildings the Mellons completed during the Depression, along with the Gulf Building, the Cathedral of Learning, and the East Liberty Presbyterian Church. In each of these projects it was R. B. rather than A. W. Mellon who delighted in the mountain of construction details, even driving at the head of the procession when some of the Mellon Institute columns were brought through the Oakland streets. The brothers had founded the institute together in 1911 as the world's first research and development center for industry. After it outgrew two other buildings, Richard Mellon and Benno Janssen carefully prepared a third home that would last a century. Janssen's prime model was probably Carl Friedrich Schinkel's Altes Museum in Berlin of 1823, with the same configuration of a hollow square fronted by a heroic Ionic colonnade and cut in two by an axial hall. The same model had already been used west of Pittsburgh for the Greek Revival capitol in Columbus, Ohio, and on the East Coast by Guy Lowell for his Boston Museum of Fine Arts, but the precedent that probably meant more in terms of Mellon dynastic interests was Robert Mills's Treasury Building of 1836 in Washington. This was exactly right as a heroic Ionic colonnade, and it conveyed to the world an architectural message the Mellons were particularly anxious to send. In 1931 the ten-year reign of A. W. Mellon as Secretary of the

Treasury was coming to an end. In the flush of the Roaring Twenties he had seemed to be a genius, but now critics in Congress were snapping at his heels, and impeachment proceedings had just started against him. Mellon quieted his critics by exchanging Pittsburgh and Washington. For Washington he built the National Gallery of Art, whose collection included several paintings from his home in Pittsburgh. For Pittsburgh he built Mellon Institute, which bore the face of his Treasury Building in Washington.

Benno Janssen designed Mellon Institute to the ultimate standard of all classical-revival buildings—the Parthenon. His Fifth Avenue elevation replicates the length of the Parthenon, and for good measure he copied the main elevation on the other three sides, even on a back alley. The colonnades rise two stories, with slit windows behind them, while the building digs down to bedrock (to minimize vibration in scientific experiments) six more stories below. Having matched the Parthenon, the Mellons exceeded it in one spectacular gesture. At the Parthenon, Ictinus and Callicrates, like all Greek and most Roman architects, were constrained to build their columns by piling up drums of marble or stone. These columns were instead hacked out of solid 125-ton chunks of Indiana limestone, then slimmed to their final weight of 60 tons. Even the capitals weigh five tons apiece. To ensure justness of proportions at such mammoth scale, a full-size replica of the corner and two columns was secretly constructed of plaster and wood at a cost of $50,000 in a cornfield north of Dorseyville in the Allegheny Valley so that R. B. Mellon could see what he was getting. R. B. was satisfied, and two weeks later the mock-up vanished.

The two handsome buildings south of Mellon Institute now appear in its architectural shadow, though each predates Mellon and the Cathedral of Learning. **The Board of Public Education** (341 S. Bellefield; Ingham & Boyd, 1927) is the more prominent of the two: a graceful Renaissance palace of exquisitely beveled limestone blocks and Michelangelesque windows, with a quiet garden court in the middle. Less prominent but no less accomplished architecturally is the middle trapezoid on the block, the old YMHA that is now known as **315 S. Bellefield** (Benno Janssen, 1924). The Kaufmann's were the mainstay of the Y in the 1920s and principal patrons of its new building. Benno Janssen was the obvious choice as architect not only because of his closeness to the family but also because he had already proved his mettle at clubhouse architecture two blocks away in his Pittsburgh Athletic Association. With his characteristic mastery of architectural history, Janssen forged a match between one facade from the Italian Renaissance (the Palazzo Piccolomini delle Papesse in Siena) and another from eighteenth-century Virginia (the Lee House at Stratford) for the Flemish-bond brick finish and the peculiarly high basement. This improbable combination works superbly both in form and in function. The high attic profile, for example, hides a flat expanse of roof where two generations of Y patrons could sunbathe in total privacy. The same mix of practicality and art extends to the interior, which combines full sports facilities and meeting rooms with one of the historic concert halls in the city (Arthur Rubinstein, Isaac Stern, Jean-Pierre Rampal, and a host of music luminaries made their Pittsburgh debuts here). Here Janssen did not shrink from wedding a Spanish stalactite ceiling with Jacobean moldings on the walls. Eight squash courts are positioned directly over the auditorium: sports enthusiasts are entreated not to play while concerts are in progress below.[1]

University of Pittsburgh Buildings on Schenley Plaza

The expansion of Pitt's physical plant in the 1960s required the demolition of Forbes Field. One of the first modern sports arenas in the country, the Pirates' famed home had stood from 1909 to 1971 on **Schenley Plaza,** where its spirit hovers ghostlike over its replacement buildings today.[2] After coal magnate John Hillman donated the land bordering the stadium to Pitt in the 1950s, the architect Max Abramovitz prepared a master plan for a sequence of classroom and professional buildings that would replace the stadium once it fell. Four buildings were placed on the site between 1967 and 1978: Hillman Library, David L. Lawrence Hall, the Law Building, and Forbes Quadrangle—none of them important as architecture, although Hillman creates a functional and pleasant environment as a research and undergraduate library for its users and its three million books.

Fortunately, the university's more recent buildings have been superior to those four in design sensitivity and practicality. The glass-walled **Mervis Hall** at the corner of Schenley Plaza and Roberto Clemente Drive was built by the IKM/SGE partnership in 1983 on another part of the Forbes Field site to house Pitt's Graduate School of Business. Its stark roofline is out of place in the Victorian environment of Bouquet Street, but the scalloped recess in the facade softens the hardness of the glass and proclaims the entrance in a way many all-glass structures forget to do. In the gentle russet tone of the vertical

1. Visitors to 315 S. Bellefield might wonder at the large blank lunettes on the upper lobby walls. In the late 1930s Edgar Kaufmann discovered the Mexican muralist Juan O'Gorman, of the same generation as Rivera, Orozco, and Siqueiros, and commissioned a set of murals from O'Gorman to fill the space. O'Gorman came to Pittsburgh and sketched out the full series, but the Y board was not enchanted with his Marxist imagery and preferred the walls bare.

2. Forbes Field was built as a partnership between Franklin Nicola and Barney Dreyfuss, who had forged the old Allegheny baseball team into the Pirates (a name bestowed not for any special nautical skills, but because Dreyfuss continually pirated away the best players in the game with high salaries). After sixty years of service, Forbes Field was finally strangled by a chaotic parking situation and was replaced by Three Rivers Stadium on the North Side in 1971. Although the old ballpark was destroyed at that time, its left-outfield wall and home plate are intact today, the latter preserved on the ground floor of Forbes Quadrangle. Forbes Field also appears regularly on television, in replays of MGM's 1951 baseball classic, *Angels in the Outfield*.

Left: Mervis Hall */Courtesy IKM/SGE Inc.* ▪ *Right:* William Pitt Union */Franklin Toker*

and horizontal accents in the glass there is even a recollection of the nearby outfield wall of Forbes Field. The effect is businesslike, as the designers surely intended, but also startlingly serene, combining the ripple effect of the glass, the profusion of greenery reflected in the mirror, and the gaggle of frame houses alongside and behind it.

The rebuilding of Franklin Nicola's old Schenley Hotel, diagonally opposite Schenley Plaza, into the **William Pitt Student Union** (Rutan & Russell, 1898; restoration by Williams Trebilcock Whitehead, 1983) also involved working with memories—in this case the legends of such national trendsetters as Diamond Jim Brady and Lillian Russell, who had lived or partied there (Russell in suite 437, now restored), of all the presidents from Theodore Roosevelt through Eisenhower who stopped there overnight, and of the famed Eleanora Duse, who on April 21, 1924, died there. The building is an elegant ten-story skyscraper of thin tawny-brown Roman bricks, and it boasts a succession of lavish public suites, which had been allowed to decay. The restoration program was functionally and philosophically complex, calling for the conservation of the major public rooms as period pieces, the conversion of the hotel rooms above into modern student activity offices, and the addition of new dining and recreation rooms in the old basement. The response of the restoration architects to this basically schizophrenic program was a basically schizophrenic building: luxuriously and meticulously Belle Epoque on the main floor, functionally modern in the office floors above, extravagantly post-Modern in the basement below. What one sees today could be mistaken for a collaboration of Stanford White in the old rooms and Giulio Romano and Robert Venturi in the new ones. Inside the basement the decor is pleasurably surrealistic: fat tubular columns with triple necking grooves, as though visitors had stumbled unaware into a gigantic Palladian pinball machine. Duse, had she lived here and not died here, would have enjoyed it.

The Pitt upper campus, with the escalator-like Learning Research & Development Center and surviving buildings of the Acropolis plan of 1908 /*Courtesy University of Pittsburgh (Norman Schumm)*

The Pitt Upper Campus

The Pitt campus divides into a lower portion on and near Schenley Plaza and an upper campus north of O'Hara Street, with various buildings on Bouquet and DeSoto streets acting as a bridge between the two parts. The most significant of the intermediary buildings are the seven blocks of undergraduate dormitories that were once the luxury **Schenley Apartments** (Henry Hornbostel & Eric Fisher Wood, 1923) that Franklin Nicola added to the back of the Schenley Hotel. On and above O'Hara Street there survive several buildings from the Acropolis project of Henry Hornbostel (1908–12), which might have produced the most dramatic college setting on earth: **Thaw Hall** and

Allen Hall on O'Hara Street and the **Mineral Industries Building** and **Pennsylvania Hall** on the hillside. Two other structures not built by Hornbostel but in accord with his master plan are **Alumni Hall** (Benno Janssen, 1920) and **Pitt Stadium** (1925).

The Acropolis scheme was one more manifestation of the overreaching ambition of Edwardian Pittsburgh to have the biggest and most dramatic of everything. It called for sixty buildings to rise in terraces several hundred feet up The Hill, whose brow would have been crowned by a full-scale reproduction of the Forum of Trajan in Rome (the 1950s Veterans' Administration Hospital now stands at the summit instead). Giant escalators were planned to move students up and down the hill. In addition to its ancient prototypes in Athens and Rome, the campus project followed two recent models: the 1893 world's fair at Chicago, and the winning scheme in the *premier grand prix* competition at the Ecole des Beaux-Arts in 1897, while Hornbostel was still in attendance. The project appears mad to us today—until we reflect that it was abandoned in favor of the still more ambitious Cathedral of Learning.

The prima donna of architecture on O'Hara Street today is not a Hornbostel building but an escalatorlike structure that houses the **Learning Research and Development Center** (3939 O'Hara Street; Harrison & Abramovitz, 1974). Regarded as the Brookhaven of education because of its lavish support by the federal government, the center is recognized worldwide in the fields of language comprehension and computer applications in educational research. LRDC is shaped like a giant staircase against the hillside because it was meant to act like one: the bare patch on the right side of the lobby was designed to carry a huge escalator to lift students to a proposed dormitory complex above. It was a last reminder of Hornbostel's escalator plan two generations earlier, and it met the same fate.

The University Health Center

Pornography and medical centers are the twin urban blights that every American city fights to keep under control. Pittsburgh tries to pen both scourges within narrow "combat zones": Liberty Avenue for the former, Oakland for the latter. In the superblock bounded or touched by DeSoto, Terrace, and Darraugh streets and Fifth Avenue, about forty buildings, the **University Health Center,** constitute one of the world's most concentrated medical complexes, where for half a century such eminences as Jonas Salk, Benjamin Spock, Erik Erikson, and Thomas Starzl have practiced medicine and allied fields. Although it would take a neurosurgeon to sort it out, there is some distinguished architecture as well as an important chapter in medical history to be found in this mass of buildings, which features **Children's Hospital** (York & Sawyer, with E. P. Mellon, 1927), the octopus-shaped **Presbyterian-**

University Hospital (York & Sawyer, with E. P. Mellon, 1930–38), and E. P. Mellon's **Falk Clinic** of 1930. (The participation of A. W. Mellon's nephew in these buildings parallels his work downtown: he appears to have been the watchdog over the Mellons' philanthropic as well as their commercial buildings.)

East of the medical superblock stands the Art Deco **Western Psychiatric Institute and Clinic** (3815 O'Hara St., NE corner DeSoto; Marlier & Stevens, 1942), a world leader in psychiatry, where Spock and Erikson collaborated in their study of disturbed children. A look-alike Art Deco counterpart to the northwest is **Jonas E. Salk Hall** (formerly the Municipal Hospital; NE corner Darraugh & Terrace Sts.; Richard Irving & Theodore Eichholz, 1940), where the Salk vaccine was developed in the early 1950s. (Salk's labs were on the ground floor and in the basement. He used rhesus monkeys in his work, and years later the walls were said to bear the paw prints of animals that had scampered out of their cages.) On the steep hillside west of Presbyterian stands **Montefiore Hospital** (3459 Fifth Ave.; Schmidt, Garden & Erickson, 1929), a Georgian Revival structure that originally descended its slope in three terraces but now lies buried under later additions. Wiser heads prevailed in the adjoining block at **Carlow College** (3333 Fifth Ave.; original Sisters of Mercy Convent by Edward Stotz, 1909), where a dozen late Gothic Revival red-brick structures have gone up since 1929 without such overcrowding. The wooded stretches of hillside between the buildings still convey a faint suggestion of what made Oakland so desirable a location in the first place.

Andrew Carnegie's Oakland: Carnegie Institute and CMU

That Andrew Carnegie had a genius for business is clear from his career. A penniless boy of thirteen when his family came from Scotland to Pittsburgh in 1848, Carnegie required only twenty years to amass a first fortune in railroads, a second fortune in oil, and a third fortune, ten times greater, in steel. But Carnegie had hardly less genius for public relations. He was richer by far than any of the other robber barons of turn-of-the-century America, but while such names as Morgan, Rockefeller, Frick, and Ford are recalled today either equivocally or with distaste, Carnegie has been regarded for a hundred years as the model industrialist. The skill in public relations that Carnegie would one day demonstrate worldwide was first seen on a grand scale in Pittsburgh with the building of Carnegie Institute and Carnegie-Mellon University, the two dominant architectural complexes of the southeast corner of Oakland. Carnegie saw the two building groups as one (there was in fact an early project

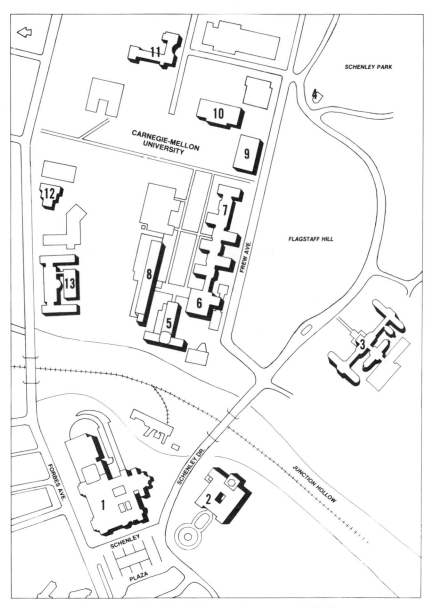

Map 7. Andrew Carnegie's Oakland: Carnegie Institute and CMU

1 Carnegie Institute & Library
2 Frick Fine Arts Bldg.
3 Phipps Conservatory
4 George Westinghouse Memorial
5 Hamerschlag Hall

6 Porter Hall
7 Baker Hall
8 Wean Hall
9 Hunt Library
10 College of Fine Arts

11 M. Morrison Carnegie Hall
12 University Computing Center
13 U.S. Bureau of Mines

to join them with a private bridge). The deep gully of Junction Hollow that runs between them was not regarded as a dividing point between Oakland and the residential neighborhoods to the east, but instead as a mirror in which the two different parts of Oakland could admire and congratulate each other. The mirror was almost obliterated in the 1960s, when Pitt proposed to fill Junction Hollow with an enormous research center. Sadly for Pittsburgh's research prospects but happily for its topographic drama, the project known as "Oakland upside-down" died at birth. Schenley Park and its romantic Junction and Panther hollows continue unimproved as integral parts of the Oakland experience.

Carnegie Institute and Carnegie Library of Pittsburgh

"We are all Pittsburghers; I have made my fortune here and by the aid of very enterprising partners I find myself busily engaged in investing it here. I link my fortunes with Pittsburghers—stand and fall with them."

In 1890 Andrew Carnegie spoke these words as a preface to his declaration of a gift to Pittsburgh of a central library, museum, and music hall. Before his death in 1919, Carnegie gave away $350,000,000, including 2,500 libraries and 7,000 church organs the world over, but none of his gifts pleased him more than this one. The **Carnegie Library** and **Carnegie Institute** building (4400 Forbes Ave. at Schenley Plaza; Longfellow, Alden & Harlow, 1895; Alden & Harlow, 1907; Edward Larabee Barnes, 1974) stretches 600 feet long on its Schenley Plaza facade and almost 800 feet long on its Forbes Avenue side—long enough that city buses are obliged to make two stops in front of it. But the importance of Carnegie Institute for Pittsburgh goes beyond its size. Architecturally, this eight-acre building is the grandest monument of Beaux Arts planning in the city, but it was recognized outside Pittsburgh, too: it appeared in the *Encyclopaedia Brittanica* of 1911 as the exemplar of the modern museum. Culturally, it marked the end of the Dark Ages for a town that had wealth but little real culture before the institute opened in 1895. (Its impact on Pittsburgh was made amply clear by Willa Cather, both in her personal correspondence and in her short story "Paul's Case," which is partly set in the library and music hall.) Today the museums of art and natural history, the library and its eighteen branches, the music hall, and the lecture hall support more varied activities than any other American cultural institution except the Smithsonian. Carnegie Institute was probably even more important to Pittsburgh in urban terms, as the flagship building to break out of the "old" city in the Triangle. So remote from town that it had to produce its own heat and electricity, it pointed a new direction physically and spiritually to a city that had been exclusively interested in production, and it gave birth not only to

Carnegie Institute and Carnegie Library of Pittsburgh, with Carnegie-Mellon University in the distance /*Maurice Tierney*

Oakland but to the residential quarters of Shadyside, Highland Park, Squirrel Hill, and Point Breeze.

The competition announced in 1891 for Carnegie Library was the most heralded contest in American architecture up to that time, and it drew 102 entries and 1,300 drawings from 96 architects in 28 cities. The winning firm of Longfellow, Alden & Harlow had built the Duquesne Club just two years before, which gave them entrée with anyone who counted in Pittsburgh, but they might have won even without that edge.[3] Richardson's courthouse had been dedicated with acclaim just three years earlier, but rather than serving up an exclusively Richardsonian design here, the three partners indulged in the lighter eclecticism of McKim, Mead & White. They looked west as well as east and were evidently taken by Henry I. Cobb's Newberry Library in Chicago, designed in 1887. The similarities of their design to Newberry Library could not be more marked in the general massing, the handling of the masonry blocks, and the late-Gothic windows. Through the Villard Houses of McKim, Mead & White in New York and the Newberry Library, the partners were led back to the Medici Palace in fifteenth-century Florence—always a nice compliment to a powerful patron. The names of the twenty-four authors that are carved above the windows were personally approved by Carnegie, who was a

3. The Longfellow, Alden & Harlow partnership (Alden & Harlow alone after 1896) is forgotten today, but in the years 1890 to 1910 it probably handled a volume of business equal to all but the very top design offices in New York. Its success was based on a combination of the social skills and connections of Alexander Longfellow (a nephew of the poet), who had apprenticed with both Richardson and Stanford White; the design skills of Alfred Harlow, another White disciple; and the managerial skills of Frank Alden, Richardson's job superintendent at the Pittsburgh courthouse.

voracious reader and probably knew at least one book or play by each. In the 1907 addition, the names in this literary pantheon were joined by several score more names in art, science, and music.

The library plan is historically unrelated to its exterior and seems to reflect the Romanesque double-transepted, double-apsed basilica of St. Michael at Hildesheim, Germany. The smaller of the two apses, toward Schenley Drive, serves today as the children's library. The larger apse projected boldly toward Forbes Avenue and was crowned with twin Venetian campanili copied from the Courthouse. This apse still stands today as the semicircular Carnegie Music Hall, but it lost its campanili when it was masked externally by the later wing of 1907. Inside the library, the rooms and halls are charmingly laid out with alcoves and Palladian arched screens in the manner of a very large but still intimate private house. Upstairs is a sequence of beautiful rooms with skylights, unfortunately now blind, in which the world's first international exhibits of modern art were held as the Carnegie Internationals, beginning in 1896. The Music Hall on Forbes Avenue is an especially successful half-Pantheon shape inside, recalling the pure geometric intensity of neoclassical France as exemplified by the renowned anatomical theater of Jacques Gondoin of 1769 in Paris. Its surface decoration refers instead to the works of the young Bramante in Milan—provincial rather than Roman Renaissance.

In November 1898 Carnegie read about extraordinary dinosaur finds in Wyoming and financed an expedition to secure the world's greatest collection of dinosaur fossils for Pittsburgh. He also resolved to quadruple the size of his library to include permanent galleries for art and natural history. Two years later Alden & Harlow drew up plans and elevations for the vast extension along Forbes Avenue that opened in 1907. They retained the old design of pillow-shaped ashlars in the Cleveland sandstone base but gave the new work the massiveness of form and scale that the critics had so applauded at the Chicago world's fair. To mask the transition between the two parts of the building, an enormous pivot was created in the pyramidal-capped roof of the Hall of Architecture that broods over the whole.

Inside, the new museum raised the spatial and textural articulation of the old portion to a level of operatic sumptuousness that rivals or exceeds its probable model, Charles Garnier's opera house in Paris. Six thousand tons of European marble—some from the very quarry that supplied Pentelic marble for the Parthenon in Athens—decorate these halls. The building contains about four miles of marble wainscoting, enough to justify Philip Johnson's quip that there is more Sienese marble in Carnegie Institute than is left in Siena. The most exuberant of the interior spaces is the **Music Hall Foyer,** built about a peripteral colonnade of mammoth Giallo Antico marble columns as the new entrance to the earlier Music Hall. The crowning entablature and the ribs penetrating the cove ceiling are covered in sheets of gold leaf and were laid out in the general rhythm of the ceiling compartments for Michelangelo's

The Hall of Architecture, Carnegie
Institute /*Maurice Tierney*

frescoes in the Sistine Chapel (as another compliment to the patron?). The
foyer is presided over by a life-size gilded bronze statue of Carnegie seated on
an Ionic throne topped by finials of Scottish thistles. Around the base is carved
his favorite motto: "All is well since all grows better."

The whole of Carnegie Institute is fascinating to explore, both for its
exhibits and for the visual experience of its enormous corridors and rooms *en
suite*. Some 10,000 exhibits of natural history are on display, with twenty times
that number kept in reserve for scientific study. The **Hall of Dinosaurs,**
unrivaled anywhere, includes a *diplodicus carnegii* and an *apatasaurus louisiae*,
which immortalize the patron and his wife. Carnegie's spirit can be caught
even more vividly in two rooms flanking the Carriage Drive vestibule: his
feminine side in a beautifully stenciled Venetian drawing room to the right; his
masculine side in the dark mahogany boardroom (briefly glimpsed in the
movie *Flashdance*) to the left, with his rolltop desk still in use. The painting
collection in the Museum of Art is strong on Impressionism and Post-Impres-
sionism and particularly good on American art between the world wars. It
contains top examples of work by Rouault, Matisse, and Monet and a repre-
sentation of the art of its native sons and daughter Andy Warhol, Philip
Pearlstein, Mel Bochner, and Mary Cassatt. The towering forty-foot-high
weathered steel sculpture by Richard Serra in front of the Scaife Gallery is
called *Carnegie*.

To connoisseurs and children alike, the most memorable works of art in
Carnegie Institute are the casts inhabiting the **Hall of Architecture.** Carnegie
had no feeling for two-dimensional art and, ever the democrat, disdained the
Old Masters that Frick and Mellon were collecting in favor of promoting
modern works that might be the Old Masters of the future. The art form that

suited him best was the plaster cast, since casts of famous buildings and sculptures appealed to his drive for excellence and passion for education. In close contact with the head of fine arts at the museum, Carnegie financed a search for approximately 1,200 of the best models in architecture and sculpture to be cast in plaster for Pittsburgh. For five years an army of agents throughout Europe worked to secure these casts, some from preexisting molds, others unique. Two men were kept busy in Pittsburgh merely translating the foreign-language telegrams that were received and dispatched. The major triumph was the cast of the Romanesque abbey church of St.-Gilles-du-Gard, the largest in the world at eighty-seven feet in length. It was made in 195 separate castings that were borne from Marseille to New York on three different steamships. The quality of the collection exceeds that of the Musée des Monuments Français in Paris, its model, and is probably second only to the Victoria and Albert collection in London on a world scale. To house the collection, Alden & Harlow prepared a hall 126 feet square, 76 feet tall to its inner skylights, and 137 feet to its outer skylights, stepped up like the Mausoleum of Halicarnassus. The effect of the casts and the colossal space is little short of hypnotic. If a single room could be said to represent the power and ambition of the Gilded Age in Pittsburgh, this is it.

Schenley Plaza and the Frick Fine Arts Building

The path from Carnegie Institute to Carnegie-Mellon University leads through **Schenley Plaza** (landscape design by Sellers & Register, 1915) and

Mary Schenley Fountain and the University of Pittsburgh's Frick Fine Arts Building
/*Franklin Toker*

past further reminders of Carnegie's partners Henry Frick and Henry Phipps. The plaza covers what had been the broad gully of St. Pierre's Ravine. In a particularly fine example of urban symbiosis, the ravine was filled in by the earth shaved off The Hump on Grant Street from 1912 to 1915. A fine stone bridge had been set over the far end of the gully in 1898, and it too was buried in 1915. Over its broad arch was constructed the **Mary Schenley Fountain** (Victor Brenner, sculptor; H. Van Buren Magonigle, architect, 1918), immediately in front of the Frick Fine Arts Building. The fountain is one of a set of sculptures erected in thanks to the three citizens responsible for the creation of Schenley Park: Schenley, Bigelow, and Magee.[4] Brenner, its sculptor, was a Russian-Jewish immigrant who is best known as the designer of the Lincoln penny. His fountain evokes the rebirth of nature through the asymmetrical opposition of the earthbound Pan hibernating and the spirit of Harmony, who wakes him with a song played on his stolen pipes. The sculpture fails to achieve its objective of organizing the loose space of Schenley Plaza as it was meant to, but as an independent object it works extremely well—tribute to a style in which neither Nature nor allegory was an embarrassment at the hand of an artist.

The true link between Schenley Plaza and Schenley Park today is, however, not the Schenley Fountain, but its neighboring Renaissance villa, the University of Pittsburgh's **Henry Clay Frick Fine Arts Building** (B. Kenneth Johnston Associates, 1965). This is one of three Frick art buildings in Pittsburgh, along with Frick's mansion and the Frick Art Museum in Point Breeze. It was created by Helen Frick, who had founded the Department of Fine Arts at Pitt in 1928. The growth of the department was unexpectedly vigorous in the rocky soil of Pittsburgh: today it is one of the best in the nation. To house it properly, Frick sought out the successors to Carrère and Hastings for a replica of the Italian *palazzo* they had constructed for her father in New York a half-century before. The commission eventually fell to a local firm that was more comfortable in concrete than Carrara, but the Renaissance image remained paramount. The prototype was Vignola's Villa Giulia on the outskirts of sixteenth-century Rome. The Frick building consists of a series of classrooms, a richly appointed library, art galleries grouped about an open cloister, and a forty-five-foot-high octagon capped by a pyramidal roof. The cloister is one of

---

4. Edward Manning Bigelow (sculpted by Giuseppe Moretti at the park entrance, 1895) secured the park for the city and built Grant (today Bigelow) Boulevard to link it for three miles to the Triangle. The memorial stele to Christopher Lyman Magee in front of Carnegie Library was designed by Henry Bacon and sculpted by Augustus Saint-Gaudens in 1908. Magee was Bigelow's cousin and the political boss of Pittsburgh. In 1904 Lincoln Steffens singled him out in *The Shame of the Cities* as among the most corrupt politicians in the country, but he got along well with Carnegie and smoothed the path for the construction of the library on city property. It was Magee's street railway that transported workers from their slum neighborhoods to enjoy the amenities of Oakland.

the delightful sights of Pittsburgh, displaying a series of meticulous fresco reproductions that the celebrated restorer Nicholas Lochoff had prepared in Italy for the Moscow Museum of Fine Arts. Stranded in Florence by the October Revolution, Lochoff appealed to Bernard Berenson, who recommended their purchase to Helen Frick. The sumptuousness of the cloister and the library, the aura of Berenson and Frick that hangs over the building, and the scholarly art exhibits in the galleries make Frick Fine Arts a rewarding place to explore.

Junction Hollow and Schenley Park

Just beyond the Frick building is the great natural drama of Oakland, **Schenley Park.** But the great drama is preceded by the little drama of **Junction Hollow.** The hollow, dividing Schenley Park from the rest of Oakland by a 150-foot-deep gorge, was known to early Pittsburghers as Four-Mile Run, and in origin it was one of many runoffs when the prehistoric Monongahela River coursed through Oakland in the last ice age. Its old name derived straightforwardly from its distance from The Point, while the current name refers to the tracks of the Pittsburgh Junction Railroad that were laid here in 1884–86. (There is also some willful confusion with the more alluring name of Panther Hollow, which lies to the south.)

Junction Hollow supports a jumble of frame houses that cling to its sides despite all the laws of gravity. Above it rises Henry Hornbostel's splendid Hamerschlag Hall at Carnegie-Mellon University, with the huge arch that was intended to be the launching point for a bridge to Carnegie Institute. Below the bridge is an evocative relic of the early days of Oakland in the **Bellefield Boiler Plant** (Alden & Harlow, 1907), which for years provided steam not only to heat Carnegie Institute but also to power the dynamos that gave the institute its own electricity. The Romanesque Revival plant still receives coal through its own trestle entrance from the railroad tracks. Although it no longer creates electricity, it does supply steam heat to about a dozen neighboring institutions. It was for this hollow that Harrison & Abramovitz projected their "Oakland upside-down" research center in 1963. Seven stories high and a mile long, the structure would have filled the gully, with railway tracks and a motor expressway tunneled through at the bottom. Five thousand scientists would have joined Pitt and Carnegie-Mellon to make this the world's largest research unit, but the promise of federal funding died with President Kennedy, and it joined the list of Pittsburgh projects that were too ambitious to be built.

The story of the creation of Schenley Park (William Falconer, landscape designer, 1890–95) is as long as the millions of years it took Nature to shape it and as short as the transatlantic race that decided who would get it. This was the heart of Mary Schenley's inherited estate, complete with two eighteenth-

Junction Hollow, with Hamerschlag Hall /*Franklin Toker*

century log houses, and Edward Bigelow raced his lawyer to London ahead of
a commercial realtor in order to persuade Schenley to give it to Pittsburgh as
park land rather than develop it as housing. Under Bigelow's guidance,
Schenley Park received Phipps Conservatory in 1893, an artificial ice rink, a
band shell, a racetrack, an electrically operated water organ, and extensive
boating facilities on the artificially created Panther Hollow Lake. Bigelow then
directed the design of four bridges to give the city access to the new park.
Two of these are now replaced, but the **Panther Hollow Bridge** arches over
its gully as Bigelow intended, complete with four splendid bronze panthers by
Giuseppe Moretti, from 1897. (Panthers—actually mountain lions—were
hunted in these woods until the early nineteenth century.) Bigelow had
enticed Moretti from Siena to play the role of court sculptor in Pittsburgh:
here he ennobled public works of all sorts for a generation.

As in its evident model of Central Park thirty years before, the scenic vistas
and dramatic contrasts in the landscape of Schenley Park were not God-given;
they had to be coaxed out of the land by human ingenuity. The artist here was
another Bigelow import, the English landscape designer William Falconer,
who gave the land its long serpentine carriage drives and shaped it in the
tradition of the eighteenth-century romantics. Particularly successful is **Flagstaff Hill,** a vast natural amphitheater ringed with trees at its periphery. It is
the city's premier spot for kiting on windy days, and it works elegantly and
efficiently for the movies, concerts, and plays that are presented there almost
every summer night.

Dreamlike and fantastic, **Phipps Conservatory** (Lord & Burnham, 1893)
stands just across the Schenley Park Bridge under the watchful gaze of
Giuseppe Moretti's Bigelow statue. In plan it is the most intricate Beaux Arts
building in the city, with a succession of major and minor axes and cross-axes

Left: Phipps Conservatory, Schenley Park /*Franklin Toker* ▪ *Right:* George Westinghouse Memorial /*Franklin Toker*

in the manner of a mid-century French insane asylum. On a national scale Phipps is much more than that: it was the first permanent demonstration of a large-scale enclosed botanical garden in the United States, and its two and a half acres still rank it as the largest greenhouse in the country. It was probably the only American conservatory of its time with such precise climate control that it could grow Victoria lilies, its most sensational exhibit. (The lilies were so large and resilient that visitors would step onto them like rafts.) The conservatory's pavilion roofs rise in billowing curves over the ogive vaults of the long halls to create the proper note of Kubla Kahn exoticism, while three fine bronze sculptures sound grace notes around it: Frank Vittor's colossal *Christopher Columbus* (1958), Giuseppe Moretti's *Hygeia* (1922), and John Massey Rhind's *Robert Burns* (1914), largely paid for by Andrew Carnegie himself.

A few moments' walk into a fertile glen near Phipps offers a reflection on Pittsburgh's most original millionaire. A pond, a jet of water, a gilded bronze youth, and a set of narrative reliefs constitute the **Westinghouse Memorial** (Daniel Chester French & Paul Fjelde, sculptors; Henry Hornbostel & Eric Fisher Wood, architects, 1930). The conception of this memorial presented a thorny problem. Unlike memorials to heroes such as Paul Revere, whose glorious deeds are known to all, the Westinghouse Memorial had to rehabilitate the memory of someone who had died humiliated, bypassed, and alone. George Westinghouse was one of the most versatile inventors in American history, ranking second only to Thomas Edison in the number of patents he filed annually during the 1870s and 1880s. He invented air brakes, signals, and switches to make railroad travel safer and more efficient; he created the first gas and electric meters and shock absorbers; and he was a pioneer in natural gas, compressed air, electric machinery, and AC electricity. But his firm had been snatched from him by New York bankers shortly before his death in 1914, and Westinghouse retreated to the Point Breeze estate he had prophetically named "Solitude" years before.

Henry Hornbostel was hired to coordinate this memorial, which was commissioned fifteen years after the death of Westinghouse by 60,000 loyal employees around the world. He evidently realized that it had to be both an icon and a narrative and serve not merely to depict the deceased but to document him, even to set the record straight. His response was to stop up a small stream, set a weeping willow (the neoclassical sign of grief) and six black Norwegian granite benches as aids to meditation around the resulting pond, and erect a monumental exedra as focus. The exedra holds a portrait medallion of Westinghouse flanked by a worker and a scientist, and six plaques documenting his exploitation or development of the railroad air brake, steam turbines, signaling systems, the harnessing of Niagara Falls for power, and the alternating-current system of electricity. Opposite, emerging from the pond as though in a magic boat, stands French's penetrating characterization of an idealistic youth studying what made Westinghouse great. Here is a memorial that does more than commemorate: it redresses the slights of history; it gives peace to the dead.

Carnegie-Mellon University

The year 1900 was a good one for Andrew Carnegie. He reorganized his steel companies preparatory to selling them the next year to J. P. Morgan for half a billion dollars; he sought plans for the enlargement of his Carnegie Institute; and he promised the mayor of Pittsburgh to build a School of Applied Industries if the city would provide the land. The Carnegie Technical Schools held its architectural competition in 1903, opened in 1906, changed its name to Carnegie Institute of Technology in 1912 and to **Carnegie-Mellon University** in 1968. CMU has had a meteoric rise among world universities in recent years and has emerged as the nation's foremost center for computer science, robotics, and artificial intelligence.

Finding the right site for Carnegie's school was no problem: once again the ward boss Christopher Magee proved helpful as part-owner of a thirty-two-acre cabbage patch on the opposite side of Junction Hollow from Carnegie Institute. Part of the land, toward Schenley Park, was ready-made for a campus, long and flat. But the other section on Forbes Avenue seemed useless: part was cut through by a deep ravine, and part rose about sixty feet in a small hill. The hill would be graded away half a century later, but for the time being it was inviolate: A. W. Mellon lived on top of it. Henry Hornbostel's winning campus design concentrated on the level land next to the park. It combined features of several campus traditions, above all the new Rockefeller-sponsored University of Chicago (itself the old Midway grounds of the 1893 world's fair), the McKim-designed Columbia University, and Jefferson's University of Virginia. As always with Hornbostel, there are fascinating mutations. Jefferson's brick-and-trim pavilions here emerge as industrial blocks projecting at intervals from two long assembly-line spines. A viewer reads the CMU campus simultaneously as Jefferson's academic village and as the rolling mills and blast furnaces of Carnegie Steel. Both Jefferson and Hornbostel intended students to look out over a steep slope at the end of the campus: the view for Jefferson was the bucolic Shenandoah Valley; for Hornbostel it was the train tracks of Junction Hollow. Both designers seemed to regard their end vistas as unfinished business that was left for students at the university to complete: westward expansion in one case, industrial expansion in the other. The sense of changing times is perfectly brought out also in the choice of the central focus of the two campuses. Jefferson chose the Pantheon as the repository of past knowledge. Hornbostel chose a boiler plant with a tremendous smokestack.

Hamerschlag Hall (originally Machinery Hall, 1912) and its smokestack introduce the theme of the campus buildings as learned but often ironic comments on the architecture of the past. The motif of paired pilasters flanking a deep niche comes from Alberti's St. Andrea at Mantua, of 1470. Hornbostel used it both front and back in this building and at several other points on campus. On top he created his finest gesture: a circular Roman temple wrapped about a tall yellow smokestack. A Tivoli-style temple had inspired Grant's Tomb, the Soldiers' and Sailors' Monument, and the top of the Municipal Building in New York a few years before. But a *smoking* temple was something else: for that, one had to look to the work of Ledoux, or Benjamin Henry Latrobe's Philadelphia Waterworks of 1800. Like their work, Hornbostel's is in the best tradition of "speaking architecture." It bespeaks his wish that CMU would marry art and technology as he had married Venus and Vulcan here.

The center of activity on the early campus was the one-eighth-mile-long corridor that slopes through **Porter Hall** and **Baker Hall** (1905 and 1914). Sloping the corridors at a 4.25 percent grade facilitated Hornbostel's accommodation of these long buildings to the considerable slope of the land, which falls off so steeply that each spring CMU students run a freewheeling buggy race next door on Frew Street. The corridors are among Hornbostel's real triumphs. We may think of them as ceremonial processionways of industrial civilization. The sconces are cast-iron pipes, the color accents emerge from different grades of factory brick, the ceiling is a gently curved segmental barrel vault of Guastavino tile. The spectacular culmination of the design is a self-supporting three-story spiral staircase of Guastavino tile set in a languorous,

Left: The Carnegie-Mellon University campus /*Courtesy Carnegie-Mellon University* ▪
Right: Tile staircase, Baker Hall /*Courtesy Carnegie-Mellon University*

indolent curve that is at startling variance with the work ethic of the institution.

On the opposite side from the Porter/Baker building is the parallel spine of Doherty Hall and Wean Hall. Hornbostel kept adding to his campus design at a furious pace until 1922, by which time Carnegie was dead and most of the intended buildings had been constructed. When construction resumed forty years later, CMU's Department of Architecture had lost its eminence, and the major new buildings (M. Edwin Green's aluminum-dressed Hunt Library and Charles Luckman's Warner Hall) were ruthless adversaries of the old. Fortunately, it was a Hornbostel student, Dahlen Ritchey, who filled in another major gap in his master's scheme with **Wean Hall** (Deeter Ritchey Sippel, 1971). Of finely poured (and some cast) concrete, and with a large projecting auditorium that continues the line of Hornbostel's pavilions, Wean is a near-exemplary model of gracious but nonservile contextualism. The same firm added the University Computing Center on Forbes Avenue in 1984, next to Hornbostel's **U.S. Bureau of Mines** building (1912), now part of CMU.

Hornbostel obviously enjoyed translating Alberti into an industrial idiom, yet on the two occasions when the program allowed it, he enthusiastically dressed his buildings in finer cloth. The first chance came in the design of **Margaret Morrison Carnegie Hall** (1907; west wing extended, 1914), the women's college that was named for Carnegie's adored mother and inseparable companion. The building is set on a side street at an oblique angle to the male-dominated campus mall and is marked by a motherly, or at least feminine, half-

Left: Margaret Morrison Carnegie Hall /*Franklin Toker* ▪ *Right*: College of Fine Arts /*Courtesy Carnegie-Mellon University*

oval forecourt of paired Doric columns that mirrors a reciprocal half-oval recession in the facade itself.

Hornbostel's slightly later **College of Fine Arts** (1912; wings, 1916) has the tall wings and low projecting central pavilion of a seventeenth-century French palace, but its sources were as much Prairie School as Paris: its main precedent was a high school in Chicago. The building cuts into a hillock and so appears low and horizontal when one approaches it obliquely from Forbes Avenue, as Hornbostel had envisioned. (He had earlier designed a viaduct to span the gully toward Forbes Avenue—an idea that died in Pittsburgh but came to life soon after in Bertram Goodhue's thousand-foot causeway approach to the San Diego Exposition of 1916.)

It is instructive to remember the close parallels in physical size, student-body size, and program between the College of Fine Arts and Walter Gropius's Bauhaus at Dessau ten years later. Hornbostel embraced neither the industrial idiom nor the open plan that so attracted Gropius, yet it is hard to imagine how a designer could have integrated the five arts more creatively than he did here, with sculpture studios in the basement, a theater and exhibition hall on the main floor, music practice rooms in the mezzanine, drafting halls for architecture and design in the upper stories, and painting studios in the attic. In the attic one also finds the *loges*, tiny rooms where the architecture students were locked up while *en concours*, competing in short design problems the way Hornbostel (and H. H. Richardson) had while attending the Ecole des Beaux-Arts. Like the Ecole building, the College of Fine Arts recalls the glory of art in frescoes, plaster casts, and building plans inlaid in the floor. Prominent are

Edfu, Chartres, the Parthenon, and Michelangelo's project for St. Peter's. The latter is missing its four front columns—but the Beaux-Arts always took an arbitrary view of history.

Franklin Nicola's Oakland: A City Beautiful and a Model Suburb

The urban glue that holds Oakland together is a central crossing consisting of an east-west arm twelve blocks long on Fifth Avenue from Morewood to Thackeray and a north-south arm of eight blocks along Craig Avenue from Forbes to Baum Boulevard. This is neither Mellon nor Carnegie territory, but mainly the preserve of Franklin Nicola, who drew up its urban blueprint in the 1890s and carefully tended it for nearly half a century. Today, its elegant churches and synagogue, clubs and civic buildings, apartments and select homes, make it a model inner-city suburb.

The planning of central Oakland actually began a generation before Nicola, in a middle-class community of the 1850s whose remnants survive today in the boutiques and restaurants of Craig Street, between Forbes and Fifth avenues. Originally part of the substantial east Oakland estate of the English settler James Chadwick, the Craig Street area was subdivided once in the 1840s, when it was purchased as a suburban retreat by publisher Neville B. Craig, and again a decade later, when Craig sold much of it to a land-speculation company headed by Edward Dithridge. Dithridge erected a turreted brick mansion on Fifth Avenue between Bellefield and Dithridge streets, with a series of other princely houses around it for other members of his family. He laid out the cross-streets of Henry, Winthrop, and Filmore and carved up the south half of "Bellefield" (the name under which the land was patented in the eighteenth century) into lots for about a hundred small houses between Craig and Boundary, Fifth and Forbes avenues. The style of such surviving houses as **4612** and **4614 Henry** might without contradiction be called vernacular Greek Revival, since they were erected by untutored builders decades after the Revival style had gone out of fashion on the East Coast. The homes along Filmore Street, particularly the sequence of 4628 to 4638 Filmore, were built in the 1870s in Italianate or High Victorian Gothic dress and indicate a change of market from the middle to the upper-middle class.

The gentrification of Craig Street in the late 1970s and the 1980s stemmed from its ideal placement as a short, cohesive district between the two major drawing points of Carnegie Institute and St. Paul's Cathedral, and from the adaptability of the large mansions and townhouses erected there a century before. What used to be fashionable drawing rooms now serve small advertis-

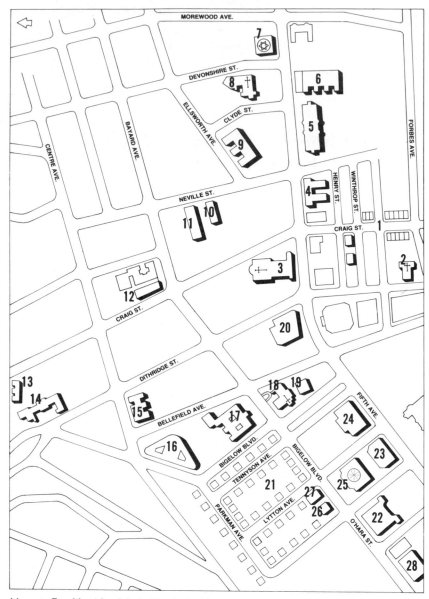

Map 8. Franklin Nicola's Oakland: A City Beautiful and a Model Suburb

1 Craig St. shops
2 St. Nicholas Cathedral
3 St. Paul's Cathedral
4 Fairfax Apts.
5 Central Catholic H.S.
6 WQED-TV
7 Rodef Shalom Temple
8 First Church of Christ, Scientist
9 Cathedral Mansions Apts.
10 Neville House
11 Winchester Condominiums
12 King Edward Apts.
13 357 N. Craig St.
14 Royal York Apts.
15 Bellefield Dwellings
16 Schenley High School
17 Western Pa. School for Blind Children
18 First Baptist Church
19 SLIS
20 Webster Hall Apts.
21 Schenley Farms
22 Soldiers' & Sailors' Mem. Hall
23 Pittsburgh Athletic Assn.
24 Masonic Temple
25 Syria Mosque
26 Twentieth-Century Club
27 Historical Society of Western Pa.
28 Gardner Steel Conference Center

ing agencies, specialty shops, and offices for the more exotic medical arts such as hypnosis, midwifery, and acupuncture. The architectural results of the transformation have been mixed, with some recycling tending to modernization and some to period restoration.

The **Carnegie-Mellon University Art Gallery** (407 S. Craig; renovation by Sylvester Damianos, 1978) is a spacious two-story exhibition space carved out of an old bowling alley. Elsewhere on the street, Second Empire and Queen Anne townhouses have been refitted with ice-cream parlors, restaurants, and offices. The rehabilitation of Craig Street also influenced the resurfacing of two larger commercial buildings that were past their prime. The more prominent of the two is the **Continental Insurance Building** (200 S. Craig, SW corner Henry; renovation by L. D. Astorino & Associates, 1984), an intrusive 1960s office block now reclad in a colorful aluminum skin of green and gray, with red accents that prove quite compatible with its polychromed older neighbors. Next door, the **University Technology Development Center I** (4516 Henry St.; renovation by Williams Trebilcock Whitehead, 1984) turned the facade of a five-story reinforced-concrete parking garage into a large-scale relief sculpture by means of stucco panels. The building houses the Pittsburgh High Technology Council, a major force in incubating new businesses in the region.

The Churches of Central Oakland

Seven important downtown churches followed the migration of their congregations to Oakland around the turn of the century: four on Fifth Avenue and three more just off the main road. The most prominent of the seven, right at the crossroads of Fifth Avenue and Craig Street, is **St. Paul's Cathedral** (Egan & Prindeville, 1906). This was the building put up with Frick money from the sale of the old cathedral on the site of the Union Trust. The designers, from Chicago, were specialists in building Gothic Revival churches for Catholic parishes across the country in the dramatic style popularized by Ralph Adams Cram. St. Paul's was their most distinguished work. The building is a hybrid of an unusual French Gothic plan of six towers and four side aisles, with a general overlay of English and German features in the elevation—an accurate reflection of its polyglot diocese. The flora and fauna carved into the limestone facade are all native to America. The cathedral quality of St. Paul's is strengthened by its attendant diocesan buildings, particularly **Synod Hall** (125 N. Craig; Edward J. Weber, 1914) and the **Rectory** (108 N. Dithridge, NE corner Fifth Ave.; Carlton Strong, 1927), which rise behind and alongside it, as well as a parish house, a convent, and two schools strung out diagonally behind St. Paul's on Craig Street.

From its traditional constituency of churches, shops, and apartment houses,

St. Paul's Cathedral /*Franklin Toker*

central Oakland began in the early 1980s to accommodate itself to an infusion of high-tech firms that were drawn to its position halfway between CMU and Pitt. Immediately in front of St. Paul's is the site of the **Software Engineering Institute** (Fifth, Dithridge, & Henry Sts.; Bohlin Powell Larkin Cywinski and Burt Hill Kosar Rittelmann, 1985–87), the home of a Defense Department collaboration with CMU that is a key element in making Pittsburgh a world capital in software expertise. Diagonally across Fifth Avenue, high-tech and religion will coexist in **Bellefield Towers** (NE corner Fifth & Bellefield; UDA Associates, 1985–87), a glass-walled and polychrome granite-tiled structure specially designed for high-tech and biotech companies. A solitary square tower of rough-hewn and irregularly coursed sandstone stands in front as a remnant of The University and City Ministries, designed (as the Bellefield Presbyterian Church) by Frederick Osterling in 1888: its congregation will meet inside the new building.

Another of the stylish neighborhood churches in Oakland is **St. Nicholas Greek Orthodox Cathedral** (419 Dithridge St., NE corner Forbes; Struthers & Hannah, 1904), built and used as the First Congregational Church until 1921. It is an unusually vigorous design in yellow industrial brick preceded by a dramatic hexastile Ionic portico. The interior of St. Nicholas should not be missed as an architectural paradigm of America itself: a cool Protestant interior heated up by a blazing iconostasis. The congregation keeps its classical heritage alive through the Ionic porch and the cardboard Erechtheion maidens who are brought out to ornament the church community center each May, when some 20,000 Pittsburghers drop in for the annual Greek Food Festival.

The **First Baptist Church,** (SW corner Bayard and Bellefield Aves, one block north of Fifth) is probably better known outside of Pittsburgh than in town as one of the masterpieces of America's most creative Gothic Revivalist of the twentieth century. The congregation dates to 1812, and for years it used the Monongahela River for all baptisms. Bertram Grosvenor Goodhue won out over sixty other contestants in the national design competition for the present church in 1910. The interior design of First Baptist has the richness of materials, textures, and volumes that keeps Goodhue's reputation so high today. On the outside, the power of the elevation and massing stems from its forced compactness, so that the church rises up as a sheer vertical cliff of limestone and glass. Unfortunately, neither the plan nor the elevation works to best advantage on this site, which is too open and detached from the street on one side and too close on the other to Pitt's muscular poured-concrete **School of Library and Information Science** (135 N. Bellefield St.; Tasso Katselas, 1965), an eight-story exercise in the late style of the California master William Pereira.

Left: St. Nicholas Greek Orthodox Cathedral, with cardboard Erectheion maidens announcing the Greek Food Festival */Franklin Toker* ▪ *Right:* First Baptist Church (Bertram Grosvenor Goodhue, architect) */Franklin Toker*

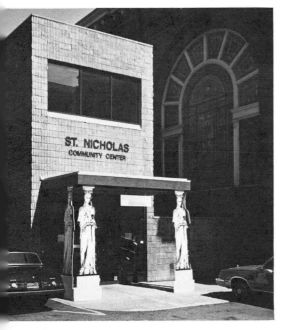

Left: Rodef Shalom Temple (Henry Hornbostel, architect) /*Franklin Toker* ▪ *Right*: Light standard, Rodef Shalom Temple /*Franklin Toker*

At the northwest corner of Fifth and Morewood avenues stands Oakland's most distinguished house of worship: **Rodef Shalom Temple** (Henry Hornbostel, 1907). This may be the best synagogue design in the United States, competing works by Peter Harrison, Frank Lloyd Wright, and other luminaries notwithstanding. Hornbostel won the commission in competition against the much better-known Albert Kahn, and the result is one of his two or three best works. The key to understanding the Rodef Shalom design is conformity. Hornbostel's solution is deliberately less conforming to church prototypes than was Harrison's Newport synagogue, but it is deliberately more conforming than Wright sought to be in his radical freeform Beth Shalom Temple in Philadelphia. What Hornbostel sought was a house of worship that would relate in some way to everyone who used or merely glanced at it. It would not be alien to the other public monuments of Oakland, but akin to them in scale and richness. It would not deny the heavy industry of Pittsburgh that was the source of its wealth, but would identify with it in its common yellow industrial brick from Kittanning and even in its (probable) model, the 1883 railroad station of Budapest. Unlike most premodern synagogues, there is nothing fake-Moorish here, although the dazzling colors on the terra-cotta bands (now faded) hint so strongly at orientalism that passersby know instinctively that this is not a church.

On the outside, Rodef Shalom divides into three component parts: the squared dome (modeled on the 1901 Great Synagogue of Rome), the sanctuary cube, and the ornamented doorway. The visitor finds inside the same shapes and motifs as outside, but the decoration is now enriched with Sullivanesque ornament and a skillful handling of natural and artificial light. Hornbostel was obviously pleased with his building and bestowed on it two small monuments that encapsulate the whole history of architecture. Left and right of the facade rise two small light standards with baskets through which grow shoots of acanthus. Surely these standards are meant to portray the origin of the Corinthian capital, as recounted 2,000 years ago by the Roman architect Vitruvius.

Grouped around Rodef Shalom are four other public monuments, which create an effective portal into the Oakland district from the residential quarters to the east. The **First Church of Christ, Scientist** (623 Clyde St., between Fifth & Ellsworth; S. S. Beman, 1904) is a small but powerful neoclassical temple marked by an elegant Ionic hexastile porch. Beman gained fame for his Chicago skyscrapers and the design of the industrial town of Pullman, but his accomplished work in the classical style was also prominently on view at the Chicago world's fair and in the string of Christian Scientist churches he built in many cities, including the Mother Church of 1904 in Boston. The effect of this tiny shrine expertly set in a concave hollow of Clyde Street is assuredly theatrical, but First Church is one of those buildings where the viewer does not mind being seduced. The nearby **Holy Spirit Catholic Church, Byzantine Rite** (NE corner Fifth & Clyde; 1961) is also dramatic in its oblique siting and triplet of sky-blue onion domes, but the effect is diminished by an internal conflict in the design between its modernist and traditionalist components.

Fortunately, no such equivocation about traditional and modern approaches

WQED studios /Courtesy WQED

affects two public buildings on the south side of Fifth Avenue. **Central Catholic High School** (4720 Fifth Ave.; Link, Weber & Bowers, 1927) recalls a late-Gothic city or castle gateway as a symbolic shorthand to suggest that education is the "gateway" to life. The building is clothed in richly diapered bricks in the tradition of William Butterfield and John Ruskin, and it adds greatly to the scale and color of the street. Immediately next door stands what might have been an intrusive neighbor, in the poured-concrete **WQED** television and radio studios (4802 Fifth Ave.; Paul Schweikher, 1970). WQED is the dean of public broadcasting stations in the country, known to many adults as the home of such specials as the National Geographic series, and to countless children as the home of "Mister Rogers' Neighborhood." This distinguished building, one of a half-dozen designed for Pittsburgh during Schweikher's residence here in the 1960s, reflects the completion of his pilgrimage from the International School of the 1930s to the New Brutalism of the 1950s. To Schweikher, brutalism was merely a formal and not a philosophical position, however, because WQED is a sensitive building both for its users and for those who pass by it. The structure is a modular construction of cavernous studios that is by necessity huge without losing sight of human scale or human delight. The concrete, for example, was poured with such care that its every joint is a small poetic statement, and the whole design presents educational television as the equivalent of the libraries, colleges, and churches that upheld civilization in the past. It richly merits inclusion among the old public monuments of Oakland that were devoted to the same beliefs a half-century before.

The Apartment Houses of Central Oakland

Multifamily buildings had existed in American architecture from the time of the early Republic, but only in the last quarter of the nineteenth century, in Manhattan, had an apartment type evolved of sufficient respectability that society leaders could live in it. Conservative Pittsburgh has never wholly approved of apartments except as *pied-à-terre's* for country residents. Franklin Nicola, ever the pioneer, broke some of this prejudice with his Schenley Hotel of 1898 (used by many as a residence), which he followed with his massive Schenley Apartments next to the hotel in the 1920s. Here were buildings of such luxury that any resident was automatically assumed to be both prominent and rich. Oakland now has several score apartment buildings, of which ten stand out as particularly good representatives of their type or period.

Henry Hornbostel set the trapezoid **Webster Hall Apartments** (4415 Fifth Ave., NW corner N. Dithridge; with Eric Fisher Wood, 1925) at a bend in Fifth Avenue, so that its eleven-story bulk appears to loom even larger than it is. It was created as an athletic club of 400 residential units, then became a hotel, and finally an apartment. Down the block is the elaborately Tudor **Hampton Hall** (166 N. Dithridge, near SE corner Bayard; H. G. Hodgkins, 1928), with just fifty-four apartments. More attuned to modernism, although still effectively ornamented with coats of arms, Scottish strapwork, and terracotta, are the **Fairfax** (4614 Fifth Ave. between Craig & Neville Sts.; Philip M. Julien, 1926) and the **Cathedral Mansions** (4716 Ellsworth Ave. at Clyde St.; John M. Donn, 1927). The modernist aesthetic partially enunciated in these two buildings and in the Webster Hall is fully pronounced in two postwar apartments just west of the Cathedral Mansions: the Le Corbusier-inspired **Neville House** (552 N. Neville St., between Fifth & Bayard; Tasso Katselas, 1958) and the jade-tile-clad **Winchester Condominiums** (540 N. Neville; Herbert Seigel, 1971).

The Irish immigrant builder John McSorley created two of Oakland's most delightful apartment blocks: the **King Edward Apartments** (4601–4609 Bayard St., between Craig & Melwood; Melwood St. corner in Tudor Revival style by H. G. Hodgkins, 1914; Craig St. corner in Art Deco style by Walter Perry, 1929), and the **Royal York Apartments** (3955 Bigelow Blvd., NE corner Dithridge St.; Frederick Stanton, 1937). McSorley had worked as a builder in both Toronto and Chicago before coming here, and his apartments combine the names of distinguished Toronto hotels with the luxury of Chicago's Gold Coast. The Royal York is one of the best Art Deco designs in the city, with buff tile walls beautifully molded into Egyptoid strips suggestive of bundled papyrus columns. The apartment was angled to give its inhabitants spectacular views across Oakland to the south and to the north across Two-Mile Run into Bloomfield.

The oldest and newest of central Oakland's apartments are within sight of each other to the south and north of the Royal York. **Bellefield Dwellings** (4400 Centre Ave., between Bellefield & Dithridge; Carlton Strong, 1904) was one of the first two apartments in the city, along with the Iroquois on Forbes Avenue. It was promoted by Robert C. Hull and Francis T. F. Lovejoy, a junior partner of Andrew Carnegie, as the most luxurious of its type in the country. The Bellefield astonished Pittsburghers with its integral garages in the basement; wall safes, telephones, automatic refrigerators, and direct access to both passenger and service elevators in every apartment; and mahogany woodwork and tapestry mosaics in the lobbies. Such interior luxuries were suggested on the outside by the vigorous color massing of the Jacobean Revival brick walls, which makes the whole block look like a private château. Still a pleasant and sunny block, it serves today as federally subsidized housing for the elderly.

The newest Oakland apartment is the **William S. Moorhead Tower** (N. Craig St., intersection of Baum Blvd.; Arthur Lubetz Associates, 1981), a sixteen-story slab that accommodates 142 apartments for the blind. Externally, the building is a curious though successful mix of practicality and whimsy. The materials are concrete block and poured concrete that has been stuccoed over and painted bright yellow. The blocky mass of the tower is relieved by a stepped parapet at the top, a vertical glazed strip indicating the elevator lobbies, and a ground-floor aedicula that seems to be made of toy blocks to signify in the most basic and totemic way the location of the main door. The scale is excellently handled so that these touches are neither overpowering nor mincing compared to the massiveness of the building itself. Of special importance to the blind inhabitants, the tower contains such ingenious features as changes of texture in the floor and walls and piped-in music for orientation toward the elevators, creating what Lubetz calls "a nonvisual conception of space."

357 N. Craig Street

It is in keeping with Pittsburgh's work ethic that its most important essay in post-Modernism is the recycling of an old garage at **357 N. Craig Street** (Arthur Lubetz, 1982). The result is a small, powerful building with a strong street facade and three whimsical doghouse gables facing a parking lot on the right. The materials throughout are mundane: ground-face cinderblock, glass block, and scored stucco. Lubetz orchestrated these simple materials to give a fair imitation of a Renaissance *palazzo* on Craig Street, with a rusticated

Left: William S. Moorhead Tower */Courtesy Arthur Lubetz Associates* ▪ *Right:* 357 North Craig Street with the Royal York Apartments behind */Franklin Toker*

basement, *piano nobile*, and attic, while he simultaneously rendered the side facade as a surreal vision in the manner of Aldo Rossi or Luis Barragán. Here, all building elements take on the totemic quality of the entrance to the Moorhead Tower down the street. None of these concepts detracts from the practicality of the building; on the contrary, the notion of miniatures within miniatures personalizes each working area and may even boost productivity.

Schenley Farms

Franklin Nicola died almost bankrupt in 1934, but he had lived to see his Oakland civic center flourish. He reasoned that a neighborhood with public monuments but without inhabitants would be no neighborhood at all, and so he developed much of Mary Schenley's estate as apartments, clubhouses, and private residences. In 1905 he designated the Schenley cow pasture bounded by Parkman Avenue on the north and west and by Bigelow Boulevard on the south and east as a residential quarter of ninety-six houses, **Schenley Farms.** East of this quarter there were already a dozen buildings for the **Western Pennsylvania School for Blind Children** (NE corner Bigelow & Bayard Street; George Orth, 1894) on land donated by Mary Schenley herself. The triangle of steep land immediately north of the school was eventually used for the mammoth **Schenley High School** (SE corner Bigelow & Centre Ave.; Edward Stotz, 1916).

What distinguished the Schenley Farms development was the care taken to secure the best architecture and the best urban context. On top of his initial investment of $2.5 million in land, Nicola spent another $1.5 million on improvements to his streets, with underground wiring (still rare in Pittsburgh today), widespread planting of shade trees, and construction of an immense retaining wall to secure Parkman Street against the hillside slope that bends around it. An additional thirty-nine fairly modest houses were created by Nicola on the hillside itself, on Centre Avenue and Schenley Farms Terrace. Without clients for his risky venture, Nicola employed architects to build eleven model houses on the west side of Lytton Street in 1906, then advertised them as a come-on for the sale of the remaining lots.[5] By 1909 half of the ninety-six lots had been filled, and by 1920 the group was complete.

5. Six of the eleven houses on Lytton can be attributed to specific architects: number 201 by Henry Gilchrist, 203 by Thomas Hannah, 213 and 219 by Rutan & Russell, 215 by Thorsten Billquist, and 217 by Vrydaugh & Wolfe. Among other Pittsburgh architects who worked for Nicola in Schenley Farms were Janssen & Abbott, MacClure & Spahr, Kiehnel & Elliott, Louis Stevens, and Henry Hornbostel. Hornbostel's house for CMU president Arthur Hamerschlag, at 4040 Bigelow Boulevard, is composed largely of uncoursed freestone, like Richardson's Ames Gate Lodge at North Easton, but it terminates in a pronouncedly horizontal Prairie School roof.

The Schenley Farms homes constitute a remarkable ensemble, not just for Pittsburgh but for any city in the nation. The construction standards set by Nicola were unheard of outside housing for the very rich. For $20,000 to $30,000, purchasers got thirteen-inch-thick brick walls with insulating air chambers, hardwood floors, finished basements, brass pipes, hot-water radiators recessed beneath windows, integral ducts for vacuum cleaning, four telephones per house, stained glass, and elaborate woodwork. The houses were less advanced in style than in technology, yet here too they are an interesting lot. Contrary to what one would find in most upper-middle-class Edwardian suburbs, only one house opted for the Beaux Arts style. In a few cases (for example, 204 Tennyson) the local architects emulated their Prairie School colleagues in Chicago. In many more cases—indeed for almost half the houses—the models were contemporary British architects of the so-called English Free Style, particularly Sir Edwin Lutyens, C. F. A. Voysey, Charles Rennie Mackintosh, and M. H. Baillie Scott, with a few followers also of the earlier Richard Norman Shaw. The other half more predictably depended on the various revivals: Tudor, Colonial, Georgian, neoclassical (including some learned quotes from Jefferson, Thornton, Ledoux, and Latrobe), and Spanish. A half-dozen houses dared to be simply vernacular. Nicola's advertising continually referred to Schenley Farms as a model community, but for once he was too modest: compared to housing conditions in the rest of the country around 1905, it bordered on the Utopian.

Parkman Street, Schenley Farms /*Franklin Toker*

Soldiers' and Sailors' Memorial Hall /*Franklin Toker*

Allegheny County Soldiers' and Sailors' Memorial Hall

In 1907 a national competition for the **Allegheny County Soldiers' and Sailors' Memorial Hall,** with such entrants as Cass Gilbert, John Russell Pope, and Ernest Flagg, produced an upset victory in favor of Henry Hornbostel for this long-delayed tribute to the Civil War veterans and dead of Allegheny County. Hornbostel designed the building to face east on Bigelow Boulevard, as the competition demanded, then convinced the county commissioners to rotate it ninety degrees to face Fifth Avenue. The design is vigorous but not so suave as Rodef Shalom or his College of Fine Arts at CMU. Its strength lies in its deft solution to a complex program that called for meeting rooms, a memorial, an auditorium for 2,500, and a banquet hall for the thinning ranks of Civil War veterans. Hornbostel also demonstrated here an excellent eye for radical structural solutions: the pyramidal roof—an allusion to the Mausoleum of Halicarnassus—is a solid mass of poured concrete, and the banquet hall (with its dangerous structural liability when used as a dance floor) is carried over the huge void of the auditorium on a bridge truss. The main ventilating duct of the hall emerges at the apex of the pyramid, so that on cold winter days the building comes alive as it puffs hot air through the roof. The coloring inside is vivid to the point of gaudy, and the piers of the banquet hall are splayed into the shape of coffins. But the message a visitor takes away is not how clever the architect was, but how noble the local war veterans were. In its heroic scale, exactness of plan, integration of the various arts, and profound expression of the institutional message, the Soldiers' and Sailors' Memorial Hall is a textbook example of what a Beaux Arts building was intended to do.

Pittsburgh Athletic Association and Masonic Temple (Benno Janssen, architect)
/*Franklin Toker*

The Clubhouses of Central Oakland

Pittsburgh society has always been gregarious. Church clubs, singing clubs, sports clubs, and general-purpose social clubs still number in the hundreds today. About two dozen clubs are regarded as "exclusive," and while a good many are in the Golden Triangle, only two occupy their own buildings there. Oakland has a half-dozen clubhouses, broadly defined, with their main concentration in the area around Soldiers' and Sailors' Memorial. The **Pittsburgh Athletic Association** (4215 Fifth Ave., NW corner Lytton Ave.; Janssen & Abbott, 1911) represents clubhouse architecture at its best. Benno Jannsen imagined the PAA as a Venetian Renaissance palace and used its giant-order pilasters and engaged columns as a screen in order to create five stories behind a two-story elevation. The main Venetian precedents seem to be Michele Sanmicheli's Palazzo Grimani and Jacopo Sansovino's Libreria on Piazza San Marco, which through synthesis have produced something entirely new here. The white limestone and terra-cotta exterior has weathered well, and the cutting of the architectural details and sculptural reliefs could not be bettered. The decoration inside includes large murals and heavily carved ceilings designed by Albert Herter of New York.

Janssen added a companion to the PAA a few years later when he designed the **Masonic Temple** (4227 Fifth Ave., NE corner Lytton Ave.; Janssen & Abbott, 1914). This severe limestone rendering of a Greek temple serves the

Syria Mosque /*Maurice Tierney*

25,000 Masons in the Pittsburgh district with a complex series of meeting and ceremonial rooms. From the outside the temple appears to be three stories high, but inside are four floors and two mezzanines. The second and third floors contain spacious and well-lighted chambers rendered in architectural motifs according to their names: Doric, Gothic, Ionic, Corinthian, Tudor, and Egyptian. The exterior is totally uninformative about these interior arrangements, as though to protect the secrecy of the rituals.

The Masonic Temple spawned a kindred building in the next block just a year later. The **Syria Mosque** (4423 Bigelow Blvd.; Huehl, Schmid & Holmes, 1915) is a building with many peculiarities, from its correctly worded Arabic inscription that declares eighteen times that "There is no conqueror but God," to its complicity in the death of Eleanora Duse, who died after she was caught in a downpour outside its locked stage door. The building represents a Hollywood view of Islamic culture: silky bronze sphinxes by Giuseppe Moretti front and back, stalactites on the cornice, and a Hagia Sofia saucer dome poking through the roof. These bargain-basement touches of exoticism aside, the building functions well as a theater and concert hall for 3,700 spectators (the Pittsburgh Symphony played here for years under Fritz Reiner) in an unusual and effective elliptical layout that maximizes acoustics and good sight lines.

Two other clubhouses stand almost in the shadow of Soldiers' and Sailors' at the northeast corner of Bigelow Boulevard and Parkman Avenue: the **Twentieth Century Club** (4201 Bigelow; G. H. Schwan, 1910; Janssen & Cocken, 1930), and the **Historical Society of Western Pennsylvania** (4338 Bigelow;

Ingham & Boyd, 1912). The former, which makes the bolder architectural statement of the two, houses a women's club that was founded in 1894 in the afterglow of the Woman's Pavilion at the Chicago world's fair in 1893. The historical society's library of 30,000 volumes is the richest and most accessible source of information on Pittsburgh and western Pennsylvania.

The grouping of clubhouses concludes with three more examples west of Soldiers' and Sailors': the **University Club** (123 University Place; Henry Hornbostel, 1926), the **Concordia Club** (SW corner University Place & O'Hara St.; 1914), and the former **Oakland Turnverein** (SE corner Thackeray & O'Hara Sts.; Kiehnel & Elliott, 1912). This last was a prominent German singing and athletic club that today accommodates Pitt's Gardner Steel Conference Center and Faculty Club. The structure itself is an unremarkable two stories of beige brick, but its cubistic cement decoration between the windows and on the doorframe seems to follow Frank Lloyd Wright's ornamental work at his Midway Gardens in Chicago, completed in the same year. Secure as Oakland's clubs were on the eve of World War I, this bold and futuristic decoration suggests that even here the winds of change were at work.

The People's Oakland: The Village on the Cliff

The upscale transformation of Craig Street in eastern Oakland and the new additions to CMU, Pitt, and the medical center are just the most recent of the successive waves of improvement that have overtaken Oakland since the 1830s. But along with these changes there still remains a goodly stretch of "old" Oakland in the trapezoid bounded by Bouquet and Dawson streets on the east, the Boulevard of the Allies on the south and west, and Forbes Avenue on the north. Here is one of the most densely packed residential neighborhoods in Pittsburgh, with an intense, sometimes melancholy appeal of its own.

The old Oakland was largely unplanned, and it derives its character today from its unpretentious streets, not from its monuments. Most of the houses lining these streets were built by speculators in the thirty to forty years following the Civil War. This was the period in which the early nineteenth-century estates were broken up by such long cross-streets as Semple, Meyran, and Atwood. The focus of Oakland after the Civil War was initially on the J&L works that dominated the Monongahela riverbank below the Oakland cliff. Passage to the Golden Triangle by horsecar began in 1859, but it was slow and expensive. Cablecar service started in 1888 (the triangle formed by Cable and Semple streets marks its old turnaround), and in the 1890s Oakland was linked to downtown by trolleys. **Chesterfield, Robinson,** and **Dunseith streets** on

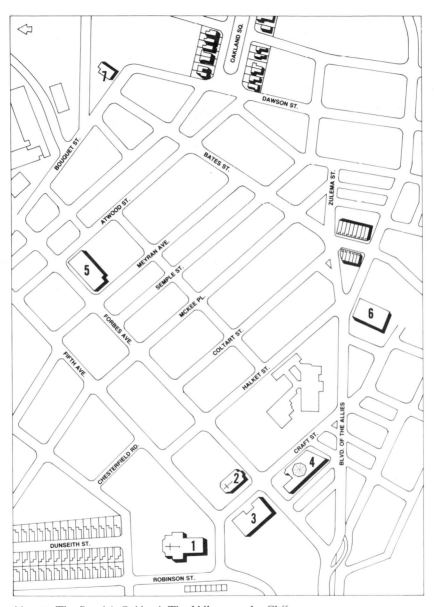

Map 9. The People's Oakland: The Village on the Cliff

1 St. Agnes' Church   3 PNMRI   5 Iroquois Apts.   7 St. Lorenzo di Gamberale
2 St. Peter's Church   4 Pittsburgh Playhouse   6 Isaly's Dairy

Residential Oakland: Dunseith Street /*Franklin Toker*

the Oakland slope of The Hill are the best survivors of the mass-housing projects from the time that Oakland was a working-class village. Chesterfield, from the 1920s, is the newest and most extensive application of the formula on these streets: a steep slope paved in Belgian blocks and flanked by a hundred identical peaked wooden houses, which are saved from monotony by their lively rhythm as they sit, two-by-two, on their own terraces like teeth on a saw. The long rows of brick houses on Dunseith and Robinson are older and squatter but still starkly effective. At the broad intersection of Robinson and Fifth Avenue sits a still-older row of eight Italianate houses of the 1870s, half with porches and half with boldly protruding three-panel bay windows. They create a lingering and effective memory of Oakland to travelers proceeding down this dramatic bend to lower Fifth Avenue and The Hill.

Visitors from the Golden Triangle cannot miss the entrance to Oakland. The long climb up Fifth or Forbes avenues ends, and the two streets level off and stretch broad and straight across the Oakland plain. The change of neighborhood is made still more decisive by two churches strategically placed like billboards at the entrance to each street. **St. Agnes' Roman Catholic Church** (3223 Fifth, NE corner Robinson; John Comes, 1917) is a carefully orchestrated and colored design in Romanesque style by the most active of Pittsburgh's church architects. One block south of Fifth, at the corner of Forbes Avenue and Craft, stands John Notman's **St. Peter's Church** of 1852, with a new porch of 1903. This church and its alter ego, St. Mark's in Philadelphia, designed by Notman a few years earlier, are among the best products of the ecclesiological, or archaeologically correct, period of the Gothic Revival in America. Notman's severe aesthetic is particularly evident in the bare plaster walls of the nave and the elegant hammer-beam ceiling. Notman also left his mark on St. Peter's in a more literal way—in two portraits of himself at the age of forty-one, flanking the entrance arch at the base of the tower.

On the southwest corner of Fifth and Craft, midway between the churches of St. Agnes and St. Peter stands the **Pittsburgh Nuclear Magnetic Resonance Institute** (Dalton & Dalton, 1985), a building that overcame a unique construction problem. The institute serves twelve Pittsburgh hospitals with diagnostic images far more precise than X-rays or CAT scans. At its heart is one of the world's largest magnets, super-cooled with liquid nitrogen so that it exerts a gravitational pull about 30,000 times greater than the Earth itself. This bizarre magnetic effect meant that the structure had to be built totally without iron or any other easily magnetized components.

An important part of the entertainment constituency in Oakland stands diagonally opposite St. Peter's Church: the **Pittsburgh Playhouse** (formerly the Tree of Life Synagogue; 222 Craft Ave., between Forbes Ave. & Hamlet St.; D. A. Crone, 1906). The neighboring street names, with Elsinore Street nearby and the corner of Hamlet and Ophelia just two blocks away, perfectly complement this group of theaters, where a different movie plays every night of the year. The main sanctuary of the synagogue was theatrical to begin with, featuring the bold mass of an octagonal pyramid and a porch of six oversized Tuscan columns. The elegant old estate fronting the synagogue has been

St. Peter's Church (John Notman, architect) /*Franklin Toker*

transformed, too. It had been "The Maples," home to Christopher Lyman Magee, who founded what is now the **Magee-Women's Hospital** (Forbes, Halket, & Craft Aves.; Thorsten Billquist, 1915). A lovely wrought-iron fence from Civil War times still encircles part of the grounds, although the Magee mansion is gone and the original hospital has been defaced by later wings.

The eight blocks of Forbes Avenue from St. Peter's Church to the Cathedral of Learning are the heart of Oakland's separate existence as a college town. Fast food, bookstores, and record outlets are the rule, but on one block of Forbes the **Iroquois Apartments** (3600 Forbes, between Meyran & Atwood; Frederick Osterling, 1901–3) dominates all else. The Iroquois was promoted by James Flannery, who followed the lead of Nicola's Schenley Hotel with this luxurious apartment building, the first in town to include prestige shops on the ground floor. (In 1911 Osterling added the Flannery Building next door—today the Parkvale Savings.) The Iroquois' shops are no longer prestigious, and its apartments are mainly doctors' offices now, but the building remains a fine piece of streetscape. It consists of five stories of brown glazed Roman brick, arranged as four separate wings over the commercial base. Osterling enlivened the huge block with exaggerated ornamental details, an undulating facade, and a massive entablature. The Iroquois is a handsome addition to Forbes Avenue

The Iroquois Apartments /*Franklin Toker*

Oakland Square and Junction Hollow, with Greenfield in the distance /*Maurice Tierney*

even on overcast days. When the sun catches Osterling's details, it becomes a universe unto itself.

Two other commercial buildings that exude confidence the way the Iroquois does are the **King's Court Theater** (3807 Forbes, between Oakland Ave. & Bouquet St.; Bickel & Brennan, 1889) and **Isaly's Dairy** (3380 Blvd. of the Allies, at Halket St.; 1929). The theater is an almost absurdly pretentious Romanesque Revival sandstone fortress that was evidently thought appropriate for its original function as a Victorian police station. Isaly's owes its commanding position as well as its function (it was an early take-out restaurant) to the automobile: its site was created when the Boulevard of the Allies bulldozed Oakland in half in the 1920s. There is a decidedly 'Twenties feel to the facade, which is covered in Art Deco terra-cotta tiles. But there is a solemnity to Isaly's in the bold piers that recall the Egyptian temple of Saqqara, whose excavation by the French was underway at that moment. Built as the main factory and showcase of the Isaly food chain, this radiant building was for years a temple to a different sort of cult: the chipped ham, Klondikes, and skyscraper ice-cream cones that were key ingredients of Pittsburgh's regional cuisine.

The crowding of Oakland's houses and the occasional flourish of an Italian-language sign give Bates, Semple, and Dawson streets the flavor of Naples. Neapolitan indeed is the quality of a score of tiny but dignified row houses of the 1920s on both sides of Bates Street between the Boulevard of the Allies and Zulema Street, where the solariums stand less than three feet from the sidewalk of a noisy street.

Oakland Square, off Dawson Street, was created in 1885 by Charles Chance, chairman of the Oakland Board of Trade, as a Boston- or Paris-style

Public steps on Diulus Way, Junction
Hollow /*Franklin Toker*

grouping of two-family frame and brick houses with mansard roofs and oriel
windows in a style close to that of Frank Furness. The square is sober and
impressive, accentuated by the developer's generosity in leaving its east side
open for a view of Schenley Park on the opposite bluff of Four-Mile Run. This
was the childhood quarter of **Andy Warhol,** whose old home stands at 3252
Dawson Street. After a steep slope, Dawson Street turns a sharp left into
Bouquet Street. The gem of Bouquet is the churchlike **St. Lorenzo di Gamberale Mutual Benefit Association** (379 S. Bouquet). Built in 1938 as the
social center of an Italian community that established itself a century ago on
this street and in Junction Hollow below, the hall is emblazoned with twin
reliefs of dogs set in its scrubbed-brick facade. Its members still live in homes
precariously set on the slopes of Joncaire Street or along the footpath called
Diulus Way. A descent deep into this haunting gully is a sobering conclusion
to any study of Oakland, offering as it does a vision of the ancient terrain
before the effects of human intervention.

The South Side, with the decommissioned LTV steelworks /*Clyde Hare*

The South Side

No one can understand Pittsburgh without a stroll through the South Side, although one can intuit its special fascination even from afar. Suddenly, a visitor in a glass skyscraper in the Golden Triangle discovers cablecars—actually funiculars, and in Pittsburgh known as inclines—scaling the long hill south of the Monongahela at two different points. The hill itself demands attention: it rises 450 feet high and stretches unbroken for five miles, from Beck's Run near Homestead to Saw Mill Run at the West End. For a hundred years this hill has been called Mt. Washington on the reasonable assumption that it was from its heights that Washington surveyed the Golden Triangle in 1753, but to the early settlers of Pittsburgh it was simply Coal Hill, and for decades it smoked from uncontrolled fires deep within its mine shafts. Draped over most of the length of the Mt. Washington cliff are hundreds of brick and frame houses, some reached by winding public stairs rather than roads. At its base is the densely settled floodplain of Old Birmingham, or South Side proper; next to it lies the entertainment and commercial district of Station Square. Just back of its cliff, Mt. Washington divides into a half-dozen neighborhood grids. Its gentle back slopes accommodate a dozen more semisuburban communities, most within the boundaries of the City of Pittsburgh, but others not.

The South Side and Mt. Washington were both included in a 3,000-acre royal grant to Major John Ormsby in 1770 for his military services in the French and Indian War. Ormsby was content to farm this land, but in 1811 his son-in-law, Dr. Nathaniel Bedford, laid it out as the village of Birmingham. The name was that of his hometown in England, but surely Bedford chose it as an augury also. He named the longest streets of Birmingham for his wife, Jane, and for her sisters, Sidney, Sarah, and Mary; Bedford Square he named for himself; Carson Street for a sea captain friend of his; and Josephine Street for his daughter. The South Side industrialized early. James O'Hara and Isaac Craig had begun producing glass there by 1797, and by the mid-nineteenth century Pittsburgh's seventy-six glass factories supplied half the nation's output. The American Iron Works opened its cold rolling mill in 1853 in the South Side, and in 1859 Pittsburgh's first successful blast furnace, the Clinton Iron Works, also began operating here.

Iron and steel transformed the South Side from a genteel village into a cauldron of activity. Its population shot up to about 30,000 (twice what it is today), and its ethnic composition changed from German and Scotch-Irish to predominantly Eastern European. It remains so today, with its main churches serving Ukrainian, Croatian, Polish, Serbian, Russian, Lithuanian, and Slovak congregations. *Kiszki, kielbassa,* and *halubki* are on sale at the food shops along E. Carson Street, and *pierogis* are made and sold by the women of St. John the Baptist and St. Vladimir's churches every Thursday and Friday. Other traditionalists celebrate the Tridentine Mass in Latin at Our Lady of Fatima Church on the South Side flats. But even the South Side cannot resist all change: only a minute quantity of steel is produced here now, and the few survivors of the eighty-five bars that once ringed the LTV mill on E. Carson Street are outnumbered by antique shops. The South Side even has a first-rate French restaurant. Whether upscale at Station Square and the condominiums on Mt. Washington or fourth-generation traditional on the flats of Old Birmingham, it is an area that presents an especially vivid cross section of postindustrial Pittsburgh.

Station Square and Mt. Washington

The richness of the South Side in topographic, social, and architectural terms stems from its isolation, or at least its separation, from the rest of Pittsburgh.

The Smithfield Street Bridge, Station Square, and the Monongahela Incline on Mt. Washington /*Courtesy Pittsburgh History & Landmarks Foundation*

The separation is underlined today by the several modes Pittsburghers use to get to or through the South Side: seven major bridges, three tunnels, and two inclines. The **Smithfield Street Bridge,** from the Golden Triangle to Station Square (Gustave Lindenthal, 1883), is the successor to a wood bridge (1818) and a wire-suspension bridge by John Augustus Roebling (1846) that once stood on the same site. Lindenthal, an Austrian-trained engineer, created here the longest and most graceful variant of a rare configuration called the lenticular or Pauli truss. The fisheye shape of the truss and its strengthening by both vertical and diagonal members make it exceptionally sleek and stable.

The other bridges nearby are newer and more prosaic: the Liberty Bridge from the 1920s, the Tenth Street Bridge from the 1930s, the Fort Pitt Bridge from the late 1950s. The Liberty and Fort Pitt tunnels (known locally as "tubes") were cut through at the same moment as their corresponding bridges,

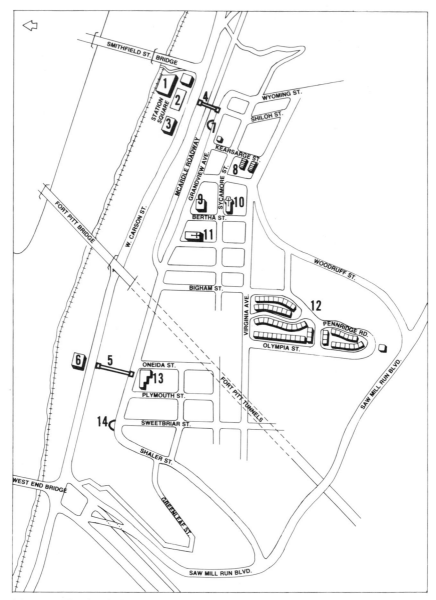

Map 10. The South Side: Station Square and Mt. Washington

1 P&LE Terminal
2 Freight House
3 Commerce Court
4 Monongahela Incline
5 Duquesne Heights Incline

6 W. W. Lawrence Paint Bldg.
7 Mt. Washington lookout
8 Hilf Houses
9 Carnegie Library, Mt.
   Washington

10 Grace Episcopal Church
11 St. Mary of the Mount
12 Chatham Village
13 Trimont Condominiums
14 Duquesne Heights lookout

while the Mt. Washington Transit Tunnel was created to bring trolleys to the
southern suburbs in 1904. There is also a fourth tunnel, out of service now,
that was built in 1904 as part of a scheme by George Gould, son of the high-
living Jay Gould, to break the monopoly of the three or four railroads that
controlled freight traffic in Pittsburgh. The bridge and the railroad terminal
that were once served by this tunnel are long gone, but the two end piers of
the old bridge still rise starkly out of the Monongahela and are crowned by a
brilliant flutter of pennants when the Three Rivers Arts Festival takes over the
Golden Triangle each June.

The forty-acre **Station Square** development, between the Smithfield and
Fort Pitt bridges (redevelopment master plan by UDA Architects, 1975),
parallels similar conversions of industrial or commercial architecture in San
Francisco, Boston, and New York. The commercial return from this investment
has been good, in the case of some of its several-score shops and restaurants
very good indeed, but the "urban return" from Station Square has been most
fruitful of all. It has stretched the retail and social boundaries of the Golden
Triangle to include both banks of the Monongahela River and has significantly
altered the buying and entertainment habits of middle-income Pittsburgh.

The creation of Station Square (the name is standard National Trust hype—
there is no square) was plotted by the Pittsburgh History & Landmarks
Foundation and funded by the Pittsburgh philanthropist Richard Scaife. The
site was the freightyard established here in 1877 by a tiny but highly profitable railroad, and its centerpiece today is the **Pittsburgh & Lake Erie Railroad Terminal** (now the Landmarks Building; William George Burns, 1901).
The terminal appears to be square but is in fact a trapezoid, because Burns
wanted its north face to parallel the Monongahela River and its east face to
parallel the nearby Smithfield Street Bridge. The cost of this excessive concern
for architectural propriety was that Burns was obliged to invent a bizarre
wedge-shaped vestibule to regularize the interior centerline of the building.
The old waiting room on the lower level was brilliantly renovated in 1977 by
the Detroit restauranteur Chuck Muer as the Grand Concourse. This palatial
room with its barrel vault of stained glass forms one of the most dynamic
volumes in the city, although everything that looks to be marble is simply
painted plaster. The only genuine thing is the side revetment on the grand
staircase, where the working drawings specified "real marble."

Behind the old terminal are the Gate House, Express House, and Freight
House, additional turn-of-the-century railroad buildings now used as office,
retail, and entertainment space, together with such attractions as a ten-ton
Bessemer converter, an Art Deco diner, and a fleet of Victorian trolleys and
railroad cars. Farther on is the dock for the Gateway Clipper fleet, the largest
excursion-boat operation in the country. The best of these other buildings is
Commerce Court (formerly the Central Warehouse, 1917; renovation by
Williams Trebilcock Whitehead, 1983), a seven-story steel frame encased in

Left: The P&LE Terminal, now the Grand Concourse restaurant */Courtesy Pittsburgh History & Landmarks Foundation* ▪ *Right:* The Monongahela Incline, W. Carson Street */Franklin Toker*

concrete. The internal recycling was radical and perhaps unnecessarily Las Vegas in character, but the brooding exterior lines of the warehouse were retained, and even with new windows punched in, the long brick walls create a solid visual anchor to the complex.

The **Monongahela Incline** (205 W. Carson St.; 1869) and the **Duquesne Heights Inclined Plane** (1197 W. Carson; 1877) are among the oldest funiculars anywhere and the sole survivors of the seventeen that once served a half-dozen Pittsburgh neighborhoods. They were inspired by the muscle-powered coal inclines that had operated on Mt. Washington for decades. The engineer for the Monongahela Incline was John J. Endres, who assembled a remarkable group of collaborators. John Roebling calculated and fabricated the cables, and Endres's assistants were his daughter Caroline, one of the first woman engineers (her sister Bertha was one of the first woman architects), and his future son-in-law, Samuel Diescher. Diescher built or rebuilt ten Pittsburgh inclines, designed steel mills all over the United States, launched boats in South America, and assisted Pittsburgh's George Washington Ferris in the spectacular debut of the Ferris Wheel at the World Columbian Exposition in Chicago in 1893. He alone engineered the Duquesne Incline.

The Monongahela incline is the shorter of the two at 635 feet, compared to the Duquesne's 793 feet, but it is steeper (35 percent, to the Duquesne's 30.5 percent). Both inclines are now powered by electricity rather than steam, but the Duquesne incline retains its original cable drum and wooden-toothed drive gear. Its cabins are also original and fantastic relics of Victoriana. The four incline stations—brick on W. Carson Street, wood on Grandview Avenue—are all period pieces, and all are delightful. The Duquesne incline lower station is joined by the fine turn-of-the-century **W. W. Lawrence Paint Company Building,** directly across the street, while its upper station is packed with curios of Pittsburgh's transportation history. Each incline has carried about one hundred million passengers without accident. The ride up is exalting, the ride down terrifying: one is obliged to try both.

The **summit of Mt. Washington** is reached by the two inclines, by the McArdle Roadway from the Liberty Bridge, or by the tortuous E. Sycamore Street, a local variant of the Burma Road that branches off Arlington Avenue just above its intersection with E. Carson. Ascending the heavily forested slopes of the hill, it is easy to think of it in George Washington's time, when fat perch weighing twenty pounds swam in the Monongahela and forty-pound wild turkeys waddled through the woods. At the top, lookouts on Grandview Avenue present vivid panoramas of the Golden Triangle directly opposite, with the Ohio River to the west and the Monongahela River to the east, fortified by miles of steelworks on both banks.

Grandview Avenue is an interesting architectural promenade in its own right. It borders two enclaves: a worker neighborhood of tiny houses packed into the saddle of land crisscrossed by Shiloh Street and Virginia Avenue, and a middle-class neighborhood of genteel late-Victorian houses along Maple, Virginia, and Bigham streets. At **201–207 Grandview Avenue,** at the southwest corner of Maple Avenue, stand four delightful Queen Anne row houses with a datestone of 1880: at **223 Grandview,** near Kearsarge Street, is a Second Empire mansarded frame house of the Civil War era, and at **520 Grandview** (within the upper curve of McArdle Roadway), stands a superbly

520 Grandview /*Franklin Toker*

preserved Queen Anne house complete with turret and octagonal gazebo. These same blocks of Grandview contain some good public buildings also: the small Academic Revival **Carnegie Library of Pittsburgh—Mt. Washington Branch** (315 Grandview, between Bertha & Kearsarge), and the dramatic but thin Gothic Revival **St. Mary of the Mount Church** (403 Grandview, between Bertha & Ulysses; Frederick Sauer, 1896). Two blocks south of Grandview stands the earlier Gothic Revival **Grace Episcopal Church** (SE corner Bertha & W. Sycamore; 1852; rebuilt 1926), an impressive rural sanctuary of finely cut ashlar blocks that served the landed gentry on Mt. Washington in the mid-nineteenth century.

The Gothic Revival survives on Mt. Washington in secular as well as in sacred architecture. The **Daniel Hilf houses** at 200–210 Kearsarge Street, between Virginia and W. Sycamore, and on Volk's Way, a little alley next to 224 Kearsarge, charmingly illustrate the possibilities of vernacular worker housing at even the smallest scale and budget. Gothic in spirit rather than in explicit style, these two groups of clapboarded frame houses, one white, one beige, were erected by Hilf, a Bavarian immigrant builder, around 1910. Another three dozen tiny houses by Hilf still stand in the semicircular hollow formed by Marne Way and Penelope and Spahrgrove streets off Saw Mill Run about a half mile to the south.

Chatham Village—the name celebrates William Pitt as the first Earl of Chatham—is not especially well known in Pittsburgh, but it is famous worldwide in planning circles as the unqualified success in low-cost housing in the twentieth century. It was built by Pittsburgh's Buhl Foundation in two stages, in 1932 and 1936. For two decades it was the official model for all federally assisted housing in the country, though none of the copies ever matched its quality. The village is bounded by Bigham, Virginia, Olympia, and Pennridge roads. It accommodates 216 families on seventeen acres of steeply terraced ground, with another thirty acres retained as woods and playground. The architecture—gracious but simple Georgian by Ingham & Boyd—is good, but the planning is brilliant. Using ground so hilly that it was regarded as unbuildable, Clarence Stein and Henry Wright laid out three clusters of homes around miniature village greens. Each cluster subdivides into smaller groups of two to eight homes, with parking either in integral garages or in hidden garage rows on the periphery of the village. Ralph Griswold and Theodore Kohankie were the landscape architects. The social center for the complex is the old **Bigham House** of 1844 on Pennridge Road. Now known as Chatham Hall, its simple Greek Revival lines and brick walls were the starting point for the design of the new houses. (Bigham House deserves commemoration in its own right, as the most important of the half-dozen stops of the underground slave railway in the Pittsburgh area.) Stein and Wright had devised middle-class housing projects before Chatham, but none achieved the social and financial success that this one did. It has always had 100 percent

Chatham Village /*Franklin Toker*

occupancy as a rental property and (since 1960) as a cooperative. A score of occupants have lived in Chatham Village since the 1930s; indeed, three families that arrived in 1932 have never left.

Two blocks west of Chatham Village, a second classic view of Pittsburgh is available on Grandview Avenue at Sweetbriar Street, in the shadow of the massive twenty-five-story **Trimont Condominiums** (Grandview, between Plymouth & Oneida Sts.; Louis D. Astorino Associates, 1985). The three rivers come into sharp focus here, with an especially dramatic view of the North Side and the Ohio River. An excellent complement to this view is the spectacular descent down the back of Mt. Washington (here called Duquesne Heights) from Grandview Avenue by way of Shaler Street to the West End, or from Grandview via Republic and Greenleaf streets down to W. Carson Street and the West End Bridge.

The Back Slopes of Mt. Washington

Pittsburgh is a confederation of villages, of which some (Oakland, Shadyside, Squirrel Hill) get more than their fair share of attention and others less. The villages on the plateau and back slopes of Mt. Washington, particularly Allentown, Arlington, Knoxville, Beltzhoover, Beechview, Brookline, Carrick, and Overbrook, are the least well known in proportion to their size and population (70,000 people, or about one-fifth of the city, and an equal percentage of the land mass). One may explain this communal low profile through history and economics, since these are among the newest and least commercially developed areas of the city. But it may be explained also in topographic terms, since the key to prestige in any city is visibility, and in

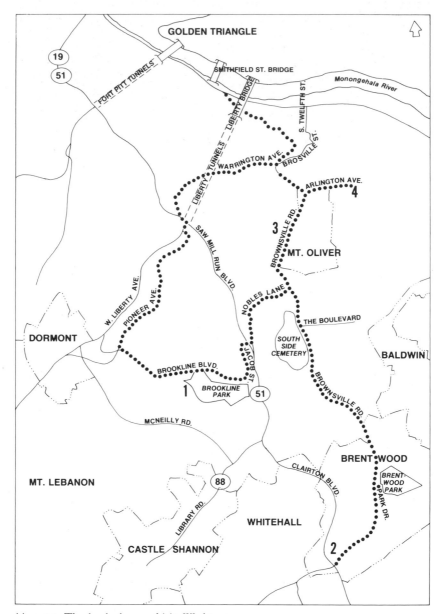

Map 11. The back slopes of Mt. Washington

1 Sam Bryen Arch   3 Carnegie Library, Knoxville
2 Whitehall Shopping Center   4 Arlington Fire Station

Pittsburgh the back slopes of Mt. Washington are effectively invisible to the other city districts. It is only when flying over Pittsburgh that one occasionally glimpses these areas, and even then they merge imperceptibly with the neighboring suburbs of Brentwood, Dormont, Whitehall, and Baldwin. A circular excursus of about ten miles can, however, catch their basic flavor.

The portal roads into the Mt. Washington neighborhoods are **Arlington** and **Warrington avenues,** the old turnpikes to Brownsville and Washington, Pennsylvania. Arlington (reached from E. Sycamore Street, the McArdle Roadway, E. Carson Street, and S. Twelfth and Brosville streets) curves up Mt. Washington on a roadbed parallel to the tracks of an abandoned incline plane. Many of the small frame houses along its path are raised as though on stilts to fit its slope. The character of this casual street changes radically at the crest of the hill, where Arlington intersects Warrington Avenue and Allentown begins.

Allentown and **Beltzhoover** were both laid out after the Civil War by Benjamin McLain and his son-in-law Thomas Maple. Like Nathaniel Bedford, they stamped the names of their children on the main cross-streets. Allentown was settled by German artisans, who came up from the South Side either on trolleys or on three inclined planes that rose over 400 feet. The social and physical cohesiveness of Allentown is dramatically revealed each year on Good Friday, when the teenagers of St. George's parish put on togas and Roman military uniforms and with a cross and crown of thorns duplicate Christ's procession to Calvary in the main streets of their neighborhood.

The isolated hilltown that had its *arx* on Warrington Avenue has lost much of its color as its residents (today numbering about 4,000) have found less fatiguing places to live elsewhere in Pittsburgh. But for a hundred years it held fast, and its relics are impressive. The three-story commercial block at **816– 818 Warrington Avenue,** between Asteroid Way and Arlington Avenue, well represents the economic history of the neighborhood. It was boldly fashioned in the High Victorian Gothic period, probably in the 1880s, with elaborately stepped corbels and wide segmental arches, then reclad at street level in the 1930s in the black-glass trademark of Art Deco.

Warrington Avenue, the Mt. Washington Transit Tunnel, and the Liberty tubes all intersect Saw Mill Run Boulevard (Route 51 South) within an eighth of a mile of each other. The old Washington Pike is now called W. Liberty Avenue (truck Route 19 South) and is a busy and unlovely thoroughfare mainly dedicated to used cars. Immediately uphill, however, W. Liberty intersects **Pioneer Avenue,** a pleasant street that cuts for 1.3 miles through the semisuburban neighborhood of Brookline.

Brookline and **Overbrook** were farmland until 1910, when both were laid out by the speculator A. P. Haaz and named for wealthy suburbs of Boston and Philadelphia. The new developments were so remote from Pittsburgh, however, that much land here and in the adjoining neighborhoods of Banksville, Beechview, and Carrick was sold cheaply as cemetery until the suburbs began

Sam Bryen Arch, Brookline
Memorial Park /*Courtesy
L. P. Perfido Associates*

to prosper in the 1920s. Long and spacious, **Brookline Boulevard** has the
storefronts and the characteristic diagonal parking of a suburban shopping
mall. The south side of the boulevard has been commercially developed, with
stores below and apartments ornamented with Spanish tile roofs above, while
the north side is largely given over to houses on high, broad lawns. If
Brookline and the other dormitory communities are unexciting for some, they
are just right for others: the home burglary rate in Overbrook, for example, is a
minimal one per thousand.

The most ingenious architectural works on the back slopes of Mt. Washington are the recreational facilities in **Brookline Memorial Park** (L. P.
Perfido Associates, 1981). The park was given to the city by developers who
could make no money out of its steep slopes and poor subsurface conditions.
Years later, the architects had the thankless task of embellishing this forlorn
land with a swimming pool and baseball diamonds. Their limited vocabulary
of colors and elements kept the project within its narrow budget and harmo-
nized with the three rows of 1930s and 1940s tract houses that stare down on
the park like bored spectators. The materials for the pool—glazed concrete
block, glass block, and brick—are handled with a severe totemic aspect, as
though they were the ruins of some nameless pueblo.

The extraordinary element of the composition is the **Sam Bryen Arch,** the
portal to the two major baseball diamonds. The "arch" is nothing more than a
gap between a garage and a maintenance shed, but the designers turned it into
something profound both in shape and function. Probably based on the Lion
Gate at Mycenae, the arch consists of brown-glazed concrete block over a
mauve base, a sturdy concrete lintel, and two 1930s-style concrete columns.
The wall rises to embrace a concrete block that is inscribed with high-minded
epigrams from the *Little League Handbook of Fair Play.* To the left, a long wall
shelters niches that will be filled over the years with plaques proclaiming the

winners of the Little League baseball season in Brookline. Here, in the middle of suburbia, rises a monument that is at once stark and lush, classic and pop, complex and contradictory.

Carrick (reached from Brookline Park by Brookline Blvd., Jacob & Whited Sts., and Nobles Lane) was once a pike town along the Birmingham & Brownsville Macadamized Turnpike to the important port of Brownsville, on the Monongahela River. Tollgates stood here as late as 1900. A middle-class district of 12,000 inhabitants today, Carrick had its brief affluence at the turn of the century, when the wealthier families abandoned the crowded South Side. One remnant of this period is **The Boulevard,** a short promenade that opens off Brownsville Road opposite the South Side Cemetery, with a half-dozen spacious Queen Anne and Colonial Revival houses.

One and a half miles south of The Boulevard, Brownsville Road becomes the center spine of the independent borough of **Brentwood,** a semisuburban district of 13,000 people. Brentwood's past and present are summed up in two buildings: the **Brentwood Senior Citizens' Center** (3423 Brownsville Rd., NE corner Park Dr., at the entrance to Brentwood Park), an Italianate farmhouse villa of the 1860s; and, farther south, the fanciful 1930s design of the **Whitehall Center** (Brownsville Rd. at DeWalt Ave.; Victor A. Regmont, 1939). Part of the first generation of American shopping plazas, the Whitehall Center is a stylish composition of a dozen low shops and two high cylindrical towers that announce the cinema at its mid-point. With this lively milestone, the "city suburbs" of Pittsburgh end and the true suburbs of the South Hills begin.

North of Carrick lie the working-class neighborhoods of Knoxville and Arlington and the independent borough of Mt. Oliver. **Knoxville** was a fruit farm established early in the nineteenth century by the Reverend Jeremiah Knox. His descendants turned the family farm into a housing development in the 1870s, but today its modest housing stock mainly dates from the early

Left: Carnegie Library of Pittsburgh—Knoxville Branch (Paul Schweikher, architect) */Franklin Toker* • *Right:* Arlington Fire Station */Franklin Toker*

twentieth century. The neighborhood thus provides a remarkable setting for Paul Schweikher's elegant and self-contained **Carnegie Library of Pittsburgh—Knoxville Branch** (400 Brownsville Rd., SW corner Matthews; 1966). This cement-block structure pulls back from the street by means of two deeply recessed vestibules that muffle traffic noises. It receives its main light not from the street but from two gray metal hoods that rise, fortresslike, from the central block of the building and terminate in skylights. The design of the library is a daring concept, elitist rather than populist in tone, since it shrinks from contact with the ragtag architecture of the street and sets itself up as a sanctuary of learning for the neighborhood residents who want one.

Schweikher's sanctuary has a counterpart a mile to the northeast in the **Arlington Fire Station** (NE corner Arlington Ave. & St. Patrick; Louis D. Astorino Associates, 1981). Glistening white and unexpectedly handsome for a utilitarian structure, the fire station derives its power from the severe geometry of its rhomboid plan and the contrast of the glass-encased machine room and the concrete block of the firemen's living quarters behind. By day and by night the sight of the bright yellow fire engine inside its glass jewel case makes one reflect on the firemen as heroic public servants, ready to lay down their lives for the public weal.

Approximately one mile to the northwest, this excursus through the back slopes of Mt. Washington returns to its starting point at the intersection of Arlington and Warrington avenues. Here also is the upper terminus of Brosville Street, which descends precipitously to S. Twelfth Street, E. Carson Street, and Bedford Square in the heart of Old Birmingham.

Old Birmingham

The 964 acres of Old Birmingham, in the heart of the South Side, are divided about equally between its "flats" and its "slopes"—that is, between the floodplain of the Monongahela River and the terraces where the cliff of Mt. Washington levels sufficiently to accommodate several hundred houses. The division of Old Birmingham into two camps was both topographical and social in origin, since the dividing point was the railroad at the base of Mt. Washington. It was an ethnic division, with Germans on the slopes and Eastern Europeans on the flats, and it was an architectural distinction as well: the slopes are covered in clusters of white frame cottages, the flats in red-brick rows. Whether on the flats or the slopes, the inhabitants of Old Birmingham are marked by their strong sense of community. To a degree hardly imaginable elsewhere in urban America, their lives revolve about their homes and their handsome churches.

It is regrettable that Nathaniel Bedford laid out **Bedford Square** on the

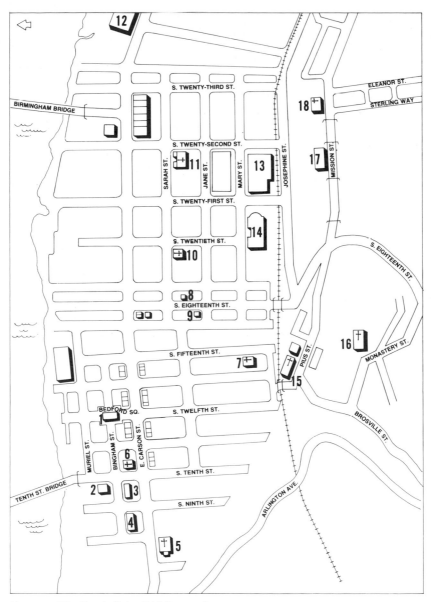

Map 12. The South Side: Old Birmingham

1 South Side Market
2 Oliver Bathhouse
3 Bedford Public School
4 Old U.S. Glass Co.
5 St. John the Baptist
  Church
6 Cleaves Temple

7 St. Adalbert's Church
8 Polish Falcons Auditorium
9 Lithuanian Hall
10 South Side Presbyterian
   Church
11 St. Casimir's Church
12 LTV Steel

13 Duquesne Brewery
14 South Side Hospital
15 St. Michael's Church
16 St. Paul Monastery
17 Mission St. Pumping
   Station
18 St. Josaphat's Church

lines of Market Square in Pittsburgh rather than those of Bedford Square in London. It is thus only a small place, cut through at the mid-points of its four sides by S. Twelfth and Bingham streets. Bedford constructed a market house there in 1813; the present **South Side Market** in transitional Romanesque-Classical style (by Charles Bickel, 1893; restored 1915) is the fifth on the site. It is one of two surviving market buildings in Pittsburgh, but since 1950 it has served as the South Side Recreational Center.

The homes around the market house in Bedford Square represent the typical mix of domestic architecture in the South Side: small row houses of two stories and an attic from the decades before or immediately following the Civil War, and High Victorian Gothic houses of three full stories or two stories and a mansard roof.

Bingham Street, leading west out of Bedford Square, was the center of glassmaking in America in the last half of the nineteenth century. Some glasshouses had been here since shortly after 1800; more moved here after being devastated by the fire of 1845 in the Golden Triangle. The chief of these was Bakewell, Pears & Company, which was founded in 1808 and soon enjoyed a world reputation for flint houseware glass. President Monroe regarded Bakewell glass as the equal of European service and ordered it for the White House. The Bakewell glasshouses occupied a full block of Bingham Street between S. Ninth and S. Tenth streets and the Monongahela shoreline until that site was taken over by Henry Oliver's ironworks. The **Oliver Bathhouse** (38 S. Tenth St., NW corner Bigham St.; MacClure & Spahr, 1915), originally sketched out by Daniel Burnham, was in the end produced by others in the Jacobean Revival mode, with a projecting bay window over the central door and handsome stone quoins at each of the reentrant angles of the brick structure. It is charmingly articulated on the attic floor by a sequence of dolphins that advertise its aquatic function. Opposite its long side stands the former **Bedford Public School** (910 Bingham St.; 1850), a large, majestic three-story construction that shows how strong and effective the language of the Greek Revival was in Pittsburgh even at mid-century.

The former factory "F" of the **U.S. Glass Company** (44 S. Ninth St., SW corner Bingham; 1891 and later), now occupied by the Salvation Army, was the headquarters of a consortium of a dozen smaller glassworks that briefly rivaled PPG. Its north wall, thirty-two bays long, reflects the older Romanesque Revival mode of factory construction, but there are also several idiosyncracies peculiar to Frank Furness, whose influence in Pittsburgh reached its height with the construction of his B&O Railroad Terminal here in 1888.

St. John the Baptist Church and Cleaves Temple

The central mile of E. Carson Street is a commercial strip of the late nine-

St. John the Baptist Ukrainian Catholic Church, E. Carson Street /*Franklin Toker*

teenth and early twentieth centuries, but the introductory note sounded by
two churches at its western entrance, toward Station Square, is decisively
spiritual. **St. John the Baptist Ukrainian Catholic Church** (109 S. Seventh
St., SE corner E. Carson; Beezer Brothers, 1895; main sanctuary, 1917) is the
most striking architectural symbol of the Central and Eastern European communities in Pittsburgh. Its plan is the proud cross-in-square of ancient Byzantine architecture, and it bears a crown of eight turquoise domes that call to
mind not only St. Mark's in Venice but the *pysanka* eggs distributed at Easter
by the Ukrainian community.

Much smaller, but still a powerful presence, is the nearby **Cleaves Temple
Christian Methodist Episcopal Church** at 1005 E. Carson, near S. Tenth
Street (1913). J. O. Keller was the builder. The red brick, the white overscaled
Ionic portico, the bright orange towers, and the onion-topped domes height-
en the impact of this charming structure. The church is both a religious and an
architectural mix: built by Ukrainian Presbyterians, it became a Greek Catholic church and is Methodist today. In its tentative accord of Eastern Chris-
tianity and mainline American Protestantism, this dashing little church symbolizes the bittersweet process of assimilation that has taken place in the
South Side over the last century.

The several hundred buildings that constitute the streetscape of **E. Carson Street** between the Tenth Street and Birmingham bridges make it an outstanding example of a Victorian commercial street. Three architectural styles predominate: Italianate, with elaborate hood molds (good examples can be found in the 1200, 1300, and 1700 blocks); High Victorian Gothic, with depressed segmental arches and elaborate bracketed corbel tables (an excellent example, though modernized, is the **Ukrainian Home** at 1113 E. Carson St.); and the Art Deco of the 1930s. Good examples of the latter are Jack's Bar at 1121 E. Carson, Pittsburgh Office Furniture at 1214, Siegel's Jewelers at 1510, Kotula's Café at 1605, and Grau Jewelers at 1734. A few sober Beaux Arts banks were also intercalated in this otherwise exuberant architectural scene: the **Iron and Glass Bank** (1114 E. Carson St.; 1926); the **Mellon Bank** branch at 1401 (originally the German Savings Deposit Bank; probably by Charles Bickel, 1896); and the **Pittsburgh National Bank** branch (originally the People's Trust Company; 1736 E. Carson; 1902, with the fine **George Trautman House** in High Victorian Gothic immediately behind, at 94 S. Eighteenth St.). In the same category as the banks is a distinguished Beaux Arts office block, the **Maul Building** (1700 E. Carson, SW S. Seventeenth St.; W. G. Wilkens Company), erected by the president of the German Savings and Deposit Bank in 1910.

The side streets of the South Side provide their own architectural accompaniment to the main theme sounded by E. Carson Street. On the short numbered streets between the river shore and the base of Mt. Washington, and on the long streets named for John Ormsby's daughters, stand hundreds of houses in almost unbroken rows, creating a living museum of nineteenth-century urban America.[1] Closely tied to these dwellings are the the ethnic community centers. The spiritual home of the Polish community is **St. Adalbert's Church** (162 S. Fifteenth St., near Breed; 1889), with its social center, parish house, and Polish school. St. Adalbert's is a striking twin-towered brick monument that was made to be seen down the whole length of Mary Street— a view that was unfortunately blocked by the prolongation of S. Seventeenth Street. The **Falcon Auditorium** (97 S. Eighteenth St., between Carey Way & Sarah; c. 1870) is the secular home of the Polish community, in a severe

---

1. Although preservationists are not yet scrambling to protect them, the KoolVent aluminum awnings of the South Side should be certified at some future point as the world's largest ensemble of the genre. The awnings were custom-built and custom-colored and featured special angled side louvers that withstood the wind-shear effect that tore off ordinary awnings. They were invented and patented in Pittsburgh in 1942, then marketed nationally through licensees. Although the rest of the country enjoyed them too, KoolVent awnings became a Pittsburgh specialty. Installed at the rate of some two dozen a day for forty-one years until their production was stopped in 1983, the awnings today adorn the windows and stoops of thousands of Pittsburgh homes. They were particularly important in the South Side, Bloomfield, and Lawrenceville, where row houses offered less individuality than the housing stock in other Pittsburgh neighborhoods.

Left: Victorian storefronts, E. Carson Street /*Franklin Toker* ▪ *Right:* S. Thirteenth Street and the slopes of Mt. Washington /*Franklin Toker*

Romanesque Revival building that was once a Methodist church. It was in this auditorium in 1917 that Ignace Paderewski inspired the delegates of the Polish Falcons to create a Polish army in the United States as part of the Allied cause—a critical step in the rebirth of modern Poland. Two blocks away, a former German social club stands today as the **Lithuanian Hall** (1721 Jane St., near NW corner S. Eighteenth St.; 1870). This tentatively Classical Revival structure was upstaged in 1908 by its annex, whose overscaled corbel brackets testify to the widespread influence in Pittsburgh of Art Nouveau.

Many of the neighborhood churches assumed corner positions on their blocks for greater visibility. The **South Side Presbyterian Church** (1926 Sarah St., SW corner S. Twentieth St.; 1893) follows the typical formula of the time in its broad twin-towered facade, but it distinguishes itself with an open Palladian arch in the belfry of its asymmetrical left tower. **St. Casimir's Church** (2130 Sarah St., SW corner S. Twenty-second St.; 1901), the oldest Lithuanian-based parish in the city, takes advantage of its corner site by raising two towers on high square shafts of brick with rusticated brick quoins. Here the tower belfries are marked by neo-Baroque paired columns set diagonally on the corners.

Sustenance of a material sort was provided to Old Birmingham by two rambling complexes on opposite sides of S. Twenty-first Street, just below the rise of the Mt. Washington hill. One was the **Duquesne Brewery** of 1899 at the southeast corner of S. Twenty-first and Mary, a rich collection of Romanesque Revival and assorted designs from the late nineteenth to the mid-twentieth century. Duquesne no longer produces beer, but it does provide accommodation for a dozen artists' studios and wholesale outlets. Atop its roof a gargantuan clock of 1933 provides the neighborhood (and half of Pittsburgh) with accurate time. Across the street, the old **South Side Hospital** is now gone, but the hospital flourishes in a new 255-bed pavilion at 2000 Mary Street, built by IKM/SGE in 1982. The new building is one of the few positive attainments of contemporary medical architecture in the Pittsburgh region. It consists of a base structure surmounted by four tapered wings, with a semicircular emergency and intensive-care pavilion at one end. The hospital's exterior skin of aluminum siding makes a startling architectural statement, but one that links the building unequivocally to the aluminum-sided homes in many neighboring rows.

The eastern end of the South Side constitutes a special group in itself, with the Birmingham Bridge, a Carnegie library, the eight-block-long Riverside Park bordering the Monongahela shore, and an especially attractive sequence of eleven Romanesque Revival buildings in the 2200 block of E. Carson Street. Rising above all else is the mass of the Pittsburgh works of the **LTV Steel Corporation** (formerly J&L) at the intersection of S. Twenty-fifth Street and E. Carson. LTV had its start here in 1853, when Benjamin Franklin Jones and Samuel Kier expanded the small ironworks firm of Bernard Lauth & Brother. The American Iron Works of Jones, Kier, and Lauth had a daily output of seven tons. Kier left to become America's oil pioneer and was replaced in 1856 by the banker James Laughlin. The South Side mill began to produce steel in its two Bessemer furnaces in 1883. By 1900 its work force of 15,000 men were pouring 3,000 tons of steel a day. Today the mill is all but deserted, and the once-powerful company store on E. Carson Street at S. Twenty-sixth Street is a Goodwill outlet.

The South Side Slopes

Bridges over the Conrail tracks at S. Twelfth and S. Eighteenth streets allow access from the flats of the South Side to its slopes. The great monument here is **St. Michael's Church** (Charles S. Bartberger, 1857–61) on Pius Street at Brosville, which extends S. Twelfth Street up a dauntingly steep hill.

St. Michael's Church and Rectory, Pius Street /*Franklin Toker*

Stirling Way /*Franklin Toker*

It was understood by the faithful in the Middle Ages that St. Michael, mightiest of the archangels, felt most at home if his altars and sanctuaries were erected at great heights. In consequence, his churches were generally perched atop mountains or surmounted by exceptionally high spires. The German Catholic immigrants on the South Side evidently understood this when they built their church of St. Michael's on this dramatic terrace overlooking Old Birmingham. The best features of the church are the superb site, the high needle spire, and the sequence of exquisitely modeled brick buttresses along Pius Street. The style is German Romanesque—the *Rundbogenstil*—which, in combination with the hillside and the river below, gives a strongly German cast to the building. Not so powerful but more lovable than the gaunt church is St. Michael's **Rectory** (1889), alongside the church. Especially seductive here are the two circular towers that are recessed into the left and right corners and topped by elegantly swirled metal domes. Probably added by the architect's son, Charles M. Bartberger, the rectory design owes a good deal to Frank Furness, particularly in the central arch, which is seemingly torn apart by the weight of the tower above it. Since World War I, the rectory has been the site of annual Lenten presentations of *Veronica's Veil*, a passion play that may be unique in America and which involves 150 men and women of the parish as actors.

The church and rectory of St. Michael's are only two elements in a complex that involves a "casino" of 1897, a community center, a large convent residence, and a school for girls (1874; rebuilt 1900), all located on Pius Street. A detached part of this complex is the **St. Paul of the Cross Monastery** (148 Monastery Ave., NE corner St. Paul St.; Charles S. Bartberger, 1853). This flourishing monastic complex on the crown of Mt. Washington is the oldest of the twenty-eight Passionist Fathers houses in America. It consists of a broad Romanesque-Gothic church encircled by monastic buildings on three sides.

Inside, the style is not medieval but classicizing: a stunning German Baroque hall-church with three naves of equal height divided by sturdy, deeply fluted Composite columns rendered in imitation marble. The chancel is the most extraordinary part of the interior, consisting of a coffered barrel vault supported by a continuous entablature that in turn rests on pilasters and cruciform piers—an arrangement that reflects the double duty of the building as both a community church and a monastic chapel.

Monastery and S. Eighteenth streets surround the St. Paul of the Cross Monastery in the manner of an encircling ramp around a Crusader castle. By means of two bridges to the east, one can leave the castle for Mission Street, which is heralded by Thomas Scott's handsome 1910 Beaux Arts **Mission Street Pumping Station.** Mission Street itself is remarkable, being another of the long terraced streets of the South Side that seem to flourish in harsh isolation. It is intersected at right angles by Sterling Way and Eleanor Street, both so steep that they need railings for winter passage. The guardian of Mission Street is **St. Josaphat's Church** (2314 Mission St., near Sterling; John Comes, 1913–17), a severe brick structure for the neighboring Polish community that mingles recollections of old Europe (a Romanesque Revival porch and a high tower with bell-and-onion dome) with stylisms of Frank Lloyd Wright and the emerging Modern Movement. Sterling Way continues for several blocks to the peak of Mt. Washington, where the houses are widely spaced amid lush gardens. It is an incredible part of the Pittsburgh experience, complete with rabbits hopping along narrow lanes. Viewing the gardens and the steelworkers' hard-won houses, one has the palpable sense of the determination that for two hundred years has sustained the South Side against its habitual adversaries of steep hills and uncertain employment.

Hillside homes on the North Side, with downtown Pittsburgh in the distance /*Courtesy* Pittsburgh Post-Gazette (*Darrell Sapp*)

The North Side

The toponymy of Pittsburgh is elegant in its simplicity: a North and a South Side, a West and an East End. The two "ends" could not be more dissimilar, but the "sides" have many parallels. Both originated as land grants in the era of the revolutionary war, both divide into flats and slopes, and both have significant industrial histories. As in the case of the South Side, there is a "greater" North Side, encompassing such communities as the Perry Hilltop, Spring Hill, and Troy Hill, and a North Side proper, consisting of the neighborhoods of Old Allegheny, Allegheny West, and Dutchtown.

The North Side was visited by a few Indian traders as early as the 1740s. In 1784 the Commonwealth of Pennsylvania paid Alexander McClain and Daniel Leet to survey a Reserve Tract of 3,000 acres as part of the "Depreciation Lands" that were to be given as farmland to the veterans of the revolutionary war as back salary in lieu of cash. (The idea of drawing up towns for war veterans instead of paying them is an old one: the Romans established Florence and other cities for the same purpose.) In 1788 Benjamin Franklin, president of the Supreme Executive Council of Pennsylvania, sent David Redick, a surveyor from neighboring Washington County, to lay out a city opposite Pittsburgh as the seat of the newly legislated County of Allegheny. This Redick did, although Pittsburgh soon appropriated the prestige of county seat for itself.[1]

In the end, the destiny of "Alleghenytown" was to be industrial and not pastoral: few veterans actually settled here, and most of the lots ended up as factories. For a hundred years the North Side yielded an industrial produce of astonishing variety: glass, rope, flour, oil, salt, cotton, woolens, iron, textiles, carriages, wagons, coaches, plows, sleighs, boats, paper, saddles, harnesses, boots, shoes, pottery, brassware, springs, locomotives, even cast-iron bathtubs. It was textiles that attracted the weaver William Carnegie to make his difficult trek here from Dunfermline, Scotland, in 1848; his wife, Margaret, stitched shoes for a North Side cobbler, while his boy Andrew changed bobbins in a cotton mill. Before its forced annexation to Pittsburgh in 1907, Allegheny City constituted a flourishing municipality in its own right. It had a university, a famous observatory, and a roster of celebrated citizens: the industrialists Carnegie, Heinz, B. F. Jones, William Thaw, Jr., and Henry Oliver; the scientists John Brashear and Samuel Pierpont Langley; and the writers and artists Gertrude Stein, Robinson Jeffers, Mary Roberts Rinehart, Mary Cassatt, and Martha Graham. Around 1900, Brighton Road and Ridge Avenue were

---

1. Redick had his doubts about the site and wrote Franklin: "[The land] abounds with high hills and deep hollows, almost inaccessible to a surveyor. . . . It would have been far more suitable for residents of the moon, than farmer or settler." He nonetheless worked the best acres of the North Side into a square of thirty-six blocks, each 240 by 240 feet and subdivided into four smaller lots. Redick left the four central blocks empty, for public use, and also provided a commons of 102 acres (most of it surviving today) that entirely surrounded the little city. Redick's design was apparently based on town plans in New England, such as that of New Haven, but its ultimate source may have been the Bible. The forty-eight Levitical cities of ancient Israel were described as squares surrounded by common pastureland, in the same proportion as Allegheny but at twice the scale.

said to have sheltered more millionaires than any two blocks in the world. Today, after two generations of neglect, the North Side is proving to be a fascinating laboratory, not for science or technology, but for the process of rehabilitation and repopulation of its old neighborhoods—a process that is being closely watched elsewhere in the nation.

Old Allegheny

The **North Shore** district, by the Allegheny River, was the part of the North Side that was hardest hit by the flight of industry decades ago. Its fortunes revived somewhat when it was designated as the site for **Three Rivers Stadium** (Deeter Ritchey Sippel, 1971), after the Pirates abandoned Forbes Field and the Steelers abandoned Pitt Stadium in Oakland. Its site, bounded by General Robinson St. W. and North Shore Drive, was already sanctified in a city that is passionate about its sports, for it was here that Exposition Park stood until eighty years ago, and here in 1903 that the Pirates played Boston in the first World Series. This enormous poured-concrete structure with a capacity of 58,000 (64,000 for concerts) has seen its own triumphs, particularly in 1979–80, when Pittsburgh took both the World Series and the Super Bowl. (The teams are not abandoned in their slumps either: Pittsburgh corporations united in 1986 to buy the Pirates rather than see them leave the city.) The stadium is handsome within a fairly conventional formula (a more

Three Rivers Stadium /*Courtesy Deeter Ritchie Sippel Associates*

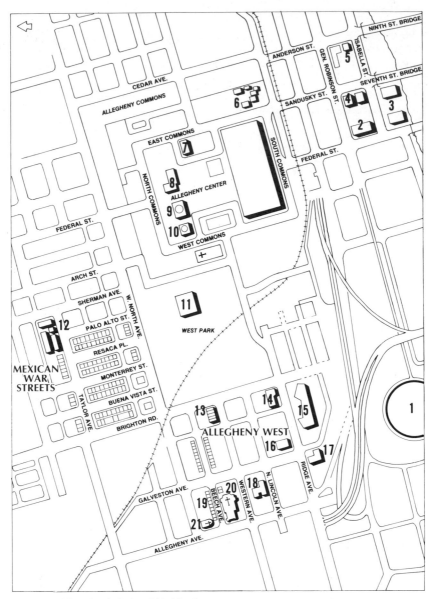

Map 13. The North Side: Old Allegheny

1 Three Rivers Stadium
2 Boggs Bldg.
3 NorthShore Center & Park
4 Volkwein Music Bldg.
5 Frederick Osterling Studio
6 Allegheny Commons East
7 IBM
8 Carnegie Library, Allegheny

9 Buhl Planetarium
10 Old Post Office Museum
11 Pittsburgh Aviary
12 Allegheny Widows' Home
13 McIntosh Row
14 B. F. Jones, Jr., House
15 Community College of
   Allegheny Co.

16 W. P. Snyder House
17 Byers-Lyon House
18 William Thaw, Jr., House
19 Stein & Rinehart houses
20 Calvary Methodist Church
21 Emmanuel Episcopal Church

NorthShore Center and Allegheny Landing Park /*Courtesy UDA Architects (Clyde Hare)*

daring horseshoe-shaped stadium was originally proposed, for which the Golden Triangle would have provided an unforgettable backdrop), with its boldly striated access ramps that recall Pierluigi Nervi's soccer stadium of 1932 in Florence. The best aspect of the stadium is its unique means of access: rather than fight traffic, hundreds of Pittsburghers sail to their baseball and football games on the Gateway Clipper fleet from Station Square.

A half-mile east of the stadium, **NorthShore Center and Allegheny Landing Park** took over another stretch of shoreline between the Sixth and Seventh Street bridges in 1984, in a significant gesture to bring Pittsburgh back to the waterways that gave it birth. The master plan and Buildings One and Three are by UDA Architects; Jackson Seay Associates were the landscape designers. Creation of the complex brought together a private developer (the builders Mellon-Stuart, who have their headquarters here), the City of Pittsburgh, and several private foundations, who invited four sculptors to create an art park linked to the new buildings. The result is a grassy knoll and a landing on the Allegheny River that recalls the neoclassical Porta della Ripetta in eighteenth-century Rome. The two low-rise buildings so far constructed are only the kernel of a projected much larger development that will extend north across Isabella Street and east to the Ninth Street Bridge. They were designed as glazed structures of a pronounced horizontality in order to reinforce their shoreline setting. The dark maroon brick is similarly keyed to the older buildings around it and was produced specially for this project to capture the hue that was once produced by the old coke-fired kilns.

Fortunately, there are enough quality old buildings left on the North Shore to enter into a dialogue with NorthShore Center. Immediately adjacent on the north is the **R. H. Boggs Building** (110–120 Federal St., NE corner Gen. Robinson St. E.; Charles Bickel, 1912; renovation by Tom Mistick & Sons,

Frederick Osterling's architectural studio, Isabella Street /*Franklin Toker*

1984), a fine Beaux Arts terra-cotta commercial block of small stores and
offices that once also housed a hotel and apartment house. Northeast of the
new buildings stands **Four NorthShore Center** (NW corner Isabella and
Sandusky; renovation by Williams Trebilcock Whitehead, 1984), a bold
Romanesque-Classical warehouse of around 1900 that is part timber-framed
and part steel cage inside. North of it rises the **Volkwein Music Building** (117
Sandusky St., NW corner Gen. Robinson St. E.; in the manner of Rutan &
Russell, c. 1915), the terra-cotta high-rise commercial block of a sheet-music
and instrument distributor that has miraculously stayed in business for almost
a century. The Volkwein block has lost its original cornice but compensates
with a series of six cornucopia-shaped consoles that drip onto the building like
giant snails from the top string-course.

One block east stands the **Frederick Osterling architectural studio** (now
Foley Electric; 228 Isabella St.; 1917), a charming diminutive building with a
glass facade covered by Gothic trefoils in the manner of Osterling's Union
Trust Building downtown. The studio provided an elegant reception room for
Osterling above and a large drafting hall below. Although not a technological
breakthrough because of its tiny scale, or an architectural milestone because of
its historicist styling, Osterling's little studio is one of the earliest glass-fronted
buildings in America, and it follows only a few years after the first curtain walls
in Europe. In its own right, this proudly independent studio speaks volumes
about the social and economic position of the architect in Pittsburgh society
early in the century.

Allegheny Center

Allegheny Center, bounded by North, East, South, and West Commons, was conceived in the optimism and expanding economy of the 1950s and aborted in the more cautious 1960s. The master plan and One Allegheny Square were designed by Mitchell & Ritchey; Mies van der Rohe did the **IBM Building** in 1966. The center was constructed by Alcoa in what had been the heart of Allegheny City, and it replaced 518 old buildings with a set of apartment blocks and office buildings, a shopping mall, and two housing complexes to the east and west. The strongest of the new building groups here is the one that was least likely to succeed: the **Allegheny Commons East** (East Commons & East Ohio Sts.; Tasso Katselas, 1966), a rent-subsidized housing development that is considerably more successful in architectural and human terms than the expensive Allegheny Towne on the west. The complex takes its architectural motifs from Italian medieval hilltowns such as Gubbio or Viterbo and, like them, ingeniously weaves its streets and ramps through the buildings. Its density is substantial: 136 housing units on just three acres, or about nine times the ratio at Chatham Village. But in these buildings the impression is not one of crowding but of a high and agreeable activity level, both for the young and the elderly of the village.

Three relics of Old Allegheny were permitted to survive on Allegheny

Left: Allegheny Center, with Buhl Planetarium at center and the Old Post Office Museum at left /*Courtesy Buhl Planetarium (Clyde Hare)* ▪ *Right:* Allegheny Commons East /*Courtesy Tasso Katselas Associates*

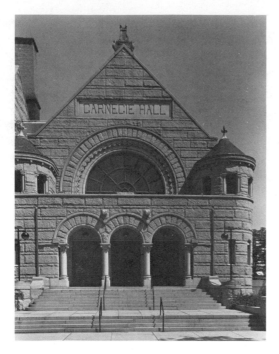

Carnegie Hall /*Franklin Toker*

Square in the heart of the new development: **Carnegie Library of Pittsburgh—Allegheny Branch** and **Carnegie Hall** (Smithmeyer & Pelz, 1889);
Buhl Planetarium and Institute of Popular Science (Ingham, Pratt & Boyd,
1939); and the **Old Post Office Museum** (William M. Aiken for the U.S.
Treasury, 1897). The library preceded the central Carnegie Library in Oakland
by six years. As in Oakland, this design was acquired by national competition,
with Carnegie personally involved in the selection. The choice of Smithmeyer
& Pelz was almost inevitable: the architects had completed the Library of
Congress the same year. The architectural idiom here is very close to Richardson's courthouse, but this is a far less interesting building. The massing of
forms is arbitrary and confusing rather than enlivening, and even the treatment of the stone is flat. The music hall today serves (after an imaginative
rehabilitation by Sylvester Damianos in 1976) as the home of the Pittsburgh
Public Theater. In front of the library stands Daniel Chester French's *Labor,* the
central figure from a destroyed monument that Carnegie commissioned in
memory of James Anderson (Henry Bacon, architect, 1904). Anderson was the
ironmaster who opened his private library to the working boys of Allegheny
City, an act of generosity that Carnegie never forgot.

Buhl Planetarium stands alongside Carnegie Library as a 1930s Art Deco
evocation of the same values that Carnegie had sought in his complex fifty
years earlier. This is a sleek, low building with fine sculpted reliefs; its walls are
rendered in smooth limestone over a rusticated base. Inside, the planetarium

offers a yearly cycle of star shows and an engrossing exhibit of "hands-on" science phenomena.

The preservation of the Old Post Office was one of the first triumphs of the Pittsburgh History & Landmarks Foundation, which then used it as its headquarters for a decade. The building is a handsome, if somewhat cold, mixture of classically derived motifs, culminating in a double dome that is imposing and Baroque on the exterior but intimate and neoclassical inside. It was restored (Williams Trebilcock Whitehead, 1975) to house an exhibit space and is now the Children's Museum of Pittsburgh. Next door is a garden of sculptural and architectural fragments from lost Pittsburgh buildings, with some astonishingly scaled bronze reliefs from the Manchester Bridge of 1915—including the legendary Joe Magarac. The artist was the Beaux Arts sculptor Charles Keck, a disciple of both Augustus Saint-Gaudens and Daniel Chester French.

West Park (bounded by N. Sherman, W. Ohio, & Brighton Rd.) is an imposing remnant of the old Allegheny Commons. For about fifty years it was used as a common grazing ground, but for fifty years after that it was dominated by the mass of William Strickland's Western Penitentiary (1826; modified by John Haviland in 1835) before the institution moved to Woods Run in 1887. Today the only building on the commons is the **Pittsburgh Aviary,** a 1950s and 1960s remake of Henry Phipps's Conservatory of 1887. Three public monuments adorn the park: an equestrian *George Washington* (Edward Pousch, 1891); Peter C. Reniers's columnar *Civil War Soldiers' Monument,* which was transferred here in a severely truncated state from Monument Hill in 1929; and the **Spanish-American War Memorial** (Charles Keck; Stanley Roush, architect, 1914). The torpedo tube and the armored porthole that are represented here as though sinking in a pool of water are actual relics from the submerged *SS Maine;* Keck designed the memorial tablets in a severe brick exedra wall behind. The effect is startlingly evocative—a testimonial to the horror of war without any glorification of it.

The Mexican War Streets

Opposite West Park lies the **Mexican War Streets** zone of about 300 houses on a dozen city blocks (Jacksonia, Sampsonia, Taylor, and W. North Aves. east-west; Buena Vista, Monterey, Resaca, and Palo Alto Sts. north-south), which was Pittsburgh's first venture in the historic preservation of an entire neighborhood. These homes were built from the 1850s to the 1890s on the small (generally twenty-foot-wide) lots parceled out by William Robinson on streets named by him for the heroes and battle sites of the Mexican War. As on the South Side, the two-story pre–Civil War houses are still strongly tied to the Greek Revival style, while the post–Civil War houses are three stories

Resaca Street, in the Mexican War Streets zone /*Franklin Toker*

high, often with mansard roofs. These homes were designed from the beginning for a higher social stratum than were the equivalent buildings on the
South Side, Lawrenceville, or The Hill. They were inhabited by professional
people, prosperous artisans, and the owners of small businesses in central
Pittsburgh, which one could reach in just a few minutes by horsecar after
1859. The rows had declined to the status of boardinghouses by the mid-
1960s, but they suffered few demolitions or modernizations. The Pittsburgh
History & Landmarks Foundation has attempted with some success to retain
the older black population that lived in these houses before the influx of white
urban professionals. The YMCA at Monterey and North Avenue, the Mattress
Factory (an art and cultural center at 500 Sampsonia Way), and the neighborhood churches have helped to nurture what might have become a reverse
ghetto into a flourishing biracial neighborhood.

Among the representative houses in the Mexican War Streets are **516 W.
North Avenue** (NE corner Monterey, opposite West Park; c. 1870), with the
standard plan of an Italianate home but ornamented with old-fashioned
Federal details; a Queen Anne house at **1201 Resaca Place** (NW corner
Eloise St.), with a pyramidal fish-scale shingle roof and a delightful corner
turret; and **1201 Buena Vista Street** (NW corner Eloise; probably by Longfellow, Alden & Harlow, c. 1890), a splendid Richardsonian Romanesque
brownstone with a three-story bay that terminates in an open loggia and
conical roof. The servants' quarters and carriage house, in wood, behind this
slab-shaped mansion are conceived instead in the Queen Anne style.

Allegheny Widows' Home

Not many American cities contain a functioning monastery in their midst, as
does Pittsburgh on the South Side. Fewer still preserve almshouses, which is
what the handsome **Allegheny Widows' Home** was until 1983. The three-

Courtyard of the Allegheny Widows' Home /*Franklin Toker*

story Greek Revival main building was erected by John Chislett in 1838 as an orphan asylum; in 1866 it became a home for widows from the Civil War. Six years later the City of Pittsburgh extended Taylor Street through the property and partially truncated the central building. In compensation, it paid for the construction of row houses—still in Greek Revival style—on three sides of the main building, where widows lived with their families in small townhouses. The institution lasted in that state for over a century. In 1984 the complex was rehabilitated (by Landmarks Design Associates) under HUD Section VIII funding as federally assisted housing for the elderly and the disabled. One hopes the same good fortune will befall the neighboring **Engine Company No. 3** (1416 Arch St., NE corner Jacksonia; 1877), a splendid Furness-style firehouse combining High Victorian Gothic and Italianate mannerisms.

Allegheny West

Situated just west of Allegheny Commons, the tiny neighborhood of **Allegheny West** consists of eight blocks bounded by W. North Avenue, Brighton Road, and Ridge and Allegheny avenues, and subdivided by Galveston, Beech, Western, and N. Lincoln avenues. The houses along these streets are better than in any other district in the North Side, and the neighborhood is also distinguished by two of the best church designs in the city. A good introduction to the neighborhood is provided by **McIntosh Row** (806–812 Western Ave., NW corner Brighton Rd.; c. 1865). This is a three-story, eight-bay-long red-brick townhouse row in Greek Revival style. Its basic lines were transcribed into a more luxurious scale by its neighbors at the end of the row: a set of two Italianate double houses at 814 and 816 and two single townhouses at 818 and 820. The windows on the ground floor of McIntosh Row were elongated during its restoration (by Carl Detwiler, 1979); they are anachronis-

The B. F. Jones, Jr., House /*Courtesy Community College of Allegheny County*

tic but elegant and add to the marketability of a block that had come perilously close to destruction.

The best of the millionaires' homes on the North Side stood on Brighton Road overlooking West Park and around the corner on Ridge Avenue. Most of these architectural dinosaurs have disappeared. The largest survivor is the **Benjamin Franklin Jones, Jr., House** (808 Ridge Ave., NW corner Brighton Rd.; Rutan & Russell, 1908), an immense forty-two-room Tudor fortress of steel-reinforced concrete (a technique evidently dear to the designers, who had used it in their Century Building downtown). Unfortunately, by the time it was built the fortunes of Allegheny City were sinking, and the Jones family abandoned it in 1931 in favor of their country home at Sewickley Heights. It is now part of the community college across the street. The house looked institutional rather than domestic to begin with, and it is almost indistinguishable from the Tudor pile of **Western Theological Seminary** (Thomas Hannah, 1912) that stands immediately alongside it.

At the west end of the same block stands the **William Penn Snyder House** (now Babb Inc., 850 Ridge Ave., NE corner Galveston; George Orth & Brother, 1911), an immense townhouse of the species that many Pittsburgh millionaires constructed in Manhattan, but only a few built here. This light-toned brownstone aims at the general impression of an eighteenth-century Paris *hôtel*, but it gives away its era with the automobile garage door on Galveston Avenue. The whole interior is finished in marble, with superbly carved overdoor decorations and jambs in mahogany. The Snyder House cost nearly a half-million dollars to construct in 1911, but it was sold just a few years later, when this family also retreated to Sewickley Heights.

The **Byers-Lyon House** (901 Ridge Ave.; Alden & Harlow, 1898) is an artless hodgepodge of Italian and French Renaissance motifs and a courtyard supposedly modeled on the Alhambra, but it is statistically impressive. It cost even more than the Snyder House and had ninety rooms and fourteen baths. Now the student union of the community college, it originally served as a double house for a family that had garnered its wealth from iron pipe, which explains the superb confectionary of the iron gate that embellishes its courtyard.

The **Community College of Allegheny County** was a pioneer of its type in the United States, and it now enrolls almost 40,000 students on four campuses. In turning the lower slope of Monument Hill into its North Side Campus in 1973, Tasso Katselas faced a challenge identical to the one resolved by Henry Hornbostel when he designed the Acropolis campus for Pitt in 1908. His solution was necessarily different from that of Hornbostel, since he could not fall back on historical precedents, nor did the economics of maintenance allow him to produce a multitude of smaller buildings, as had Hornbostel. Katselas created instead a sequence of interlocking buildings in

Left: Community College of Allegheny County—North Side Campus /*Courtesy Tasso Katselas Associates* ▪ *Right:* Gertrude Stein's birthplace, Beech Avenue /*Franklin Toker*

poured and cast concrete with a warmly textured brick facing for an effort that suggests the pluralism of the worker-students who study here.

The **William Thaw, Jr., House** (930 Lincoln Ave., between Allegheny & Galveston) is an architectural palimpsest of the years 1875 to 1900, with the original Romanesque Revival building on the right, a later segment with an unusual recessed porch in the middle, and a third wing in Colonial Revival style on the left. The brickwork triangles on its crow-step Dutch gable are a quote borrowed from Richardson's Emmanuel Episcopal Church a few blocks away. The charming Italianate house with a verandah, immediately left of the Thaw House, has been home for almost fifty years to the owner of the Pittsburgh Steelers.

Two streets north of Lincoln is **Beech Avenue,** with a charming series of three-story houses of the last quarter of the nineteenth century, many adorned with spacious verandahs. Two famous names attach themselves to houses on this short block: **Gertrude Stein** (who "always remained firmly born in Allegheny, Pa") was born in 1874 in the richly adorned two-story Italianate brick house at 850; **Mary Roberts Rinehart** lived for years in the substantial brick house at 954 Beech, at the northeast corner of Allegheny Avenue. It was here in 1907 that Rinehart wrote *The Circular Staircase,* one of America's pioneer mystery stories. Next door, at **948–950 Beech,** stands a delightful double house that is an eclectic mix of Italianate, Second Empire, and High Victorian Gothic detail.

Calvary Methodist Episcopal Church and Emmanuel Episcopal Church

Separated by just a city block and only six years apart in date, the distinguished **Calvary Methodist Episcopal Church** and **Emmanuel Episcopal Church** take diametrically opposed positions in both architectural and ideological terms. Calvary (NE corner Allegheny & Beech Aves.; Vrydaugh & Shepherd, with T. B. Wolfe, 1892) represents the best in the luxurious churches of the Gilded Age. It speaks the highly charged language of High Victorian Gothic that Ralph Adams Cram would soon turn into something more mellifluous, but honesty is not its strong point. What appear on the outside to be small half-octagonal side chapels protruding off the nave turn out to be mere conversation points inside, with no liturgical function at all. Rather than the long nave with transept and apse anticipated from a reading of the exterior, the church has an undivided nave followed by an apse-shaped Sunday school. The sanctuary is dominated by a wooden barrel-vaulted ceiling that converges over the space in a complex, sixteen-sided vault reminiscent of the octagon crossing at Ely Cathedral. Everything about the church inside and out is rich, textured, and above all, comfortable. To enter it is to

Left: Calvary Methodist Episcopal Church /*Maurice Tierney* ▪ *Right:* Emmanuel Episcopal Church (H. H. Richardson, architect) /*Franklin Toker*

intrude on a sumptuous private drawing room. The *Apocalypse, Resurrection,* and *Ascension* windows are among the best products of Louis Comfort Tiffany, who exhibited them at the Chicago world's fair prior to their installation here.

H. H. Richardson's Emmanuel Episcopal Church (NE corner Allegheny & W. North Aves., 1886) looks at first glance to be nothing more than the power plant for Calvary. This completely unpretentious building (its neighbors call it the bake oven) cost only $25,000 to construct—one percent of the expense lavished on his courthouse. The two buildings are chronologically intertwined, but whereas Richardson's courthouse explores the integration of a complex series of shifting geometries, Emmanuel is reductionist and minimalist, perhaps more than any American church of the nineteenth century. The richness of Calvary a block away is one of vocabulary; the richness of Emmanuel is one of syntax. Richardson here ignored the two venerable crutches of American church design—the spire and the transept—and conceived Emmanuel with nothing more than the vividness of the brickwork and the power of a severe triangular gable set low on an arched and battered base. The brickwork designs are richer than any Richardson had designed before, which shows his trust in the skilled Pittsburgh laborers who executed them. The designs called for five concentric circles of brick around each of the three entrance arches; a zone of complex basketweave on the gable wall above; and *muisetanden,* or "mouse teeth," infill triangles along the gable edge (Richardson surely copied this feature from Dutch Colonial architecture in the Hudson River Valley, which he knew from his work on the New York State capitol at

Albany). To the shape, texture, and color of the exterior shell Richardson added his expertise at rhythmic groupings, so that the interior of the church, with its three bays demarcated by laminated wood arches, is perfectly expressed in the one-over-three rhythm of the exterior windows. Entering this dynamic space, the worshipper feels enwrapped in a spiritual cocoon.

Manchester, Perry Hilltop, and Fineview

Manchester was founded on the right bank of the Ohio River in 1832 to rival Birmingham on the South Side. It flourished for nearly a century as an industrial center, specializing in ships and locomotives, but then it rapidly declined. Manchester was severed from the rest of the North Side over a century ago by what are now the Conrail tracks and then cut off in the 1960s from the industrial plants on the Ohio River by the construction of the Chateau Street Expressway (Route 65). Its population then dropped from 15,000 to about 3,000. It became an almost exclusively black community after the resettlement of residents from the Lower Hill in the 1950s, and it suffered badly in the riots and racial tensions of the late 1960s. By 1970 it had become a slum.

Manchester is hardly free of problems today, but beginning in the 1970s the area dramatically turned itself around with an unusual experiment in both social and architectural engineering. The rebirth of Manchester followed the discovery by the Manchester Citizens' Corporation that it could rehabilitate hundreds of owner-occupied or rented homes using federal loans or subsidies if they were certified according to historic-district guidelines. The Urban Redevelopment Authority of Pittsburgh secured about $25 million in federal housing monies, the Pittsburgh History & Landmarks Foundation set the rehabilitation guidelines, and the restoration firm of Tom Mistick & Sons rebuilt hundreds of structures with an intensity unmatched in the nation. As a result, Manchester now glows with meticulously restored facades on N. Sheffield, Pennsylvania, and Liverpool streets and on the long cross-streets of Manhattan, Fulton, and Allegheny avenues.

The main portal to the fifty blocks of Manchester is the intersection of Allegheny and North avenues. The intersection includes an empty lot, symbolic in its way of the unfinished business that still remains to be done in Manchester, but a half-block to the north and west are dozens of fine restorations that show the new spirit of the place. The three-story, U-shaped double house at **1313−1315 Allegheny Avenue,** between W. North and Sheffield streets, resembles a Mississippi steamboat in the gingerbread age. Its two best features are a lovingly restored entablature of minuscule brick brackets flanking four panels of basketweave terra-cotta and an elaborate

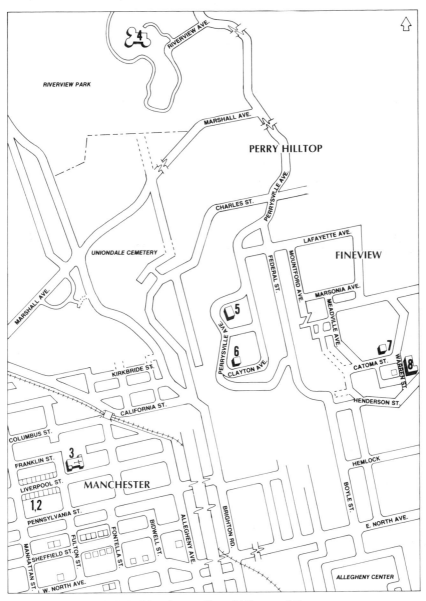

Map 14. The North Side: Manchester, Perry Hilltop, and Fineview

1 Stifel House   3 St. Joseph's Church   5 John Brashear factory   7 Heathside Cottage
2 Langenheim House   4 Allegheny Observatory   6 Brashear House   8 Henderson House

spindled verandah. The **1100** and **1200 blocks of W. North Avenue** from Bidwell to Fulton contain fine three- and four-story Italianate and Second Empire townhouses of the late 1860s and early 1870s (especially good examples are at 1102, 1110, 1112, and 1116–1118 W. North). The double house at **1203–1205 W. North Avenue** has been superbly renewed, with its dark blue porch supported by fanlight quadrant consoles and ornamented with glass discs imported from France. Another double house, at 1211–1213, features six individual gables crowning the third-floor windows. The mansions to the west reflect another wave of prosperity in Manchester in the 1880s and 1890s. The townhouses at 1229 to 1241 W. North Avenue are excellent examples of the Romanesque Revival, while the superbly detailed **Wertheimer-Sipe House** (1220 W. North; 1892 and later) is a fine example of Queen Anne—a witty balance of a conical tower of brick on the right and a shingled polyhedron of wood on the left.

Sheffield Street, a block to the north, was built up mainly during the "Queen Anne decades" of the 1880s and 1890s. The street suffered badly during its period of decay, but the conjoined houses at **1324–1326 Sheffield,** between Manhattan and Fulton streets, have emerged radiantly from their restoration with a renewed mansard roof and endearing checkerboard

Left: Sheffield Street: part restored, part replaced, part awaiting reconstruction /*Franklin Toker* ▪ *Right:* 1324–1326 Sheffield Street /*Franklin Toker*

fretwork on the gables. The **1200 block of Sheffield,** from Fulton to
Fontella, has also been rebuilt, but according to three different ideologies of
renewal. Several of the elaborate old double houses on the north side of the
block have been given a period restoration. On the opposite side of the block
sit a dozen split-level houses from the 1970s, the result of an earlier give-the-
people-what-they-want philosophy that produced suburban houses in the
middle of an urban context. On the north side of the block are also fourteen
award-winning passive-solar houses of 1983–84 by UDA Architects, with
solar engineering by the Department of Architecture at CMU. Here too the
intent was to create something intimate and enjoyable for the tenants or
purchasers, but in an architectural language that would mirror more faithfully
the density of the surrounding blocks and even some of the decorative
detailing of the older homes.

Pennsylvania Avenue, one more block to the north, reflects the same
generational approach to urban redevelopment: the homes on the 1200 block
were plowed under and replanted with suburban split-levels in the 1970s,
while the houses of the 1300 and 1400 blocks were preserved and renovated as
they were. The most interesting of the homes on the street is **Calliope House**
(1414 Pennsylvania, between Manhattan & Chateau), an Italian villa constructed in 1876 in the manner of designs published years before by Andrew
Jackson Downing and Samuel Sloan. This imposing brick mansion has had
only four owners in 110 years: its current name derives from the spirited
gatherings of folk musicians that are held here, including the annual Smoky
City Music Festival.

Flanking Calliope House on the north side of the block are more villas of
the same period, plus one suburban interloper of the 1970s, while the south
side of the street harbors modest two-story frame and brick workers' housing.
The affluent character of the patrician side of the block is splendidly upheld
by Calliope House's back-to-back neighbor, the **James Anderson House**
(today Anderson Manor, a residence for the elderly) at 1423 Liverpool,
between Chateau & Manhattan. Poorly documented, this appears to be the
house that the ironmaster James Anderson, Carnegie's benefactor, built around
1830. It was enlarged and radically resurfaced in Georgian Revival style in
1905, but the distinctive two-story porch may be original: late Georgian
rather than fake Georgian. More appropriate to Jeffersonian Virginia than to
Jacksonian Pittsburgh, the porch would have had a personal significance for
Anderson: his father, William, was a professional builder who had worked on
the White House in the 1790s.

The **1300 block of Liverpool Street** is one of the chief glories of
Manchester. After decades of neglect its spiky rows of Second Empire and
High Victorian Gothic mansions have now been brought back to life. This
exceptionally vivid block, with one bright verandah outshining the next, was
known as "North Jerusalem" to its neighbors in the 1880s because of the high

Left: 1300 block of Liverpool Street, with St. Joseph's Church /*Franklin Toker* ▪ *Right:* The Gustave Langenheim House /*Franklin Toker*

proportion of Jews on the street. (The North Side had two synagogues—one still stands as a Gospel church in Dutchtown—and the original Concordia Club, which was organized here in 1874, a year behind the Duquesne Club.) Of special note are the **Stifel House** (1319 Liverpool; Charles S. and Charles M. Bartberger, 1885) and the **Gustave Langenheim House** of 1882–83, at 1315 Liverpool. The Langenheim house (restored as eight rent-subsidized apartments for the elderly; Tom Mistick & Sons, 1984) consists of three stories of brick shot through with curved lintels of stone and brick that continue as wraparound string-courses. Its style is High Victorian Gothic with a bow to Queen Anne in its incongruous Corinthian-topped pilasters. Frank Lloyd Wright would have loathed it, but the way each element of the building grows from a preceding one is nothing if not organic.

The Liverpool streetscape is effectively closed by Frederick Sauer's **St. Joseph's Church** (NE corner Liverpool & Fulton; 1898), a more dynamic Gothic composition than Sauer usually achieved, with a gabled corner tower (shorn of its needle spire) lifting above the rooftops of the neighboring mansions. The tower is the main landmark of central Manchester as well as of a secondary offshoot that lies northeast of the Conrail tracks in a small quarter of houses—many of them dramatic in conception and ornament—on both sides of Kirkbride Street (reached by Columbus Avenue). Passing through Kirkbride to Brighton Road, or reaching Brighton by returning to Allegheny and W. North avenues, it is a short and lively ride up to the Perry Hilltop.

Perry Hilltop

The **Perry Hilltop** derives its name from an incident in the War of 1812, when Commodore Perry used Perrysville Avenue—then called the Franklin Road and before that the Venango Indian Trail—to transport supplies for his naval victory over the British on Lake Erie. Today its 1,000 acres provide a lush setting for about 15,000 Pittsburghers, who can enjoy breathtaking views and some of the more picturesque frame houses in the country. As is so often the case in Pittsburgh, the greenery of the Perry Hilltop was the gift of Nature rather than of human foresight. The 96 acres of Uniondale Cemetery and the 275 acres of **Riverview Park** are verdant today simply because nothing could be built on them. Still, the natural topography has been intelligently tended. The park is, or appears to be, virgin forest. Careful planning has inserted numerous hiking trails, picnic groves, and a swimming pool without spoiling it, and there is the obligatory early settler's log cabin for historical interest.

Allegheny Observatory

The University of Pittsburgh's **Allegheny Observatory** (159 Riverview Ave.; Thorsten Billquist, 1900–1912) is the unexpected bonus of a visit to Riverview Park. One of the world's important astronomical centers, it occupies an elegant palace of buff brick walls and terra-cotta columns that breathes the tranquillity of the eighteenth-century Enlightenment, on which its design is based. The fame of the observatory was established well before the construction of the present building because of the oldest of its three telescopes, a thirteen-inch refractor that had been purchased by a group of Pittsburgh

Allegheny Observatory, Riverview Park /*Courtesy University of Pittsburgh (Ray Cristina)*

businessmen in 1861. The observatory was also nationally known because it was the early timekeeper of the railroads and the federal government. Its director was Samuel Pierpont Langley (later head of the Smithsonian), the aviation pioneer whose unmanned heavier-than-air machine took to the air before the Wright Brothers. He was succeeded by James Keeler, who established by observations here that the rings surrounding Saturn were composed of particles rather than being solid. Keeler's successor, John Brashear, was a South Side millwright who ground lenses as an avocation and later produced them for observatories all over the world. Brashear personally established the world standard for the length of the meter, and through the application of his telescopes other scientists discovered 300 new planets. Brashear built the two other famous instruments that are housed under Billquist's domes: the thirty-inch Thaw refractor telescope, regarded as the most accurate of its type in the world, and the thirty-one-inch Keeler reflecting telescope, which photographs the spectra of the stars in double and multiple star systems. In recent years the Allegheny Observatory has entered the computer age as the world center for astrometry, which plots the mathematical coordinates of the stars by computer simulation. Two-thirds of the known star distances have been determined through astrometrical calculations on the Thaw telescope here.

Brashear joined the Swedish-trained Billquist in solving the immense technical problems presented in the design of the observatory. Each of the telescopes was set below its own dome, with movable floors below the Thaw and Keeler instruments, so that viewers or cameras can look through them comfortably no matter how they are angled. For perfect accuracy, these two telescopes were built on independent foundations of bedrock and do not touch the observatory walls. But the observatory is no spartan lab: it is exquisitely, even palatially finished in costly woods and marbles (William Thaw, Jr., financed it all), and it boasts a fine stained-glass window of *Urania*, the muse of astronomy. Nor is it a building devoid of the human spirit. At the base of the Keeler telescope is the somber crypt that contains the tombs of Keeler and his son and of John Brashear and his wife, Phoebe. Brashear's epitaph (from a poem by Sarah Williams) reads: "We have loved the stars too fondly to be fearful of the night."[2]

---

2. For those not enamored of crypts, there are recollections of Brashear in two other Perry Hilltop buildings. His old telescope factory stands in ruins at **2016 Perrysville Avenue,** about a mile and a half south of the Allegheny Observatory, while at **1801 Clayton Avenue** stands the house that William Thaw, Sr., built for him in the 1880s. Both home and factory were immediately adjacent to the observatory, which was in use before 1912. On this hilltop also the University of Pittsburgh (then the Western University of Pennsylvania) had erected an entire campus of Romanesque Revival buildings, which was still more convenient for Brashear when he served as university chancellor *pro tem* in 1901–4. The Brashear house is made of wood but in imitation of rusticated masonry blocks. It is a charming building, with a fine three-panel oriel lookout over an elaborate porch and, fittingly for the visionary Brashear, a mountaintop view that encompasses not only Pittsburgh but half the horizon as well.

Fineview

The **Fineview** neighborhood is so small that its entire shopping district consists of two corner stores. It occupies its own hilly outcrop a quarter of a mile to the east of the intersection of Perrysville Avenue and Federal Street at an average elevation of about 400 feet above the Allegheny. (It is reached from Federal Street by Lafayette, Mountford, Marsonia, and Meadville avenues.) Its highest point today is marked by the WPXI television studio and antenna at the top of Rising Main Avenue. This is the most intractable of the many hilltop areas of Pittsburgh, and public steps rather than roads seem to predominate. In the nineteenth century the central area, known as Nunnery Hill, was served by its own 1,100-feet-long inclined plane, one of four on the North Side.

Three homes in Fineview are particularly remarkable. One is the brick **Heathside Cottage** of about 1855 (416 Catoma St., NE corner Myler), which may have been the gatekeeper's lodge to an old Catholic cemetery. The structure is currently painted light brown and is distinguished by its fish-scale slate roof and the lacy carving of its bargeboards. Particularly gracious outside are the hood molds and diamond-pane windows set in the three-panel bay, while inside the detailing is miniaturized and luxurious.

A moment's walk downhill from Heathside Cottage stand two other Gothic Revival structures: the imposing **Henderson House** (1516 Warren St.) and the board-and-batten **Henderson Cottage** (1521 Warren St., NE corner Lee). The cottage is the more intriguing, with its cross-gable plan and ogive-arch porches. It is close in spirit to the four cottages created in 1851 at Evergreen Hamlet, about two miles farther upstream on the Allegheny River. The ten-

Heathside Cottage, Fineview /*Franklin Toker*

room Henderson House (c. 1860; restoration by Tai+Lee, 1984) consists of ashlar blocks elegantly set off with finely worked sandstone quoins. Like the guest cottage, the plan of the main house is cross-gabled, but it also incorporates sets of staggered axes. Next to it stand a carriage house and a springhouse in the same elaborate style. The rehabilitated building provides seven apartments (one in the former carriage house), so even in its second century it continues to be a useful member of a fascinating hillside community.

Dutchtown, Spring Hill, and Troy Hill

The districts of Dutchtown, Spring Hill, and Troy Hill are geographically dissimilar—the first is all flats, the others all slopes—but together they constitute the heart of Pittsburgh's German community. **Dutchtown** (city planners call it East North Side, though no one else does) is a flat area of about 250 acres comprising several dozen small city blocks. Its nucleus lies between the Allegheny Commons and the Heinz plant on the Allegheny River. Formerly a major center for the tanning, meat-packing, and brewery industries, it declined along with the collapse of its economic base. As in the Mexican War Streets and Manchester, it owes its current rebirth to the high quality of its housing stock, which includes fine examples of Romanesque Revival and Queen Anne, together with a few Greek Revival homes of the canal era. Its ethnic ties are strong, although hardly comparable to the era before World War I, when Dutchtown had the major share of the seventy German singing societies in town. (It is still the headquarters for the *Teutonia Maennerchor*.) Although the primary language of Dutchtown was German, it was also a haven for Croatian immigrants, who called the area east of Chestnut Street *Mala Jaska* for their native region. It was no less a haven for blacks, who flocked to the Avery Institute (now destroyed) that the white manufacturer Charles Avery had established in 1849 as an educational, social, and religious center for the community.

Much of Dutchtown consists of quiet residential streets. The most prominent of these is Cedar Street, with a score of proud townhouses between Suismon and Pressley streets, overlooking East Park. The best of these is a Queen Anne double house at **814—816 Cedar** that brings together walls of deep red pressed brick, a stubby, slate-covered mansard roof, two pyramidal towers decked out in fish-scale patterns, and ornamental molded brick. The facade stretches over five bays in a receding/projecting rhythm, with a passageway in the middle that leads to servants' quarters in the rear. A bonus on the facade are three reliefs from Greco-Roman mythology: Medusa in a fine panel on the second floor, Neptune on the string-course above, and a radiant Minerva at the top. The house appears to date from the late 1870s or

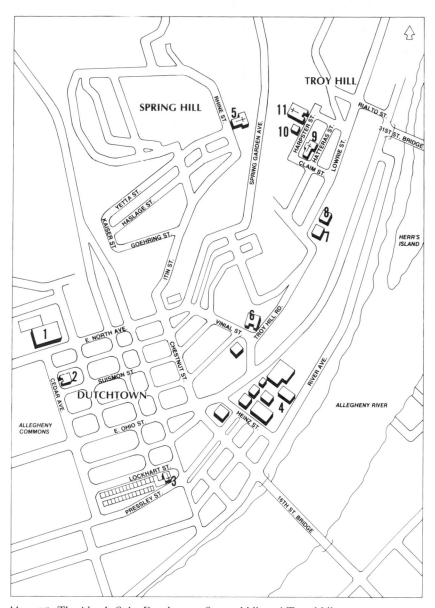

Map 15. The North Side: Dutchtown, Spring Hill, and Troy Hill

1 Allegheny General Hospital
2 814–816 Cedar Ave.
3 Old St. Mary's Church & Priory
4 H. J. Heinz Co.

5 Spring Hill United Church
6 Eberhardt-Ober Brewery
7 Ober House
8 Reineman House

9 Most Holy Name of Jesus
   Church
10 Suitbert Mollinger House
11 St. Anthony of Padua Shrine

814–816 Cedar Street, Dutch-town /*Franklin Toker*

the 1880s and may be the work of the Bartbergers, who specialized in scenographic fronts.

Many of these mannerisms, suggestive of the same architect or builder, appear a short walk away at **602 Pressley,** between Cedar and Nash, in a three-story mansarded house with a central frontispiece that seems to staple itself onto the second floor with corbeled brackets. Here again the ornament is in molded brick: two portrait heads flanking a hoary lion. The gable is lovingly articulated in a series of raised brick circles that recall similar ornament in wood in the contemporary houses of Manchester. Some of the qualities of this and the Queen Anne house at 814–816 Cedar have been captured nearby, if only by analogy, in the thirty-two three-story townhouses of **Deutschtown Square** (Avery, Cedar, & Lockhart Sts.; Larry Gessner, 1984), one of the developments that is infusing young urban professionals into this staid old neighborhood.

Chestnut Street, at the base of Spring Hill /*Franklin Toker*

For those who want to buy the real thing in nineteenth-century townhouses for a fraction of the cost of these imitations, many are still available at the upper end of Dutchtown in the six blocks centered at the intersection of Chestnut and Tripoli streets. Here frame dwellings alternate with the somewhat more prevalent brick rows, with the houses as tightly packed together as the bright red bricks that form the roadway. At the end of the vista, looking south, is the silver halo of the Civic Arena dome, beckoning from a Pittsburgh that is of surprisingly little interest to the women who pause to chat at a nearby door stoop, as did their mothers and grandmothers before them.

The homes of Dutchtown are guarded by three imposing institutions: one charitable, one religious, one industrial. The most visible of these, **Allegheny General Hospital** (320 E. North Ave.; York & Sawyer, 1929–36), long enjoyed the status of the most fashionable charity in Pittsburgh, as is made clear at once by the august names on the donor plaques in the lobby. This society connection is made still more evident in the outer dress of the hospital. When York & Sawyer designed Presbyterian Hospital in Oakland in these same years, their design was sober Beaux Arts. Here they flirted instead with Art Deco and produced something that is more frivolous but also more significant on the Pittsburgh skyline. The hospital was large for its time— 1,200 rooms on seventeen stories of standard yellow industrial brick. York & Sawyer exploited its dramatic contrast with Fineview Hill immediately behind,

Entrance portico, Allegheny General Hospital /*Franklin Toker*

giving special care to the Greek temple that crowns it. This marvelous feature is floodlit at night and seems to float like a vision of Valhalla through the Pittsburgh sky. For the passerby at street level, the best part of the design is the entrance portico, which is three bays long and both rib- and barrel-vaulted internally. Its columns, radiant shafts of granite and marble, terminate in basket capitals or highly stylized acanthus leaves in an architectural mix that is part Venice, part Constantinople, and part Cecil B. De Mille. Externally, the porch sallies forth with an arched corbel table infilled with blue and green terra-cotta in a *tableau vivant* of physicians and fake-Byzantine saints.

St. Mary's Roman Catholic Church and Priory (Lockhart, Nash, & Pressley Sts.; here attributed to Charles S. Bartberger, 1853–54) offers a fascinating glimpse into the social history of Pittsburgh (and America) at the mid-nineteenth century. The church was constructed without windows because of the constant vandalism of virulent Know-Nothing partisans, yet it proudly bore its Catholic and German heritage in its two broad Romanesque-style towers, which originally ended in bulbous Bavarian domes. The achievement inside is even more astonishing for a working-class immigrant parish: four giant Composite columns support a Greek cross of transverse barrel vaults, which rise sixty-five feet at the center to an umbrella vault and skylight. One of the sources for the design was surely the German Baroque, but the other was probably Christopher Wren, in his intimate City Churches for London, such as St. Mary at Hill.

The pious local attribution of the design to the second pastor of the congregation, Fr. John Stiebl, is decisively to be rejected. No amateur thinks in terms of such sophisticated volumetrics as these, and the Redemptorist Fathers were known to hire top architects for their churches, such as Robert Cary Long, Jr., who did their convent in Baltimore. More likely, the architect was Charles S. Bartberger, just arrived from Germany and busily at work both on old St. Paul's Cathedral on Grant Street and on the Passionist Fathers' convent on Mt. Washington. It was probably also Bartberger who returned here thirty years later to design the priory, which is a lively and ingenious solution to a dark, cramped site. Deconsecrated now, this important and moving building will reopen shortly as a hotel.

H. J. Heinz Company Factories

Henry John Heinz had the same relationship to food that Henry Ford had to the automobile. Inventing nothing, he nonetheless changed the way the world lived by packaging and marketing food better than anyone in history. Heinz was born in Birmingham in 1844, the son of two recent German immigrants. He grew up in Sharpsburg, four miles upstream on the Allegheny from the future site of this factory, and there he entered his father's brickmaking

The Heinz factories, E. Ohio Street /*Franklin Toker*

concern before branching out in 1869 to grow horseradish on the family land. Like Thomas Mellon in the same year, Heinz could not help but flourish because everything he needed for bottling and canning his foods was right in Pittsburgh: the glass, the corks, the pottery crocks, and the tinned steel cans. Even the inspiration for his "57 Varieties"—surely the most famous and the most instantly recognizable slogan in the history of marketing—seems to have come to him from the toponymy of Pittsburgh.[3] In 1889 Heinz built the world's first modern food-processing complex on the Allegheny shore at Heinz and E. Ohio streets between the tracks of the Pennsylvania and the Pittsburgh & Western railroads. It was an industrious German-Swiss neighborhood, ideal for recruitment of the 1,500 male and 2,000 female employees he needed.

The first stage of the factory involved seventeen buildings; eventually there were thirty-two. Heinz himself oversaw the construction of these Romanesque Revival blocks, demanding walls of the finest glazed and pressed brick and solid concrete and stone foundations, generally three and a half feet thick. Once, dissatisfied, he ordered an entire factory covered with new walls because he regarded the original brickwork as substandard. The buildings contained kitchens, plants for bottling, packing, and canning, an electricity plant with its own dynamos, a restaurant, an indoor swimming pool, a gymnasium, and classrooms for employee self-betterment. Newspapers called the stable building "an equine palace" and reported in awe on its cork floors imported from England, its steam radiators, its warm hoofbaths for tired horses, its hospital wing, and its jail (for horses prone to kicking).

Today, about a dozen of the founder's buildings are still in use. The **Sarah Heinz House** (SW corner Heinz & E. Ohio Sts.; R. Maurice Trimble, 1913) announces the whole complex with a luxurious Tudor settlement house that serves the children of the neighborhood. Immediately below the Conrail

---

3. In his old age Heinz recounted that he had modeled his slogan on one he had seen in 1892 while riding an elevated train in New York. There a manufacturer had advertised his 21 different styles of shoes. Apart from a lame reference to "lucky 7," at odds with his staunch Presbyterianism, Heinz could never explain why he had fixed on the number 57, which was not the number of Heinz products on sale in 1892 (well over 60), or the number of the Manhattan street where the el had stopped (28), or his age at the time (48). The number 57 was evidently stuck so deeply in Heinz's psyche that he could subconsciously but not consciously think about it. Where had he come by it?

The answer may lie in the place of invention: a public train moving past a sequence of numbered streets. But the streets that gave birth to the slogan were in Pittsburgh, not New York. Heinz lived not far from Pittsburgh's 57th Street, which was—and is—the last in a long line of numbered cross-streets along Penn Avenue and Butler Street that ends opposite his hometown of Sharpsburg. (The Robert Fleming Bridge on the Allegheny River between Sharpsburg and Pittsburgh is popularly known as the 62nd Street Bridge because in 1867, when the streets received their numbers, 62 streets were projected. Only 57 of these were realized, however, and the theoretical 62nd Street, opposite the bridge, is today no more than a lane.) Heinz knew the sequence of 57 streets intimately, even painfully: six days a week for eighteen years (1872–90), he left his home in Sharpsburg, crossed the bridge to Pittsburgh, and took the five-mile, fifty-seven-block ride on the horsecars of the Citizens' Passenger Railway Company to his office and plant on Second Avenue in the Golden Triangle. There was no other route, since the trains of the Allegheny Valley Railroad, which Heinz might have used later on, also passed the same cross-streets. Fifty-seventh would have been the first street Heinz counted in the morning and the last in the evening, on a trip he took between seven and ten thousand times. It was a number his subconscious would never let him forget.

tracks the plant itself begins, with the enormous **Employee Service Building** (NW corner Heinz & Progress Sts.), which the famed industrial architect Albert Kahn designed in 1930 in an old-fashioned style to blend with the 1889 buildings. It contained a lavishly appointed auditorium for employee presentations (modernized in 1953 by Skidmore, Owings & Merrill and much diminished in scope) and dining rooms for male and female employees. East of this, in a row on the north side of Progress, stand the **Meat Products Building** (R. Maurice Trimble, 1920), the **Bean Building** (1912), and the **Bottling Building** (1896 and 1905), all in the same austere industrial style but with corner turrets and handsome corbel tables. Opposite them rises the **Cereal Building** (SE corner Heinz & Progress; 1926). Farther inside the complex are two more buildings by Kahn: the **Administration Building** of 1905, a reinforced-concrete structure with Heinz's favorite mottoes etched in stained glass, and the **Administration Annex** of 1930, a severe industrial white-brick building facing the Allegheny.

In later years, as the firm grew to produce 1,200 varieties, it commissioned three new buildings from Skidmore, Owings & Merrill that became instant classics of the 1950s: the **Research Building** on the Allegheny shore, the eight-million-cubic-foot **Warehouse,** and Gordon Bunshaft's celebrated **Vinegar Works** opposite E. Ohio Street, with one of the most refined glass curtain walls in International School architecture. Today, although the schoolchildren of Pittsburgh no longer come by for the "pickle tour" that they and 50,000 adults a year used to take, the Heinz Company retains its close ties to the city of its birth, and to H.J.'s magical number: the telephone number at the world headquarters in Pittsburgh is 237–5757.

Spring Hill and Troy Hill

About 6,000 Pittsburghers live on **Spring Hill** at an elevation of about 450 feet above the Allegheny shore. The hill is almost totally cut off from the rest of the city by the East Street Valley to the west and the Spring Garden Valley to the south and east. (It is most easily reached by Itin [the hillside continuation of Chestnut Street] and Rhine streets, circling back by way of Yetta, Wilt, Haslage, Kaiser, and Goehring streets.) The area is strikingly German even today—in its people, its street names, and its fastidiously neat white frame houses and Italianate brick homes of the mid- and late nineteenth century. It is wholly residential, with few public or commercial buildings and only four churches. The **Spring Hill United Church of Christ** (1620 Rhine, opposite Yetta St.; 1902) is the smallest but the most memorable of the group. Built of common red brick, this charming structure with a miniature crow-step gable and pseudo flying buttresses recalls Dutch or northern German architecture of the fifteenth century as understood in the age of Art Nouveau.

Spring Hill United Church of
Christ /Franklin Toker

One can see but not reach **Troy Hill** from Spring Hill. To reach it requires a
descent down Itin to Spring Garden Avenue and an immediate right after the
Deutschtown Fire Station to Vinial Street, which cuts across the upper terrace
of Dutchtown to Troy Hill Road. Standing at the base of Troy Hill Road is the
High Victorian Gothic **Eberhardt-Ober Brewery** (800 Vinial; Charles S.
Bartberger, c. 1880), a remnant of a once-sprawling complex of a dozen
buildings. Across the street is another brewery relic, in Romanesque Revival
style, while behind the main plant are ruins of the old beer vaults that had
been cut into the hillside. (Almost all the breweries in Pittsburgh—here, in
Lawrenceville, and on the South Side—were built next to hills or in valleys in
order to construct such vaults.)

Troy Hill is the most isolated of Pittsburgh neighborhoods. The village of
New Troy—the name derived from the hometown of its original owner,
Elizabeth Seymore of Troy, New York—was founded in 1833, but its early
growth was not auspicious: after ten years it had attracted only three cemeteries to its side. (One of these, Voegtly Cemetery, is the site of an annual
Memorial Day commemoration with bands and a parade. There, for a fleeting
moment, one can picture the gregariousness of the German community as it
must have been, with its *Liedertafeln* and *Turnverein's*.) The railroad shops and the
Heinz plant at the base of the hill provided a few new settlers each year, and
the occasional devastating flood at the Allegheny shoreline induced still more
to climb to its windswept plain. By 1900, when it had its own trolley run and
inclined plane, Troy Hill had reached its peak population of 10,000. It is home
today to about 4,000 people.

Troy Hill Road follows a long but fairly comfortable grade of half a mile
along a steep cliff. Over it peer white frame houses like silent sentinels. At the
crest of the hill stands the **John Ober House** (1501 Lowrie St., NE corner
Troy Hill Rd.), a rare example of the Stick Style in a Pittsburgh home, built in
1877 and purchased by one of the partners in the Eberhardt-Ober Brewery a
few years later. The skin of the building is composed entirely of wood siding
that has been arranged in fish-scale and diamond patterns, while the corners

Left: Troy Hill, from the Allegheny /*Franklin Toker* ▪ *Right:* Goettmann Street houses, Troy Hill /*Courtesy* Pittsburgh Post-Gazette (*Mark Murphy*)

and string-courses stand out boldly as green wooden strips. In plan, the Ober House is an Italian villa (close to that of Calliope House, one year older), but such details as its detached and bracketed eaves reveal its links to the fashionable houses that were being built at the same time in Newport and Tuxedo Park. More exuberant still is the **Reineman House,** two doors away at 1515–1517 Lowrie Street. This huge double house of the 1870s in brick and bright wood trim has been meticulously preserved, from its spindled verandah to its slate mansard roof, excepting only the loss of its wrought-iron cresting.

The home of Troy Hill's most eccentric inhabitant has also withstood a century of change. The **Suitbert Mollinger House** (today the Rectory of the Most Holy Name of Jesus parish, 1700 Harpster St., intersection with Tinsbury) is a richly crafted Second Empire house of brick with elaborate door and window surrounds of stone. It was built in 1876 by a wealthy Belgian nobleman who, after a stay in Padua for medical and theological studies, took holy

Left: The John Ober House /*Franklin Toker* ▪ *Right:* Suitbert Mollinger House and the Shrine of St. Anthony of Padua /*Franklin Toker*

orders and settled in Pittsburgh. The house was superbly crafted throughout, but its glory is the dining room. Here in a state of sanctity are preserved Mollinger's massive oak furniture, crystal chandelier, carved ceiling medallion, and the animal and bird murals on the ceiling and walls.

Next door stands the object of Mollinger's special attention: the **Shrine of St. Anthony of Padua** (1704 Harpster St.; 1880–90). The exterior of this light sandstone Gothic Revival chapel with flanking needle spires is picturesque, but it is below the usual high standard for such work in Pittsburgh at the time. It is not the outside, however, but the inside that makes the chapel so remarkable and probably unique outside of Europe. St. Anthony's harbors some 5,000 relics of Early Christian saints and martyrs that Mollinger had purchased in Europe, together with their yellowed—but now computerized—attestations of authenticity. The presence of such a bountiful harvest of relics beckoned thousands of pilgrims to the top of Mt. Troy in an earlier, more credulous age. The miracles that were proclaimed with regularity at the shrine have ceased now, but the collection (open Tuesdays and weekends) is still a fascinating sight. A half-block away stands the **Most Holy Name of Jesus Church** (1500 Claim St., NE corner Harpster; 1863 and 1898), a gaunt Germanic brick church with a tall central tower that is powerfully effective as it stands out against the open hilltop.

The American cities that were most strongly influenced by their German populations (Milwaukee, St. Louis, Cincinnati, and Pittsburgh) all had in common superb waterfronts and good and hearty taste in their food, their beer, and their architecture. In the case of Pittsburgh the food was solidly centered in the North Side even before Heinz located his plant here. **Herr's Island,** in the Allegheny River at the base of Troy Hill, was for almost a century the site of an enormous stockyard, now mostly derelict and awaiting redevelopment. The stockyard was in part established in conjunction with the many slaughterhouses on Herr's Island, but in the main it was a holding and feeding pen for the livestock on the Pennsylvania Railroad main line between Chicago and New York. To get down to Herr's Island (or to cross over it in the direction of The Strip on the Pittsburgh side of the Allegheny) from Troy Hill is easily done, though not by the faint-hearted. **Rialto Street** (the former Pig Hill, reached from St. Anthony's shrine via Harpster, Froman, & Ley Sts.) leads straight down 370 feet to East Ohio Street and the Thirty-first Street Bridge, but the descent is at a 24 percent angle. Although there are four steeper streets in Pittsburgh, Rialto is vertiginous enough to give drivers the sensation that they are flying down a track—and rightly so, since it is the old track bed of the Mt. Troy incline plane.

The Strip, between The Hill and the Allegheny River (1980) /*Courtesy* Pittsburgh
Post-Gazette *(Paul Slantis)*

Penn Avenue and the Railroad Suburbs

It is six miles by air and seven and a half miles by car from The Strip, an
industrial district of Pittsburgh on the south bank of the Allegheny, to the
heart of the residential suburb of Wilkinsburg. The two areas are physically
and socially remote and separated by a dozen neighborhoods that also seem to
lack any connection from one to another. Yet two links should be obvious:
first, in a city marked by a score of hills, these dozen neighborhoods are all
flat; second, the entire route from The Strip to the end of Wilkinsburg follows

a single street—Penn Avenue. Whoever drives its full course has traveled the whole length of "mainland" Pittsburgh, past half the city's land mass and population. With the addition of just one more street, Braddock Avenue, a driver can follow a ten-mile crescent from the Allegheny River to the Monongahela by way of the four additional suburbs of Edgewood, Swissvale, Rankin, and Braddock. Both Braddock and Penn avenues are based on old Indian trails that were used in part in General Edward Braddock's abortive assault on Fort DuQuesne and General John Forbes's successful capture of it in 1755 and 1758. Unlike many Indian trails, these streets are straight and flat, because they run through the temporary riverbed created millennia ago by the Monongahela River.

Pittsburghers, always keen as Adam at naming things, never gave a name to this riverbed (we might call it the "Monongahela Plain"), because at first they failed to recognize it as such. The nameless plain nonetheless stuck out as an obvious feature to the scouting parties of the Braddock and Forbes campaigns, and on two other occasions when it proved a godsend: in 1852, in the construction of the Pennsylvania Railroad through Pittsburgh's daunting hills, and in 1983, when the Pittsburgh bus system used parts of the Pennsylvania/Conrail track bed for a busway that moves commuters from Wilkinsburg to The Strip in seventeen minutes.

Recognized or not, the Monongahela Plain and its water-course runoffs have had an incalculable impact on the urban development of Pittsburgh. It was the runoffs that gave many Pittsburgh neighborhoods their special identities. Four-Mile Run cut off Squirrel Hill from Oakland on the east, while Nine-Mile Run cut it off from Point Breeze on the west. Heth's Run cut off Highland Park from Morningside on the east, and Negley's Run cut it off from Lincoln on the west. Similarly, Two-Mile Run distinguishes Shadyside from Bloomfield and East Liberty and Lawrenceville from Polish Hill. The Monongahela Plain also determined which neighborhoods would develop first and which later. Wilkinsburg, seven miles east of the Golden Triangle but linked by rail, was a flourishing village by 1860, while Squirrel Hill, three miles closer to downtown Pittsburgh but not linked to it by rail, was still only half-settled in 1910. The Monongahela Plain not only encouraged industrial development, but it was itself a moneymaker. There was scant profit to be made in the urban development of the hilltops of Pittsburgh, where homes had to be custom-built to the quirks of topography, but creating rows of cheap houses on the flat plain was lucrative and easy. Scions of several pioneer families—particularly the descendants of one Caspar Taub—made fortunes by cutting up their ancestral estates into the smallest possible lots. One obscure branch of the Taub clan, the Winebiddles, squeezed a respectable fortune from their lands in Bloomfield, Friendship, and Garfield. But other Taub descendants did even better, slicing up great-great-grandfather's land with such exactitude that they laid the foundations of a colossal fortune. They did so well that history has forgotten their link to the Taub clan and records them on their own, as the Mellons.

The Strip and Polish Hill

Like most Pittsburgh districts, **The Strip** defines itself with precision: its boundaries are Eleventh Street, Penn Station, and the Golden Triangle on the west; the Allegheny River to the north and the wooded slopes of The Hill to the south; and Doughboy Square and the packed row houses of Lawrenceville to the east. In these 300 acres, a literal "strip" a mile and a half along Penn and Liberty avenues, an important part of the world's industrial history was born. In fact, when James Parton crafted his famous metaphor in 1868 about Pittsburgh being Hell with the lid off, he was looking down on The Strip from Cliff Street on The Hill. The quantum leap to the Carnegie and J&L mills on the Monongahela and Ohio shores had not yet taken place. Certainly no tract of land on earth was better formed to be an assembly line than The Strip, and it was no accident that the man who bought the whole of it in 1773 was James O'Hara, Pittsburgh's pioneer manufacturer. The Strip was on the main road to Philadelphia and in time would be served by the Pennsylvania Canal and three separate railroad lines. Nearby were four residential areas (including The Hill, which was linked to The Strip by the Penn Incline until 1953) that accommodated thousands of workers with minimal travel time.

The Strip handsomely repaid those who believed in its industrial future. It was The Strip, and its continuation along the Allegheny shore in Lawrenceville, that nurtured the growth of the earliest iron foundries in Pittsburgh. Here the fledgling Republic produced much of its artillery and bullets in the War of 1812; here, during the Civil War, the Union cast its sixty-ton Rodman cannons, capable of blasting thirty-pound cannon balls three miles; here Thomas Armstrong cornered the world market on the production of cork; and here Westinghouse and Charles Martin Hall put to work their revolutionary inventions of air brakes and aluminum.

The Strip today counts a mere 285 inhabitants, yet its story is one of human as well as industrial triumph. Before the settlement of The Strip, virtually all Pittsburghers were either English or Scotch-Irish. Around 1800 the Catholic Irish entered Pittsburgh as its first immigrant group, and here in 1808 they built St. Patrick's, the city's first non-Protestant church. The Strip later became the point of entry for German, Polish, and Slovak immigrants, who lived alongside the factories in long rows of brick houses. Fragments of Greek Revival and Second Empire rows still stand on the 2500 block of Penn Avenue and south of it on Spring Way, on Twenty-seventh Street at the corner of Mulberry Way, and on the 2900 block of Penn. The struggle to create a

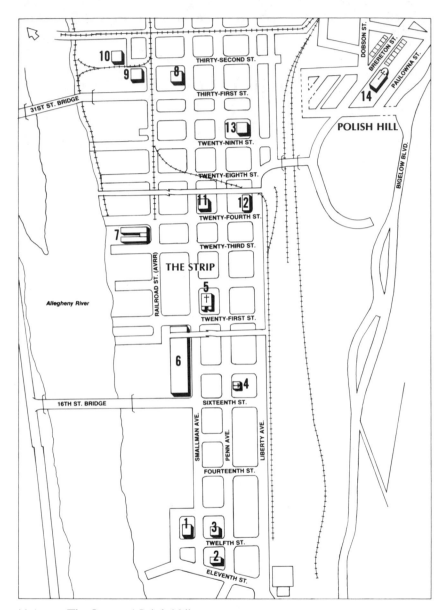

Map 16. The Strip and Polish Hill

1 Allegheny Steam Heat Plant
2 1133 Penn Ave.
3 Sack Store Fixture Co.
4 St. Elizabeth of Hungary Church
5 St. Stanislaus Kostka Church

6 Pa. RR Fruit Auction Bldg.
7 Armstrong Cork Plant
8 Old Crucible Steel foundries
9 Cyclops Steel plate mill
10 LectroMelt Corp.

11 Phoenix Brewery
12 Old Westinghouse Air-Brake Co.
13 Pittsburgh Ballet Theater
14 Immaculate Heart of Mary Church

livelihood was bitter for these immigrants, yet The Strip was touched at least twice by living saints: Saint John Neumann was pastor of St. Philomena's Church here in the 1830s, and Mother Mary Katharine Drexel served The Strip fifty years later as a novice with the Irish-based Sisters of Mercy.

While most of The Strip's churches left the district when its houses were ground into industrial plants, four remain. **St. Stanislaus Kostka** (57 Twenty-first St., NE corner Smallman; attributed to Frederick Sauer) was founded in 1875 and built in 1892 as the mother congregation of the several hundred thousand western Pennsylvanians of Polish origin. This powerfully detailed and splendidly sited church closes a five-block-long "piazza" (actually a former rail switching yard) from the Sixteenth Street Bridge to Twenty-first Street with the self-possession of a Renaissance cathedral. It is an elaborate and capacious building inside, with rich frescoes of biblical and Polish history. The mother church of the Slovak community, **St. Elizabeth of Hungary** (1620 Penn Ave., SE corner Sixteenth St.; 1895), is a charming building nearby that matches an entrance porch and window pediments from American house architecture with the central tower of a fortified church in Eastern Europe. There are also two twentieth-century churches in The Strip: **Good Samaritan** (NW corner Penn & Fourteenth St.) and **St. Patrick's** (1711 Liberty, between Seventeenth & Colville), both constructed in 1935 in more severe dress, although St. Patrick's permitted itself a high conical tower that recalls the heroic Irish monasteries of the Dark Ages, complete with a fragment of the Blarney Stone inside. Today these four churches are grace notes to the main anthem of The Strip, which is sung to commerce and industry.

The visual character of The Strip is fixed at its west end by a half-dozen buildings near Penn Station. Among the more prominent of these are the

St. Stanislaus Kostka Church and its five-block-long "piazza" /*Franklin Toker*

electric substation (1907) and the boiler house (1927) of Duquesne Light's decommissioned **Allegheny Steam Heat Plant** (Etna, Smallman, Twelfth, & Thirteenth Sts.), with its immense rooftop stack, and the old six-story brick loft of the Byrnes & Kiefer Company at **1133 Penn Avenue** (Frederick Osterling, 1892; recycled as professional offices by UDA Architects, 1984), with an elaborate sandstone facade in Richardsonian Romanesque style. Another two powerful buildings stand a block to the east: one is now the **Sack Store Fixture Company** at 1201 Penn, a vividly articulated Romanesque Revival warehouse with staring lunette windows punched deep into its thick walls. At the opposite end of the block stands the fortresslike **Consolidated Ice Company** (SW corner Smallman & Thirteenth; c. 1900), whose low masonry vaults and riveted steel beams supported the enormous weight of the ice blocks once piled on the floors inside.

What makes The Strip the most alluring of the Pittsburgh industrial districts today is its devotion to food, which it has stored up and distributed to the rest of the city since the Pennsylvania Railroad tracks were ripped out of the Golden Triangle in 1906. The railroad then relocated its food sheds in The Strip, in huge switching yards stretching from Thirteenth to Twenty-first Street. Trucks soon began to appear in The Strip, particularly after the construction of the **Sixteenth Street Bridge** in 1923. This lovably pompous

Fruit and vegetable market, Penn Avenue near Twenty-first Street /*Franklin Toker*

The Armstrong Cork factory (Frederick Osterling, architect), with The Hill behind
/Courtesy UDA Architects (Clyde Hare)

structure was designed by Warren & Wetmore, architects of Grand Central Station in New York, and was given its bronze seahorse ornaments by the sculptor Leo Lentelli. It was to coordinate trains and trucks that the **Pennsylvania Railroad Fruit Auction & Sales Building** was erected in 1926. It is an immense building, five blocks in length, but relieved by touches of Art Deco on the caps of its miniature buttresses. Fortunately, when rail traffic ended, the City of Pittsburgh bought this behemoth and had it entirely renovated (by The Design Alliance, 1983), and it continues to be an important part of the local produce trade.

For private consumers looking for fruits, vegetables, plants, and the best in imported foods, the heart of The Strip is the impromptu market on Penn Avenue between Seventeenth and Twenty-first streets, with an extension of lesser intensity to Twenty-eighth Street. From six until ten o'clock each morning these blocks of ramshackle Federal, Greek Revival, and Italianate houses thrive with the rhythm of an Oriental bazaar. The classic triad of restaurants and take-outs in The Strip are Wholey's and Benkovitz's for fish, and the all-night Primanti's for colossal sandwiches, but there are also a dozen others that make The Strip the best district for good eating—not necessarily dining—in the city. The food stores with the largest cult followings are Parma Sausage; Rubino's, Galioto's, Alioto's, and Weisberg's for fruit and vegetables; Stamoolis Brothers for pita bread, phyllo dough, and spanakopita; Pennsylvania Macaroni; the Pittsburgh Cheese Terminal; Panini Bakery; and Sam Bok Oriental Foods.

The heavier business of The Strip has retreated nearer to the Allegheny shore, particularly to a strip road along the Allegheny Valley Railroad tracks that is officially Railroad Street but invariably called AVRR. The most impressive industrial installation here is the **Armstrong Cork Factory** (Twenty-third

St. & AVRR; Frederick Osterling, 1901–12). Thomas Armstrong, a clerk in a Pittsburgh bottleworks, applied new mechanical techniques to the millennial trade of cutting corks. His first factory on the site, of 1879, gave way to this sequence of a dozen buildings as his company pioneered in cork as a building material. Osterling's earlier buildings here have masonry bearing walls, but the later ones are entirely steel-framed, with brick serving only as a veneer. Stylistically, the factories evolve from Romanesque Revival to a kind of industrial classicism, with three-story-tall pilasters of brick crowned with Ionic capitals. This vivid industrial complex is now the object of a proposed conversion into a complex of shops, offices, and apartments.

The most important factories still in operation in The Strip stand east of the Armstrong Cork plant, on the dozen blocks between the Allegheny River shore and Smallman Street, from Twenty-eighth to Thirty-third streets. Used by a number of industrial companies today, more than a few of these buildings date from before the Civil War, when the Park Brothers and the Kloman-Phipps works merged as Andrew Carnegie's Union Iron Mills. Four parts of this venerable industrial complex are particularly arresting. The **Crucible Steel foundries** (now the Ralph Meyer Company; Spruce Way, SE corner Thirty-first St.), are three century-old brick basilicas supported internally by triangular trusses of iron and wood. Somewhat newer is a corrugated-steel building that housed the **Iron City Tool Works** (now Western Pennsylvania Waste Paper Company; Thirty-second Street between AVRR & Spruce Way), a broad-gabled structure with brooding ventilating hoods on the roof. Two larger units of the old mill stand at the dead-end of Thirty-second Street next to the riverbank: on the west, the **Cyclops Steel finishing plate mill,** a cavernous union of four steel basilicas that are sewn together lengthwise (it fabricates super-alloys for the aircraft and aerospace industries); and on the east, a factory of the **LectroMelt Corporation,** a steel-frame cantilevered

The Cyclops Steel finishing plate mill (*left*) and LectroMelt Corporation /*Franklin Toker*

structure with long strip windows that must have been one of the more advanced factory designs in the nation when it was built, around 1920.

These industrial facilities are museum pieces now, but one has to view The Strip—and all the old mills of Pittsburgh—as being on the cutting edge of Victorian high-tech. This is forcefully brought home by a large plaque around the corner from the Crucible buildings, at 3220 Smallman, which commemorates the site of the Pittsburgh Reduction Company, better known to the world as Alcoa (legend holds that the name was changed because of confusion with a Pittsburgh garbage-disposal firm). Here the first ingots of commercially made aluminum were poured on Thanksgiving Day, 1888. A few streets away, on Liberty Avenue between Twenty-fourth and Twenty-fifth streets, stands a block-long plant where the Civic Light Opera Company builds its stage sets, but which was constructed in 1870 as the first headquarters of the **Westinghouse Air-Brake Company.** By 1870 trains had been operating for half a century, but their potential was hamstrung by their crude brakes, which had to be set by hand in each car. George Westinghouse solved the problem by applying to it the new invention of compressed air. He then moved from upstate New York to Pittsburgh to find financial backers who would begin production of his invention, exactly as Charles Martin Hall would do a decade later for aluminum. Westinghouse specified this handsome factory, twenty-five bays long, as the last word in industrial design, then labored frantically here with his employees to satisfy the worldwide demand for his invention. In five years he turned out 2,000 locomotive brakes and 7,000 car brakes. In 1871, a year after production began, Westinghouse declared Saturday a half-holiday—the first in the United States. World demand continued to be so intense that this plant, big as it is, gave way to another on the North Side in 1881, and to a third, twenty times as large, east of Pittsburgh in Wilmerding, in 1890.

Visually richer to look at, though less revolutionary in its implications, is a

The original Westinghouse air-brake plant (1870), Liberty Avenue /*Franklin Toker*

near-neighbor to Westinghouse, the 1893 **Phoenix Brewery** (later Otto Milk; today the Ironrite Company), at the southeast corner of Smallman and Twenty-fourth Street. This six-story factory is an especially fine example of the more pretentious industrial architecture of the last two decades of the nineteenth century, with a stone platform and three sturdy classical arches of brick at its base, three stories of elongated Romanesque arches above, and a corner tower with a pressed-brick phoenix rising from the flames. The half-Classical, half-Romanesque look constitutes a sort of Queen Anne school of industrial architecture, and it was used to ennoble not only this brewery but the three other key breweries in town, on the South Side, the North Side, and Lawrenceville.

What almost killed The Strip a century ago was its own success: it was too small to contain all the flourishing enterprises to which it had given birth. Reconciled to its scale now and reoriented to service and consumer sales, the area is in the middle of a vigorous economic and architectural rebirth. An old bus garage at 2900 Liberty Avenue provides excellent rehearsal facilities for the **Pittsburgh Ballet Theatre** (renovation by IKM/SGE, 1984). Two blocks away, an old warehouse at 2837 Smallman Street became a Roman *domus*, with a central light court and perimeter offices, for the **Air Tool Parts and Service Company** (Sylvester Damianos, 1984). New buildings have begun to rise among the old, starting with the headquarters of **Ironworkers Local Union 3** (2201 Liberty; Klaus Associates, 1979), a mix of aggregate panels and stainless steel. As the Convention Center, Liberty Center, and the recycling of Penn Station take hold, and particularly if ambitious plans for a Faneuil Hall-type complex materialize, these will be only the beginnings of a profound transformation of what is already a delightful area.

Polish Hill

Around 1880, ten years after their arrival in Pittsburgh, the Poles who worked in the foundries and mills of The Strip began to settle in new row houses on what had been an empty 139 acres on the north slope of The Hill, where the almost vertical cliff gives way to a gentler but still-steep rise. In this narrow district, sharply marked by the gully of Two-Mile Run on the north and east, the terrace of Bigelow Boulevard on the south, and the Twenty-eighth Street Bridge over the Conrail tracks on the west, about 2,000 of their descendants still live today. (The day of the monolithic Pittsburgh neighborhood is over, however: the main celebrity born in Polish Hill—at 1040 Herron Avenue, in the three-story Arnd apartment house of 1885—was the famed quarterback Danny Marino.) The Poles called this haven *Polskie Gory*, or **Polish Hill,** and on it they built hundreds of tiny frame and brick houses during the next twenty years, many burrowed so far uphill that they are reached only by flights of wooden or concrete steps.

Left: Polish Hill, with the Immaculate Heart of Mary Church /*Franklin Toker* ▪ *Right*: Cargill Street, Polish Hill /*Franklin Toker*

Over this hamlet reigns the majestic **Immaculate Heart of Mary Church** (3058 Brereton Avenue; William P. Ginther, 1906), the best-sited church in the city. The plot of land purchased by this poor congregation was rich in scenographic possibilities, being immediately below the new carriage drive of Bigelow Boulevard and at the crest of Brereton and Dobson streets, with sight lines across several miles of the Allegheny Valley. Functionally, however, the site was a nightmare: the hillside was so precipitous that normal placement of the nave was impossible, and the church had to straddle the hill broadside. Ginther always seemed able to rise to this sort of challenge, and he did so with brilliance here. Like Hornbostel's Rodef Shalom, this building is really two churches, or even three: from the back it is St. Peter's in Rome, even to the detail of Michelangelo's peculiar attic windows; from the front it is Borromini's S. Agnese on Piazza Navona in Rome; inside it is based on the City Churches of Sir Christopher Wren in London. After Ginther handed in his design, the men of the parish built it themselves.

God's house is not the only one to shine on Polish Hill. All the houses here seem blessed by inner peace. The earlier ones stand three and four stories tall, either of brick or of clapboard that has given way to aluminum siding or imitation brick. The ground floor is often a shop, but a tiny archway gives promise of a garden behind. The homes are oriented for the best views over the Allegheny Valley, even if they must crane around their neighbors to get it, like spectators at tennis. Walking on Paulowna, Herron, Brereton, or Dobson streets, and on Pulaski or Flavan ways, one can only be moved by this proud community that never amassed material wealth but "made good" on this hillside on its own terms a century ago.

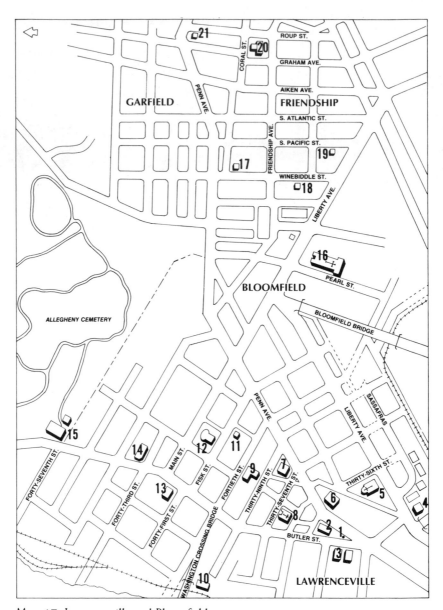

Map 17. Lawrenceville and Bloomfield

1 Doughboy Square
2 Old Pa. National Bank
3 Lawrenceville Bathhouse
4 Pittsburgh Brewery
5 St. John the Baptist Church
6 3600 Penn Ave. (Foster site)
7 Cinderella Apts.
8 St. Augustine's Church

9 Allegheny Arsenal powder
  magazine
10 Allegheny Arsenal machine
  shop
11 Brown House
12 Carnegie Library, Lawrenceville
13 Pittsburgh National Bank
14 Arsenal Bank

15 Allegheny Cemetery
  gatehouse
16 St. Joseph's Church
17 Ursuline Academy
18 Winebiddle House
19 Bartberger House
20 Friendship School
21 Lackzoom Acidophilus

Lawrenceville and Bloomfield

Lawrenceville is an important district, but it is less cohesive than others along Penn Avenue, and its participation in Pittsburgh's renaissance has been limited because of it. One of the largest city neighborhoods, with 1,300 acres, its borders are well defined only on the north and south, by the river and by Two-Mile Run. On the west and east it trails off without punctuation into The Strip and Bloomfield. Its character, too, is mixed: its flat land is industrial and its slopes residential, with a population of some 12,000 inhabitants of Central and Eastern European origin.

Lawrenceville is the only part of Pittsburgh that we can envisage as populated by Indians. A number of colonists—George Washington included—visited the Delaware village of "Shannopin's Town" on Butler Street, but the natives had gone by the time Joseph Conrad Winebiddle started his tannery in the area in 1771. In 1814 Colonel William Foster purchased 121 acres between the roads to Butler and Greensburg and laid it out as Lawrenceville, in memory of the naval commander who had died with the shout of "Don't give up the ship!" the year before.

The heart of Lawrenceville, then as now, was the Forks of the Road, where the Butler and Greensburg pikes split. Since 1921, Pittsburghers have generally called this triangle **Doughboy Square** for the neighborhood war memorial (by the New York sculptor Allen Newman) that stands there. The square has a lessened intensity today because of the demolition of some of its constituent buildings, but it still has a strong architectural as well as social character. The floridly Beaux Arts **Pennsylvania National Bank** (Beezer Brothers, 1902) rises as a triangular backdrop to the Doughboy; a muscle-bound Romanesque Revival undertaker's castle of 1888 (now a garage) stands alongside at **3441 Butler;** and the triangle ends at 3445 Butler with the former **Lawrenceville Bathhouse,** which opened in 1904 as part of a string of public gifts from Henry Phipps. The building had eighteen showers on the first story and ten tubs on the second; on a typical Saturday several thousand millworkers and their families would line up outside it.

Doughboy Square /*Maurice Tierney*

Left: Pittsburgh Brewing Company, Liberty Avenue /*Franklin Toker* ▪ *Right:* St. John the Baptist Church, Liberty Avenue /*Franklin Toker*

The pronounced visual monument of Lawrenceville is the sprawling **Pittsburgh Brewery** (originally the Iron City Brewery; 3340 Liberty Ave., between the Herron Avenue Bridge & Sassafras), once the third largest "beer trust" in the United States and still an important brand nationwide. In 1962 the brewery joined with Alcoa to create a significant artifact in American material culture: the first flip-top can. Its dozen buildings all date from the second half of the nineteenth century, some as early as 1866, when Edward Frauenheim and Leopold Vilsack built Iron City here. The Queen Anne-style administration building dates from the 1880s and is a finely detailed brick structure featuring a bust of Ceres, goddess of grain, with sheaves of wheat for hair. On the opposite side of Liberty stand two other Lawrenceville landmarks: the **Lawrence Square Apartments** (3417–3429 Liberty), a triangle of worker flats from the end of the nineteenth century that wraps around the site of the Iron City wagonworks, and the Italian Romanesque **St. John the Baptist Church** (3501 Liberty; John Comes for Beezer Brothers, 1902–7), with its polychromed facade, striped (but now truncated) campanile, and exuberant diaper work on the apse.

Through a thicket of streets from Liberty one can reach **3600 Penn Avenue,** opposite Thirty-sixth Street, a curious relic of Stephen Foster. William Foster chose this commanding site on the Greensburg Pike in 1814 for the "White Cottage," which seems to have been designed for him by Benjamin Henry Latrobe. There, on July 4, 1826—the day on which John Adams and Thomas Jefferson lay dying—William's son Stephen was born. Failing to prosper in Lawrenceville, the father moved the next year to the North Side, where America's most beloved composer spent most of his life. It was a brief life—just thirty-eight years—and its end coincided with the destruction of the "White Cottage," which was replaced in 1864 by this proud Second

Empire mansion, built by Andrew Carnegie's partner, Andrew Kloman.[1] Fifty years later, in 1914, the Pittsburgh philanthropist James Park bought the mansion as an intended refuge for Foster's aged and impecunious daughter, Marion Foster Welch. In 1980 music returned to the site when the house was bought as an artists' residence and as lodging for musicians in the American Wind Symphony.

Diagonally across Penn Avenue from the Foster site, at the northeast corner of Penn and Thirty-seventh Street, stands an apartment block that gained its fame in another way. Held up by a bricklayers' strike in 1903, its builder, John Fink, constructed it out of coal ashes that were mixed with cement and ground brick, then poured into a wooden framework. The innovation gave the block its obvious title: the **Cinderella Apartments.**

St. Augustine's Church (220 Thirty-seventh Street, between Bandera & Butler Sts.; John Comes for Rutan & Russell, 1901) is a large Munich-style Romanesque Revival church squeezed into a narrow site but dominating Lawrenceville with its high towers and octagonal crossing. The hammer and tongs sculpted among the Instruments of the Passion over the entrance were artifacts of daily use for the German millworkers who constituted the parish. Another half-dozen buildings on the same block support the activities of the church and the Capuchin friars who minister to it.

Fisk Street, four blocks east of Thirty-seventh, is another good introduction to the public and private architecture of Lawrenceville. Wedged into this narrow way is the imposing **Carnegie Library of Pittsburgh—Lawrence-ville Branch** (279 Fisk; Alden & Harlow, 1898), the first branch in the Pittsburgh library system and the prototype for several Carnegie libraries in other cities. It appears to have been the first library anywhere with a children's section, and the building plan is particularly gracious and efficient, with the book stacks radiating like spokes in the half-circle of the apse. Even on a slim budget, the architects concocted a fine portal of gray terra-cotta plaques set in alternation with thin courses of Roman brick. Diagonally across the street at 294 Fisk is the Civil War-period **Brown House,** a Gothic Revival brick cottage with fantastic drooping gingerbread designs on the gables.

Western Pennsylvanians who grumble that their region is shortchanged in the Defense Department budget can only lament the passing of the **Allegheny Arsenal,** which stood from 1814 to 1907 between the Allegheny River and Penn Avenue at Thirty-ninth and Fortieth streets. The arsenal produced ammunition through four wars, spewing out 30,000 bullets a day during the Civil War. Its nucleus of a dozen main buildings was designed by Benjamin Henry Latrobe, who came to Pittsburgh in 1811 at the request of Nicholas

---

1. Another old house at 3414 Penn was for years erroneously pointed out as the Foster birthplace. Henry Ford, to whom history was bunk, came to Pittsburgh in 1934, heard the tale, and bought the fake house for his Greenfield Village in Dearborn, Michigan.

Machine Shop, Allegheny Arsenal (Benjamin Henry Latrobe, architect, 1814) /*Franklin Toker*

Roosevelt to design the first steamboat ever built inland. When Lafayette took breakfast in the arsenal with his old comrades-in-arms in 1825, it was one of the best neoclassical groups of buildings in the country. A respectable half-dozen buildings survived until the 1950s, but just three stand today: the L-shaped, barrel-vaulted **powder magazine** buried in the hillside of Arsenal Park, a thick-walled brick structure in Allegheny County's Clack Health Center nearby, and the old **machine shop** next to the Washington Crossing Bridge. This last, cut back in 1923 when the bridge was set over it, now serves the Arsenal Terminal Warehouses as a depot for "Mr. John" brand portable toilets. Its material is brick, with a sandstone entablature and Doric capitals on its severe pilasters; the elegant proportions are those of a Greek temple. No American architect but Latrobe could have designed a structure that would look so noble despite the ill-treatment it has endured.

Apart from its specifically military role, the Allegheny Arsenal must be regarded as the largest of the early factory complexes of Pittsburgh. It employed hundreds of workers and produced a boom in Greek Revival houses in Lawrenceville in the 1830s and 1840s. Scores of them survive around the intersection of Thirty-eighth and Foster streets and elsewhere in the lower town, each marked by severe stone lintels over the windows, and many with sidelights by the doors. As Lawrenceville expanded east, the new homes took on the Italianate lintels of the 1860s and later the High Victorian Gothic corbel brackets of the 1880s, but the sense of intimacy on its crowded streets was never lost.

The noisy commercial thoroughfare of **Butler Street** is the main pathway to Lawrenceville's mills, serving as the counterpart to E. Carson Street on the South Side or Second Avenue in Hazelwood. In fact, the architecture of all three streets is essentially interchangeable. The stores are jammed together, at least three stories high, often four, and they reflect the national taste in commercial architecture in the decades after the Civil War. Special prominence falls, as always, to the banks: the High Victorian Gothic **Arsenal Bank** (SE corner Butler & Forty-third Sts.) and the elegant **Pittsburgh National Bank** branch (the former Metropolitan National Bank; 4105 Butler, NE corner

Forty-first St.; Beezer Brothers, 1903). Inside this hushed Beaux Arts temple of Mammon shine eight stained-glass windows in veneration of the principal gods of Pittsburgh industry.

A few blocks east of the commercial strip, the mills themselves begin. For Lawrenceville the first of the colossal mills was the predecessor of the H. K. Porter Locomotive Works, opened in 1866 on Harrison Street and Hemlock Alley, between Forty-ninth and Fiftieth streets. A dozen low brick structures of that complex are used today by the Pittsburgh Commercial Heat Treating Company and the McConway-Torley Corporation. The second came in 1877 and was even larger. Between Forty-seventh and Fifty-second streets Carnegie, Kloman & Company built the Lucy blast furnace, named for Carnegie's sister-in-law. Lucy engaged in a fierce production race with the competing Isabella furnace across the river in the appositely named town of Etna, until she hit the phenomenal output of 1,400 tons a week in 1881. Worn out, Lucy was demolished in the 1930s. The Crucible Steel works and Heppenstal Forge cover most of the site, in desuetude today.

In just a moment's walk from this sad industrial graveyard, the visitor to Lawrenceville can enter the 300 acres of **Allegheny Cemetery** (4734 Butler St., east of Forty-seventh St.), which is by contrast a pleasant and almost

Left: Lawrenceville row houses, Foster and Forty-first streets /*Courtesy* Pittsburgh Post-Gazette *(Darrell Sapp)* ▪ *Right:* Outdoor mattress sale, Butler Street /*Franklin Toker*

Tombstones in Allegheny Cemetery: William and Stephen Foster /*Franklin Toker*

hopeful place. It is the fourth of the rural cemeteries of the United States in chronological order, after Boston, Philadelphia, and Brooklyn, and not the least of these in terms of historic and artistic interest. Like the neighborhood of Stanton Heights behind it, the cemetery was part of the Bayard and Croghan summer estates, and its gorges and peaks give it an appropriately romantic spirit. John Chislett was the designer of both the grounds and the gatehouse in 1844–48; Henry Moser added the Gothic chapel in 1870. Within the cemetery lie eighteen mayors of Pittsburgh and a fair number of international celebrities: Harry Thaw, Lillian Russell, Stephen Foster, and a host of the industrial kings of Pittsburgh in mausolea ornamented with fine Tiffany windows. Briefly making his appearance among them was A. W. Mellon, who was buried here in 1937 but was later disinterred by his son Paul to a quieter resting place in Virginia.

Bloomfield

Bloomfield is a feast, as rich to the eyes as the homemade tortellini and cannoli in its shop windows are to the stomach. It stretches along Penn and Liberty avenues from the Bloomfield Bridge to Negley Avenue in East Liberty, and from Garfield Hill on the north to the dip of Two-Mile Run and the Conrail tracks on the south. Its 658 acres encompass three villages: Bloomfield proper (10,000 residents, mainly Italian in origin, with roots in five towns in the Abruzzi); Friendship (2,000 residents, mainly German in origin, living in the triangle between Liberty and Penn); and Garfield (8,000 residents, mainly black, on Penn Avenue and Garfield Hill). The urban organization of Bloomfield departs from the Pittsburgh norm in having these separate subdistricts, each distinct socially and topographically, and also in having not one, but two, spine streets. Penn is the older of the two by a century, and it is markedly narrower and quieter, as befits a matron 200 years old. Liberty was laid out in the 1880s, about the time Italian immigrants began to arrive in Bloomfield; its 100-foot width gave it the aspect of a market street from the beginning. It is lined with two solid walls of three-story Gothic Revival shopfronts with apartments overhead. Breaking them up visually are a few key public monuments, notably **St. Joseph's Church** (4712 Liberty, SE corner Pearl; 1886), a Gothic Revival mass of tan brick walls, deeply pointed and crisply patterned, with two asymmetrical towers, and the **Plaza Theater** (4765 Liberty, NW corner S. Mathilda), an odd but engaging match of an Art Deco body and a Beaux Arts top.

It requires only a moment to step from the crowding of Liberty Avenue to the quiet elegance of **Friendship,** the late nineteenth-century community organized by Caspar and Harriet Winebiddle on a portion of the 600 acres their ancestors had amassed a century before. These handsome streets, particularly Winebiddle, S. Pacific, and S. Atlantic, testify to the rising wealth of middle management in Pittsburgh around 1900, and they are as much a document of the beginnings of corporate culture here as are the high towers downtown. One finds houses of exactly the same four-square plan, with its telltale Palladian window in the upstairs front bathroom, in the three other neighborhoods to which the corporate managers swarmed from 1890 until 1910: Shadyside, Highland Park, and Squirrel Hill. Some of the Friendship homes were architect-designed, but the majority were produced by developers. The formula at 328 Roup Street is identical to that at 316 Roup, for example. The best of the older homes in Friendship is the Henry Lynch House of 1868, now the **Ursuline Academy** (201 S. Winebiddle, SE corner Coral), a textbook example of a Second Empire mansion, with a central tower and asymmetrical wings under proud mansard roofs. The **Winebiddle House** at

Left: Bloomfield rooftops /*Maurice Tierney* ▪ *Right:* 4500 block, Liberty Avenue /*Maurice Tierney*

Architect Charles M. Bartberger's
home, S. Pacific Avenue /*Franklin Toker*

340 S. Winebiddle is a fine example of the Romanesque Revival homes found in the area, while the High Victorian Gothic, with characteristic touches of Queen Anne ornament, is best exemplified by the **Charles M. Bartberger House** (408 S. Pacific; by Bartberger himself, 1883).[2] The Winebiddle lands were parceled out from west to east, so the homes near East Liberty display later turns in style: a large New England Colonial home with an overscaled gambrel roof, at the northeast corner of Friendship and S. Aiken; a Renaissance Revival mansion with obvious links to the Prairie School, at 240 S. Graham; and the Colonial Revival twins at 316 and 328 Roup, mentioned earlier. These grand homes were constructed just before the motorcar age and so have no garages. The heart of the Friendship subdistrict is the **Friendship School** (5501 Friendship, between S. Graham & Roup; Charles M. Bartberger, 1899), an accomplished Beaux Arts palace characterized by ornamental columns and corner pilasters of terra-cotta, and by windows that are broadly grouped almost like strips.

2. The Bartberger house, along with Osterling's studio on the North Side and Hornbostel's two dozen buildings in Oakland, is an important document of the culture of the Pittsburgh architectural community at the turn of the century, and it gives us insight into the finances and social life of the typical designer of the period. Bartberger stamped the building three times: his monogram is on the gable, the Masonic seal is on the second floor, and his coat of arms is on a stained-glass window on the upstairs landing. Everything about the house suggests an owner whose social aspirations exceeded his budgetary reach. The interior detailing is fastidious to the point of claustrophobia, as though one of the marble palaces of Newport had been caught in the rain and shrunk.

Garfield was laid out in 1881, beginning on the day the martyred president was buried. Its lower streets are monotonous rows that barely acknowledge their hilly site, but the uppermost streets are curved and shady and lined with pleasant brick cottages. The Garfield streetscape along Penn Avenue is fairly mundane, but it has some once-elegant housing, particularly in a long row of Queen Anne townhouses with verandahs on the 5100 and 5200 blocks from N. Evaline to N. Atlantic streets. Here too is the old **Lackzoom Acidophilus** store (5438 Penn Ave., near S. Graham), a small building as remarkable for its name as for its luxurious classical terra-cotta facade, complete with cherubs. It dates from around 1920 and was the modest progenitor of the General Nutrition Corporation of today. It is a sunny, quirky building, in its odd way one of the most memorable on Penn Avenue.

East Liberty, Highland Park, Larimer, Lincoln, and Homewood

East Liberty is a classic example of a pike town that developed step by step with the roads and transportation systems that passed through it: first the Forbes Road and Greensburg Pike to Philadelphia; later the railroad, the horsecar, the trolley, and the automobile. There is much to be learned from East Liberty, particularly from its struggle to overcome the straitjacket of the well-intentioned urban-renewal specialists who almost killed it in the 1960s. But its urban history yields another bonus: the unexplored story of the foundation of the Mellon fortune, not in oil or aluminum, but in land—specifically, huge parcels of land along Penn Avenue.

One remembers the Mellons in the Horatio Alger mode in which Americans normally think about Great Wealth. The legend is half right: A. W. Mellon's father, Thomas, lifted himself out of the dire poverty that had forced the family to emigrate from Northern Ireland. One forgets, however, that Mellon's mother belonged to a clan that controlled about 3,300 acres of choice Pittsburgh land—nearly everything that today comprises the neighborhoods of East Liberty, Highland Park, Larimer, Lincoln, and Homewood. The story of its acquisition is as simple as the workings of compound interest. It begins with the German immigrant Caspar Taub, who in 1762 was granted 303 acres in the Highland Park district by Colonel Henry Bouquet in exchange for a promise to deliver one-third of his crops to feed Bouquet's soldiers at Fort Pitt. Taub married his daughter Elizabeth to Joseph Conrad Winebiddle, Sr., who owned even more land in Lawrenceville and Bloomfield. In the third generation, the Winebiddles married their daughter Barbara Ann to Jacob Negley, who, through this marriage, owned virtually all the land from Highland Park to Point Breeze. Around 1810 Negley laid out the town of East

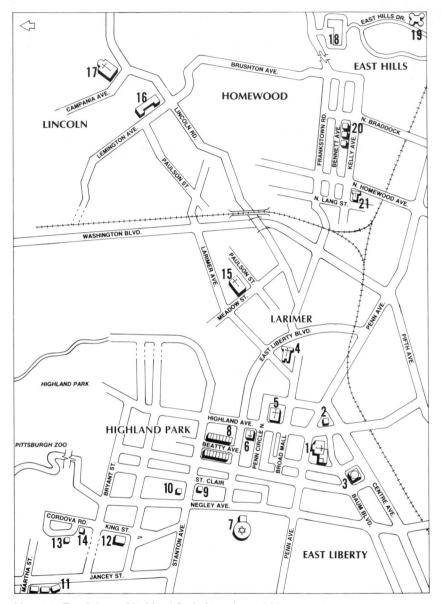

Map 18. East Liberty, Highland Park, Lincoln, and Homewood

1 East Liberty Presbyterian Church
2 Highland Bldg.
3 Liberty Market (Motor Sq.)
4 Sts. Peter and Paul Church
5 Eastminster United Church
6 Emery United Methodist Church
7 B'Nai Israel Synagogue

8 Alpha Terrace
9 Stanton Castle
10 5655 Stanton Ave.
11 Vilsack Row
12 1147–1155 King St.
13 Bendet House
14 Best House

15 Our Lady Help of Christians
16 Lemington School
17 Cornerstone Baptist Church
18 East Hills Shopping Center
19 East Hills School
20 Syria, Kismet, & Nelda Apts.
21 Rosary Church

Liberty on his land (an English "liberty" meant grazing land around the city: Pittsburgh had a North and West as well as an East Liberty), and a few years later he paved and widened the two-mile stretch of the Greensburg Pike that ran through the property.

In 1843 Jacob Negley married his daughter Sarah Jane to Thomas Mellon, who began to build the cornerstone of his fortune on Negley land. Mellon used the land in four ways: he sold it outright, he built houses on it, he gave mortgages on it, and he foreclosed on property when the mortgages were not repaid. Some observers—not his friends—said that Mellon was the happiest man in Pittsburgh after the Great Fire of 1845 because of all the foreclosures and investment possibilities it would bring. Mellon also involved himself in numerous transportation ventures connected with land. In 1859 he was one of the main proponents of the two horsecar lines that connected East Liberty through Oakland and Lawrenceville to the Golden Triangle. When these lines were electrified around 1892, they consolidated East Liberty as the trolley nexus of Pittsburgh. The Mellons played no less a role in East Liberty's last spurt of growth, early in the century, as the center of Pittsburgh's motor culture. A dozen car or parts dealers opened on Baum Boulevard in the first years of the century, and Henry Ford established a subsidiary assembly plant in a factory that still stands on the southeast corner of Baum and Morewood. Three-quarters of a mile away, the head of Gulf, Thomas Mellon's grandson William Larimer Mellon, established one of the first drive-in gas stations in 1913 on Mellon land at the intersection of St. Clair and Baum Boulevard. The next year Gulf published the world's first motoring roadmap.

Most Pittsburghers today are familiar not with East Liberty's urban history, but with its problematic urban renewal. Beginning in 1960, the Urban Redevelopment Authority pumped $68 million into the center of this 500-acre district. In the process it destroyed 1,500 old homes and created 2,000 new ones in apartments and townhouse clusters, it plowed under a dozen old roads and opened up a dozen new ones, and it transformed a tight urban knot into an *ersatz* suburban shopping mall. The decline of East Liberty as a retail center had set in before this aggressive redevelopment, but the cure aggravated the disease. The number of shops in East Liberty declined from 242 in 1963 to 98 in 1977, although it has now rebounded to 140. In ten years the population fell from 7,000 to 4,000, although it too has since edged up. Today the street furniture of the 1960s is being ripped out, one-way and pedestrian-only streets are being returned to the traffic patterns they had twenty-five years ago, and everything is being done to encourage the irregularity and unstructured casualness that marked this community when it was still a flourishing enterprise.

The **East Liberty Presbyterian Church** (116 S. Highland Mall, SW corner Penn; Ralph Adams Cram, 1931–35) is the most luxurious of the Mellon buildings constructed in Pittsburgh during the Depression, not excluding the

Cathedral of Learning and Mellon Institute. Old-timers in Pittsburgh referred to it as the "Mellon fire escape," because R. B. Mellon and his wife seemed to be building it for the redemption of their souls (the doors to their tombs are in fact thrown wide open on Easter Sunday). But East Liberty Presbyterian is only indirectly a Mellon monument: as the fifth church to have stood on this land since Jacob Negley donated it in 1819, it is a *Negley* monument, and it was designed to reinforce the Mellon image as part of Pittsburgh's landed aristocracy. It was, per square foot, probably the most lavish church commission ever given to Cram or any other American architect. Since the neighborhood had already begun to decay by 1930, when he designed the church, Cram placed the greatest emphasis on its high Spanish Gothic spire, which can be seen straight across town from Bloomfield to Homewood—exactly that part of Pittsburgh that the Mellon ancestors once owned.

Immediately behind East Liberty Presbyterian stands the thirteen-story **Highland Building** (121 S. Highland Ave., NE corner Baum Blvd.; Daniel Burnham, 1910), a Frick monument that, oddly, copies features of two buildings by Burnham's nemesis, Louis H. Sullivan. The models were the Carson-Pirie-Scott store in Chicago for the detailing of the bead-and-reel ornament channeled through the terra-cotta skin, and the Guaranty Building in Buffalo for the splayed-out cornice. Along with the Highland Building, there are other significant remains from the salad days of East Liberty, particularly in the three main blocks of Penn Mall—the old Penn Avenue before it was suburbanized—

Left: The Mellons' East Liberty Presbyterian Church (Ralph Adams Cram, architect) /*Franklin Toker* ▪ *Right:* The Highland Building (Daniel Burnham, architect) /*Maurice Tierney*

Commercial buildings of the 1930s, Penn Mall /*Maurice Tierney*

from Beatty Street to Sheridan Avenue. Notable are the Richardsonian Romanesque **Liberty Building** from the 1880s, the Art Deco shopfronts of the 1930s, particularly the F. W. Woolworth Store, and the elaborate facades of the Regent and Sheridan Square theaters.

Some blocks to the west stands the Mellons' second most prominent monument in East Liberty, the **Liberty Market** (popularly known as Motor Square Garden; 5900 Baum Blvd., SE corner S. Beatty St.; Peabody & Stearns, 1900). The Mellons built it as a city market after one of their subdivisions failed to sell enough houses. It failed as a market and as a sports arena, but current plans aim to revive it as a shopping mart. The Mellons entrusted its design to a suave Boston firm that did so much business in Pittsburgh that it established a branch office here. Peabody & Stearns produced a fanciful mix of an industrial interior, with exposed steel girders, and a Roman exterior with an enormous skylit dome and thermal windows worthy of the Emperor Caracala. Inside, the viewer can almost palpably feel the sweep of its enormous volume and dynamic structure, reminiscent of the glorious iron-and-glass concourse of the old Pennsylvania Station in New York.

The skyscape of East Liberty is dominated about equally by its churches and its business blocks, which is not surprising since East Liberty was never a government or a cultural center, but functioned as a true crossroads, meeting the everyday needs of the East End and the eastern suburbs. Either intentionally or through timidity, the urban planners left most of East Liberty's churches intact. Next to East Liberty Presbyterian, the most prominent of these is **Sts. Peter and Paul Roman Catholic Church** (130 Larimer Ave., between East Liberty Blvd. & Broad St.; 1890). The prototype of this church for a German congregation was probably the historic St. Elizabeth at Marburg, which the replica recalls in the leap of its twin spires, but not in its lackluster detailing and the concrete blocks that pretend to be stone. Substantially better is the **Eastminster United Presbyterian Church** (250 N. Highland Mall, SE corner Penn Circle North; William Fraser, 1893), a vigorous

Richardsonian Romanesque building by a Pittsburgh architect who was even more astute at designing commercial than spiritual blocks.

One of the few new buildings of the last half century in East Liberty that is not devoted to housing or fast food is also a church, for a congregation that has served the neighborhood since 1832: the **Emery United Methodist Church** (325 N. Highland Ave.; Stotz, Hess, MacLachlin & Fosner, 1973), a handsome, semitraditional design in the Modern Romanesque style that Harry Weese made famous in his First Baptist Church (1965) in Columbus, Indiana. The chain of East Liberty churches includes a "safe" Colonial Revival chapel at the **Pittsburgh Theological Seminary** (616 N. Highland Ave.), which sits on the farm where Charles Lockhart began by refining kerosene and ended up owning a major block of Standard Oil. Farther on is the dramatic half-Byzantine, half-Renaissance **B'Nai Israel Synagogue** (327 N. Negley Ave., opposite Rippey; Henry Hornbostel, with Alexander Sharove, 1923), standing out as a blaze of color against the east slope of Garfield Hill.

Highland Park

Highland Park derives its name both from Robert Hiland, the county surveyor who laid out Highland and Negley avenues through the Negley homestead in 1837, and from the Chicago suburb of the same name. It is a paradox in urban terms: a community of 10,000 residents on 1,000 acres that dead-end on the west, east, and north on the steep slopes of Heth's Run, Negley's Run, and the Allegheny Valley. Such isolation proved crippling to Manchester, Garfield, East Hills, and Homewood, but it made Highland Park flourish, with

The Alpha Terrace on Beatty Street, Highland Park /*Franklin Toker*

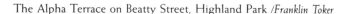

a score of handsome streets and a thousand of the best houses in Pittsburgh. The answers to the paradox lie north and south of Highland Park: to the north, in **Highland Park** itself, the 360 acres that Edward M. Bigelow acquired for the city in 1893 and that Christopher Magee developed further with his fine **Pittsburgh Zoo** in 1898; and to the south, where for a hundred years East Liberty functioned as a vigorous heart, pumping into Highland Park whatever urban amenities the little community could not develop on its own.

Although Highland Park is nothing but houses, many of these are of high interest, particularly the **Alpha Terrace,** a collection of two dozen town-houses on both sides of N. Beatty Street that once formed a private green between Stanton and Hayes. It was built by several Mellon cousins in 1885 (the architect seems to have been James Steen) as rental property, and the units were sold off only in the 1950s. The west side of the development is Romanesque Revival, in solid granite, while the east side is Queen Anne, much more fanciful (several homes sprout Ghibelline machicolations) and intimate, with shingles above the stone walls. Overall, it is one of the distinctive experiments in multifamily housing in late-Victorian America.

The more conventional detached houses of Highland Park represent a century of styles in domestic architecture from Italianate to Wrightian. Those in the first category, such as a farmhouse with Italianate details at **1317 Sheridan Avenue,** from a few years before the Civil War, are survivors from the era of the Negley farm. A half-dozen homes represent the Second Empire period and the flush of industrial prosperity after the Civil War. The best of these is **Baywood** (1251 N. Negley, reached through Elgin Street). Its builder was the glass magnate Alexander King, father of Jenny King Mellon and thus an ancestor of the Scaife branch of the Mellon clan. The house dates from around 1872. The several castellated towers nearby were added as an instant ruin by King's son Robert in 1898.

Much more prevalent than these rare survivors are the homes that were built after 1890, when Magee brought his trolley lines through the community (hence his gift of the zoo at the north end of the tracks, which boosted ridership on the trolleys). At the crossroads of Highland Park, in the 5600 block of Stanton Avenue between Mellon and N. St. Clair streets, stand two of the outstanding homes in the district. One is **Stanton Castle** (5652 Stanton Ave., SW corner St. Clair), a twentieth-century medievalizing brick house that features a low segmental arch at its center, possibly in emulation of Richardson's house for Sir Hubert von Herkomer in England. Across the street, at **5655 Stanton Avenue,** stands a fine Shingle Style house, dating from around 1890. Not far away, the northern Renaissance is represented at **935 N. Highland** in a brick house with pressed brick trim and picturesque Flemish scroll gables at the front and sides. Typical of the large Colonial Revival homes is an elegant example in Roman brick with Queen Anne trim, at **944 Sheridan Avenue.**

Vilsack Row, Morningside (Frederick Scheibler, architect) /*Franklin Toker*

In the adjoining neighborhood of Morningside are the best modern homes of the district, which are the eighteen units of **Vilsack Row** (1659–1693 Jancey St., SW corner Martha; reached from Highland Park via Stanton and Morningside Aves.). These five-room units were erected in three separate rows for the Vilsack estate in 1914 by the man who brought Modern architecture to Pittsburgh: Frederick Scheibler.[3] The rows have deteriorated and the central

3. The life of Frederick Gustavus Scheibler, Jr. (1872–1958), creates an almost exact chronological parallel with that of Frank Lloyd Wright (1867–1959), although they had little in common apart from their passionate love of creating human shelter. Scheibler was born in Pittsburgh, the grandson of a German bookbinder. He lived his whole life here and almost never left western Pennsylvania either to travel or to build. His architectural education was no less parochial: an apprenticeship in 1888 with Henry Moser, several more years with the minor architect J. Lewis Beatty, then his own career as an independent designer for twenty-five years. He had little interaction with his colleagues; one will not even find his face among those of the thirty-two architects who bought their way into the pages of *Palmer's Pictorial Pittsburgh* in 1905. But through magazines he knew what his English, German, Austrian, and American colleagues were designing in the years 1900–1920, and he could study their renderings firsthand in the annual exhibits of the Pittsburgh Architectural Club at Carnegie Institute. The architectural world knew about Scheibler, too: his works were published nationally and even overseas, in Germany.

Scheibler designed more than a hundred homes in Pittsburgh. Almost all are still standing—in Morningside, Highland Park, Shadyside, Squirrel Hill, Point Breeze, Wilkinsburg, and Homewood. (With some practice one can distinguish them fairly easily from the designs of two pseudo-Scheiblers, Edward B. Lee and Edward Weber.) Scheibler's homes are generally adaptations of European prototypes—preeminently the English Free Style of C. F. A. Voysey, Charles Rennie Mackintosh, and M. H. Baillie-Scott and the Vienna Secession school. These prototypes he transformed into an American vision that over the years became more romantic than the originals. His career was marked by a proto-Modern phase, with his fascinating insight and even prescience of the International School, from about 1905 to 1915, and then a second, more romantic interpretation of the earlier themes, to about 1925. Scheibler's national and international reputation had largely evaporated by 1915; by 1925 there were few even in Pittsburgh who had heard of him.

group has been changed by the addition of a continuous patio and an overhanging porch, but what is left has exceptional clarity and uncompromising geometric boldness. Vilsack Row derives its power from a simple projection/recession rhythm that is intensified by the massive simplicity of its cavelike arched entrances and strip windows. It is unfair—but inevitable—in the presence of a provincial masterpiece to ask how this work compares to Wright and the Prairie School in the Midwest and to Gropius, Mies, Le Corbusier, and the beginnings of the International School in Europe. Vilsack Row is so simply composed (in brick, stucco, and wood trim) that it appears to leapfrog over Wright's designs and find its main parallel in the concrete houses of Irving Gill on the West Coast. Whatever its parentage, the economy of scale and materials shown here, the social concern manifested for housing the lower middle class, and the foreknowledge of what lesser architects would be designing a half-century afterward make Vilsack Row one of the most revealing documents of early Modernism in the United States.

The more picturesque domestic architecture of the 1910s and 1920s in Highland Park is effectively represented by the row of five homes at **1147– 1155 King Street,** below Bryant (1914), a low ski slope lifted up on splayed bungalow piers. Scheibler himself showed his picturesque side a little farther north, in the **Best House** (1315 Cordova Road, near the corner of Bryant & King), a half-timbered and pseudo-thatched cottage of around 1915. Very close by stands the **Bendit House** (1321 Cordova Road; c. 1927), by the delightful Pittsburgh architect Theodore Eichholz, who ended his days twenty years later designing huge works such as hospitals and the Greater Pittsburgh International Airport. This "Mother Goose" cottage reflects his more characteristic playful mood, with a high-pitched shingle roof and a conical entrance that echoes Benno Jannsen's just-completed Kaufmann House in Fox Chapel.

Larimer

The working-class district of **Larimer** borders Highland Park on the east, but it reflects in its long rows of modest brick and frame homes an earlier moment of settlement and a poorer clientele. The houses are plain: the older ones have some features of the Queen Anne style from the 1890s, whereas the newer ones are low bungalows from the 1920s. Larimer was created for the first wave of Italian immigration at the same time as the larger community in Bloomfield, but for families who were already prosperous enough to buy a freestanding house and a garden around it. The Italian community today is only a small enclave in a neighborhood that is predominantly black, yet it still supports a dozen shops at the intersection of Larimer and Meadow streets. A few blocks away stands the community's great monument, **Our Lady Help of Christians Church** (6513 Meadow), an exuberant Italian Baroque structure of 1892.

Like the communes of medieval Italy, in which the upkeep of the bridges was critical, Larimer depends on its bridges to keep it from being cut off from Highland Park and Lincoln. The three bridges over nearby Negley's Run (Washington Boulevard) are among the most powerful and lyrical sights in the city. The earliest, from 1903, is the **Pennsylvania Railroad Bridge,** which carries the Conrail tracks over Lincoln Avenue, on the east side of the boulevard. It consists of six ponderous arches that are faced with stone over an internal structure of concrete. Under the northernmost of those six arches, at a right angle to the bridge, pass the two semi-elliptical stone arches of the 1906 **Lincoln Avenue Bridge.** A quarter of a mile farther to the north, Washington Boulevard is crossed again by the elegant **Larimer Avenue Bridge,** this time a concrete structure of 1912. In the gully itself, at the northwest corner of Washington and Negley Run boulevards, stands a strange building with the character of a circus prop. It is the blackened four-story tower of the **firemen's training school,** which is set on fire again and again to simulate actual fire conditions. Its purpose is serious, but as architecture it is one of the more incongruous sights of the city.

Lincoln

The neighborhood of **Lincoln,** known also by the names of its Belmar and Lemington subdistricts, is an attractive district high on a plateau that over-looks the Allegheny Valley to the north, Negley's Run and Highland Park to the west, Penn Hills to the east, and the flats of Homewood to the south. Lincoln is a middle-class black neighborhood with houses of World War I

Lemington School, Lincoln
/Franklin Toker

vintage that are spaced more generously than one finds even in older and wealthier neighborhoods such as Shadyside. Its spine, Lincoln Road, is not what one generally finds in the older neighborhoods of Pittsburgh either: it twists through the area with the breeziness of a suburban highway (it in fact leads to the suburb of Penn Hills), rather than affecting the sobriety of a city street.

Part of the appeal of Lincoln stems from its hills and near-suburban character and from two monuments of architectural delight. The **Lemington School** (7060 Lemington Ave., opposite Paulson; Marion M. Steen, 1937) is, in decorative terms, the most striking school in Pittsburgh. It is constructed of beige industrial brick but in Classical Revival proportions, so that the piers between the windows affect the approximate height and girth of the columns of a Greek temple. Above, a frieze of brown, cream, blue, red, and green terracotta tiles creates a similar evocation of the triglyphs and metopes of a temple entablature. The blaze of color in the two large polychromed overdoor reliefs evokes more exotic cultures, however: Islam, the Aztecs, and Hollywood. A few blocks to the northeast stands the equally grandiose **Cornerstone Baptist Church** (NW corner Lincoln & Campania Aves.; 1928). This was constructed as St. Walburga's for a German-Catholic congregation and passed to the black community in the 1960s. It is a flamboyantly sited hillside building of finely dressed, irregularly coursed sandstones of varied hues and has a charming open space before its facade. A moment's drive up Campania Street leads to an ideal viewing point from one side of Pittsburgh to the other, including Oakland and the tops of several skyscrapers in the Golden Triangle.

Homewood

Through the deep shadow under the railroad bridge and he knew he was in Homewood again. Sure he had made it back. This was the exact place. This daylight after the dark tunnel, this door you push through to get into Homewood, this line you stepped over, danced over if you were the 501 Engineer Corps returning from the war. You stopped marching and started dancing because this was the edge, the very moment you knew you'd made it home one more time.

There are many ways to enter **Homewood.** The most dramatic points of entry are the underpasses that cut below the Conrail tracks at N. Homewood, N. Dallas, and N. Braddock avenues. This was the way Albert Wilkes entered in John Edgar Wideman's lyric novel of Homewood, *Sent for You Yesterday* (New York: Avon Books, 1983), quoted above. It is the approach to Homewood that most forcefully shuts out the white world and embraces the black. One can also enter Homewood on the historic route that leads from East Liberty along Frankstown Avenue, following the north branch of the eighteenth-century Forbes Road. But there is still a third entry, by following Lemington Avenue in Lincoln to the top of Brushton Hill at Mohler Street. This is the only point in

Homewood, from Brushton Hill /*Maurice Tierney*

Pittsburgh where it is possible to see a neighborhood in its entirety, with every last house and garage. Looking down on Homewood, even the most prosaic traveler must think himself or herself a second Moses, or Balboa overlooking the Pacific.

The flat land of Homewood (sometimes known also as Brushton, a sub-district once served by a separate railroad station), so unusual in Pittsburgh and so perfect for building row houses, originally belonged to James Kelly, a civic-minded entrepreneur who was a major landowner also in Wilkinsburg, Point Breeze, and Edgewood before the Civil War. To finance a town here, Kelly borrowed from Thomas Mellon, who foreclosed on him after the Panic of 1873, and began to lay out row houses in strips parallel to Frankstown Road. The lots sold for about sixty-five dollars each and the homes for a few hundred dollars more. By 1900 or 1910 the entire valley was filled with these repetitive shapes. They were intended for Irish-immigrant railway workers, but some also went to blacks, the descendants of a small community that had estab-

Row houses, Kedron Street /*Courtesy* Pittsburgh Post-Gazette (*Harry Coughanour*)

lished the Homewood African Methodist Zion Church here in 1871. Some of those early settlers were well-to-do businessmen; others were jockeys or workers at the Homewood racetrack. The population of Homewood shifted from Irish to black during the Depression; the redevelopment of the Lower Hill forced hundreds of other black families into Homewood, and by 1960 it was a ghetto of 20,000.

Homewood's population is lower today, about 13,000, as those residents leave who can. The most ambitious attack on the problems of Homewood was the creation of the **East Hills** housing development (reached by Frankstown Road and the East Hills Shopping Center), an enclave east of Homewood-Brushton that replaced the Turner Dairy farm. Nearly 1,000 housing units were created here in the 1960s by ACTION-Housing, Inc., mainly by Pittsburgh architect Tasso Katselas, in garden apartments and townhouses that were laid out to achieve maximum privacy on their winding hillside streets. The development has worked well in architectural terms, but it was undermined in urban and social terms by the isolation of the site from all parts of the city except Homewood itself, and it switched from a racially mixed to a solidly black neighborhood. Two civic centers were established for the development. One was the **East Hills Elementary Magnet School** (2150 East Hills Dr.; Tasso Katselas, 1966), a loosely grouped series of two- and three-story pavilions, each articulated by a distinctive feature on its roof. Racially balanced, it is regarded by parents all over Pittsburgh as one of the best schools in the city. The other civic complex was the East Hills Shopping Center, a mall that has taken twenty years to get on its feet. Difficult to reach because of its hilltop—the Pittsburgh Acropolis complex again—and crippled by competi-

East Hills Elementary Magnet School /*Courtesy Tasso Katselas Associates (John Hobbs)*

tion from the glittering malls to the south and east, it bides its time, with many of its stores padlocked and vacant.

Vacancy is also a prime characteristic of Homewood today. Three of the four corners at the intersection of Frankstown Road and Braddock Avenue are simply fields, and once-crowded streets such as Tioga have virtually returned to a rural state. Homewood seems to have put its worst years behind it, however, and its prognosis for the future seems to be guardedly optimistic. There are a number of new, rent-subsidized apartments, and some good older blocks are being restored. The 7000 block of Bennett, for example, with its homes and lawns set on hillocks, rivals any other middle-class neighborhood in the city. Homewood preserves a number of buildings by Frederick Scheibler: his **Syria, Kismet,** and **Nelda Apartments** at the southwest corner of Bennett and N. Braddock enhance the street with their two-story porches arranged like Greek temple fronts. Scheibler also built two terraces in Homewood: **Meado'cots,** at the corner of Madeira and Rosedale streets, and **Inglenook Place.** Homewood has several handsome public buildings: the **Carnegie Library of Pittsburgh—Homewood Branch** at the corner of Hamilton and Lang avenues is one of the most elegant libraries in the city. The parish church of Homewood, **Holy Rosary** (7160 Kelly, SE corner Lang; 1930), has the best facade of Ralph Adams Cram's three churches in Pittsburgh and an austerely dramatic Catalan Gothic nave. If Homewood regains its urban health, it will be in part because of the more generous instincts that architects or patrons such as Scheibler, Carnegie, and Cram showed toward it. The rest of Homewood was built as cheaply as traffic would bear, and a bad urban legacy, like a good one, will endure for years.

Left: The Kismet and Nelda apartments, Bennett Street /*Franklin Toker* ▪ *Right:* Holy Rosary Church (Ralph Adams Cram, architect) /*Maurice Tierney*

Point Breeze

The last three miles of Penn Avenue cut broad and straight toward Wilkins-burg. In **Point Breeze,** just a few blocks from Homewood, Penn Avenue became one of the most opulent millionaire rows of nineteenth-century America. Armstrong, Heinz, Frick, and Westinghouse—the kings of cork, pickles, coke, and electricity—lived here; so did Andrew Carnegie, his mother, his brother, and a half-dozen partners. Lillian Russell was here, and the Thaws and R. B. Mellon lived around the corner, making about three dozen millionaires in all. The area was known alternately as Point Breeze or Homewood. Point Breeze was the name of a tavern that stood from 1800 to 1886 at the crossing of Penn and Fifth avenues. "Homewood" was the estate of 650 acres (today cut up into Homewood Cemetery and Frick Park), where Judge William Wilkins lived in a Greek Revival mansion that was not much smaller than the White House.[4]

Point Breeze was remote from Pittsburgh when Wilkins moved there in 1836, but by 1860 it was being served by two railroad stations and was the ideal location for Pittsburgh businessmen. Among the first to arrive was Andrew Carnegie, in 1862, with a residence on Homewood Avenue not far away from Judge Wilkins. When the aristocratic Wilkins died in June 1865, his mansion was ostentatiously taken over by Carnegie's partner and mentor, the coal and oil king William Coleman, who two years later became father-in-law to Carnegie's younger brother Tom. The move decisively signaled the transfer of power in Pittsburgh from the pioneer aristocracy to the new iron-and-steel elite.

The flowering of Point Breeze was both glorious and shortlived. The Westinghouse, Heinz, and Tom Carnegie estates (Andrew had left for New York in 1867) were cut up in the 1920s; the Mellon, Thaw, and Armstrong

---

4. William Wilkins (1779–1865) was a judge, a diplomat, and a banker in addition to being president of the Greensburg Pike. He was a U.S. Senator and Representative, Minister to Russia, and Secretary of War in President Tyler's cabinet. His brother-in-law was George Mifflin Dallas, the Vice-President under Polk. Wilkins bought his land in 1832 and completed Homewood four years later. He claimed to have designed the mansion himself, although the plan was evidently assimilated from several plates in Minard Lafever's *Modern Builder's Guide* of 1833, and a professional architect must have at least consulted on the project. Wilkins knew three good architects: John Chislett of Pittsburgh; John Haviland of Philadelphia, who in 1834 had built the Bank of Pittsburgh, of which Wilkins was the leading director; and Robert Mills, the chief federal architect at the time Wilkins was in the cabinet. There seem to have been several models for this huge house: its conceptual model was The Hermitage, the mansion built outside Nashville by Wilkins's political mentor, Andrew Jackson. The name "Homewood" was taken from the estate of Charles Carroll, Jr., in Baltimore, but Wilkins specifically likened his house to Thomas Jefferson's Monticello. Like Monticello, Homewood was filled with gadgets. The house played a crucial role in the architectural and social history of Pittsburgh, and it remained an object of curiosity even after it was replaced in 1924 by a dozen brick homes at the intersection of Edgerton and Murtland.

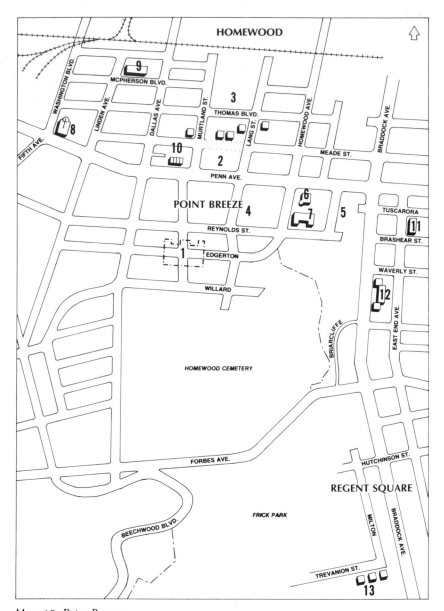

Map 19. Point Breeze

1 Site of Wilkins's "Homewood"
2 Site of Heinz's "Greenlawn"
3 Site of George Westinghouse House
4 Site of Andrew Carnegie House
5 Site of Thomas Carnegie House

6 H. C. Frick's "Clayton"
7 Frick Art Museum
8 Point Breeze Presbyterian Church
9 Linwood Apts.
10 Parkstone Dwellings

11 201 East End Ave.
12 Old Heidelberg Apts.
13 7506–7510 Trevanion St.

Clayton, the Henry Clay Frick House
/*Franklin Toker*

houses fell in the 1940s and 1950s. Today the uninitiated will see almost nothing of the Gilded Age on Penn Avenue apart from H. C. Frick's house and two lesser castles that are used by evangelical churches. With a little detective work, however, one can quickly discover where other estates used to be: a dozen cul-de-sacs record the location of once-private driveways, while other estates are recorded by wrought-iron fences (the one on the north side of Penn between N. Murtland and N. Lang marks the front of the Heinz estate, "Greenlawn"). The elaborate Queen Anne shingled cottage at 209 N. Lang was used by the Heinz estate manager. The cinderblock—but elegant—structure at 7033 Meade Place is the garage in which Heinz stored his prize fleet of limousines, and the odd house at 7035 Meade is his former museum of watches and curios. The Shingle Style house at 222 Carnegie Place was Tom and Lucy Carnegie's carriage house. The Westinghouse mansion, "Solitude," has become Westinghouse Park, and there remains no sign of the private well that Westinghouse drilled 1,600 feet deep to supply his house with natural gas (he became so fascinated with it that he invented the gas meter and founded the Equitable Gas Company). But two splendid houses that Westinghouse built as gifts do survive. Both are Prairie School designs, although overlaid with Renaissance detailing. Their materials are long Roman bricks of the type Frank Lloyd Wright preferred in his contemporary houses in the Chicago suburbs. The home Westinghouse gave his son is at **201 N. Murtland;** the mansion he gave his personal physician stands at **7100 Thomas.**

Just one Point Breeze mansion survives in all its glory today: Henry Clay Frick's **"Clayton"** (7200 Penn Ave., SE corner S. Homewood), which is now being prepared as a public museum of his life. (The same estate houses the **Frick Art Museum,** a Brunelleschian villa of Alabama limestone with an intimate collection of Renaissance panels and bronzes and eighteenth-century canvases.) It is not by coincidence that "Clayton" stands while all the other mansions have fallen, for few men in America gave more thought to their public persona than Frick. His daughter Helen also spent most of her ninety-six years (she died in the house in 1984) polishing his memory until it shone with flawless luster. The house remains today exactly as it was when Frick left Pittsburgh for his greater mansion in New York early in the century. At its core is an Italianate villa of around 1870 that Frick bought in 1882 and transformed into a French château eleven years later. With Judge Wilkins dead and Andrew Carnegie in residence in New York and Scotland, Frick was lord of Point Breeze. He began to buy large parcels of the Wilkins estate, beginning at his back door on Reynolds Street and extending south through the gully of Nine-Mile Run, until he had acquired nearly 500 acres. Around 1900 Frick commissioned Daniel Burnham to design an art gallery for the Beechwood Boulevard side of the estate, but in the end Frick took his Raphael and his Bellinis, Holbeins, and Rembrandts to New York, saying that Pittsburgh's smoke would damage them. No one seems to have asked who contributed more to the smoke than the "King of Coke" himself. Today Frick's estate is the virgin forest of **Frick Park.** The rustic but noble pavilions at the park entrances on Beechwood Boulevard, Forbes Avenue, and Reynolds Street are by the Beaux Arts master John Russell Pope and date from the extension of the park by Helen Frick in 1935.

There are no millionaires among the 4,500 residents of Point Breeze today, but it is a flourishing, racially balanced community that, along with the adjacent district of Regent Square, is one of the most attractive and accessible areas in Pittsburgh for younger homeowners. The focus of restoration and preservation efforts in Point Breeze is not on the millionaire row but on the western half of the neighborhood, on such architecturally varied streets as Linden, Reynolds, Hastings, and Gettysburg, and on McPherson and Thomas boulevards, which were laid out in imitation of Baron Haussmann's Paris in 1885. In this latter sector stand a half-dozen works by Frederick Scheibler, allowing a visitor to gain insights into early Modern architecture that can be had in only a few other neighborhoods in the country. The appropriate beginning in this study would be the **Linwood Apartments** (6801 McPherson, NE corner N. Linden; 1907), a three-story brick structure coated in Portland cement. It is constructed without ornament and has an unmistakable kinship with the contemporary Viennese work of Joseph Maria Olbrich and Adolph Loos. The broad white planes and their contrast with the wood trim also recall the contemporary work of Frank Lloyd Wright. Peculiar to Scheibler, however, and much in keeping with Pittsburgh, is the expression of structure: the bowing of the two-story wooden piers holding the balconies,

Left: Old Heidelberg Apartments (Frederick Scheibler, architect) */Franklin Toker* ▪
Right: Parkstone Dwellings, Penn Avenue */Franklin Toker*

the concealed/revealed steel beams sunk into the soffit of the ground-floor porches, and the graphic detail of the dowel-ends protruding through the piers, as though they were ready to slip.

The same concern for mass, projection, and detail animates two more Scheibler apartments in Point Breeze: **201 East End Avenue** (SE corner Tuscarora; 1907) and the masterly **Old Heidelberg Apartments** (401–423 S. Braddock, SE corner Waverly; 1905, with additions of 1908). The East End block is less daring than the Linwood because of the "safer" pediments over the porches and the conventional Art Nouveau detail of the wave motif over the central door. Scheibler's skill as a decorator is more apparent in the Old Heidelberg block, with its art glass, mushroom wall reliefs, and stumpy piers on the third floor, with heart-shaped capitals borrowed from Olbrich.

The transition in Scheibler's work from a romantic rationalist to a rational romanticist can be followed in three other groups of his work in Point Breeze. These are a three-unit row house of 1913, around the corner from the Old Heidelberg, at **420–422 East End Avenue;** two houses of around 1910 and 1916, at **579** and **592 Briarcliffe Road,** just west of the intersection of Forbes and Braddock avenues; and three detached cottages at **7506, 7508,** and **7510 Trevanion Street** in the Regent Square/Swissvale neighborhood, constructed in 1905, 1917, and 1915–16, respectively. These intermediate designs prepare us, but only in part, for the overt picturesqueness of Scheibler's last major work, **Parkstone Dwellings** (6937–6943 Penn, near NW corner N. Murtland; 1922). The irregularly coursed schist walls, the exaggerated slope of the slate roof, and the pronounced decoration (giant mushrooms at the doors, mosaic "rugs" hanging from the porches) at Parkstone give evidence of Scheibler's growing discomfort with the Modern Movement. By 1922 Pittsburgh's leading Modernist seems to have looked into the future—and decided not to join it.

Wilkinsburg, Edgewood, and Swissvale

A borough of about 25,000 people symmetrically disposed on both sides of the last stretch of Penn Avenue, **Wilkinsburg** is a residential town so similar to the contiguous parts of Pittsburgh that it, like Edgewood and Swissvale beyond, is a suburb in a legal sense only. The area has been identified by four names in its bicentennial history: "Jewstown," after Levy Andrew Levy purchased almost the entire area in his warrant for 266 acres in 1765; "Rippeyville," from the name of its leading tavern-keeper two decades later; "McNairstown," after Colonel Dunning McNair laid it out as a village in 1790; and Wilkinsburg, when it incorporated as a borough in 1887. Its best years were probably in the 1920s and 1930s, when it had a large commuter population on the Pennsylvania Railroad line. It declined along with the railroad but is now in a marked revival as a new generation of Pittsburghers discovers its low-cost housing, particularly after the busway restored its attractiveness as a commuter town in 1983.

Wilkinsburg is a middle-class and working-class town, evenly split between its white and black residents. The town has little great architecture, but it is conservative enough to have preserved a dozen vernacular "monuments" that would have been torn down elsewhere. Among them is **Scotty's Diner** (7714 Penn, actually within the Pittsburgh city limits), the last functioning streamlined diner in the city; a Classical Revival train station; a set of neocolonial borough buildings and post office; a half-dozen good commercial buildings in the downtown; and **The Crescent** (724–734 Kelly Ave., south of Rebecca), an ambitious sequence of commercial and housing units that were tied together around 1904 by an amateur designer who had evidently seen a photograph of the crescents of London or Bath.

North of Penn Avenue, on the slopes of the Wilkinsburg Hill, stand some good survivals of Victorian housing. One of the more memorable is the **Gibbs Rest Home** (1300 Wood, NE corner Hill St.), a standard Colonial Revival mansion of around 1900 with a semicircular portico of outlandish scale. Up the hill, at 1318 Singer Place, stands the **John Singer House** of around 1865. This is the prime Gothic Revival home in Pittsburgh; and, along with William Coleman's takeover of the Wilkins mansion, it was a striking indication of the drive to ostentation of the iron-and-steel elite. John Singer made his fortune in Singer, Nimick & Company and chose to spend it in baronial splendor on a thirty-acre estate with this mournful castle. The house cost $75,000—the price of three good-sized churches at mid-century—and contained eighteen rooms and two bathrooms, as well as a private chapel that is now gone. There is a tradition that Joseph W. Kerr was the architect, although all features of the plan and elevations could easily have been derived from the Victorian patternbooks of architects such as Isaac Hobbs or Samuel Sloan, or from the fashionable *Godey's Lady's Book and Magazine*. The material is sandstone, hammer

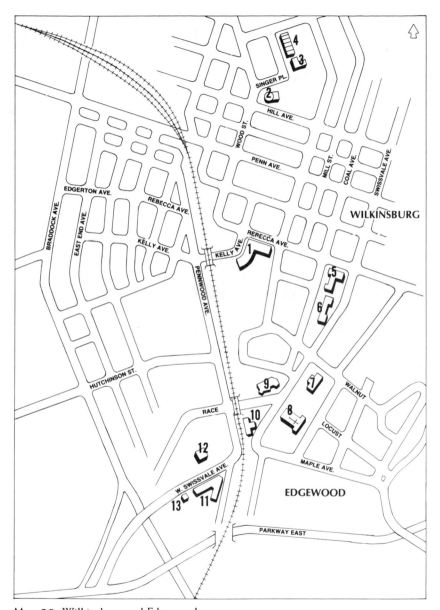

Map 20. Wilkinsburg and Edgewood

1 The Crescent
2 Gibbs Rest Home
3 Singer House
4 1330–1368 Singer Place
5 Rebecca House
6 Jane Holmes Residence
7 Western Pa. School for the Deaf

8 Edgewood Presbyterian Church
9 Edgewood Municipal Bldg.
10 Edgewood RR Station
11 Edgewood Club/Mellor Library
12 Gardner-Bailey House
13 Grubbs-Kerr House

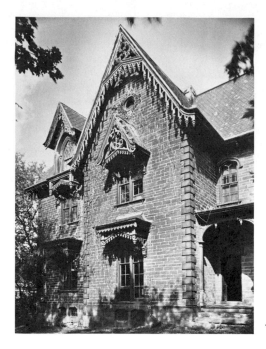

The Singer House /*Maurice Tierney*

dressed and regularly coursed, with finely polished ashlar blocks as quoins. The roof is slate, in fish-scale and variegated designs; the bargeboards drip almost menacingly with spindled lacework.

Conservative and tranquil by comparison is the neighboring row of twenty homes by Frederick Scheibler at **1330–1368 Singer Place,** from 1913–14. Effective also against the slope of the Wilkinsburg Hill is a wood frame Gothic Revival villa of the 1860s at **813 Hill Avenue** (NE corner Mill) that was probably copied from designs of Isaac Hobbs. The emphasis on struts, brackets, braces, and eaves characterizes the Stick Style mansions that were coming into prominence in the 1860s and 1870s in Newport and the watering holes of the East Coast.

At the end of its commercial strip in Wilkinsburg, Penn Avenue intersects Ardmore Boulevard and begins a long climb up Wilkinsburg Hill, where it enters the borough of Churchill and changes its name and character to become a suburban highway. Swissvale Avenue, intersecting Penn just before this fork, becomes the spine road for the southern half of Wilkinsburg and its link to **Edgewood** and **Swissvale.** Here is another set of impressive civic monuments: **Rebecca House** and the **Jane Holmes Residence** (900 Rebecca and 441 Swissvale Aves., respectively; the first definitely and the second probably designed by Henry Moser, 1871 and 1882), which are adjoining old people's homes of dignity. They are both in the Italianate style, with the broad verandahs, spreading oaks, and extensive lawns that one expects of their building type. A block south, within the boundaries of Edgewood Borough,

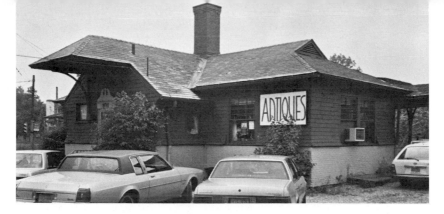

Edgewood Railroad Station (Frank Furness, architect) /*Franklin Toker*

stands the **Western Pennsylvania School for the Deaf** (SE corner Swissvale & Walnut; Alden & Harlow, 1903), a Beaux Arts building with eight overscaled Ionic columns and a top-heavy porch. South of them is the civic center of Edgewood, consisting of the **Edgewood Presbyterian Church** of 1918, an unusual medieval German *Westwerk* of two huge towers with a bridge-arch between them; an elegant war memorial; and the **Edgewood Municipal Building** (Clifford Lake, 1938), a picturesque grouping of a Cotswold-style tower and outbuildings.

Adjacent to the war memorial stands the Shingle Style **Edgewood Railroad Station** (101 Swissvale Ave., at the Conrail tracks; 1905), now a realty office and an antique shop. This was the real heart of the community that from 1864 to 1964 sent half its menfolk to work in the Golden Triangle by train each day. According to a note in the *Philadelphia Inquirer* in 1902, the author of this modest structure was Frank Furness, and there is little reason to doubt it. Furness built scores of suburban railroad stations, as well as central stations in Philadelphia and Pittsburgh. Even with a tiny budget, and in the years of his decline, he was incapable of delivering a dull building. Admirable here is the tight symmetry of the plan, the way in which the shingles of the upper wall are battered out from the bricks of the lower wall, and the complex rake of the shingled roof. Even the support system for the long shed at trackside goes far beyond what was demanded of Furness. It consists of eight sets of back-to-

The Edgewood Club and C. C. Mellor Library /*Franklin Toker*

back iron quadrant arches—precisely the kind of detail Furness had soaked up
from his reading of Eugène-Emmanuel Viollet-le-Duc's *Entretiens sur l'Architecture*
thirty years before. What a pleasure to discover a surviving building after all
else has gone by the master who had such influence on Pittsburgh architecture
in the late nineteenth century.

The last of the public monuments of Edgewood is the **Edgewood Club/
C. C. Mellor Library** (Edward B. Lee, 1916), across the tracks at the southwest corner of W. Swissvale and Pennwood avenues. Diminutive in size, it
combines a library, a community center, and a swimming and tennis club with
a Mediterranean sophistication appropriate to a wealthy suburb. Exactly fitted
to its triangular plot, the building is a white stucco mass held low to the
ground, with a bright Spanish tile roof and a pergola and a line of stubby
columns on the Swissvale Avenue side—altogether one of the best public
buildings in the city.

Edgewood contains many of the finest homes in Pittsburgh, set on lush side
streets named Locust, Maple, Hawthorne, and Beech. It is the best place in the
city to study, or to buy, Shingle Style homes of the 1890s, or infill houses in a
number of revival modes that were added in the 1910s and 1920s. Three fine
homes of the early twentieth century on Maple Avenue provide a sample of
Edgewood's riches: at **200 Maple,** a distinctive Prairie School house of fine
sober lines and characteristic eaves; at **361 Maple,** an imposing Georgian
Revival mansion; at **431 Maple,** a Craftsman-style low stucco house with
many of the features of Edward Lee's Edgewood Club.

The half of Edgewood that lies west of the railroad is older than the eastern
half. It was laid out in 1864 by John Grazier on land purchased from James
Kelly, with a plan designed to maximize the romantic vistas of its curving
streets. W. Swissvale Avenue ends here with two dozen homes that make it
one of the most handsome Victorian streets in the city. Particularly outstanding is the **Gardner-Bailey House** (124 W. Swissvale) of 1864, an Italianate
farmhouse of flush wood siding carrying a delightful square cupola that gives it
an air of majesty far beyond its modest scale, and the **Grubbs-Kerr House**
(235 W. Swissvale), a board-and-batten home from the time of the Civil War.

At the foot of W. Swissvale Avenue is an intersection with the Parkway East,
affording quick access either to the Golden Triangle to the west or to the
eastern suburbs of Pittsburgh. Braddock Avenue also cuts through Nine-Mile
Run here and links Edgewood to Swissvale. The latter, a residential-industrial
town of 13,000, has as its chief treasure George Westinghouse's huge brick and
concrete **Union Switch & Signal** (original complex 1886; rebuilt 1917), at the
intersection of Braddock Avenue and the Conrail tracks. Swissvale thus marks
a transition point between the bedroom suburbs of the Pennsylvania Railroad
line and the industrial towns of Homestead, Rankin, Braddock, McKeesport,
Duquesne, and Clairton, which extend out from Pittsburgh in a string along
the Monongahela River.

The Civic Arena /*Courtesy Public Auditorium Authority of Pittsburgh & Allegheny County* (*Ken Balzer*)

Fifth Avenue and the Streetcar Suburbs

Just as Penn Avenue and the railroad combined to create Wilkinsburg, Point Breeze, and East Liberty, so Fifth Avenue and the streetcar gave birth to the four important inner-city suburbs of Oakland and The Hill, Shadyside, and Squirrel Hill. The railroad and streetcar suburbs developed according to two different patterns. Penn Avenue became a thoroughfare through the inevitability of geography; Fifth Avenue became one by fiat. It was at first an unconnected sequence of purely local streets: Fifth Avenue in the Golden Triangle; Beelen's, Watson's, and Braddock's Field roads in Uptown; and Pennsylvania Avenue in Oakland. Not until the mid-nineteenth century did these streets amalgamate into the Farmers' and Mechanics' Turnpike from the Golden Triangle to Point Breeze. Fifth Avenue was also the preeminent streetcar route in Pittsburgh. In the 1840s it played host to the omnibus service from the Golden Triangle to The Hill, and it was later the route for the horsecar service of 1859 to Oakland, which was extended in 1872 to Shadyside and East Liberty. In 1889 Fifth Avenue was used by the steam-driven cablecars to Point Breeze and in 1892 by the electric trolley to Shadyside and East Liberty, which reached Point Breeze in 1896. The four streetcar suburbs created along Fifth Avenue all had become part of Pittsburgh by 1867, but they pursued separate destinies. Oakland became a civic center, The Hill became black, Shadyside WASP, and Squirrel Hill heavily Jewish. The latter three "suburbs" continue to focus internally on their residents rather than reach outward to the city as a whole. They defy the admonition of John Donne and remain islands entire of themselves.

The Hill, Uptown, and The Bluff

There are so many memories stored in **The Hill** that its existence in the mind is as vivid as the physical reality of its 15,000 inhabitants and its long plateau set between the Golden Triangle and Oakland. Pittsburgh's writers and artists, including Willa Cather, have recorded it; Stephen Foster (who was taken to a black church on The Hill as a child) had his main encounter with black life there; and television's "Hill Street Blues," which was conceived by a producer and actors trained in Pittsburgh, attempted an electronic facsimile of it. Like Pittsburgh's other streetcar suburbs, The Hill has no industry and plays no significant role in commerce beyond its local retail stores. The only product manufactured there today is the smoked fish that is still cured in wood-fed ovens at Cantor and Smolar's on Bedford Avenue. What The Hill has produced, and abundantly, is people. Such main-stage entertainers as Adolph Menjou, Lena Horne, Billy Eckstine, Erroll Garner, Art Blakey, and Oscar Levant got their start in The Hill. O. Henry lived here too, when he was a journalist for the Pittsburgh newspapers. It was a waystop for almost all the ethnic groups in Pittsburgh, particularly the Germans, Italians, Russians, Slovaks, Armenians, Syrians, Lebanese, Greeks, and Chinese, and it was the cradle for two groups who lived here for generations: Pittsburgh's blacks, now numbering 100,000, and its Jews, about one-third that number. This social diversity always gave The Hill a radical strain, first as a center of Abolitionist sympathies, later as a hotbed of Socialism. Oral tradition insists that both David Ben-Gurion and Leon Trotsky proselytized for their causes on The Hill.

The Hill gave hospitality to so many groups because within the ridge that

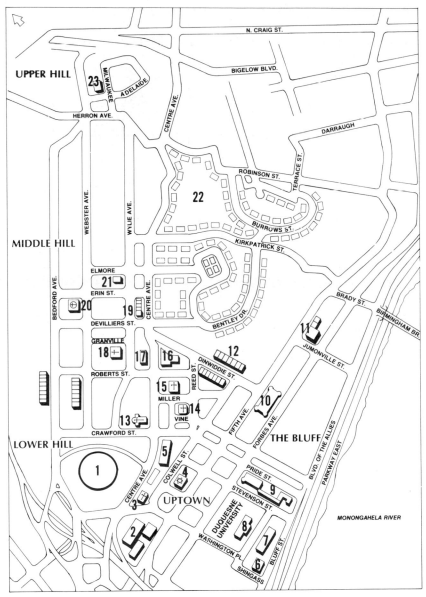

Map 21. The Hill, Uptown, and The Bluff

1 Civic Arena
2 Chatham Center
3 Epiphany Church
4 Beth Hamedrash Synagogue
5 Washington Plaza Apts.
6 Duquesne Univ. Old Main
7 Mellon Hall of Science
8 Duquesne Univ. Union

9 Mercy Hospital
10 Fifth Ave. High School
11 2000–2004 Fifth Ave.
12 Townhouses, Dinwiddie St.
13 St. Benedict the Moor Church
14 St. Michael's Cathedral
15 Miller Street Baptist Church
16 Hill/Phoenix Shopping Center

17 Hill House
18 Mount Rose Baptist
   Church
19 New Granada Theater
20 Zion Hill Baptist Church
21 Crawford Grill
22 Terrace Village
23 Madison School

stretches two miles from the Golden Triangle to Oakland are several little hills and the remnants of three isolated villages. On the Lower Hill was Hayti, a village of runaway slaves that had a black church by 1818; on the Middle Hill—an amalgam of Gazzam's, Goat, and Ruch's hills—was Lacyville; and on the Upper Hill (known also as Coal, Quarry, or Herron's hills) was Minersville. For its first hundred years The Hill was mainly populated by Germans and Scotch-Irish. It changed to Eastern and Central European, particularly Jewish, in the 1880s and became entirely black in the 1940s. The blacks who live there now represent a community that appeared at the start of Pittsburgh—in the British army that took Fort DuQuesne in 1758. Because of western Pennsylvania's Virginia connection, there were also black slaves in Pittsburgh—150 appeared in the census of 1790—but all were free within a generation. The black community here went on to become one of the most stable in the United States. By the early twentieth century it included businessmen, small manufacturers, and about 1,600 steelworkers; the Pittsburgh *Courier* was the leading black newspaper in the country. Today, a century and a half after they first established themselves on The Hill, Pittsburgh's blacks still regard it as the heart of a community that has spread out to a score of urban and suburban neighborhoods.

The Lower Hill

The Hill today retains its old configuration of three basic subdistricts: the **Lower Hill** from Grant to Crawford Street, now entirely redeveloped; the **Middle Hill** from Crawford to Herron Avenue, near Pitt; and the **Upper Hill,** from Herron to Bigelow Boulevard. The reconstruction of the Lower Hill began in 1955 with $17 million in federal grants. In an area of 100 acres, 1,300 buildings housing 413 businesses and 8,000 residents (a majority of them black) were displaced in an attempt to extend the revitalization of the adjacent Golden Triangle. Even were one to overlook the devastating social impact of the Lower Hill redevelopment, its success could only be judged as minor. The new complex failed to graft on to the Golden Triangle because of the intrusion of the Crosstown Expressway and the misalignment of the street grids of the Golden Triangle and The Hill. Some bad luck also dogged the Lower Hill redevelopment, particularly the bankruptcy of William Zeckendorf, one of its major supporters, and the decision by the Heinz foundations to locate their new concert hall in the Triangle rather than on The Hill. But the major cause of its failure was the animosity between the developers and the black community. When that animosity boiled over as part of the nationwide racial riots of 1968, Pittsburgh's dream of a cultural Acropolis on the Lower Hill ended.

All that is left of the old Lower Hill today is one building: **Epiphany Church** (SE corner Centre Ave. & Washington Place; Edward Stotz, 1903;

interior decoration by John Comes), a strongly articulated Romanesque Revival structure in deep red brick with plentiful terra-cotta trim outside and a richly frescoed interior. (Two blocks east of it stands another spiritual center, the small **Beth Hamedrash Hagodol Synagogue** at 1230 Colwell Street, a 1960s building that amalgamated several of the two dozen congregations formerly scattered over The Hill.) The heart of the Lower Hill today is the shimmering **Civic Arena** (Mitchell & Ritchey, architects; Ammann & Whitney and Robert Zern, engineers; 1962). This extraordinary building had its origins in the late 1940s, with Edgar Kaufmann's enthusiasm for summer opera. It began as a project for a cable-supported opera tent that would have opened like a Japanese fan, and evolved into an opera hall with a retractable dome for summer performances in the open air. After a decade of false starts, the construction of the Civic Arena was linked to an older project for the clearance of the Lower Hill. It opened in 1962 with a stainless-steel dome 415 feet in diameter (the world's largest at the time) composed of eight sections that are supported by a cantilevered tripod—technically a space-frame box girder—that holds six of the sections when they are swiveled back. The base of the dome is bound with an enormous ring girder of concrete and buttressed by diagonal struts. Each of its sections weighs 220 tons; all six can be opened in a little over two minutes. The capacity of the building is 18,000. The opera hall is now mainly devoted to sports events and popular concerts (which it accommodates well) because of the difficulty of rigging stage sets in a roofless structure. It is a pity that the failure of the development around it denied the Civic Arena the acclaim it deserved as one of the triumphs of engineering in the postwar period. Its failure to do so does, however, underline the fact that great architecture demands more than the solution of technical problems.

Most of the Lower Hill is taken up today by a proverbial sea of parking lots around the Civic Arena, although another half-dozen new buildings stand nearby. Two famous names in the late International School were involved in their design: William Lescaze at **Chatham Center** (NW corner Washington Place & Fifth Ave., 1966; Chatham II tower added by Burt Hill Kosar Rittelmann, 1981), an apartment block and combination office building and hotel (now the Hyatt Pittsburgh), and I. M. Pei at the **Washington Plaza Apartments** (SW corner Centre Ave. & Crawford St.; with Deeter & Ritchey, 1964). Efficiently planned and beautifully textured in poured concrete, this tower of 400 units is the epitome of the refined design of the 1960s, but it looks forlorn without the two other projected towers, which were aborted by the Zeckendorf bankruptcy in 1962.

Uptown

The **Uptown** district is a trough, one and a half miles in length, that separates

The Hill from The Bluff. The main corridor between the Triangle and Oakland, it consists of hundreds of nineteenth-century row houses on Fifth and Forbes avenues and their cross-streets. To these were added several scores of commercial blocks, which by the first half of the twentieth century accommodated more wholesale distributors (mainly of dry goods) than any similar complex between New York and Chicago. Uptown decayed in the 1950s and 1960s, along with the decline of The Hill and of the wholesale trade itself; today, under the new banner of the Midtown Corridor, it has joined in the city's urban revitalization. The late nineteenth-century architecture on the four long blocks of Fifth Avenue between Chatham Center and Pride Street is excellent, and good private homes stand farther east on Fifth Avenue between Dinwiddie and Jumonville streets, with a once-fine row of Queen Anne townhouses on the 200 block of Dinwiddie. Particularly elegant are three homes at **2000–2004 Fifth Avenue** (SE corner Jumonville): a Romanesque Revival and a High Victorian Gothic townhouse next to the elaborate former Methodist Episcopal Deaconess' Home of about 1890.

Along with the homes, Uptown has an imposing public structure in **Fifth Avenue High School** (1800 Fifth, opposite Dinwiddie; Edward Stotz, 1894), a handsome Romanesque/Gothic Revival structure in orange brick with characteristic Ruskinian diaper work. Its construction was an attempt to reach out to at least a part of Pittsburgh's foreign-born population, since it was built in a ward populated entirely by immigrants. It was the first fireproof school in Pittsburgh and is still in excellent condition, recycled now into a retail mall called Uptown Plaza. With the revival of the school and some of its adjacent homes and the transformation of many of the storefronts of lower Fifth Avenue into law offices, Uptown may reassume its old status as the proud link between the Golden Triangle and Oakland.

Renovated Victorian storefronts
on Fifth Avenue, Uptown
/Franklin Toker

Mellon Hall of Science (Ludwig Mies van der Rohe, architect), Duquesne University /*Courtesy Duquesne University (Hedrich-Blessing)*

The Bluff

First known as Ayer's or Boyd's Hill, **The Bluff** is a high plateau 1.5 miles long with such a commanding view of the Monongahela River that several British officers preferred it to The Point as the site for Fort Pitt. Today it is a crowded neighborhood of several thousand people that conjoins the early settlements of Pipetown, Riceville, and Soho. The Bluff's street grid was laid out on top of the plateau around 1830, and the majority of its houses date from the three following decades. The district enjoyed the services of the Fort Pitt Incline from Second Avenue up to Bluff Street from 1882 to the 1930s. For over a century The Bluff has been home to **Mercy Hospital** (Blvd. of the Allies, Stevenson, Locust, & Pride Sts.). The original hospital block that the architect or builder Haden Smith constructed in 1848 was destroyed in 1982, but Mercy's remaining Second Empire and High Victorian Gothic buildings form a handsome complex, including an anatomical theater of 1906.

The westernmost portion of The Bluff is occupied by **Duquesne University,** established here in 1878 by the German-based Fathers of the Holy Ghost. Today it educates approximately 6,000 undergraduate and graduate students and is distinguished for its liberal arts and schools of law and communications. Three campus buildings are particularly outstanding: **Old Main,** a dramatic six-story High Victorian Gothic brick block of the 1880s; the **Richard King Mellon Hall of Science** (Ludwig Mies van der Rohe, 1968), a standard Miesian temple in black steel; and the **Duquesne University Union** (Paul Schweikher, 1967), a gracious poured-cement structure with a series of wraparound ramps outside and several elegant and imaginatively lit volumes inside.

Conkling Street, on the Middle Hill
/*Franklin Toker*

The Middle Hill

The **Middle Hill** extends a mile and a half from Crawford Street to Herron Avenue along the three long residential streets of Wylie, Webster, and Bedford and a commercial strip on Centre Avenue. As the only place in Pittsburgh with views of both the Allegheny and the Monongahela valleys, it was destined to be a fine residential suburb, and until the 1840s it was parceled into a dozen estates with handsome Greek Revival mansions. It received a regular street pattern and several hundred townhouses just before and after the Civil War. A census taken in 1877 listed 300 professional people—doctors, lawyers, and judges among them—as residents in the Middle Hill before it lost its social standing with the arrival of thousands of Central and Eastern European immigrants. Decayed now, and with some gaps between them, the townhouses in which the old families lived are still handsome. Among the best preserved groups are the Italianate homes on Webster Avenue near Roberts Street (these were built by Thomas Mellon, who lived there in the 1850s) and the High Victorian Gothic rows nearby on Bedford Avenue. Incongruous, but in their odd way a sign of the nascent revival of the Middle Hill, are the hundred suburban-style ranch houses constructed in the 1970s on Roberts Street and in other pockets on The Hill. Fortunately, the newer homes are townhouses that are more respectful of their context.

The Middle Hill retains its significant old public monuments as well. The most striking of these is **St. Benedict the Moor Roman Catholic Church** (NE corner Crawford & Centre; Henry Moser, 1895). This elaborate Gothic Revival structure was built for the German-based Holy Trinity parish; its name was changed to St. Bridgid's when the parish became Irish and then changed again in 1971 by its black parishioners. A block and a half to the southeast is the picturesque **St. Michael's Russian Orthodox Cathedral** (43 Reed, NE corner Vine; 1903 and 1910), with its high flight of wooden steps and

Left: St. Michael's Russian Orthodox Cathedral, Reed Street */Franklin Toker* ▪ *Right:* Zion Hill Baptist Church */Franklin Toker*

bejeweled interior. In the same district are a half-dozen old synagogues, easily identified by their Hebrew cornerstones, that now serve the black community. Three of the most interesting are the **Miller Street Baptist Church** (23–25 Miller, opposite Foreside Place), the old Beth David/Shaaray Tefillah Synagogue; the **Mount Rose Baptist Church** five blocks to the north (1845 Wylie Ave., NW corner Granville; 1911), the former Machsikei Hadas Synagogue, a tall, square building that clearly owes more than a little to the Baroque fortress synagogues of seventeenth-century Poland; and the monumental domed **Zion Hill Baptist Church** (2043 Webster Ave., NW corner Erin, 1920), the former Kether Torah/Agudas Achim Synagogue—all congregations that migrated long ago to Squirrel Hill or Highland Park.

The social and commercial center of The Hill has for generations been the dozen blocks between Roberts and Kirkpatrick on Centre Avenue. Here stands **Hill House** (formerly the Irene Kaufmann Settlement; 1835 Centre Ave., near Roberts). Its old swimming pool by Joseph Urban has been destroyed, but it retains a classicizing auditorium of 1928 (possibly by Benno Janssen) and has added a handsome 1973 building of laminated wooden girders by Walter Roberts. The transition from the old to the new Hill is also manifested a few blocks to the east in the late-Victorian storefronts on the 2000 block of Centre Avenue and the nearby **Hill/Phoenix Shopping Center** of 1976 at Centre and Dinwiddie. The outstanding building of Centre Avenue is the **New Granada Theater** (NE corner Centre & DeVilliers; 1927), an elaborate Art Deco entertainment palace with a facade of enamelized metal

The New Granada Theater /*Franklin Toker*

plaques that once blazed with color. Now shuttered, it is a building full of memories of the vaudeville performers, Yiddish actors, and black entertainers who once held forth there. One block uphill is another communal monument that flourishes still: the **Crawford Grill** (2141 Wylie Ave., NW corner Elmore; 1917), a nationally renowned jazz club housed in a buff brick structure with an ornamental parapet and a modernized ground floor. Sarah Vaughan, Nat King Cole, and Miles Davis were among the hundreds of jazz performers who played here, and it was the cradle for Pittsburgh's own renaissance in jazz.

The commercial district of The Hill ends at Kirkpatrick Street, which leads south to Kennard Playground and the dozens of severe blocks that make up the federally subsidized housing project of **Terrace Village** (Marlier, Lee, Boyd, and Prack; 1937–41). Constructed at a cost of $14 million, this was the second largest of the pioneer federal housing projects in the United States, and it was important enough that President Roosevelt himself came to Pittsburgh to open part of it in 1940. Terrace Village was preceded by several years by Bedford Dwellings, a series of cul-de-sacs north of Bedford Avenue, whose original list of rules, unimaginable today, included lights out at 10:00 P.M., no pets, no signs, no laundry in the windows, and no cooking of cabbage. In all, 3,073 housing units in 155 buildings were constructed on The Hill, with an enlargement in the 1960s to 3,727 units in 191 buildings.

The three-story brick blocks on Bentley Drive and Burrows Street and uphill on Robinson Court near the Pitt campus are plain but not quite grim.

Terrace Village /*Franklin Toker*

They were largely modeled on the award-winning development of Chatham Village, and their severity is lightened by ornamental touches in the 1930s Moderne style. The landscape architect for the development was in fact a veteran of Chatham Village, Theodore Kohankie. Terrace Village was made by leveling Gazzam's, Goat, and Ruch's hills, which were cut down and used to fill in the deep valley that is now covered by Kirkpatrick Street. (This extensive earthmoving operation uprooted a coal seam in the three hills, which provided two years of free winter fuel for the project.) The earthmoving unfortunately created a barren site where the natural topography had once been rich and varied; it also made Terrace Village an enclave that was detached from the street grids of Oakland and The Hill, so that the development became an orphan to both of the older centers. Despite these drawbacks, the federal housing on The Hill is still serviceable after forty-five years and has already lasted three times the life span of St. Louis' Pruitt-Igoe housing development, which was dynamited after only fourteen years. Nonetheless, Terrace Village is a period piece from the Roosevelt years, and few would want to see such behemoths built again.

The Middle Hill ends with a valley at Herron Avenue, east of which is the middle-class black area of the **Upper Hill**—Lena Horne's old neighborhood. There are older nineteenth-century homes here too, particularly on Webster Avenue, with a dozen elaborate Romanesque Revival and Queen Anne mansions, but for the most part it is a district of small, well-tended homes from the early twentieth century. **Madison School** (NE corner Milwaukee & Orion Sts.; Ulysses Peoples, 1902), a peculiar amalgam of classical and Romanesque Revival motifs by an apprentice of Daniel Burnham, serves as its main landmark. At its peak is the Robert E. Williams Park and the Herron Hill Reservoir, bounded by Milwaukee and Adelaide streets, from which one can spy nearly every quarter of Pittsburgh. The progression from the slums of the Lower Hill to the tenement blocks of the Middle Hill and the green avenues of the Upper Hill is almost a diagrammatic outline of the American dream.

Shadyside

Shadyside has always seen itself as a village. The image was valid in the 1850s, when Shadyside was a settlement of twenty families on the Pennsylvania Railroad line. Today the village image is cultivated whether valid or not. The village myth has proved useful in protecting Shadyside from the fate of Homewood, which is its near-twin in size and topography. Even the heavy traffic that surrounds Shadyside on four sides has been turned to advantage, so that Fifth Avenue on the south, the Conrail tracks on the north, Penn Avenue on the east, and Neville and Craig streets on the west seem to form a protective cordon around it.

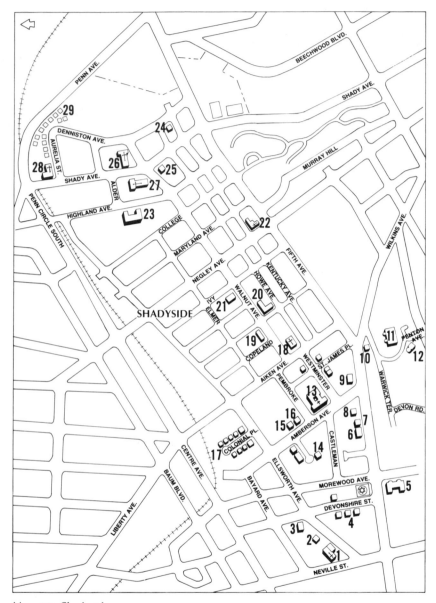

Map 22. Shadyside

1 Church of the Ascension
2 4841 Ellsworth Ave.
3 Hunt House
4 Childs House
5 Mudge House
6 Hillman House
7 Moreland-Hoffstot House
8 Gwinner-Harter House
9 McCook House
10 McClelland House, "Sunnyledge"

11 Clifford Heinz House
12 Steinberg House
13 Shadyside Presbyterian Church
14 David Aiken House
15 MacBeth House
16 Spencer House
17 Colonial Place
18 Shadyside Adventist Church
19 Minnetonka Bldg.
20 Bellefonte Place

21 Walnut Mall
22 Third Presbyterian Church
23 Highland Towers
24 424 Denniston Ave.
25 Sellers House
26 Calvary Episcopal Church
27 Sacred Heart Church
28 Christian Church of North America
29 Village of Shadyside

The future of Shadyside would have been quite different had its brief experiment with industry been a success. In 1792 the Alsatian immigrant George Anshutz teamed with Anthony Beelan and William Amberson of Shadyside to create the first blast furnace in Pittsburgh on what is now Amberson Avenue, but within a year or two it ceased operations because of a lack of wood and good iron ore. Shadyside might have industrialized with the coming of the Pennsylvania Railroad to its doorstep in 1852, but its land-holders—above all the Castleman/Aiken clan, which had owned most of it since 1780—carved their estates into a variety of lot sizes to prevent it: not all narrow, so that Shadyside would not join Bloomfield, Lawrenceville, and Homewood as worker suburbs, nor all grand, so its estates would not end up as the white elephants of Point Breeze. The transformation of Shadyside before and after the Civil War is still evident on the map today. The Aikens subdivided their land into a few broad estates in the 1850s, from Neville Avenue on the west to Aiken on the east; the McFarland land from Aiken Avenue to College Street was developed by Thomas Mellon and other entrepreneurs in narrow lots of 25 by 100 feet in the 1860s; and the east end of Shadyside, from College to Penn Avenue—easily recognized by a set of grids on deviant axes—was developed by another group of Pittsburgh businessmen, who had their estates there in the 1870s and 1880s.

Today, Shadyside counts 14,000 residents on 750 acres and is probably the wealthiest district per capita in Pittsburgh. It is the site of Sacred Heart Church, the most prominent Catholic parish in the city. Two wealthy Episcopal churches (Ascension and Calvary) mark its western and eastern boundaries, and two wealthier Presbyterian churches (Shadyside and Third Presbyterian) mark its mid-point. The latter two denominations are socially equal, although certain liturgical distinctions reflect their different origins. In the Lord's Prayer, the congregants at Shadyside Presbyterian forgive their debtors,

The Episcopal Church of the Ascension, Shadyside /*Franklin Toker*

for they are descended from merchants. The worshipers at Calvary derived their wealth from land, and so they forgive those who trespass against them.

The portal building to Shadyside on the west is the **Episcopal Church of the Ascension** (NE corner Ellsworth Ave. & N. Neville St.; William Halsey Wood, 1898), an imposing mass of irregularly coursed sandstone that is dominated by an enormous Tudor Gothic tower. Alongside the tower is a long nave, sumptuously articulated in an open timberwork roof and enriched by elegant side aisles and subsidiary chapels. East of the church, Shadyside displays one of the better collections of Victorian domestic architecture in the nation, spoiled only by the extraordinary degree to which even the wealthiest Pittsburgh streets crowd their homes together.[1] Almost any street in this district is a revelation: turn-of-the-century Queen Anne mansions on Wallingford, two Greek Revival frame houses on Bayard Street, an Italianate villa in the style of Andrew Jackson Downing at **4841 Ellsworth Avenue,** and the **Alfred Hunt House** at 4875 Ellsworth (NW corner Devonshire; Edward Grenzbach, 1976). In this mansion for an Alcoa heir aluminum was used wherever possible, even in its raw form as the anorthosite boulders of aluminum ore that form its base. Devonshire Road, linking Ellsworth and Bayard with Fifth Avenue, constitutes a small museum of Victorian homes in its own right. Particularly interesting is the New England Colonial shape of the **Childs House** at 718 Devonshire (Peabody & Stearns, 1896). It is followed by an elaborately textured wooden Queen Anne house at 808 and then, at 820 Devonshire, a somber Romanesque Revival/Queen Anne house with black sandstone walls and wooden porches and gables.

Fifth Avenue, the major public thoroughfare in Shadyside, was less saturated with millionaires than was Penn Avenue in Point Breeze, but its length of two miles made it collectively more impressive. Mansions began to be erected here before the Civil War and continued into the 1920s, with the last in date being one of the most interesting. The **Pauline and Edmund Mudge House** (now Mudge Graduate House of CMU; SW corner Fifth & Morewood; Henry D. Gilchrist, 1922) is a neoclassical design featuring an elegant double-bow facade in smooth limestone as an inside-out rendering of Sir Edwin Lutyens's "Nashdoms" of 1908. The Mudges would have enjoyed its local associations

---

1. Crowded urban streets are the rule in older and poorer neighborhoods in American cities, but they are unexpected in newer and wealthier districts such as Pittsburgh's East End (Highland Park, Shadyside, Point Breeze, and Squirrel Hill). The explanation for such crowding among wealthy Pittsburghers seems to involve Henry George, the little-remembered nineteenth-century reformer. George argued (in *Progress and Poverty* and other works) that inequality in the distribution of wealth could be eradicated by a single tax based on the value of land alone. The theory was widely admired in the late nineteenth century (George outpolled Theodore Roosevelt in the contest for mayor of New York—which both lost—in 1886). Pittsburgh, with a greater inequality of wealth than any American city, embraced George's concept enthusiastically but perversely, taxing land at twice the rate of buildings and for a good while not taxing homes in the East End at all. As a result, Pittsburgh's gentry built their great mansions on the smallest possible lots.

Left: Moreland-Hoffstot House, Fifth Avenue /*Franklin Toker* ▪ *Right:* Sunnyledge, the McClelland House /*Maurice Tierney*

also, as a transformation of John Shoenberger's old double-bow Greek Revival mansion of 1847 on Penn Avenue in the Golden Triangle. Internally, the building is a diagram of a 'Twenties marriage, with a "his" wing on the north and a "her" wing duplicating everything on the south.

A half-dozen important mansions follow on Fifth Avenue between Morewood and Wilkins: the **Hillman House** (now condominiums; 5045 Fifth Ave.), a Second Empire mansion that was reclad in Georgian style by E. P. Mellon in 1922; the Newport-style neo-Rococo **Moreland-Hoffstot House** (5057 Fifth; Paul Irwin, 1914); the **Gwinner-Harter House** (5061 Fifth), a dilapidated but grand Second Empire mansion that was built in the 1870s for William B. Negley; a baronial Tudor castle for the industrialist **Willis McCook** (NE corner Fifth & Amberson; Carpenter & Crocker, 1906); and **Sunnyledge,** a combination house and office for the society doctor James McClelland (5134 Fifth, SW corner Wilkins; Frank Alden for Longfellow, Alden & Harlow, 1887). This is a luxurious brick home in the manner of the continuous spatial envelope that H. H. Richardson created so brilliantly in wood in the Stoughton House in Cambridge and in stone in the Glessner House in Chicago. At $49,000, the McClelland home was cheap by Pittsburgh's millionaire standards, since William Thaw paid fifty times more for his house farther east on Fifth Avenue in 1889, but it was still an expensive house for the times. Theodore Roosevelt's "Sagamore Hill" on Long Island cost only one-third as much in the same decade.

Shadyside extends into several hamlets on the slopes of Squirrel Hill, north of Fifth Avenue. One is **Morewood Heights** (known also as Devonshire or Wilkins Heights), reached by narrow lanes that wind off Wilkins, Forbes, and Beeler streets. Among the score of excellent homes on this private hilltop, the most lavish is the **Clifford Heinz House** (5090 Warwick Terrace, 1924) in Jacobean Revival style, but the most inventive is the small **Abraam Steinberg**

Shadyside Presbyterian Church
/*Franklin Toker*

House (NW corner Penton & Dorset, near Beeler; 1952). This is one of the homes built in the Pittsburgh area in the interwar and postwar years by Peter Berndtson and Cornelia Brierley, two architects trained in the Taliesin Fellowship by Frank Lloyd Wright. The Steinberg house was constructed on a sloping and heavily wooded site using battered brick walls and redwood trim around a wedge-shaped open courtyard. The house plan involves a complex integration of circles and rectangles as the two basic geometries of the design.

With the destruction of many of the mansions east of the intersection of Wilkins and Fifth avenues, the main monument of this stretch of Shadyside today is the **Third Presbyterian Church** (NE corner Fifth & Negley; Theophilus P. Chandler, Jr., 1896–1905). Third Presbyterian is a mountainous sandstone Gothic structure with a rush of pinnacles, and it gives the sensation of being an entire city in itself. Funding for this superbly rich building came in equal parts from Henry Frick (who paid to have the congregation's old church destroyed to make way for his William Penn Hotel) and from Josiah Thaw, whose less pious brother Harry entered into tumultuous matrimony with Evelyn Nesbit here on April 5, 1905. The church interior is alternately severe and rich, with its unplastered sandstone walls enframing some of the best stained glass in America. Represented here are Louis Comfort Tiffany, the fresco painter Kenyon Cox, Robert McCausland, and William Willett, one of the two Pittsburghers who launched the revival of Gothic glass in America.

A half mile to the west, **Shadyside Presbyterian Church** (807 Amberson, NE corner Westminster Place; Shepley, Rutan & Coolidge, 1889–92) rises massive and pyramidal in its black-sooted sandstone blocks in a powerful restatement of Trinity Church in Boston, the early masterpiece of the founder of the firm, H. H. Richardson. Shadyside Presbyterian is, however, fenestrated much more amply than its Boston model, in the desire to catch whatever light was available from the black sky over Pittsburgh a century ago. The congregation was born in 1866 at a meeting in the handsome Italianate villa of the former owner of this neighborhood, David Aiken, Jr.: **5020 Amberson Place,** built in 1864. The villa was subsequently modernized with a stucco finish to harmonize it with the smooth walls of the homes that were built during the final dismemberment of the Aiken estate two generations later. The best of the newer homes are the **Roy Hunt House** (5050 Amberson Place; Maximillian Nirdlinger, 1913), a restrained and Lutyens-like horizontal villa by a disciple of Frank Furness, and the **Louis Brown House** (704 Amberson Avenue; Edward Weber, 1913), a poured-concrete home with pseudo-thatched roof that is an artfully contrived simulation of an English cottage.

The gracious ambience of the Shadyside Presbyterian neighborhood is completed by two of the best Queen Anne houses in the city: the **George MacBeth House** and the **Charles Spencer House** at 717 and 719 Amberson Avenue. The first house was designed by Charles M. Bartberger and E. G. W. Dietrich in 1884; the second by George Orth in 1886. Both have a scalene quality, as though their upper walls were imitating the smooth skin of a fish. As always in the Queen Anne style, the buildings are restless, with multiple gables, multiple inserts and projections, and a highly complex sequence of planes. The MacBeth House recently came alive with an imaginative reconstruction of its porch. The Spencer House came alive in another way in 1983 with the publication of Ethel Spencer's memoir of her childhood there eighty years ago.

The Amberson Avenue neighborhood even has a "mass" housing project of the Victorian age on **Colonial Place,** one block east of the intersection of Amberson and Ellsworth. In this short dead-end next to the railroad tracks, George Orth designed five pairs of mirror-image houses in 1897. The result is a triumph of Victorian eclecticism: nine hybrids (the tenth house was destroyed) from the grafting of the Renaissance Revival, Dutch Colonial, and Virginia Georgian architectural trees. The attractive homes of the Shadyside Presbyterian Church district continue to the east as well, in a sequence of Shingle Style and Queen Anne homes in the 5200 and 5300 blocks of

MacBeth and Spencer houses,
Amberson Avenue /*Franklin Toker*

Left: Minnetonka Building (Frederick Scheibler, architect), Walnut Avenue /*Franklin Toker* ▪ *Right:* Highland Towers Apartments (Frederick Scheibler, architect) /*Franklin Toker*

Westminster Place, and in the charmingly miniaturized **Spinelli House** (5302 Westminster, SE corner St. James; c. 1865), a Gothic Revival frame cottage that is one of the best relics of old Shadyside. Westminster Place ends at Aiken Avenue nearly opposite **Shadyside Seventh Day Adventist Church** (formerly First Methodist Church; 821 S. Aiken Avenue; Frederick Osterling, 1893), a collection of Richardsonian motifs, including a quote from his Chestnut Hill Railroad Station outside Boston.

The commercial side of Shadyside breaks through on Walnut Street, a magnet for shoppers and diners through the whole East End. Most of the buildings on Walnut were originally homes or modest storefronts before they were converted into boutiques. The best of the older structures is the **Minnetonka Building** (5425–5431 Walnut; Frederick Scheibler, 1908). This, one of Scheibler's few commercial buildings, makes an interesting connection with his apartment work, since it also contains living quarters over a set of ground-floor shops. It is a svelte, complex design with a classical bias but without the elements of a classical vocabulary. It can best be compared to the Vienna work of Olbrich and Loos in the same period. Diagonally across from the Minnetonka, a short block away, is **Bellefonte Place** (SE corner Walnut & Bellefonte; L. P. Perfido Associates, 1982), a post-Modern structure that picks up some features of Scheibler's building, such as the exposed I-beams and the Palladian windows and other details of the older mansions on the street. The commercial strip ends with another use of the Palladian motif, here blown up into a three-story scale, in the **Walnut Mall** (NW corner Walnut & Ivy; Carl Becker, 1984), a historically attuned but nonimitative design that attempts to balance some of the clutter of Walnut Street with a simple exterior wall pattern.

The most interesting of the dozens of small apartment blocks in Shadyside is Scheibler's **Highland Towers** of 1913 (340 S. Highland Ave.). This four-story brick apartment building shows Scheibler at the point in his career when he was most influenced by Frank Lloyd Wright. The proportioning of the volumes and the use of decorative tiles on the building certainly recall Wright.

Like Wright, too, Scheibler was interested in the spareness of Japanese buildings, which are recalled in the broad fenestration of the central block. Along with these debts, there is a close connection between Scheibler and the Dutch architects of the Amsterdam School and the De Stijl movement after World War I. The strongly Expressionist and even Cubist aspects of Highland Towers never impinge on its functionality. Each floor contained four apartments of eight large rooms in a tight and effective plan that minimized wasted space. Subdivided into much less grand units today, the apartments at Highland Towers are still greatly in demand.

Shady Avenue, two blocks east of Highland, is the original thoroughfare that linked Shadyside to East Liberty and to Squirrel Hill. It marks one side of the triangle formed with Penn and Fifth at the easternmost point of Shadyside. The homes in this triangle are newer than those in the rest of Shadyside and to a degree more exuberant, especially in such Shingle Style houses as **424 Denniston Avenue** (NW corner Kentucky; 1892). Here the texturing of the dark brown shingles and the arbitrary mix of gable ends, porches, oriel windows, projecting bays, and a corner *tourelle* is most effective. At the intersection of Shady and Walnut streets stand two distinguished churches. The better known is Ralph Adams Cram's **Calvary Episcopal** (1906), a dramatic limestone pile in thirteenth-century English Gothic that also weaves in a half-dozen other historical periods. It dominates its corner with the enormous block of the central crossing tower and a needle spire that is brutally but dynamically set atop it. The interior glass is inventive and casts a rich light on the rough texture of the cove timber roof and the austere stone walls. Cram was forty-three when he completed Calvary, and it is generally recognized as one of the landmarks of the mature period of his career. (The superbly

Shadyside Shingle: 424 Denniston Avenue /*Franklin Toker*

preserved **Francis Sellers House,** an 1858 Italianate villa diagonally across from Calvary, has served as a rectory to the church.)

It is worth noting that **Sacred Heart Church** on the opposite corner of Shady and Walnut (Carlton Strong, 1924 and later) is better related to its site than is Calvary, and it carries out some of Cram's objectives better than he did himself. One has the impression that Cram's design, fine as it is, was mailed from Boston by someone who had only a haphazard knowledge of its intended placement, whereas Strong appears to have sat for days at the site, like a painter before his easel. The two fine churches at the corner of Walnut and Shady have a third partner in the dynamic but less sophisticated **Christian Church of North America** (originally the First Cumberland Presbyterian Church; 241 Shady Ave., NE corner Aurelia; c. 1900), a dramatically articulated Romanesque Revival/Queen Anne design that incorporates some of the most vivid passages of brickwork in the city.

It is fitting that the village qualities that are so pronounced in Shadyside should have been captured in the successful **Village of Shadyside** housing complex (Penn, Aurelia, & Denniston Aves.; UDA Associates, 1982–87). This vacant nine-acre site is being transformed into 215 housing units in sixty-seven townhouses and seven condominium blocks of three to five stories. Part of the development faces the south side of Aurelia Street, which is a solid wall of elaborate Queen Anne homes. (Willa Cather used Aurelia as the model for Cordelia Street in her story "Paul's Case": "It was a highly respectable street, where all the houses were alike and where business men of moderate means begot and reared large families of children . . . all of whom were as exactly alike as their homes.") The new townhouses on the north side of Aurelia relate well to their Victorian prototypes and restore an urban density to an area that had lost it in earlier redevelopment schemes. The result is a post-Modern but nondialectical solution to the problem of creating instant tradition in architec-

Calvary Episcopal Church (Ralph Adams Cram, architect) /*Maurice Tierney*

The Village of Shadyside /*Courtesy UDA Architects*

ture. The project could be subtitled "Learning from Shadyside" because it renders a fit conclusion to an exceptionally handsome residential colony.

Squirrel Hill and Greenfield

Squirrel Hill, south of Fifth Avenue, is such a stereotypical bedroom community that one would not think to look here for architectural or urban features of distinction. But that would be a mistake, for part of the lore of Squirrel Hill is its roster of notables, who include Harry Thaw, Perle Mesta, Marjorie Merriweather Post, Willa Cather, Gene Kelly (his dance studio survives at 5824 Forbes Avenue), Jonas Salk, and five of the most important Mellons: A. W. and his son Paul, R. B. and his son Richard King Mellon, and Gulf founder William Larimer Mellon. Even the tragic heiress Sunny von Bülow lived here, as plain Martha Crawford. Squirrel Hill is a neighborhood of surprises: it has no significant history, and yet it preserves log houses from the eighteenth century and a cemetery in which Indians are buried. It is an area without significant artistic or aesthetic impact, but among its homes are designs by Walter Gropius, Richard Meier, and Robert Venturi. It is the largest and most populous Pittsburgh neighborhood (1,700 acres; 36,000 residents), but it is split into two halves socially: a wealthy Scotch-Irish and German-Jewish half, north of Forbes Avenue, and a middle- and working-class half of tiny row houses and a dozen kosher butcher shops, south of Forbes.

Squirrel Hill has a feature that is unique among Pittsburgh neighborhoods and a rare phenomenon anywhere: in a nearly literal sense it turned itself around. It was born as a pioneer farming community in the 1760s, with an

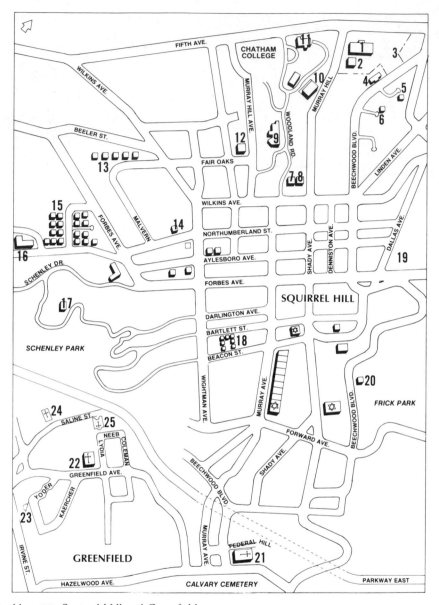

Map 23. Squirrel Hill and Greenfield

1 Pittsburgh Center for the Arts
2 Scaife House
3 Site of R. B. Mellon House
4 Frew House, Beechwood Hall
5 Site of Thaw House, "Lyndhurst"
6 Site of Perle Mesta House
7 18 Woodland Rd. (Meier)
8 18A Woodland Rd. (Venturi)
9 A. W. Mellon Hall

10 Frank House
11 Howe-Childs House
12 Willa Cather House
13 Robin Road
14 5553 Northumberland St.
15 Schenley Road townhouses
16 Pittsburgh Golf Club
17 Neill Log House
18 Hamilton Cottages

19 Homewood Cemetery
20 Harter House
21 Mary F. Brown Mem.
   Church
22 St. Rosalia's Church
23 Yoder Street lookout
24 St. Joachim's Church
25 St. John Chrysostom
   Church

admixture of Indian traders. The original village fronted south on the Monongahela River, toward Homestead, and its center of activity was the present-day intersection of Brown's Hill Road and Beechwood Boulevard. Nearby, in what is now the 3400 block of Beechwood, was John Turner's estate of Federal Hill (1778). Nearby too, at the sharp bend of Beechwood Boulevard, William "Killymoon" Stewart built a tavern in 1819 that hosted generations of travelers to Pittsburgh, and it was not destroyed until after World War II. Because of its inaccessibility (only three minor lanes entered Squirrel Hill—from Shadyside, Hazelwood, and the Monongahela shore), it remained for another century as a district of a few dozen large estates. It finally changed character and became both fashionable and populous with two milestones: the introduction of the electric trolley along Forbes and Murray avenues in 1893, and the rebuilding of Beechwood Boulevard by Frederick Law Olmsted, Jr., in 1903.

The trolley system sparked the building of hundreds of large but nearly identical homes for the middle management of the steel companies, such as those on Shady and Denniston avenues near Aylesboro. The opening of Beechwood Boulevard occasioned the building of still-larger mansions in the northeast corner of Squirrel Hill, which became an extension of the millionaire row in Point Breeze. The population of Squirrel Hill jumped again between 1922 and 1927, when the Boulevard of the Allies linked it directly to the Golden Triangle. The new residents, mainly from Oakland and The Hill, moved into modest infill rows of brick homes on the cross-streets of Murray Avenue, south of Forbes. By the 1930s nearly all the available land of Squirrel Hill had been filled; barely a hundred homes have been built there since.

No one thinks of Squirrel Hill as a river town on the Monongahela today because the south edge of the settlement declined in vigor as its north edge expanded to meet the contiguous neighborhoods of Oakland and Shadyside. One of the prominent portals to Squirrel Hill is Shady Avenue, specifically at the point where the hill begins just above Fifth Avenue. The corner has an impressive anchor in the neo-Georgian mansion occupied by the **Pittsburgh Center for the Arts** (the former Charles Marshall House; 6300 Fifth Ave., SE corner Shady; Charles Barton Keen, 1911). Donated in 1945 and now Pennsylvania's largest arts center, the house bursts with activity in classes, recitals, lectures, conferences, exhibits, happenings, and outdoor concerts. The concerts take place on the lawn of its auxiliary building, the former **Alan and Sarah Scaife House** (1081 Shady; Alden & Harlow, 1904; renovated 1927), a Tudor Revival mansion that was a wedding present from Sarah Scaife's father, R. B. Mellon. Mellon's own house stood next door, on the 10.5 acres that now constitute **Mellon Park.** The Mellon house was by no means the largest in Pittsburgh, but it was impressive: twenty-two servants maintained its sixty-five rooms, its organ, its sumptuous Tiffany windows (exhibited in fragments today in Carnegie Institute), its lavish marble (later recut to provide altars for St. Peter's Church in New Kensington), and its magnificent formal gardens. Alden

Sunday concert and brunch at the Scaife House, Pittsburgh Center for the Arts
/*Franklin Toker*

& Harlow built it in 1907; Richard King Mellon lived in it briefly, then had it destroyed in 1941. An idea of the sumptuousness of the structure is provided by the surviving carriage house, the wrought-iron spiked fence by Samuel Yellin, and the remaining gardens. The designer of the terraced Renaissance garden of the late 1920s was the landscape architect Gilmore D. Clarke of New York, who next worked in Pittsburgh twenty years later on a far wider scale as the landscape architect of Gateway Center.

The curve-filled **Beechwood Boulevard,** beyond Mellon Park, was used as an impromptu racetrack for a decade after its rebuilding in 1903. Had decisions gone differently, it would have served also as the grand approach to H. C. Frick's intended art museum in Frick Park. Next to the Mellon estate there survives the ponderous neo-Georgian portico of **Beechwood Hall,** the home of the civic leader William Nimick Frew (1054 Beechwood; Alden & Harlow, 1902). Opposite Beechwood Hall stand the thirty-two modest postwar homes that replaced **Lyndhurst,** the mansion that railroading tycoon William Thaw built in 1889, the last year of his life.[2] Thaw's widow, Mary,

2. "Lyndhurst" was designed by Theophilus P. Chandler, Jr. Its name derived from a mansion built by Alexander Jackson Davis at Tarrytown, New York, which had been purchased in 1880 by the railroading giant Jay Gould. The Pittsburgh "Lyndhurst" was a huge Gothic mansion that spread over its hill and seemed to resemble a half-dozen different buildings glued together. Containing only forty-two rooms, it nevertheless cost $2.5 million—the same price as Richardson's courthouse and jail, and ten times the cost of the contemporary eight-story German Savings Bank on Sixth Avenue downtown.

The builder of "Lyndhurst," William Thaw, Sr., fathered ten children in two marriages. His offspring represented the best of the Pittsburgh industrial elite. Three of the boys—William, Jr., Benjamin, and Josiah—were respected community leaders; one of the daughters became the Comtesse de Perigny; another the Countess of Yarmouth. Although he inherited only a few million of the family fortune, it was their younger brother Harry who obscured all the illustrious deeds of the clan with the murder of Stanford White in 1906.

lived at Lyndhurst forty more years, until her death in 1929. A slight impression of its magnificence can be garnered today by the powerful brick surrounding wall along Lyndhurst Drive on the left side of Beechwood Boulevard. The intriguing Queen Anne miniature house with diamond-pane windows and a scalloped upper story at 1065 Lyndhurst Drive was the family playhouse. The former estate stable stands at 1071 Lyndhurst, complete with ventilator hoods still in place on the roof.

William Thaw was not the only builder on Beechwood Boulevard to die before he could enjoy his house. Several hundred yards uphill on Beechwood, again on the left, George and Perle Mesta constructed an immense limestone neoclassical residence in 1925. When the husband died the same year, his widow (who survived him by half a century) installed a Mesta relative in the house, then destroyed it thirty years later. The garage and a caretaker's house survive at the top of Beechwood Lane. Apart from the destruction of the Mellon, Thaw, and Mesta houses, Beechwood Boulevard stands almost unchanged from the turn of the century, with a lively mix of Spanish Revival and more traditional Tudor and Colonial Revival houses. After several curves, Beechwood intersects Wilkins Avenue, which leads two and a half blocks west to Woodland Road and the Chatham College campus.

Woodland Road District

Immediately after the Civil War, a half-dozen interrelated families of Pittsburgh's industrial elite created houses on the fifty-five forested acres of the Woodland Road district between Fifth and Wilkins avenues. The families were

Andrew W. Mellon Hall, Chatham College /*Courtesy Chatham College*

joined in 1869 by a women's college that was the predecessor to **Chatham College,** which today occupies a score of buildings here. Some of these the college has built for itself in various revival modes; others are large Shingle Style mansions it has inherited. The oldest of the buildings is the **Howe-Childs House** at the southeast corner of Woodland and Fifth Avenue, a delightful Stick Style clapboarded house of the late 1860s. Larger than all the rest is **Andrew W. Mellon Hall** at the mid-point of Woodland Road. Mellon's home was constructed in 1907 (by MacClure & Spahr) for the steel millionaire George Laughlin; he tripled it in size ten years later when he moved in, as usual employing his nephew E. P. Mellon as architect. What had been a fake-Tudor house now received trainloads of authentic Tudor and Jacobean work from crumbling manor houses in England. Among the luxurious additions made to the house were a solarium, an all-aluminum office (including the drapes, destroyed now along with the rest of the aluminum decor), a bowling alley, and an indoor swimming pool vaulted in Guastavino tile. Paul Mellon occupied the house for a few years after his father died in 1937, then gave it to Chatham in 1941.

What shocked Woodland Road in 1937 was not the death of A. W. Mellon but the construction in the same year of the nearby **Frank House** (96 E. Woodland Rd.) by Walter Gropius and Marcel Breuer. Gropius had just come to teach at Harvard, making this only his second building in America after his own house in Lincoln, Massachusetts. Regarded as little more than a curiosity at the time and generally overlooked today as one of the half-dozen major buildings of the International School in the United States, the Frank House deserves a thorough investigation. What is fascinating in social terms about this avant-garde house is the way in which it functions in exactly the same mode as the old mansions on Woodland, particularly the Mellon house, with its indoor swimming pool, vestibule, salon, servants' quarters, and even a *porte-cochère*. The Frank House bears the clear imprint of its patrons, who were close

Left: The Frank House, Woodland Road (Walter Gropius and Marcel Breuer, architects) /*Franklin Toker*

Opposite left: 18 Woodland Road (Richard Meier, architect) /*Franklin Toker*

Opposite right: 18A Woodland Road (Robert Venturi, architect) /*Franklin Toker*

friends of Edgar and Lilianne Kaufmann and had watched the building of Fallingwater from its inception. Cecilia Frank chose the architect; Robert Frank, an engineer, oversaw all aspects of its construction and insisted that the house be welded—almost all previous steel buildings had been riveted—out of consideration for the tranquillity of his neighbors.

The Frank House sits on a thickly wooded rise and consists of three parts: a three-story entrance pavilion, a gently curved two-story bow window over a fieldstone base, and a long wing with a recessed porch and a projecting hangar for the swimming pool. It is a contradictory building by reason of its great size, which links it to the nineteenth rather than to the twentieth century, and in the inconsistency of its materials: fieldstone, concrete, wire link fence, glass block, and stainless steel. Gropius and Breuer instilled some eloquent passages in its facade, such as the concrete stair reinforcement (a pure piece of Cubist sculpture), but its industrial hardness makes it problematic as a human habitation even now, half a century after it was built.

The Gropius house can be usefully contrasted with a home in the neo-International School vocabulary that **Richard Meier** designed in 1981–83 at 18 Woodland Road, toward Wilkins Avenue. The house, which has received much international attention, is a Cubist theorem that glistens white in its stucco and porcelained steel panels. It creates an extension of its hillside with a grassy patio that masks the garage underneath. An isolated gateway points across this patio to the public rooms of the house, with private accommodations on two levels above and below.

By an extraordinary coincidence, immediately next to the Meier house, at 18A Woodland Road, stands a house built at the same time by the prophet of populist architecture, **Robert Venturi.** Venturi's response to the hilly site was to yield to Nature rather than to synthesize man and Nature as Meier did. He set the house over a creek that ran through the old estate that these two new houses dismembered. Allusions to the creek reappear in the form of the house,

Left: Willa Cather's home in Pittsburgh, 1180 Murray Hill /*Franklin Toker* ▪ *Right:* 5553 Northumberland Street /*Courtesy Arthur Lubetz Associates*

which resembles a mammoth paddlewheel digging itself out of a trough. The structure is clad in green and white wooden clapboards, enamel panels, and stucco. The cacophony of materials and its irregular fenestration and profile make an unforgettable contrast to Meier's Cartesian purity next door.

Bordering the Chatham College campus on the west, and accessible through a side outlet of Woodland Road, stands an ample Colonial Revival house at 1180 Murray Hill Avenue, at the northwest corner of Fair Oaks, where from 1901 to 1906 **Willa Cather** lived as a guest of the family of Judge Samuel McClung. The seven years that Cather spent teaching and editing a magazine in Pittsburgh were especially fruitful in her development as a writer, and she reciprocated by giving Pittsburgh a prominent role as the backdrop to her short stories of these years. To honor this good feeling, a group of Cather devotees dine in the house each year on December 7, her birthday. Murray Hill Avenue would be a fine street even without Cather's presence, however. Its charm is considerably enhanced by the irregularities that have developed over the years in its Belgian-block roadbed, and it boasts a lovely sequence of speculator-built Queen Anne houses with eyebrow dormers in the manner of H. H. Richardson.

Fair Oaks, at right angles to Murray Hill Avenue, is a good representative of the prosperous interwar period in house building in Squirrel Hill. West of its intersection with Wilkins Avenue, the street enters the **Murdoch Farms** district, which was dairy land until the early twentieth century. The most interesting homes here are five Cotswold houses grouped together on **Robin Road,** a private lane that opens off of Fair Oaks just before its juncture with Malvern Avenue. All five were built in the late 1920s by Benno Janssen and William Cocken on a precipitous slope that descends toward Beeler Street.

Special emphasis was placed on the picturesqueness of the slate roofs and on the textured walls, either of stone or of brick.

The homes in Squirrel Hill are by and large less venturesome than the contemporary houses of Shadyside or Highland Park, but some designs in Murdoch Farms are well done. The Renaissance-style **Marcus Aaron House** at 5564 Aylesboro Avenue (SW corner Wightman) stands close to a massive three-story Roman brick mansion at **5605 Aylesboro** that artfully combines mannerisms of both the Prairie School and the Colonial Revival. A half block to the west, the English decorated cottage at **5530 Aylesboro** is an accomplished building in the Voysey manner, with an exaggerated chimney that terminates in an obelisk. There are modern buildings, too: the **Speyer House** (NW corner Wightman & Northumberland; c. 1970) is a Miesian block in cool gray brick, glass, and steel that the Pittsburgh-born Mies associate A. James Speyer designed for his mother. Standing out a good deal more violently from its older neighbors is a post-Modern house at **5553 Northumberland,** near Wightman. It was constructed in 1982 by Arthur Lubetz in obvious reference to Gropius's nearby Frank House in its use of such industrial materials as stainless steel and sections of aluminum siding (the house was built for an Alcoa executive). The house is split in two by its steps, by its windows, and by its main chimney, so that its appearance is not structural but antistructural. While most buildings emphasize what holds them together, this one proposes an architectural entropy that makes one reconsider the structure both of architecture and of domestic life.

The western extension of Northumberland Street, across Forbes Avenue, leads to Schenley Park and the neo-Palladian clubhouse of the **Pittsburgh Golf Club** (1896). On the way to the club stand sixty-two neo-Georgian townhouses that have been packed, a little too energetically, in the **Schenley Road** development (Northumberland, Gladstone, & Forbes; The Design Alliance, 1979–85). The construction of this complex was the most radical change in the topography of Squirrel Hill in half a century. Two mansions had occupied the site. The larger was the seven-acre estate of the retailer Nathaniel Spear, which comprised a fine house by Henry Hornbostel and a Chinese garden with ponds and a picturesque bridge. Several proposals for high-rise condominiums had been defeated by the neighbors, who accepted instead this concept of an instant Downing Street. The result is inferior in imagination to the Village of Shadyside and can scarcely be compared with Chatham Village two generations ago, and yet it represents a general victory for neighborhood values and neighborhood self-determination.

Schenley Park contains two affecting relics of pioneer days in Pittsburgh: the **Robert Neill Log House** (Serpentine Drive, in the Schenley Park municipal golf course) was probably built in 1787. About half a mile away is the **Martin House** (Overlook Drive, between the Schenley Park oval and swimming pool), which may have been built by the first owner of the Neill land,

The Neill Log House, Schenley Park /*Franklin Toker*

Ambrose Newton, in the 1760s. The Neill House, which is the more interesting, consists of massive wooden planks with interspaces filled with mud and small fieldstones. The logs are notched at the ends and show the marks of the adze that hewed them. Internally the building is a single room with an attic loft.

Beacon Street, the continuation of Boulevard of the Allies after it leaves Schenley Park, was conceived as a promenade of equal width and elegance as Beechwood Boulevard, but it never received its expected rich clientele and for the most part is lined with ordinary middle-class houses. The best architectural products on Beacon Street are the **Hamilton Cottages** (5635–5663 Beacon, between Wightman & Murray; Frederick Scheibler, 1910–14), a sequence of simple units in common industrial brick. Each unit is enlivened by such unexpected touches as a slate roof and interior detailing in the manner of the Craftsman style. A half block farther east, Beacon intersects Murray Avenue, which is part of a commercial district that continues around the corner on Forbes. The appeal of the dozens of food stores that make a hillside market out of Murray Avenue is strictly gastronomic: the stores themselves, mainly in 1930s Moderne styling, offer little of visual interest, although the layering of buildings that has taken place in the last two generations is often picturesque. **Bageland** at 2120 Murray Avenue, for example, is a 1950s Miesian rebuilding of a 1930s Moderne storefront that in turn stands in front of an Edwardian Tudor-style double house. The food sold on Murray Avenue is Chinese and Italian as well as Jewish; in the ecumenical spirit, Mineo's Pizzeria closes on Yom Kippur and Passover. There are about a dozen synagogues in Squirrel Hill, a few in fairly elaborate buildings but others ingenious adaptations of old Tudor Revival mansions, including three close together on the 5700 block of Bartlett, just west of Murray. These literal "houses of worship" mingle but also clarify the special qualities of both domestic and ecclesiastic architecture.

East of Murray Avenue, Beacon Street climbs to the peak of Beacon Hill, about 500 feet above the Monongahela River level, then ends beyond Shady Avenue with a rich colony of houses that include a 1920s neo-Greek design by

Henry Hornbostel at **6515 Beacon,** and **Rosewall** (6530 Beacon; Frederick Merrick, 1912), the grand neo-Georgian former residence of Marjorie Merriweather Post in the 1950s and 1960s, when she was married to her fourth husband, Pittsburgher Herbert May.

An eighth of a mile downhill, Beacon intersects Beechwood Boulevard at **Homewood Cemetery,** Pittsburgh's second most prestigious burial ground. In its 205 shaded acres are buried H. J. Heinz and H. C. Frick, along with a score of Mellons and members of other industrial dynasties; Perle and George Mesta, in a chaste mausoleum opposite Dalzell Avenue; and Pittsburgh's most astute collector of modern art, G. David Thompson, who is buried below his stainless-steel cast of the famous *Bird in Space* by Constantin Brancusi.

Half a mile south of Homewood Cemetery stands Frederick Scheibler's **Harter House** of 1923 (2557 Beechwood, near Forward), one of the best of his attempts at organic architecture, complete with pseudo-thatched roof and bollards in the shape of mythological beasts. An overlook opposite 3024 Beechwood, farther south, gives a dramatic view of the steelworks at Homestead. Three-quarters of a mile beyond this Beechwood curves back on itself and enters the district covered by John Turner's Federal Hill estate two centuries ago. Here is located the oldest congregation in Squirrel Hill, the **Mary F. Brown Memorial Methodist Church** (3424 Beechwood Blvd.; George Orth, 1903), which serves as custodian of the cemetery next door, with its Indian graves and recollections of the early pioneers.

Greenfield

Greenfield, like Squirrel Hill (the two areas are topographically indivisible), was another of the favored locations for summer estates in the nineteenth

Coleman Avenue, Greenfield /*Franklin Toker*

century, and it still has a scattering of farmhouses and Queen Anne mansions on its slopes. Overwhelmingly, however, its homes date from the explosive growth of the steel industry after the Civil War: several thousand of them are proudly maintained in Greenfield by their Italian, Irish, and Russian owners. The community's spine road is **Greenfield Avenue,** an old trolley route that links Greenfield by various intermediary roads to Squirrel Hill and Hazelwood at one end and to the Golden Triangle at the other. The more inaccessible slopes of Greenfield were covered with houses only in the 1950s, when the Eliza Furnaces and the J&L coke works at Hazelwood were still in full production. At the mid-point of Greenfield Avenue stands **St. Rosalia's Church** (411 Greenfield, NW corner Lydia; probably by John Comes, 1923). This modern adaptation of the Romanesque tradition is well set back on its own piazza and creates a fine piece of theater for its mainly Italian parish. The interior is a single, cavernous barrel vault covered in frescoes, as an Italian church ought to be. Behind St. Rosalia's one can look a hundred feet down to Greenfield's Eastern European community in Four-Mile Run, which is known locally as "The Run" or Russian Valley. Here stand several dozen old houses and two churches of a steelworker community. One church is the maroon brick **St. Joachim's** (301 Saline; 1910), for the Polish and Slovak community; the other is the Carpatho-Ruthanian **St. John Chrysostom** (506 Saline St.; W. Ward William, 1931–35), a twin-towered church whose gold domes sparkle over the Parkway that invaded this quiet valley in the 1950s.

Greenfield is built like a two-horned pyramid and has extraordinary views from almost every street. From Bigelow Street, Winterburn, or an ironically named alley called Parade, one can see the downtown skyscrapers five miles away and the steelworks upriver and downriver on the Monongahela; on Yoder Street there is also a vivid panorama across Schenley Park into Oakland. Greenfield Hill is unusual in the local geography in having two peaks rather than one. The peaks appear to hail each other from a distance, like the two washerwomen in *Finnegans Wake*. Whoever stands on Coleman Avenue, Lydia Street, or Neeb Avenue has the odd sensation of viewing a neighborhood from within. These internal views vividly convey the depth of feeling in Pittsburgh's insular neighborhoods. The young urban professionals have not yet discovered Greenfield—is it unfair to hope they never will?

The Monongahela, with the LTV coke works in Hazelwood /*Clyde Hare*

Around Pittsburgh:
The Three Rivers and Inland

Pittsburgh is so resolutely urban that it is hard to think of it also as a suburban experience, yet here, as elsewhere, a strong urban context created a strong suburban response. Certainly the buildings and settlements that surround Pittsburgh are formidable: they include a score of industrial towns, a Utopian commune at Ambridge, America's first romantic suburb at Evergreen Hamlet, a planned community by Walter Gropius at New Kensington, and Rachel Carson's ancestral home at Springdale. Farther afield is Frank Lloyd Wright's Fallingwater and another score of sites in the surrounding counties of Southwestern Pennsylvania that form the Pittsburgh periphery. These are extraordinary creations in their own right, but they attain added meaning in relation to the metropolis, for until recently Pittsburgh treated its surrounding countryside not in the modern American way, as something inferior that buckles under urban sprawl, but in the medieval European way, as a co-partner in a development of mutual benefit. Pittsburgh's satellite towns are neither inferior nor superior to the city, but they are necessary to it. Pittsburgh could not be Pittsburgh without them.

The Pittsburgh region is like the city itself: well defined and disinclined to sprawl. Symmetrically disposed around the city are the three smaller cities,

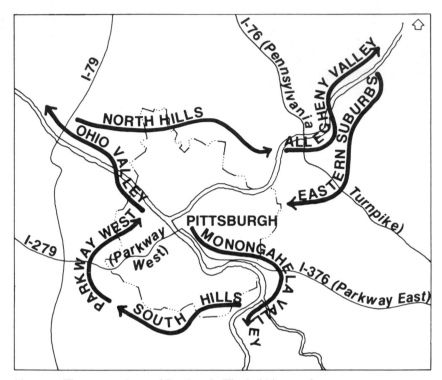

Map 24. The surroundings of Pittsburgh. The bold lines indicate itineraries.

eighty-four boroughs, and forty-two townships that together form Allegheny County. The county covers 728 square miles (an area half the size of Rhode Island and twelve times that of Liechtenstein) and has a population of about 1.5 million. Symmetrically disposed around Allegheny County are the eight other counties of southwestern Pennsylvania: Beaver, Lawrence, Butler, and Armstrong to the north; Westmoreland to the east; and Fayette, Greene, and Washington to the south and west. The nine counties co-sponsor Penn's Southwest, a development organization that has brought Volkswagen and several hundred other foreign firms to establish themselves here.

Although the river system and the old Indian trails pointed prophetically to Pittsburgh as the dominant city of western Pennsylvania, during the first century of its existence it was no more than a regional coordinating center for the hundred agricultural settlements and river towns around it. It assumed a dominant status only with the coming of the railroad and the second industrial revolution that J&L, Carnegie, Westinghouse, the Mellons, PPG, and Alcoa created between 1870 and 1900. During those years, a single decision made in the boardrooms of the Golden Triangle could radically transform such old river towns as Hazelwood, Braddock, and McKeesport, or create a new satellite overnight. (Naming the new towns was an art in itself: A. W. Mellon's steel town of Donora immortalizes both his wife, Nora, and his partner William H. Donner.) The industrial suburbs on the rivers were backed up a generation later by residential suburbs to the north, east, and south. These dozens of middle-class or affluent clusters were created by the trolley and the motorcar, but many of them, including such important ones as Churchill, Bethel Park, Mt. Lebanon, Fox Chapel, and Monroeville, grew up around old country churches. Thus the suburbs around Pittsburgh, like the city itself, developed according to an urban logic that left little room for disorder.[1]

The Monongahela Valley: Hazelwood, Homestead, Braddock, and McKeesport

For 130 years, from 1853 to 1983, the **Monongahela Valley** meant "Steel Valley" not just in America but in many countries of the industrialized world. Ten huge steel mills were shoehorned into a twenty-three-mile segment of this

1. The Pittsburgh region is given structure by three expressways—I-79, the Pennsylvania Turnpike, and the Parkway—that form a triangle around the city; and by five "color belts" that link the back country roads by means of color-coded signs. The color belts are indicated on all motoring maps of Pittsburgh and in the driving instructions and maps in this chapter.

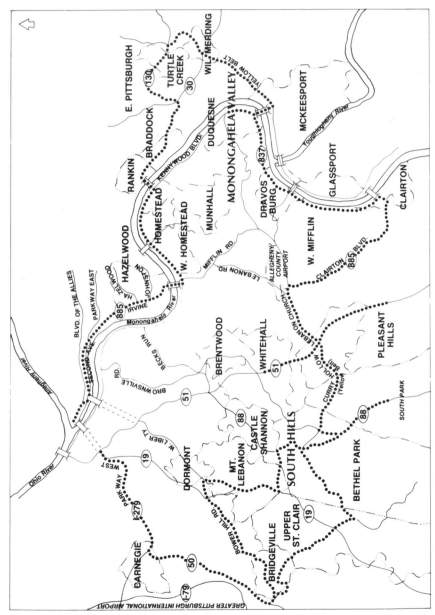

Map 25. The Monongahela Valley, the South Hills, and the Parkway West

serpentine valley between Pittsburgh and Clairton. One hundred thousand workers labored in these mills at their peak during World War II; employment today is about three percent of that. While it lasted, this ribbon that smoldered by day and glowed by night was one of the sublime sights on earth. From the air, the smoke and fire of the Mon Valley was so distinctive that airplane pilots between New York and Chicago habitually fixed their bearings by it. On the ground, the steel towns could be bleak and ugly, but they bustled with the intensity of a gold rush. The work schedule was twelve hours a day for about twenty-six days a month, with a swing shift of twenty-four hours of work once a fortnight. The steelworkers who came here from the British Isles, Central and Eastern Europe, Scandinavia, the Middle East, the Mediterranean, the Baltic, Mexico, and from black hamlets in the South probably worked harder than any free people in history.

The Mon Valley achieved world dominance in steel because it formed an immense assembly line, importing iron ore from the north and west, coal and limestone from the south, and laborers from the east. Mass and energy were fused in a process that was physically brutal and filthy but intellectually elegant. Inventors in many countries contributed to steelmaking, but it became a golden goose at the hands of five men who came to Pittsburgh: Benjamin Franklin Jones, James Laughlin, Andrew Carnegie, Henry Frick, and Charles Schwab. The J&L (now LTV) Pittsburgh Works served as the prototype: the rolling mills of Jones's American Iron Works on the South Side (1853) were linked to Laughlin's Eliza blast furnaces across the Monongahela at south Oakland (1859) and their joint coke works upstream in Hazelwood (1884). Carnegie applied the same formula a little farther upriver, when he started one steel mill and captured four others that earlier Pittsburgh entrepreneurs had built. These five, with two later mills, eventually became the Mon Valley works of U.S. Steel. Coke was produced at Clairton and sent downriver to the blast furnaces at Rankin, Braddock, Duquesne, and McKeesport. The pig iron from these mills was then charged in steelmaking furnaces, and the steel ingots produced were rolled and finished locally or sent on to the Homestead or Irvin plants for specialized work. Putting the mills along the river provided the enormous quantities of water needed for steelmaking, cheap transportation for the raw and finished materials, plentiful hillside land where the workers could build, and deep valleys where the slag heaps could pile up.

The fragmentation of the Mon Valley works into independent units along the river (unthinkable today, and one cause of their decline) suited Carnegie, who ran them as two dozen separate companies before selling them all to U.S. Steel in 1901. Fragmentation neutralized his partners and prevented the unionization of his workers. Linked but not yoked, the plants had the flexibility to exploit fluctuations in the American economy. The steel rails of Braddock cashed in on the post–Civil War railroading boom of the 1870s; the girders of Homestead responded to (and made possible) the American sky-

Hot strip mill, U. S. Steel Irvin Works
/*Courtesy U. S. Steel*

scraper boom of the 1880s; in the 1890s McKeesport rode the American oil boom as the world's greatest supplier of tubes and pipes; and in 1938, as the Depression bottomed out, Irvin was created to supply flat-rolled steel to meet the upsurge in appliance and automobile sales. For years the technology of these plants was the most advanced anywhere, with succeeding generations of Bessemers and open-hearth, basic oxygen, and electric furnaces. Say what you will of the recent decline of Smokestack America and the Rust Belt: one hundred years ago the Mon Valley was—except in labor relations—the perfection of enterprise in this country. It remains the ideal, at least sub-liminally, that all later forms of American enterprise have tried to emulate.

The Steel Valley begins where it was invented—at Pittsburgh. Second Avenue, which starts underneath the Boulevard of the Allies ramp east of Grant Street, was extended along the east bank of the Monongahela to Hazelwood early in the nineteenth century, then as a plank road to Braddock. Here, south of Oakland, was James Laughlin's Eliza Furnaces (named for his daughter, who was Duncan Phillips's mother). Today, most of the mill has been cleared away for an industrial and research park, where the main project is expected to be robotics: so begins a new chapter in Pittsburgh's production history.

Hazelwood

Hazelwood is part of Pittsburgh, though its grim brick rows and hillside cottages give it the look of an independent steel town. As "Scotch Bottom" it

Left: Church of the Good Shepherd, Hazelwood /*Franklin Toker* ▪ *Right:* St. Stephen's Church, Hazelwood /*Franklin Toker*

had its share of summer estates until shortly after the Civil War, when its industrial expansion took place. That transformation is vividly documented at the entrance to town, in an Italianate villa of the Civil War days at **4527 Irvine** (an offshoot of Second Avenue) that became a factory in the 1930s. Nearby, two blocks up Hazelwood Hill, stands the **Woods House** (4604 Monongahela St., SW corner Tullymet), built in the 1780s or 1790s by the family of the surveyor who laid out Pittsburgh in 1784. The house is Georgian in design, although crudely built of erratically squared sandstone. Several blocks east, at **121−123 East Elizabeth Street,** stands a sparkling Second Empire mansion done up in white clapboard. Better than anything else, it testifies to the delights of the Hazelwood slope in its preindustrial days. At the base of the slope is Hazelwood's badly decayed commercial strip on Second Avenue. Below it are the **LTV coke works,** marked by gigantic coal bunkers and larry cars that ride back and forth as they feed the batteries of coke ovens.

Like all steel towns, Hazelwood has two classes of public monuments: its factories and its churches. The oldest of its three main churches is the **Church of the Good Shepherd** (SE corner Second Ave. & Johnston St.; 1891), by the nationally prominent William Halsey Wood. Founded in 1870 by a wealthy and ritualistic Anglo-Catholic congregation that still had enough members to rebuild two decades later, it is a surprisingly playful building, with a fantastic pagoda spire that is scalloped in five stages. About 150 congregants can fit in its intimate sanctuary, over which hovers a richly detailed hammer-beam roof.

If Good Shepherd represents Hazelwood's mill owners, then **St. Stephen's Church** (5115 Second Ave., SE corner E. Elizabeth; Frederick Sauer, 1902) represents its Irish-origin middle managers and laborers. Sauer chose a ponderous Baroque style for the facade, which he rendered in buff industrial brick with decorative trim in molds of fine-grained cement. The interior of St. Stephen's uses a good deal of poured concrete, which links it in objectives (if not in quality) to the "industrial" churches that Auguste Perret later built in France. The Eastern European work force of Hazelwood is represented by the **First Hungarian Reformed Church** (221 Johnston, near NW corner Gertrude; 1903), which bears the name of its architect, the fiercely original Titus de Bobula, in elegant Art Nouveau letters on its cornerstone.[2] The church is small, with a sandstone facade and buff factory brick on the side walls. The step-gabled facade is perforated by two strange ovoid windows left and right of the central tower. The Art Nouveau style is particularly marked in these windows and in the flower shape of the light fixtures inside.

West Homestead, Homestead, and Munhall

The industrial river town of **Homestead** and its satellites of **West Homestead** and **Munhall** were laid out on the south bank of a substantial bend in the Monongahela River. It is reached on the Homestead High-Level Bridge from Pittsburgh, on Route 837 South from the South Side, or by the Glenwood Bridge from Hazelwood on Route 885 South. Homestead and Munhall filled up overnight with the homes of 7,000 workers when the Pittsburgh Bessemer Steel Company set up its blast furnaces and blooming mill there in 1881. Carnegie bought the operation in 1883 and linked it to the blast furnaces he had built at Braddock a decade earlier. The Homestead Works grew phenomenally after its first open-hearth furnaces were added in 1886. Its rolling mills specialized in structural steel, and the columns, girders, and beams rolled there supported the top floors of the Home Insurance Building in Chicago (the first true skyscraper), as well as the Empire State Building in New York

---

2. Only scant information is available on de Bobula and no personal document beyond his photograph in *Palmer's Pictorial Pittsburgh* of 1905, in which he peers out enigmatically from under a hat, like Toulouse-Lautrec. In the spontaneity of his style, particularly his interest in languid, sinuous curves, his predilection for the clashing of smooth and rough materials, and his outrageous handling of the classical orders, Titus de Bobula must be regarded as an authentic Art Nouveau architect—possibly the only true devotee of that style in the United States. He was evidently Hungarian, and his style suggests that he was trained in the Vienna Secession school. He worked in Pittsburgh from about 1900 to 1910 (in 1920 he designed a house in New York and probably resided there), leaving behind three churches and designs for a group of free-flowing monuments that, if executed, would have made him a sensation among American architects.

Left: The Mesta House, West Homestead /*Franklin Toker* ▪ *Right:* 201 E. Tenth Avenue, Homestead /*Franklin Toker*

and the massive Hancock and Sears towers in Chicago. The plant eventually grew to 430 acres and a work force of 20,000.[3]

West Homestead is dominated by the mile-long bulk of the **Mesta Machine Company** plant between Seventh Avenue and the river. For a generation this was the world's largest machine shop under one roof, and Mesta was regarded as the most versatile creator of machinery in the world. Its supreme product was the seven-story 50,000-ton hydraulic press that was used to form the sheet metal for Air Force jets in the mid-1950s. George Mesta built the factory here in 1898; rebuilt after he died in 1925, it yielded high profits for a half-century until its collapse in 1983. Today, Mesta has vacated the old mill and has been reborn in the Pittsburgh suburbs as a computer services firm.

A more personal recollection of Mesta's glory days is the nearby **George and Perle Mesta House** (540 Doyle Ave., reached by Eighth & Basic Aves.). This clapboarded Colonial Revival mansion of about 1890 forms part of a proud hillside terrace where the Mesta superintendents lived. To its left stands the elaborate and beautifully scaled ballroom that launched Perle Mesta's career as a socialite, just an eighth of a mile from her husband's factory.

Homestead Borough, east of the Mesta plant, has **Chiodo's Tavern** (107 W. Eighth Ave., next to the Homestead High-Level Bridge) as its social center. Steelworkers still cluster around the memento-choked bar at Chiodo's, though

---

3. Homestead is as famous for its 1892 strike as for its role in construction history. The steelworkers' union that was created in 1876 reluctantly agreed in 1889 to a new wage scale in exchange for official recognition by the company. (The old wage scale was tied to productivity, but when production topped record after record, Carnegie proposed to pay the men by the hour instead.) When the 1889 contract expired, Frick, as chairman of Carnegie Steel, vowed to break the unions and hired 300 Pinkerton men to open the mill to strikebreakers. On July 6, 1892, about a dozen Pinkertons and strikers died during a fierce battle. The union lost this strike and the next big strike in 1919, after which U.S. Steel issued a poster of Uncle Sam telling the men, in eight languages, to get back to work. Final certification of the union did not come until the 1930s.

they seem outnumbered at times by the journalists and anthropologists who come here to report on their demise. There is a colorful row of mom-and-pop stores along Eighth Avenue, particularly in the three blocks between West and McClure streets, which were a gold mine in the days when thousands of steelworkers and their families crowded here on payday. The more prosperous steelworkers lived in small brick and frame houses that were built by Carnegie's land company. These houses still survive by the hundreds, along with a score of larger homes for the mill managers. One that was possibly built for this purpose is a blue Stick Style clapboard cottage at **201 E. Tenth Avenue** (NE corner Amity) from the 1880s, with a set of false gables around the eaves.

Homestead bears no sign now of its dreadful tenements or "courts" for the immigrant workers, where 15 people would crowd into a flat and 100 drank from a single fetid pump. What testifies to the immigrant experience today is a cluster of churches within the radius of two blocks from the intersection of Ann Street and E. Tenth Avenue. There are sixteen in all, giving Homestead a sacred density to rival Rome and Jerusalem. Two are now deconsecrated; of the fourteen in service, one is Catholic, two are evangelical, one Methodist, one Episcopalian, one Presbyterian, and one Jewish. The rest serve ethnically based congregations of blacks, Hungarians (two), Russians, Italians, Slovaks, and Carpatho-Ruthenians. It was this last community that erected **St. John's Greek Catholic Cathedral** just over the border in Munhall (913 Tenth Ave., NE corner Dickson; Titus de Bobula, 1903). This Art Nouveau design is one of the more erratically brilliant structures in Pittsburgh. Its facade is marked by two fantastic towers that begin in arches of exaggerated sandstone voussoirs and end in neoclassical columned tholoi. The towers are bridged by a cavelike arch in the basement and by two columnar walkways. Both here and in the parish house next door, de Bobula jumbled classical and industrial elements in

Homestead churches, with U. S. Steel Homestead Works /*Franklin Toker*

Left: St. John's Greek Catholic Cathedral, Munhall (Titus de Bobula, architect) */Franklin Toker* ▪ *Right:* St. Michael's, Munhall (John Comes, architect) */Franklin Toker*

a style that recalls *fin-de-siècle* Vienna but is American in its assemblage of bits and pieces of architectural history. De Bobula would have been an ideal partner for Bernard Maybeck, who was building in the same spirit around San Francisco, or for Julia Morgan as she concocted William Randolph Hearst's castle at San Simeon.

Another outstanding Munhall church is the Slovak community's **St. Michael's** (NE corner Ninth Ave. & Library Place; John Comes, 1927), which is the dramatic outcome of its author's long search for an integration of traditional European church types and modern styling. On the wooded slope above the church stands the **Carnegie Library of Homestead** (510 Tenth Ave.; Alden & Harlow, 1898), Carnegie's conciliatory gift to his striking workers in the form of a French Renaissance palace with a music hall, library, gymnasium, swimming pool, and four lanes of duckpin bowling alleys.

Rankin and Braddock

The flats and slopes of the right bank of the Monongahela, diagonally upriver from Homestead, are occupied by the industrial towns of Swissvale, **Rankin,**

Edgar Thomson Steel Works, Braddock /*Courtesy U. S. Steel*

and **Braddock.** Rankin grew around the Carrie Furnace, which began operations here in 1884 and was taken over by Carnegie in 1898 as a source of pig
iron for the steelmaking furnaces of Homestead. The blast furnaces were shut
down in 1983 and will probably be demolished. The town has a dramatic site,
with the three gilded onion domes of **St. Michael the Archangel Greek
Catholic Church** (Third Ave.; 1910) standing out against the slope of the hill
and green cemeteries at its crest.

The broad flood plain of Braddock, east of Rankin, entered history in 1755,
when it provided a perfect musket range for the French and Indian massacre of
General Edward Braddock and his Coldstream Guards. Braddock's defeat was
an epochal event: it launched the Seven Years' War and George Washington's
military career (he was Braddock's aide-de-camp), and it was even an indirect
cause of the American Revolution. In 1873 Carnegie bought one hundred
acres where the plain was crisscrossed by Turtle Creek and three railroad lines,
and there he built the **Edgar Thomson Steel Works** (Alexander L. Holley,
engineer), which marked a quantum leap in American industrial technology.
The mill still functions for U.S. Steel today, but below its historical levels of
production.

Many a Pittsburgh fortune was made in the hundred shops that lined
Braddock Avenue in the blocks leading up to the mill. Most of the shops are
now boarded up, and the population numbers just one-fifth of the 22,000 it
once was. Without a dramatic reversal the only record of Braddock a generation from now may be three works of art: Emanuel Leutze's *Braddock's Defeat,* a
heroic painting (by the artist of *Washington Crossing the Delaware*) that is temporarily stored in the Mellon bank here; Thomas Bell's 1941 novel *Out of This
Furnace;* and a set of *cinema verité* films on Braddock made by Tony Buba in the
1970s and 1980s.

The most vigorous of the many handsome but decayed buildings in Braddock is the vacant **Carnegie Library of Braddock** (416 Library St., a block

north of Braddock Ave.; William Halsey Wood, 1888), a Romanesque Revival design executed in sandstone blocks now turned black with smoke. It was the first of Carnegie's gift libraries in America (he had given a small library to his hometown in Scotland in 1881), and it set the pattern for the others in the Pittsburgh milltowns, with a gym, a pool, and baths, in addition to a music hall and books. Wood skillfully broke up the mass of the building into five separate components so that it would resemble a rich man's private house and thus propagate the image of Carnegie as a benevolent father living in the midst of his workers.

Carnegie himself had abandoned Pittsburgh early on, but he insisted that his superintendents live hard by the mills. The **Charles M. Schwab House** (541 Jones Ave., uphill from the library; Frederick Osterling, 1889) is a charmless Queen Anne hulk that Carnegie's most flamboyant associate built the year he was made superintendent of the Braddock works. Schwab was then twenty-seven; just six years had passed since he had joined the plant at one dollar a day. The presidencies of both U.S. Steel and Bethlehem Steel still lay ahead of him, but already he was seized by his well-known mania for opulence. His castle in Braddock was evidently a practice run for Riverside, the mansion he built twelve years later in New York, with its six elevators and ninety guest bedrooms. At **817 Kirkpatrick,** a block from the Schwab house, stands the so-called Superintendent's House, an opulent Queen Anne house in wood, with art-glass windows, fish-scale shingles in the dormers, and delightful octagonal and circular protuberances to the left of the main block. A third prodigy house, in Queen Anne with strong accents of the Stick Style, stands a few blocks away at **522 Verona Street,** just above the Conrail tracks.

Left: Carnegie Library of Braddock (W. Halsey Wood, architect) */Franklin Toker* ▪ *Right:* Charles Schwab House, 541 Jones Avenue, N. Braddock */Franklin Toker*

East Pittsburgh, Turtle Creek, and Wilmerding

A mile east of town, Braddock Avenue passes under the **George Westinghouse Bridge** (Vernon Covell & Stanley Roush, engineer & architect for Allegheny County; George S. Richardson, structural engineer; 1932), which is the portal to the Turtle Creek Valley and the huge electric works that George Westinghouse opened here in 1894. With the longest concrete arch in the country (many accounts claimed in the world), the Westinghouse Bridge was a sensation when it opened. Half a century later it remains the paradigm of what a good bridge should be. Even after repeated viewings one does not tire of the elegant proportions of the piers, the effortlessness of the semi-elliptical arches, the heroic Art Deco reliefs (by Frank Vittor, 1934), and, above all, the perfect match of the man-made and the natural wonder of the site.

The **Westinghouse Electric Corporation East Pittsburgh Works** extends about two miles along Turtle Creek, north of the bridge. George Westinghouse achieved the first practical application of alternating current for electric-power transmission in 1886 with a demonstration wire between the Golden Triangle and Lawrenceville. Realizing what an immense demand his system would create for generators and electric machinery, Westinghouse purchased 500 acres of land in the Turtle Creek Valley in 1887 as the site for a giant factory complex, but fierce opposition from Edison and the partisans of direct-current electricity forced him to stay his hand for six years. In 1893 Westinghouse scored two decisive triumphs over Edison by supplying AC electricity to the Chicago world's fair and exploiting the water power of Niagara Falls; the next year the East Pittsburgh works opened to national and international acclaim. The plant employed 20,000 workers at its peak, many of whom lived in the small homes that were built for them by the Westinghouse land company in the nearby valleys and mesa tops of East Pittsburgh, Turtle Creek, Trafford, and Wilmerding. An impressive group of these wooden homes and boardinghouses stands north of the plant on Brown Avenue (Route 130 North), toward Churchill. From the plant came the world's first electric locomotive, the first regular radio broadcast (on Pittsburgh's KDKA), and the first electronic television camera. Much of the old complex was clad in a metal skin in 1957 (one manufacturing aisle was seven stories high and three football fields in length), but Thomas Rodd's French Renaissance administration building, where Westinghouse worked, is still intact.

It is two miles from Westinghouse Electric to the **Westinghouse Air-Brake Works** in **Wilmerding** (reached via Route 130 South on the Yellow Belt). Frederick Osterling designed and Westinghouse himself supervised the building of these handsome brick foundries and machine shops in 1890. Around the factories Westinghouse laid out the model industrial town of Wilmerding (the name recalls Johanna Wilmerding Negley, whose family had farmed this valley for generations). Atop a little rise in the center of town was a library and

Top: George Westinghouse Bridge, Turtle Creek */Franklin Toker* ▪ *Center:* Worker housing near the Westinghouse Electric plant, East Pittsburgh */Franklin Toker* ▪ *Bottom:* Westinghouse Air-Brake General Office Building, Wilmerding */Franklin Toker*

community center with a swimming pool and baths, evidently inspired by
Carnegie's prototype at Braddock. When the library burned in 1896, Westinghouse directed Osterling to rebuild it in grander style, without the public
facilities, as the **Westinghouse Air-Brake General Office Building.** Janssen
& Cocken added the wing on the left in French Renaissance style in 1927.
Superannuated in 1984, it is now destined to be a conference center for the
nonprofit American Production and Inventory Control Society.

McKeesport

The Yellow Belt (Routes 130 and 148 South) connects Wilmerding with
McKeesport, an old river town at the confluence of the Monongahela and
Youghiogheny rivers, 3.7 miles to the south. The city was dominated by the
blast furnaces of the National Tube Company from 1873 to 1983, when the
"hot end" of the mill was shut down. As the major supplier of tubes and pipes
to the oil industry, McKeesport grew in spurts with the various oil booms, but
always along the lines of the grid that its founding father, John McKee, and his
surveyor, Andrew McCullock, had set down for it in 1795. Once linked to
Pittsburgh by a trolley line, and now by bus and train, McKeesport was
nonetheless far enough away to create its own vigorous economy and culture.
A poignant testament to its early days still stands in the rows of frame houses
that were set up for immigrant workers in the 500 block of Mulberry Lane and
the 700 block of Strawberry Lane, parallel to the Youghiogheny River shore.

McKeesport is one of a sextet of industrial towns that clusters around a
pronounced double S-curve in the Monongahela River. South of it, on the
same side of the river, are **Glassport,** a town created by the old U.S. Glass
Company when it was still a rival to PPG, and the once-flourishing **Elizabeth,**
which was a major force in boat-building in the late eighteenth century. On
the opposite bank are the industrial towns of Dravosburg, Duquesne, and
Clairton, and the U.S. Steel Irvin Works.

Pipesmoke, McKeesport /*Pamela Bryan*

"Dorothy Six," Duquesne /*Pamela Bryan*

Duquesne and Clairton

Duquesne (reached by Route 837 North from the McKeesport Bridge) is a town of yellow brick roads and long tree-shaded streets with superb views over the Monongahela River. It has an intimate and lively scale and provided a warm domestic counterpart to the slavish work at the mill. Duquesne was created overnight by the Duquesne Steel Company in 1886 and is the site of a mountainous twenty-eight-story blast furnace named "Dorothy Six."

Clairton, 5.8 miles south of Duquesne, grew up around the coke plant created by Henry Frick's St. Clair Steel Company as a threat to Carnegie in 1900. Until the 1970s this was the largest coke plant anywhere: 13 percent of the world's coke was produced in this one plant. The mill is still active and belches forth huge plumes of smoke day and night. Unlike most steel towns, there is no "lower town" in Clairton, apart from the mill: the whole city is built on a high terrace above the Monongahela.

Along with its obsessive devotion to work, the Mon Valley permitted itself a single installation made for fun: **Kennywood Park,** halfway between Homestead and Duquesne on Route 837 South. Its chief promoter was, of all people, A. W. Mellon, who created it in 1899 to promote ridership on his Monongahela Street Railway Company. But it flourished long after the trolley line folded, and it continues today on 100 acres as a delightful family park. Its carousel is a period piece of Art Nouveau, and its Shingle Style casino now serves as the main restaurant. Connoisseurs of such things rate the Thunderbolt Roller Coaster as one of the classics in the nation. One is not obliged to ride it, but the careful student of the Mon Valley should, because just before the cars take their sickening downward plunge, they stop for an instant at the top. From that height one sees the mills at Braddock and Duquesne as though lifted up by an angel. And who is to say that the ghosts of Jones and Laughlin, and of Carnegie, Schwab, and Frick, do not hover there also?

Fishing in the Monongahela, between Dravosburg and Clairton /*Pamela Bryan*

The South Hills and the Parkway West

Between the industrial developments along the Monongahela and Ohio rivers there stretches a crescent of agricultural land about twenty-five miles long that is collectively, if only approximately, known as the **South Hills** and the **Parkway West.** For a century this agricultural district, isolated from Pittsburgh by two rivers and the bulk of Mt. Washington, was strongly influenced by Virginia, which claimed and actually administered it in the 1770s. In 1871, however, the Pittsburgh & Castle Shannon Railroad cut into the heart of the South Hills with a track that later connected with an inclined plane over Mt. Washington. The charming but deserted **Linden Grove Dance Hall** that the railroad built is still standing next to the PAT tracks in Castle Shannon, at the intersection of Library and Grove roads. Other train and streetcar lines followed, either going over Mt. Washington or around it on Saw Mill Run, until the opening of the Mt. Washington Transit Tunnel in 1904 turned the South Hills into a full-fledged suburban extension of Pittsburgh. Brentwood, Whitehall, Castle Shannon, Dormont, and Mt. Lebanon developed as trolley suburbs, while West Mifflin, Pleasant Hills, Bethel Park, and Upper St. Clair grew as motorcar suburbs, following the opening of the Liberty Tunnels below Mt. Washington in 1924. The South Hills preserves several monuments of what might be termed the pioneer phase of suburbia in America: two early shopping centers, an airport, and a cloverleaf traffic circle from the 1930s, and even earlier tract houses erected near Bridgeville by William Ryan, whose family firm later built suburban homes all over the country.

West Mifflin and Pleasant Hills

The South Hills/Parkway West district begins and ends with an airport: the one most local travelers know is the giant on the Parkway, but Pittsburgh's corporate jets use the **Allegheny County Airport** in **West Mifflin** (Lebanon Church Road at Route 885; Stanley Roush, 1925–31). The airport plan is standard Beaux Arts in its symmetry, but the more fanciful Art Deco style emerges in the overlay of Aztec designs and the streamlined corners of the building, and in a set of memorable green and black terra-cotta planters decorated with eagles, propellers, and squadrons of planes. Unexpectedly, the borough also contains three outstanding homes from the years 1939 and 1947–50 by Frank Lloyd Wright's two Pittsburgh-based disciples, Cornelia Brierley and Peter Berndtson, on Lutz Lane, 1.3 miles north of the airport (reached by Route 885 North, Noble Drive & Irwin Run Rd.). The most imposing monument of the area is not a building at all, however: it is **Browns Dump,** a heap of seventy million tons of slag (a nonferrous waste that separates out from pig iron in the blast furnaces) that was poured out for years in red-hot streams by the nearby U.S. Steel plants into a deep valley south of the airport, between Routes 885 and 51. By the time the liquid pouring ceased in 1969, and the dumping of hard slag a few years later, the valley had become a towering mountain. In 1979 the Century III Shopping Mall was built over

Left: Allegheny County Airport, West Mifflin */Franklin Toker* ▪ *Right:* Slag heap with movie theater, West Mifflin */Franklin Toker*

Holy Trinity Serbian Orthodox Church, Whitehall (John Tomich, architect) /*Franklin Toker*

the flattened lower slopes of the mountain, so that today one has the superimposed images of plastic mall architecture and the man-made peak that looms over it like a prehistoric mesa.

A mile away in the borough of Whitehall, just off Route 51, stands the **Holy Trinity Serbian Orthodox Church** (4920 Old Clairton Rd., SW corner Maxwell Drive; John Tomich, 1967–71). Neither ignoring nor slavishly imitating the historical precedents for Orthodox churches, Tomich fashioned a poured-concrete, Brutalist structure that has an extraordinary degree of self-assurance and nobility. The basic scheme is a rectangle with three apses—the venerable triconch plan used in the time of the emperors Constantine and Justinian—surmounted by two intersecting barrel vaults and a high watchtower. The facade has in addition an isolated barrel vault that recalls Alberti's S. Andrea at Mantua. The detailing is thoughtful and engaging—for example, in the thin panels of glass that separate the apses from the main rectangle. Not everything at Holy Trinity is successful: the interior effects were never resolved, and the social hall/school is perhaps too overtly modeled on the work of Louis Kahn. But the church is one of the most majestic buildings of postwar Pittsburgh, and it will endure when the ephemeral structures around it have returned to pasture.

The **Pleasant Hills Cloverleaf,** uniting Route 51 (Clairton Blvd.), Curry Hollow Road, and Lebanon Church Road, is the first of its genre in the region and probably among the first half-dozen in the nation (its dedication plaque, of 1939, quaintly calls it a "grade separation bridge"). Next to it stands another early milestone of Pittsburgh suburbia, the Bill Green Shopping Center, and south of it lies the borough of Pleasant Hills. While not large in population (about 10,000), **Pleasant Hills** stands out as the first Pittsburgh district to be developed entirely as tract housing, with a half-dozen projects between 1929 and the early 1970s. In its period of greatest growth, during the Eisenhower years, developers were putting a new home under roof every three days.

Along with the cloverleaf and the shopping center, Pleasant Hills has a third typically suburban component: the **Jefferson Memorial Park** (Curry Hollow Rd., one mile west of the cloverleaf), a motor-age cemetery from the 1920s that is considerably more restrained than Los Angeles' Woodlawn, but it is nonetheless filled with attractions to mitigate the atmosphere of death. Three of these attractions are architectural relics: the rebuilt but valid **Jacob Beam log house** of 1782; the stone-walled **John Work House** of about 1800; and, the sensation of the place, the resurrected portico columns of George Post's **Bank of Pittsburgh** from the Golden Triangle, rebuilt here in a tholos shape in 1956.

West of Pleasant Hills, the Yellow Belt changes its route name to Broughton Road, which borders the 2,000-acre **South Park** (main entrance from Baptist or Library Rds. to Corrigan Dr.). This magnificent greenspace and the twin North Park in the North Hills were established in the 1920s by the former mayor of Pittsburgh and county commissioner Edward V. Babcock, who (taking his cue from an earlier park pioneer, E. M. Bigelow) bought much of the land from his personal funds. South Park contains the pioneer **Oliver Miller Homestead** (Stone Manse Dr., just east of the Corrigan Dr. roundabout). The stone house, on Georgian lines similar to the profile of the Woods House in Hazelwood, was built by James Miller in 1808 on the site of his father's log house of a generation earlier. To its right is a later addition of 1830, with an enormous rubble chimney. The building was inhabited by five generations of Millers until 1927, after which the interior was preserved as a museum. In the late 1930s Franklin D. Roosevelt's Civilian Conservation Corps left a second architectural monument in South Park: **Fort Bonham** (McConkey Rd., west of Corrigan Dr.), a concrete-block park service center that dreams of being a French château and is altogether charming.

Oliver Miller Homestead, South Park /*Franklin Toker*

Bethel Park, Upper St. Clair, and Mt. Lebanon

Two itineraries lead from South Park to Bridgeville and the Chartiers Valley, which is the dividing line between the southern and western suburban districts of Pittsburgh. The shorter route passes through the boroughs of **Bethel Park** and **Upper St. Clair,** with their rich heritage of country farms and estates; the longer explores twentieth-century suburbia in Mt. Lebanon. Representative of Bethel Park is the wooden **Peter Bover House** (5679 Library Rd., 1.1 miles on Route 88 South from the South Park main gate), one of the richest Greek Revival private houses in the Pittsburgh district, with a striking two-level Ionic portico and meticulously carved details of the 1830s or 1840s. About a mile to the northwest stands **Bethel Presbyterian Church** (2999 Bethel Church Rd., 1.4 miles west of Route 88, at Marshall Rd.), the fifth building of a congregation that was organized here in 1776. Next to the church stretches a graveyard with fourteen tombs of Revolutionary War veterans. Pioneer days are also remembered nearby in the elegant brick **Marshall House** (3000 Oakhurst Rd., NW corner Marshall Rd.). Dating from 1838 (except for the anachronistic giant-order portico that was added in the 1930s), it was built by President John Adams's grandson George Marshall, who was then pastor of the church.

In Upper St. Clair, west of Bethel Park, a good number of early farmhouses survive amid the elaborate housing complexes of the 1970s and 1980s. The township symbol is one of them: the **1830 Log House** on McLaughlin Run Road, immediately west of the Route 19 overpass. A mile and a half farther west, toward Bridgeville, stand two of Allegheny County's most photogenic farm buildings: the **Tustin-Harrison House and Octagonal Barn** (2333 Lesnett Rd., south of McLaughlin Run Rd.). The clapboarded early Victorian farmhouse (c. 1840) is charming despite its aluminum skin. The Shaker-style barn, dated 1897, is an even more striking relic of Upper St. Clair's farming days.

The longer route to Bridgeville passes through **Mt. Lebanon** (six square miles in area, with a population of about 35,000), which is the archetype of

Tustin-Harrison house and farm, Upper St. Clair /*Franklin Toker*

St. Bernard's Church, Mt. Lebanon
/*Franklin Toker*

the wealthy Pittsburgh suburb. (Four roads—Library, Connor, Washington, and Bower Hill—are required for this itinerary, but one can follow them with directional ease, since all but the last are part of the Yellow Belt.) Settlement of the township began in the 1770s, when it was a tavern stop on one of the two routes between Pittsburgh and Washington, Pennsylvania. The population grew as access to Pittsburgh improved, with railroad tracks installed to the north and south in 1871 and 1878, a trolley link to Saw Mill Run added in 1902, and the streetcar tunnel cut under Mt. Washington to Pittsburgh in 1904.

The first large housing project constructed in Mt. Lebanon, in 1901, was urban rather than suburban in character, and it held close to the projected trolley line on Washington Road. The next wave of housing, following World War I, was east of Cochran Road and was designed for homeowners with cars. A third wave, in the 1920s and 1930s, created the luxurious homes of the Mission Hills, Virginia Manor, and Hoodridge/Terrace Drive districts. In these areas Mt. Lebanon's early street grid gave way to contoured streets, and the homes changed from standard builders' vernacular to Cotswold, neoclassical, or Federal designs. Despite their elevated prices, these homes were still part of a "development": most were designed by a half-dozen architects who were retained by the developers, and their stone and slate seems to have come from just a few quarries, possibly sources controlled by the developers. Successive complexes filled up the unbuilt areas of the borough between the 1940s and the 1960s, with infill projects still going on today. In all, about forty separate tract-housing plans have gone up in Mt. Lebanon in the past eighty years.

Mt. Lebanon's streetscape avoids monotony because the housing developments are broken up by several early homes (the best of these is the Greek
Revival **Snyder-Bockstoce House** of around 1835, at the edge of Mt. Lebanon Cemetery on Shady Drive East); by a variety of Art Deco and Tudor
Revival storefronts on Washington Road; and by three fine churches at the
summit of Mt. Lebanon Hill, within the triangle formed by Scott and Washington roads and the Mt. Lebanon Cemetery. The churches create a triplet of
variations in the so-called Second Gothic Revival style: the rock-faced **Mt.
Lebanon Methodist Church** (Charles W. Bier, 1923); **Mt. Lebanon United
Presbyterian Church** (J. Lewis Beatty, 1929), in English Decorated Gothic
style modeled on York Minster; and—the best of the group—the muscular
but delicately colored **St. Bernard's** (Comes, Perry & McMullen; 1933–47), in ,
transitional Romanesque-Gothic style.

Bridgeville, Carnegie, and the Parkway West

Mt. Lebanon's triad of churches stands opposite Bower Hill Road, a curving
route that descends 4.4 miles down the slopes of the Chartiers Valley. Around
1790, Brigadier-General John Neville built the richest mansion in western
Pennsylvania on Bower Hill, only to have it burned to the ground in 1794 by
farmers in the Whiskey Rebellion. (Neville, an aristocratic Virginian, had
earlier commanded Fort Pitt, but the farmers vented their fury at him in his
later capacity as collector of the excise tax on whiskey that was instituted in
1791.) Today the road leads without incident to **Bridgeville,** a lively old town
on a great bend in Chartiers Creek, set up originally between two eighteenth-
century bridges on the Washington Pike. To the north, the boroughs of
Heidelberg and Carnegie also occupy bends along the creek, whose name
derives from a French half-breed who set up a trading post at the mouth of this
valley in the 1740s.

Two miles north of Bridgeville, at 1375 Washington Pike (Route 50 East),
immediately before the entrance to Woodville State Hospital, stands **Woodville,** a log house begun by John Neville around 1780 at the center of the
7,000 acres he owned in and near the Chartiers Valley. Neville expanded the
house in the Tidewater Virginia hall-and-parlor tradition a few years later,
adding two bedrooms on the upper floor. The original log house was retained
as the kitchen, and its old fireplace was extended in a Y shape to serve two
adjacent rooms. Neville went on to build his ill-fated mansion on Bower Hill,
then lived out his days at his estate on Neville Island in the Ohio. Woodville
passed to his son Presley and his descendants, who added the early Gothic
Revival dormers and the gently swelling eaves that give the house a Mississippi or Tennessee profile. In 1973, after the house had passed through six
generations of Nevilles and the parlor had acquired sixteen coats of paint,

Left: "Woodville" /*Franklin Toker* ▪ *Right:* Sacred precinct: Ukrainian, black, and Russian Orthodox churches in Carnegie /*Franklin Toker*

Woodville was purchased by the Pittsburgh History & Landmarks Foundation. A charming touch to the house are the names and dates of guests that have been scratched in the glass since 1811. In 1825 a revolutionary-war commander visited the house to pay homage to Presley Neville, his former aide, and he, too, followed this custom. The glass pane he selected was lost or stolen a generation ago, but until then one could clearly read the signature of the Marquis de Lafayette.

Half a mile north of Woodville, on the east side of Chartiers Creek, stands another key monument of the pioneer days of Pittsburgh: **St. Luke's Episcopal Church** (SW corner Old Washington Pike & Church St.; reached by Greentree Rd.). This rustic Gothic Revival church in uncoursed masonry was constructed in 1851 as the third building of a congregation that was organized here around 1770. (James Van Trump attributes the design to John Notman, who was then in town for construction of St. Peter's Episcopal Church.) It is a skillfully crafted building with a charming board-and-batten wood vestibule (reproduced from the original according to photographs) and an impressively severe aspect inside.

One mile north of Old St. Luke's is the borough of **Carnegie,** the main industrial town of the Chartiers Valley, which was created in 1894 in the consolidation of the two settlements of Chartiers and Mansfield. The **Mansfield Brown House** of around 1820 or 1830, the severe stone Greek Revival home of the major landowner of the district, still stands near the center of town, at 602 Poplar Alley (reached by Washington Rd. & Trimble Ave., behind the Episcopal Church of the Atonement). At the heart of town, in a dense industrial and residential district, stands another of Titus de Bobula's exuberant churches: **Sts. Peter and Paul Ukrainian Orthodox Greek Catholic Church**

(200 Walnut, SE corner Mansfield Blvd.; 1906), a brilliantly crafted building of concrete and industrial brick with two side domes and a high central octagonal belfry that is crowned by a double onion dome. Churches for the black and Russian communities follow in a row to the west. The extraordinary feature of Carnegie is the Acropolis that rises just south of Main Street. Here the mill superintendents once lived, in elegant Colonial Revival houses that still stand on Beechwood and Library avenues. The slopes of the hill are eroded and overgrown with vegetation now, so that it does not make the clamorous topographic statement it must have made in the days of Peter Chartiers. But the Acropolis does feature a temple: Struthers & Hannah's Renaissance-style **Andrew Carnegie Free Library** of 1899.

At Carnegie there is an interchange of the **Parkway West** (a combination of Routes 279, 22/30, and 60), at which point Pittsburgh is five miles distant to the east, and the **Greater Pittsburgh International Airport** (Theodore Eichholz for Allegheny County, 1946–51) lies ten miles to the west. The construction of the airport and the Parkway in the early 1950s fueled an explosion of office building in what had been the least-developed area of the Pittsburgh region. High-tech companies began to build here soon after, either in the two office parks of the Regional Industrial Development Corporation, west and north of the airport, or in private clusters such as those of the Mobay Chemical Corporation, Penn Center West, Foster Plaza, or the Parkway Center. These buildings were the nucleus of a corporate suburbia that is physically close to but conceptually remote from the soot-blackened steel towns where many of the tenant firms had their beginnings.

The Ohio Valley: The West End, McKees Rocks, Sewickley, Ambridge, and Aliquippa

The Ohio River begins at the confluence of the Monongahela and Allegheny rivers, just as generations of schoolchildren were taught, but it does not *look* like the Ohio until a mile downriver from The Point, where it flows under the **West End Bridge** (Vernon Covell, engineer; George S. Richardson, structural engineer; 1930–32), with a striking 770-foot parabolic arch that seems to leap in the air above the river and the modest houses on its banks. The bridge connects the North Side and the West End, a section of Pittsburgh that contains a dozen hilly neighborhoods such as Elliott and Sheraden on a high plateau that was cut through over the centuries by the turbulent Chartiers Creek and the smaller but still treacherous Saw Mill Run. The West End developed as the beginning of the thirty-five-mile Steubenville Pike, which led

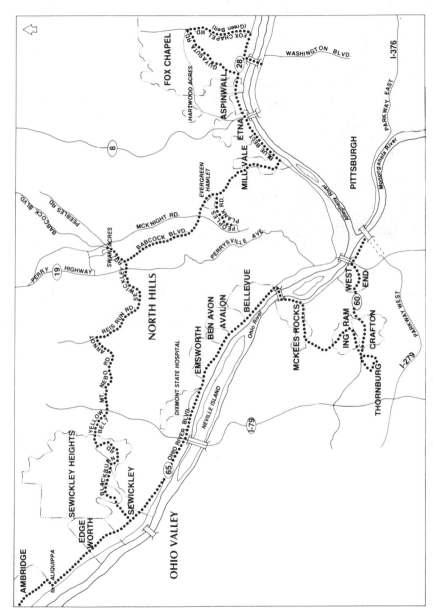

Map 26. The Ohio Valley and the North Hills

The West End Bridge /*Maurice Tierney*

from Pittsburgh along an old Indian trail across a narrow strip of Virginia (now West Virginia) to Steubenville, Ohio.

Steuben Street, the successor to the Steubenville Pike, leads directly from the West End Bridge to the lively urban neighborhood of **Temperanceville,** on the flats of a hill next to Saw Mill Run. Here once stood the water-powered saw that cut the logs for Fort Pitt in 1760, which was later joined by a saltworks, a glassworks, iron mills, oil refineries, and railroad shops. The reformers John Warden and John Alexander founded a refuge from alcohol here in 1837 and expanded it into the 100-acre village of Temperanceville ten years later. The experiment failed, of course, and observers noted that Temperanceville soon had more bars than any other part of the city. From Steuben Street it is a short drive via Chartiers and Lorenz streets to the attractive wood cottages on the hilly checkerboard grid at the upper portion of Temperanceville. At the top lies the improbably named **Rue Grande Vue,** which affords the broadest and best of all the views of Pittsburgh, particularly at dawn and in the late afternoon. Downtown Pittsburgh rises at the confluence of the three rivers to the right, Manchester lies directly ahead, and the Ohio River flows vast and broad to the left.

Crafton, Thornburg, and Ingram

The delightful situation of the Chartiers Valley, which cuts around the West End to link with the Ohio Valley at McKees Rocks, was confirmed as early as

1777, when Brigadier-General Edward Hand established a hospital on the Steubenville trail next to what is now the Crafton Athletic Field on Steuben Street, two miles beyond Temperanceville. Numerous other settlers followed, especially after the trail became an improved turnpike in 1818. The farming village along the Steubenville Pike transformed itself into a suburb in the 1860s, when James Craft abandoned his estate in Oakland—now Craft Avenue—and moved here. Craft promoted the building of the Pittsburgh, Chartiers & Youghiogheny Railroad through the valley and left a substantial tract of land to his son Charles, who laid out the village of **Crafton** around 1873.

West of Crafton, W. Steuben Street (Route 60 West) crosses a bridge high over the Chartiers Creek and resumes its historic name of Steubenville Pike. Immediately after the bridge, a road on the left leads to the idyllic early twentieth-century settlement of **Thornburg,** which was laid out in 1899 (probably on the model of New York's Tuxedo Park) by two grandsons of the Thomas Thornburg who had farmed 1,000 acres here in the days of the early Republic. With its score of ample mansions, curving streets named for early colleges, a direct rail link to Pittsburgh, and a private golf course, Thornburg was one of the prestige addresses of Edwardian Pittsburgh. Especially attractive today is a Shingle Style house at **1137 Cornell Avenue** (NE corner Hamilton; c. 1905), with its Queen Anne details, high Dutch gambrel roof, and striking cobblestone chimney. Remarkable too is the Colonial Revival mansion at **1080 Stanford Road** (NW corner Yale; C. E. Willoughby, 1906), which is a faithful copy of the Morris-Jumel mansion of 1765 in Harlem Heights. Farther uphill is the **Frank Thornburg House** (1132 Lehigh, NE corner Harvard; 1906), a handsome, pronouncedly horizontal Richardsonian Romanesque house that has an uncoursed fieldstone base but is shingled above in the manner of the Newport-area homes of McKim, Mead & White.

Ingram, on the Crafton side of Chartiers Creek, developed in the same way as Thornburg. Here it was Thomas Ingram who laid out a town in 1880 on the hill that his grandfather had bought as farmland in 1823. Ingram and W.

Left: 1137 Cornell Avenue, Thornburg */Franklin Toker* ▪ *Right:* High Victorian Gothic: 80 Berry Street, Ingram */Franklin Toker*

Prospect avenues are its two spine roads: the former in the valley and the latter high on a hill. The dramatic views over the Chartiers Valley induced several suburbanites to build elaborate Italianate and Gothic Revival villas on W. Prospect Avenue. The street dips at its west end to a sumptuous turn-of-the-century Colonial Revival home at number 315 that now serves as the **Allegheny Valley School—Patricia Hillman Miller Campus.** Another Ingram house of distinction stands high on a hill at **80 Berry Street,** a block and a half north of the intersection of Berry and W. Prospect. This cruciform-shaped summer house of the 1870s features a number of motifs from the High Victorian Gothic style, such as sunburst brackets, that seem to derive from the famous *vade mecum* of the Victorians, Charles Locke Eastlake's *Hints on Household Taste,* published in London in 1868 and republished with great success in Boston four years later. A half-block downhill from the house, Wind Gap Avenue intersects Berry and leads northwest in a breezy course through the quintessentially 1920s and 1930s neighborhoods of Sheraden and Wind Gap to the Wind Gap Bridge over Chartiers Creek and into McKees Rocks.

McKees Rocks

Not many visitors to Allegheny County stop to study **McKees Rocks.** Those who do will find it to be a marriage of a superb natural site and powerful industrial buildings, almost a paradigm of the Pittsburgh steel towns. The **rock** in McKees Rocks is a huge sandstone outcrop on the Ohio, so prominent that it was a rival to The Point as the location for Fort Pitt. When Colonel Alexander McKee received the rock as part of a 728-acre land grant in 1766, it consisted of both the natural formation and a mound that the Adena- and Hopewell-culture Indians had erected and used from the first millennium B.C. until after A.D. 500. The site was quarried for years and is now engirdled by an oil refinery and an asphalt plant. McKee enjoyed his rock only briefly, since he fled Pittsburgh as a Tory in the Revolution, but his brother James laid out a town on "The Bottoms" that became a major industrial center about 100 years later.

The packed streets of McKees Rocks, with their jumble of frame and brick homes, provide the perfect foil for its public and industrial architecture. A landmark of the upper town is **St. Mary's Church** (St. John St., south of Chartiers Ave., between Church St. and the Pittsburgh, Chartiers & Youghiogheny Railroad tracks; William P. Ginther, 1901), a Gothic Revival design with three needle spires and a facade of deep-toned brick. Less effusive but beautifully rendered is its **convent** (Comes, Perry & McMullen, 1930), a self-possessed stone building shaped like a medieval bishop's palace, which stands immediately next to the railroad tracks but is wholly oblivious to the twentieth century. Two blocks farther east stands **St. Francis de Sales Church** (810

Convent of St. Mary's Church, McKees
Rocks /*Franklin Toker*

Chartiers Ave., NW corner Margaret), a dramatic, if somewhat preposterous,
1899 design melding an Alberti-derived sandstone portico with a high nave of
irregularly coursed rock-faced stone and a cupola that miniaturizes the dome
of S. Maria del Fiore in Florence.

The McKees Rocks bottoms, where the busy railroad shops and ironworks
of a dozen firms used to be, is reached by a ramp at the start of the McKees
Rocks Bridge. The Pittsburgh & Lake Erie Railroad Yards here consisted of a
dozen buildings, of which the most impressive is the old **P&LE steam
locomotive repair shop,** a twenty-four-bay Roman basilica of around 1910
with grandly scaled thermal windows. The commercial strip of the lower town
was Helen Street, today a depressed area of bars, churches, and funeral homes,
but for fifty years a flourishing center for retail stores. Parallel to it on the west
is Munson Street, with the same kind of ecumenical sacred precinct that one
finds in Mt. Lebanon and Carnegie. Here stand St. Mark's church and convent,

P&LE steam locomotive repair shop, McKees Rocks bottoms /*Franklin Toker*

and **St. Nicholas Russian Orthodox Greek Catholic Church** (1914), marked by six onion-domed towers outside and a brilliant fresco treatment of the walls inside. Until 1980 the sequence concluded with a picturesque Baroque Revival synagogue next to St. Mark's, where there is now a park. The parting image of the town is the mile-long **McKees Rocks Bridge** over the Ohio (George S. Richardson, structural engineer, 1931), with its central through-arch of steel backing up against four noble pylons of stone.

Sewickley and Edgeworth

Ohio River Boulevard (Route 65 North, incorporating parts of the old road to Beaver) links the Brighton Heights neighborhood of Pittsburgh, opposite McKees Rocks, with **Sewickley,** eight miles downriver. The drive involves a dramatic mix of industrial and natural views through a district that was the heart of the Depreciation Lands that Pennsylvania parceled out in 300-acre lots to its unpaid revolutionary-war veterans in 1784. The boulevard—itself a dramatic work of 1920s engineering—borders the suburbs of Bellevue, Avalon, Ben Avon, and Emsworth, with their many large Italianate and Shingle Style homes. In the river is **Neville Island,** five miles of farmland so rich that as late as 1926 the old Waldorf-Astoria Hotel in New York featured Neville Island asparagus on its menu. The island experienced frantic industrial growth during World War II, when the Dravo Corporation launched hundreds of landing craft from its shipyards here. By the 1970s there were more than fifty different firms in heavy industry on the island. Today these plants are either vacant or dedicated to other uses, and only the blast furnaces of Shenango Incorporated represent the old days. Beyond Emsworth, on a high rise above the Ohio River Boulevard that is reached by Huntington Avenue, stands the former **Dixmont State Hospital,** built in 1862 by the Pittsburgh architect Joseph W. Kerr for the mental-health pioneer Dorothea Dix. Three miles downriver from Dixmont, the old Beaver Road splits from Ohio River Boule-

Left: Pine Road villas, Sewickley */Franklin Toker* ▪ *Right:* "Newington" */Franklin Toker*

vard, passes several blocks of fine High Victorian Gothic and Shingle Style homes, and enters Sewickley.

Sewickley—the collective name for the three interlocking boroughs of Sewickley, Edgeworth, and Sewickley Heights—is the only place in the western half of Pennsylvania that is approved for habitation by *The Official Preppy Handbook*. Sewickley was a river town of the late eighteenth century that prospered as a summer refuge when the railroad reached it in 1851, and soon it became an autonomous Victorian settlement. Its two main monuments today are its churches: **St. Stephen's Episcopal** (NW corner Frederick Ave. & Broad St.; Charles M. Bartberger, 1894), a vigorous uncoursed brownstone approximation of early English Gothic, and **Sewickley Presbyterian** (SE corner Grant & Beaver Sts.; Joseph W. Kerr, 1859), a regularly coursed, hammer-dressed design of austere Gothic with an elegant and airy country-church interior.

Like Shadyside in the city, the scores of homes in Sewickley constitute a virtual museum of mid-Victorian design. Among the more notable homes is a handsome Gothic cottage of the Civil War period with picturesque irregular turrets and gables, at **66 Beaver Street** (SW corner Beaver & Grant), opposite the Presbyterian church. Diagonally across from St. Stephen's Church, at **246 Broad Street,** is an elaborate Italianate clapboarded and shingled villa of 1877. Alongside the same church are two excellent Gothic Revival cottages: a board-and-batten wood frame house at **422 Frederick** (1845) and the Atwell-Christy House at **403 Frederick** (1862), an intimately proportioned Gothic Revival cottage of tightly lapped vertical wood siding. Unusual and charming are the four identical **Smith Houses** (Peebles St., south of Beaver St., between Thorn & Graham), constructed around 1872 for four sisters. Each varies slightly in detail but keeps to a basic plan of a main block with a central tower and polygonal bays extending left and right. At the two ends of the village, on Nevin Avenue and Pine Road, are some of the newer homes of Sewickley, including neo-Shingle Style bungalows of the 1920s.

Pine Road, just north of Sewickley Presbyterian Church, extends northeast from Beaver Street as a link to the elegant, tree-lined **Woodland Road** in the neighboring borough of **Edgeworth.** The homes on Woodland bear distinguished architectural pedigrees from such society architects as Charles Barton Keen and Benno Janssen, but they are relatively new, from the 1910s and 1920s. The older homes of Edgeworth line the Beaver Road, a block closer to the Ohio shore. The **John Way House** at Beaver and Quaker roads dates from the Federal period, around 1810, with a Greek Revival addition; the adjoining **Abishai (Nicholas) Way House** (108 Beaver, at the entrance to Edgeworth) is an elegant Greek Revival home of 1838. The Ways resided in these homes for generations and still live nearby. Even more conservative is the six-generation ownership of **Newington** (SW corner Beaver Rd. & Shields Lane). Daniel Leet of Washington, Pennsylvania, surveyed all of Edgeworth in

1776, when it was claimed by Virginia, and again in 1783–84 as part of the Depreciation Lands of Pennsylvania. Pennsylvania gave the Newington estate to him for services rendered, and he passed it on to his son-in-law, David Shields. Shields built the modest first block of Newington in 1816, then added a large Federal house seven years later. It was this house and its luxurious eleven acres of gardens that set the model for the grander homes that the iron-and-steel barons later built on the Sewickley hills, much as Judge Wilkins's mansion was the lightning rod that drew many of them to establish their city homes in Point Breeze. Wilkins, however, enjoyed Homewood only for thirty years, while the Leet/Shields family has been at Newington for more than two hundred. The clan worships together one block to the south, at the **Shields Presbyterian Church** on Church Lane (Joseph W. Kerr, 1869), and their dead are buried all together in the Romanesque Revival **Shields Mausoleum** next door.

Ambridge (Economy) and Aliquippa

It is hard not to lapse into clichés at the contrast between the austere homes of the communitarian settlement of **Economy** at **Ambridge,** on the right bank of the Ohio, and the massive scale of the Aliquippa Works of LTV Steel, directly opposite on the left bank. But the difference between these neighbors is less than meets the eye, because Pittsburgh's passion for industry affected even the Utopian ideals of Economy, which became one of the important industrial centers of the early Republic. The story of Economy begins with the emergence of George Rapp as leader of the pietistic Harmony Society in Württemberg, Germany, around 1785. Rapp brought his flock to America in 1803, and from 1805 to 1815 a few hundred of them lived on 9,000 acres of land centered at the town of Harmony, twenty miles northeast of here. The Harmonists then migrated to New Harmony, Indiana, where they lived another decade before selling to a fellow Utopian, Robert Owen. They settled at Economy in 1824 and had all their buildings up by 1831; the architect was Father Rapp's adopted son, Frederick.

The fervor of Economy proved to be more commercial than spiritual. Here and in nearby satellites, the Harmonists operated some of the first steam-driven textile mills in America, flourished in the wine and distilling trades, and even began drilling for oil immediately after Drake at Titusville. The society owned stock in five different railroads and soon amassed so many shares in the Pittsburgh & Lake Erie Railroad that it could install its leader, Jacob Henrici, as president in 1881. A celibate sect, the Harmonists died out rich but depopulated in 1905, by which time the American Bridge division of U.S. Steel had built the world's largest bridge and structural steel and fabricating plant over much of their land. Pennsylvania took over the remaining dozen buildings of Economy in 1919, and Charles Stotz restored them twenty years later.

Left: Granary at Economy (Ambridge) /*Franklin Toker* ▪ *Right:* The Feast Hall, Economy /*Franklin Toker*

The publicly accessible buildings of the Harmonists are bounded by Ohio River Boulevard and Thirteenth and Church streets in Ambridge, near several score more Harmonist houses that are now in private hands. The buildings are in the finely proportioned Federal style that was in vogue when the sect came to America in 1803, but they are overlayed with touches of German vernacular. This mix is immediately recognizable in the village chapel, now **St. John's Lutheran Church,** with its distinctive bell-shaped dome over an otherwise standard American Protestant church body. The **Granary,** in which the colony kept a full year's supply of food for the coming of the Millennium, has a half-timbered stone base that is also a medieval German throwback. In addition, there are workshops, stores, dormitories, the **Feast Hall** (where the 800 adherents would gather for "love feasts" about eight times a year), a formal garden, an herb garden, and the **Great House** of Father Rapp.

Two blocks south of Economy, the Eleventh Street Bridge crosses to **Aliquippa** on the opposite shore of the Ohio and to the astonishing mass of the **Aliquippa Works** of LTV Steel. This four-mile-long facility occupies 725 acres of a total site that extends seven miles toward Monaca at the bend of the Ohio River. It was built in 1907–12 and was several times extensively modernized.[4] It had five blast furnaces and was a totally integrated process, with its

4. The town of Aliquippa has always been secondary to the steelworks, but even in its current depression it is an interesting phenomenon. Its chief monument, copying Carnegie, is the **B. F. Jones Memorial Library** (663 Franklin St.; Brandon Smith, 1929), an exquisite Renaissance marble and limestone *palazzetto.* The town was laid out by the J&L land company in thirteen districts, each with a specific house type. The districts matched the number of ethnic groups in the hierarchy of the mill.

LTV steelworks, Aliquippa (1984) /*Courtesy LTV Steel*

own coke ovens, blast furnaces for making pig iron, steel furnaces, and a cold rolling mill that spun out sheet steel at the speed of seventy miles an hour. It regularly employed 14,000 workers, and as late as 1981 it shipped out three million tons of steel a year. Today all but a fraction of it is shut down. It would be simplistic to speculate here how such a disaster could have overtaken this magnificent steelworks so suddenly, but the architectural history of the plant suggests that its rise was as quick as its fall. Before 1907 Aliquippa had been a small village called Woodlawn, whose only attractions were a small steelworks and an amusement park that was run by the P&LE Railroad. When J&L took over the site in 1907, it temporarily placed its administrative offices in what had been the dancehall of the amusement park. Three-quarters of a century later they are still there.

The North Hills: Sewickley Heights, Evergreen Hamlet, Millvale, and Fox Chapel

The term "North Hills" specifically refers to the postwar suburbs in and around McCandless, Hampton, Ross, and Shaler townships, but by extension it also applies to the two dozen boroughs and townships that lie within the obtuse angle formed by the intersection of the Ohio and Allegheny rivers. Its population is about 150,000, smaller than that of the eastern or southern suburbs, but growing at a faster pace. The growth of the North Hills may be measured by certain milestones: the transformation of the old Venango Indian trail into the Franklin Road or Perry Highway (Route 19) in 1809, the opening of the Butler Road (Route 8) in 1823, the construction of the railroad to Erie in 1864, a local oil boom from 1890 to 1915, the creation of North Park in 1927, and the paving of the McKnight Road commercial strip in the 1930s.

Sewickley Heights

The population of **Sewickley Heights,** a mile inland from the Ohio, is well under 1,000, but it is important as the wealthiest local suburb per capita and among the most affluent in the nation. It is difficult to view the buildings of Sewickley Heights, because its homes are set far back from the stone walls and wood fences that line its country roads. A suggestion of its past and present opulence is, however, afforded by a two-mile drive on Blackburn Road (the Orange Belt), which passes the half-dozen servants' houses of **Fairacres,** the B. F. Jones estate on the left. On the right is **Wilpen Hall,** the William Penn Snyder estate, which is best viewed from Water Works Road, just south of the intersection of Blackburn and Scaife roads. George Orth, who designed Wilpen in 1898, perhaps had in mind the image of Noah's Ark at rest on the mountain peaks of Ararat. It is a huge Shingle Style mansion at the top of its own hill, with brownstone walls and shingled gables that rise over a rough stone base and are capped by a mammoth Dutch gambrel roof and a dozen chimneys. From this point, Scaife Road winds back 1.3 miles through a score of other estates to rejoin Blackburn as it meanders east to the I–79 expressway.

One of the major fixed points of the North Hills is the intersection of Route 19 and Three Degree Road, where a stagecoach inn stood 180 years ago. (The

Wilpen Hall, Sewickley Heights /*Franklin Toker*

intersection is reached by car from Sewickley Heights via the Yellow Belt, Reis Run Road, and the Green Belt, through 5.5 miles of woods, hills, and streams.) Babcock Boulevard, an early motorcar road from the F. Scott Fitzgerald years, passes a quarter of a mile east of Route 19 and links several sites of national importance. **Swan Acres,** a quarter-mile uphill on Babcock from Three Degree Road, became fleetingly famous across the United States in the 1930s as the first all-Modern housing development in the nation. The original twelve of these thirty-six houses were built between 1934 and 1936, mainly to the designs of Pittsburgh architect Harry C. Clepper, and set on thirty-five acres of wooded drives. These homes have the unadorned walls, flat roofs, glass block, casement windows, and rounded corners that were the hallmarks of the International School of the 1920s and the 1930s. Each is different (prices varied from $12,000 to $22,000), but most homes relate to a basic formula. The home at **111 Circle Drive** is unusual in being of stone rather than concrete, and **127 Circle Drive** is different from the rest in being derivative of Frank Lloyd Wright in its brickwork and intersecting planes. Forgotten today even in Pittsburgh, and looking somewhat timid compared to the radical Modern of Le Corbusier in the same years, Swan Acres is still a fascinating note to the nationwide battle of architectural traditionalists and modernists between the wars.

Evergreen Hamlet

It is a fitting historical coincidence that the ground-breaking Swan Acres lies just 3.7 miles north of another epochal community on Babcock Boulevard: America's earliest romantic suburb at **Evergreen Hamlet** (Rock Ridge Rd., just before the intersection of Babcock Blvd. and Evergreen & People's Plank Rd.). The question of when and where Americans created a community that was neither urban nor rural is of major significance for our social history. The usual answer is that the first true suburb in America was Alexander Jackson Davis's Llewelyn Park of 1853 in West Orange, New Jersey. That colony appears to have trailed behind Evergreen, however. At Evergreen, seven lots were purchased in 1851, and four homes were ready the next year. Although the Evergreen experiment parallels Thoreau's communion with Nature at Walden Pond in the same years, its leaders were major industrialists and not philosophers. Among them were the iron barons William Scaife and William Shinn and the oilmen Samuel Kier, Robert Sellers, and Wade Hampton.

Unlike the earlier extensions of the Golden Triangle into the fresh air of The Hill or Oakland, Evergreen Hamlet was a suburb in every sense. Its isolation on a mountaintop six miles from Pittsburgh had been decided both for the social benefits of the eighty-five-acre site and for its picturesque view of the Allegheny Valley 250 feet below. It was laid out (by Heastings & Preiser of

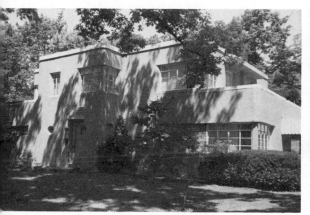

Left: Swan Acres /*Franklin Toker* ■ Right: Hill House, Evergreen Hamlet /*Franklin Toker*

Pittsburgh) in conformity with the natural contours of the hill. Nor was it a summer colony: the businessmen of Evergreen Hamlet left it every morning and returned each evening—as American commuters have done ever since.

Just four villas were constructed at Evergreen before disharmony tore the colony apart. The architect to whom the four have been attributed is Joseph W. Kerr, but their real author formally and spiritually was Andrew Jackson Downing, particularly in his *Treatise on the Theory and Practice of Landscape Gardening* (1841), his *Cottage Residences* (1842), and *The Architecture of Country Houses* (1851). Downing's books paint the picture of Americans living harmoniously with Nature in villas that expressed their personal individuality. The villas at Evergreen Hamlet fit that program exactly. The **Hampton** and **Sellers houses** are four-square Regency villas of formidable bearing inside and out, although the latter has a relaxing latticework verandah. The **Shinn House** is a more adventuresome building, almost a Swiss chalet, with drooping bargeboard ornaments and a pronounced verticality to its board-and-batten frame construction. The design is an amalgam of various A. J. Davis plans that Downing had published. (The cross-gable roof was an important element in the Gothic Revival home, because the sign of the cross was thought to ensure domestic purity and growth.) Grander than the rest is the **Hill House,** again in board-and-batten and correctly painted in pastels rather than the white that Downing despised. It is nonetheless a big and formal house, with a library and parlor opening left and right of the central hall to create a cross-axis fifty-seven feet long. The plan mixes features of two different plans in Downing's *Country Houses,* but the author seems to have been aware, too, of Joseph C. Wells's much-admired Roseland Cottage in Woodstock, Connecticut (1846), in the detail of the twin pseudo-gables on the sides. There seem to be a number of references to Jefferson's Monticello as well. All four villas are beautifully maintained, and a visit to Evergreen is mandatory preparation for a trip to America's foremost villa at Fallingwater, for Wright, too, was a child of the mid-Victorian passion to escape the city.

Millvale

The final two-mile stretch of Babcock Boulevard follows Girty's Run to the south, over six little bridges from Evergreen Hamlet to the worker suburb of Millvale. Millvale's residents are mainly Central European, particularly Croatian, in origin. They left two monuments here: their own homes, perched tenaciously on the sides of a valley that opens like a vast amphitheater on the Allegheny River shore, and the frescoes inside **St. Nicholas Roman Catholic Church** (24 Maryland Ave., reached from the Blue Belt via Grant & Sheridan Sts.; Frederick Sauer, 1901 and 1922). The frescoes were executed by the Yugoslav painter Maximilian Vanka in 1937–38 and (after a break attributed to his torment by a ghost on the scaffolding) in 1941. In these vivid scenes, executed in true fresco, Vanka combined Socialist realism, the Expressionism of his Mexican contemporaries such as Orozco, and traditional Byzantine iconography. Among the most affecting scenes are those in the short transepts, showing the disasters befalling Croatia in the twentieth century: war and death in the homeland, and explosions and starvation amid the blast furnaces of Pittsburgh.

The parallel town to Millvale, two miles up the Allegheny, is **Etna** (reached by Route 28 North on the Blue Belt), from which a side excursion of six miles may be made up Route 8 and Saxonburg Boulevard to Allegheny County's cultural center at **Hartwood Acres.** Mary Flinn Lawrence's 629-acre estate boasts elaborate stables and a mansion in Stockbroker Tudor by Alfred Hopkins (1929); it has played host to as many as 50,000 spectators at its free concerts. After **Sharpsburg,** which is the next town up the Allegheny and the

Millvale /*Franklin Toker*

scene of H. J. Heinz's first triumph, the Blue Belt crosses over the Highland Park Bridge into Pittsburgh, while the Green Belt continues upriver to Fox Chapel.

Fox Chapel

Fox Chapel is regarded as the second wealthiest of Pittsburgh suburbs, and it is the greenest and loveliest to visit. In terms of urban development it is not its wealth that is remarkable, but the rapidity with which it assembled all the urban institutions that usually take generations for new towns to develop. Like Sewickley, which is a downriver replica of old Allegheny City, Fox Chapel replicates the East End of Pittsburgh as it was on the eve of World War I. It began as part of the Depreciation Lands of 1784, but within a generation nearly all of it fell within the 1,200-acre estate of the financial speculator (and U.S. Senator) James Ross. The chapel donated in 1889 in memory of the early settler John Fox was the nucleus of the future suburb. Today its replacement, the **Fox Chapel Methodist Church,** marks the north end of the borough. This first church spawned two others: the neo-Georgian **Fox Chapel Presbyterian,** at the crossing of Fox Chapel and Field Club roads, and **Fox Chapel Episcopal Church** on Squaw Run Road East, which was originally a house designed by the society architect Brandon Smith, a disciple of Stanford White. Secular institutions migrated from the city along with the spiritual: the Pittsburgh Field Club (1915), Shady Side Academy (1922), the Fox Chapel Golf Club (1923), and the Pittsburgh Hunt Club (1926). Several of their buildings can be inspected on a two-mile drive along the Green Belt North on Fox Chapel Road.

"La Tourelle," the Kaufmann House in Fox Chapel (Benno Janssen, architect) /*Franklin Toker*

The homes of Fox Chapel are secluded in the woods, but a score of Colonial Revival and other traditional-style structures are visible west of Fox Chapel Road on Field Club Road and its continuation (as Guyasuta Road) southwest of Squaw Run Road. Here, particularly on the steep hill south of Guyasuta, are dozens of superbly rendered homes by Brandon Smith, Theodore Eichholz, and Benno Janssen, in front of which one expects at any moment to see Douglas Fairbanks, Greta Garbo, or even the great Gatsby. The best of them is **La Tourelle,** Janssen's 1922 fantasy for Edgar Kaufmann, which resembles three different fragments of a Cistercian monastery that some giant has randomly stuck together.

The fantasy theme of the homes in Fox Chapel does not end there, but has an unexpected coda a half-mile to the west in Aspinwall. There, halfway down a steep hill from the intersection of Guyasuta Road and Center Avenue, stand the **Frederick Sauer houses** (615–627 Center Ave., just uphill from the Route 28 overpass), which is the most bizarre collection of buildings in western Pennsylvania. Sauer was one of the many German-born or German-origin architects who dominated the middle ranks of Pittsburgh designers early in this century. He was educated in Stuttgart but came from Heidelberg, and one look at these houses on their steep hillside by the water makes clear that he carried the image of the ruined castle of his hometown with him all his life.

Sauer came to Pittsburgh around 1880 and built a dozen Catholic churches here. In 1904 he began to construct rental properties on this plot of land, acting as his own designer, mason, bricklayer, and carpenter. Sauer started conventionally with the house at 625 Center, which is made of ordinary Kittanning brick in a four-square Colonial Revival mode. He continued to build through the 1920s and 1930s, with each new structure more fantastic than the last. His usual materials were irregularly coursed stone and yellow brick, to which he added hundreds of strange inserts—lopsided keystones, turkeys and eagles, roundels of Benjamin Franklin, lions and Roman gods— that contribute to the fantastic nature of this miniaturized village. The buildings are a little more stolid than the supreme American fantasy structure, Simon Rodia's Watts Tower in Los Angeles, but only because they had to serve a practical purpose. Each apartment grows in an easy organic manner out of its designated materials and out of its hillside niche, until the whole group culminates in a fantastic mailbox that seems to have been made by bands of hobbits from J. R. R. Tolkien's The Lord of the Rings.

Opposite: Frederick Sauer houses, Aspinwall /*Franklin Toker*

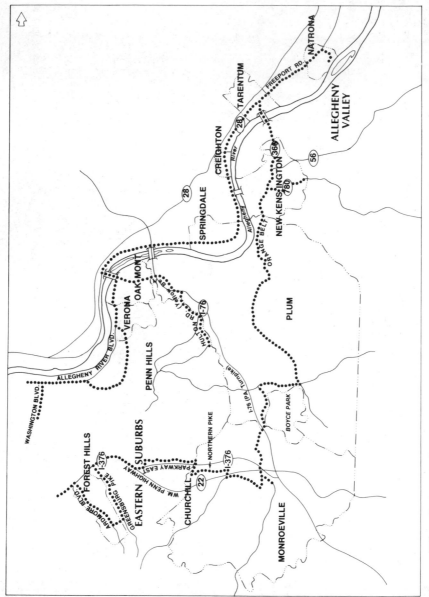

Map 27. The Allegheny Valley and the eastern suburbs

The Allegheny River: Verona and Oakmont in the distance /*Franklin Toker*

The Allegheny Valley: Oakmont, Natrona, and New Kensington

The Allegheny is neither so heroic a river as the Ohio, nor so important to industry as the Monongahela, but it is more beloved by boatmen, who delight in sailing or cruising its swift-flowing waters. It is a visual delight for motorists also: from Pittsburgh it is best approached by Washington Boulevard, which snakes through Negley's Run toward the river like a tributary. At the river's edge it joins Allegheny River Boulevard (Route 130 South, on the Green Belt), for an easy passage of five miles to Verona and Oakmont. One can take the boulevard directly to Oakmont, or leave it at Nadine Road to see the Allegheny Valley from the high grounds of the **Longue Vue Club** (imme-

The Longue Vue Club, Penn Hills
(Benno Janssen, architect) /*Franklin Toker*

diately west of the intersection of Nadine & Lincoln Rds.; Janssen & Cocken, 1925). Longue Vue is one of Benno Janssen's most genial inspirations: a Cotswold-style rambling structure in the shape of a stretched and curved double H, with two bridge-tunnels that allow cars to pass through it to the parking lot in the rear. By turns formless and formal, the clubhouse rises at points in great peaked chimneys and elsewhere hugs low to its rolling ground. The walls are made of local sandstone, often thinly sliced like Roman bricks, and set in thick cement beds like a peasant farmhouse. The Vermont slate on the roof is likewise thick and richly textured. The whole building is brilliantly choreographed, and it was probably this work that led Richard King Mellon to choose Janssen for his opulent Rolling Rock lodge at Ligonier a year or two later.

Oakmont

Three miles upriver from Longue Vue is the railroading town of **Verona,** whose name is a melodic corruption of that of James Verner, the entrepreneur who laid out the town. A mile beyond is **Oakmont,** which also began as an industrial settlement by the river but developed into an elegant residential quarter. The gracious homes on Hulton Road include a half-timbered house by Brandon Smith at **728 Hulton,** the Colonial Revival **Wade House** at 833 Hulton, and a much-reworked Frederick Scheibler stucco home of 1907 at **1204 Hulton.** The glory of Oakmont, diagonally opposite the Scheibler house, is the **Oakmont Country Club** (Edward Stotz, architect; Henry Fownes, course designer; 1904). Oakmont became famous within the international golf world within a few years of its opening because of the treacherousness and speed of its clay-based course. The PGA Open has been held here once, the USGA six times.

Hulton Road extends 2.7 miles inland beyond the club to a fork with Unity Road in Penn Hills Borough. A tenth of a mile south of this fork, on Unity Road, lies the **Newfield Mine,** a bituminous deep-shaft coal mine with a half-dozen Romanesque Revival basilical structures that date from 1921. One of the few mines still operating in the county, it is an affecting monument to the industry on which the prosperity of the district was once based.

From Oakmont, the Yellow Belt crosses to the north bank of the Allegheny River on the Hulton Bridge, then curves briefly along the north shore of the Allegheny on Freeport Road. Four miles upriver and a little inland is the borough of **Springdale.** At the shore itself stands the huge steam-generating plant that the West Penn Power Company built here to take advantage of water transportation and the presence of a coal mine directly across the river. The extraordinary monument of Springdale is, however, not the plant but the **Rachel Carson House** (613 Marion Ave., near the NE corner of Colfax St., at

Left: The Newfield Mine /*Franklin Toker* ▪ *Right:* Rachel Carson House, Springdale /*Franklin Toker*

the top of Colfax Hill). This charming frame farmhouse was built by Rachel Carson's ancestors in 1840 at the center of their forty-three-acre farm. Carson was born here in 1907, graduated from high school in nearby New Kensington in 1925, and took her science degree from Chatham College in Squirrel Hill. The house is preserved as it was when she left it in the 1920s. It is a low-ceilinged house with tiny bedrooms, and it presents the same forthright integrity as its famous occupant. Carson did not write her epochal *Silent Spring* of 1962 here, but the site undoubtedly served to raise her ecological consciousness. The hilltop provides a striking view of the green mantle of the opposite side of the Allegheny Valley, which is despoiled only by the red-and-white striped smokestack of the Springdale power plant. The plant that spoils this sylvan view was put up in 1920, when Carson was at the impressionable age of thirteen.

The bend in the Allegheny River beyond Springdale was the cradle of three important American innovations of the nineteenth century: plate glass (Creighton), oil (Natrona), and aluminum (New Kensington). Glassmaking was an ancient technique that had resisted automation and large-scale production before its center transferred to Pittsburgh. Here for the first time it was fired by coal, and later by natural gas, and here many of the critical steps toward mechanization were taken (all the machines that produced Coca-Cola bottles were made in Pittsburgh, for example). It was the presence of coal mines on both sides of the Allegheny that led the directors of the new Pittsburgh Plate Glass firm to build their huge glassworks at **Creighton** in 1883. In the fifty buildings that once employed 6,000 workers here, PPG became the world's first successful producer of plate glass. The old mills with their high-peaked roofs (to dissipate the intense heat) have been leveled to accommodate a new glass plant, but a dozen of the old company houses still stand nearby on Ferry and Railroad streets.

"Pigeon Row," Natrona /*Franklin Toker*

Natrona

Four miles east of Creighton (reached by Spring Hill Road from Natrona Heights, on Old Route 28) is **Natrona,** America's first oil producer and an excellent example of an early Victorian company town. In 1850 the Pennsylvania Salt Manufacturing Company set up an important plant here for the production of caustic soda through the heating of salt brine (the town name derives from the Greek word for salt). The location was ideal, with both coal and good salt wells nearby, and the Pennsylvania Railroad had built its tracks over the bed of the Pennsylvania Canal in the center of town. Along with its industrial buildings, Penn Salt constructed about 150 houses in wood and brick between 1850 and 1857. For nearly a century the company rented the homes to its employees, then sold them in 1941 when it left town. Most of the homes are still standing, wedged between the river, the towering plants of the Allegheny Ludlum Steel Corporation at either end of town, and a massive slag heap inland. The oldest units stand on Blue Ridge Avenue, facing the tracks. Long, grim row houses of brick, they are an unintentional parody of the elegant Philadelphia streets that the company founders had left behind. The wooden houses, particularly those on Federal Street ("Pigeon Row" to the residents) are almost unimaginably small, with just two rooms below and one above, but they are detached and bespeak a certain independence in their gabled peaks and (where not covered) their vertical board-and-batten siding.

The salt wells of Natrona were also the birthplace of the American oil industry a decade before Titusville. In 1849, annoyed at the petroleum seeping into his wells, the industrialist Thomas Kier helped his son Samuel bottle it as "Kier's Petroleum or Rock Oil." Young Kier sold what he could of the petroleum as medicinal oil and as a lubricant, then began in 1853 to refine it as an illuminant, producing twenty-five barrels of "carbon oil" a day at his still on Grant Street in the Golden Triangle. The next year he pumped oil out of wells in Natrona and Tarentum that were 400 feet deep; six years later he was exporting oil as far away as London. Although Edwin Drake, attracted by Kier's success, brought in oil in much greater quantity at Titusville in 1859, the heart of the industry in its early years lay in the refineries of Pittsburgh. It was the Mellons' familiarity with the local oil business that induced them to prospect for oil on a vastly greater scale with their Gulf operation in Texas.

New Kensington

Aluminum was first produced in Pittsburgh not because the city had bauxite or hydroelectric power, but because Pittsburgh entrepreneurs agreed to back Charles M. Hall's new process after Boston capitalists had rejected it. In 1891, three years after its first beginnings in The Strip, Alcoa moved to a giant plant in **New Kensington.** The reduction operations later left Pittsburgh for Niagara Falls, Tennessee, and Canada to obtain cheaper electricity, but the finishing plant remained here until after World War II. Today, Alcoa's operations in and around New Kensington are mainly in research, but there remains one unique monument of the years when it employed 7,000 workers here: the once-famous **Aluminum City Terrace** of Walter Gropius and Marcel Breuer (reached from Natrona and Tarentum via Route 366 South; then on Route 780 East uphill to East Hill Drive).

Much of the fame that Gropius enjoyed when Harvard University brought him to the United States derived from his 1920s housing estates at Dessau and Berlin, yet this is the only such project he managed to build once he got here. Constructed in 1941 for wartime workers in the aluminum plant, it reflected its low budget ($3,200 per unit) in its austere use of brick and wood and in the spartan dimensions of each unit. Gropius and Breuer broke the 250 units into 38 rows that are scattered at random over the uneven ground. These International School rows reflected the clarity and unblinking rigor of the European designers, but in 1962 they were radically Americanized: the backs of the rows were transformed into fronts through the addition of porches and the designation of private gardens; the inefficient wooden sunshades were replaced in aluminum at the same time. With these changes, the residents in effect became their own architects, and today the unit owners (it is now a cooperative) are delighted with their homes. The restructuring of Aluminum City Terrace may thus be regarded as a conflict between its European architects and its American residents, but one can see it less drastically as a partnership between them in forging what Gropius sought all his life—a community.

Aluminum City Terrace, New Kensington (Walter Gropius and Marcel Breuer, architects) /*Franklin Toker*

Cross Roads Presbyterian Church,
Monroeville /*Franklin Toker*

The Eastern Suburbs: Monroeville, Penn Hills, and Churchill

So much of importance to Pittsburgh has come from the east—the British troops that conquered it, the railway that transformed it, the immigrants who peopled it—that one would expect its eastern suburbs to be its oldest and most settled district. While there is much that is old here, not everything is settled in this still-growing seven-mile stretch between the city border and the Pennsylvania Turnpike. Even Plum Borough (reached directly from New Kensington on the Orange Belt), one of the oldest settlements in the county, is so sparsely populated that it still has large stands of virgin forest. The passage through Plum is a lovely one: the road follows a series of creeks, and rabbits, chickens, and deer peek out from the farmlands and woods.

Monroeville, at the southern border of Plum, at first appears to be all highways and shopping centers (one of these, the Monroeville Mall, was immortalized in George Romero's film *Dawn of the Dead*). Five highways cut through the borough: the Pennsylvania Turnpike, the Parkway East, the William Penn Highway, and the superseded Old William Penn Highway of 1924 and the Northern Pike of 1810. On the Northern Pike (at one point also called Monroeville Boulevard) stands Monroeville's key historic site: the **Cross Roads Presbyterian Church** (NE corner Monroeville Blvd. & Stroschein Rd., one mile west of the Orange Belt). A congregation was organized on this hillock in 1836, with the farmer Andrew Mellon—grandfather of A.W.—as one of its elders; the cemetery next to the present church dates from a generation earlier. The current church building is not particularly old or distinguished, but it is a hearty survivor and resists the encroachment of three high-speed boulevards, several fast-food outlets, a trailer park, and the high-

Left: The Sri Venkateswara Temple, Penn Hills /*Courtesy* Pittsburgh Post-Gazette (*V. Campbell, Jr.*) ▪ *Right:* Beulah Presbyterian Church, Churchill /*Franklin Toker*

tech gloss of a neighboring office block. Immediately west of the church, the path of the Northern Pike has been obliterated by later highways, but by crossing a small bridge over Route 22 opposite the Municipal Building, one finds a good stretch of the old road and even the **Rising Sun Stagecoach Inn** of 1827, a major pike stop that is now a doctor's office at 3835 Northern Pike. The old road proceeds west, toward Pittsburgh, for a delightful mile and a quarter of country road, until its intersection with Thompson Run Road.

Both the **Beulah Presbyterian Church** and the **Sri Venkateswara Temple** were built by pioneer congregations: the former in 1837 on the hill on which their ancestors first gathered to pray in 1758; the latter by the Indian scientific and professional community of Pittsburgh in 1979. Coming from Monroeville, one reaches the temple first (S. McCulley Road, left off Thompson Run Road). It stands in **Penn Hills** on the forested west slope of the cool and humid Thompson Run valley. It was the second Hindu temple in the nation when it opened; a third was built five years later, also in Pittsburgh, on Illini Drive in Monroeville. The model here was the Tirupathi shrine from seventh-century southern India; the Pittsburgh variant is dedicated to the Lord Venkateswara, best known in the West as Vishnu or Krishna. The two spire-towers, or *sikhara,* and the two domes are made of inch-thick stucco over a brick and concrete base. When the sun catches the encrusted walls, they light up as a white-hot fire. Inside, a skylighted atrium leads to the central sanctuary and three recessed shrines for the images of Vishnu and the goddesses Padmavathi and Andal. A lotus pond completes the temple in the conch of the hill below.

The elaborateness of the temple contrasts well with the sturdy lines of Beulah Church three miles to the west (Beulah & McCrady Rds., at the **Churchill** interchange of the Parkway East; reached from the temple via Old

The Westinghouse Atom
Smasher, Forest Hills /*Franklin
Toker*

William Penn Highway and Rodi Rd.). Here the British troops made their last
encampment before marching on Fort DuQuesne in November of 1758. A
contingent that remained here to tend the cattle supply for Fort Pitt built a
church and laid out a graveyard in the years following. The graveyard was
already in use by 1773, and thirty-four veterans of the revolutionary war were
later buried there. The Flemish-bond brick walls, the gentle slope of the roof,
and the two-door arrangement of the facade show that the builders of the
present church thought in terms of the old Federal style, although the Greek
Revival makes its appearance in the slender window frames. It is one of the
perfect works of architecture in the Pittsburgh region—sensitively cradled in
the earth, superbly proportioned, and vigilantly preserved. Most of the glass
panes are original, and the only concession to modern taste are the cushions
on the hard wooden pews.

The main industry of the eastern suburbs today is thinking. George Westinghouse put a premium on research in his plants in the Turtle Creek Valley a
century ago, and as the ranks of manual workers in the valley declined, the
number of scientists and engineers at the nearby Westinghouse laboratories
grew to many thousands. Much of their work now is in nuclear energy, in
which Pittsburgh is a world leader. One of the crucial milestones in this work
is the **Westinghouse Atom Smasher** of 1937, decommissioned but reverently
preserved in the old Westinghouse Research Laboratories in Forest Hills. (The
atom smasher is easily, if incongruously, reached from Beulah Church: a half
mile west on William Penn Highway, 2.6 miles south on the Greensburg Pike,
then downhill on West Avenue to its intersection with North and F avenues.
Avenues A and B lead from the atom smasher to Ardmore Boulevard, which
leads to the Parkway East and Penn Avenue in Wilkinsburg.) The atom
smasher—properly termed a Van de Graaff nuclear accelerator—is a benign-
looking steel tank shaped like an upturned pear. It was the first testing ground
for the industrial applications of nuclear physics, and it was used to observe
the action of particles that were shot through a vacuum tube at a speed of 100
million miles per hour. From it came the first fission of uranium atoms by

gamma rays, an important step in the science of nuclear energy. Building on the discoveries made here, in 1957 Pittsburgh became the world's first nuclear-powered city. It is providential that Westinghouse preserved the old atom smasher rather than scrapping it, as the steel firms did with their early blast furnaces. Today, Ground Zero at Hiroshima symbolizes the birth of the Nuclear Age. Some centuries from now, if the peaceful applications of the atom prevail over the military ones, the appropriate symbol may be this steel tank in Pittsburgh.

Fallingwater and the Pittsburgh Periphery

In strictly geographic terms, the Pittsburgh periphery includes the whole of western Pennsylvania, every part of which can be reached from Pittsburgh in a single day's excursion. Some of western Pennsylvania's cities and towns, such as Erie and Bedford, acknowledge only a marginal relationship to Pittsburgh, but most stand as figurative and sometimes literal reinforcements to the metropolis. The environment of the Pittsburgh periphery is rich and varied. It includes buildings by Louis Kahn and Frank Lloyd Wright, a sanctuary for Pittsburgh's rich at Ligonier, John Augustus Roebling's workshop at Saxonburg, an Amish colony at New Wilmington, and industrial landmarks at Shippingport and Titusville.

South and East

The lifeblood of the southeastern segment of the Pittsburgh region is Route 30, an Indian trail known to explorers as the Raystown Path and to colonial settlers as the Forbes Road, after its enlargement by British engineers in 1758. Greensburg, the seat of Westmoreland County, lies on this road thirty-one miles southeast of Pittsburgh. On Cabin Hill Drive in Greensburg, off Main Street, stands the fortresslike **Greensburg *Tribune-Review*** (1959–61) of

Tribune-Review offices, Greensburg (Louis Kahn, architect) /*Courtesy* Tribune-Review

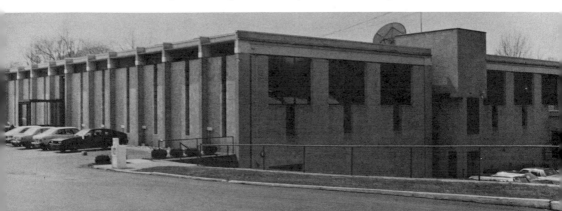

Fallingwater in winter /*Courtesy Western Pennsylvania Conservancy (Harold Corsini)*

Louis I. Kahn. Here America's most distinguished architect of the mid-twentieth century struggled with a sloping site and the need to integrate a printing plant and editorial offices. Kahn was not entirely successful in his design, but he was better at searching for answers than finding them, and the building is a profitable lesson in the accommodation of functions, materials, and human responses to architecture. Nearby is the Westmoreland Museum of Art, which offers an excellent introduction to the arts of western Pennsylvania.

Seventeen miles farther inland on Route 30 lies **Ligonier,** heralded by the lush forests along Loyalhanna Creek. Fort Ligonier is a scholarly restoration of the stockade erected in 1758 by General John Forbes in his victorious march to take Fort DuQuesne, while the town itself is a Mellon-financed reconstruction of a western Pennsylvania settlement of preindustrial days. About a score of Mellon heirs and several hundred heirs to other Pittsburgh fortunes live around Ligonier or at nearby Laughlintown and Rector, on Route 381. The heart of this colony is the private Cotswold-style **Rolling Rock Club** on Route 381, designed by Benno Janssen in 1928 as the private retreat and stables of Richard K. Mellon. (Charles M. Schwab, the perennial outsider, built his lavish estate at Loretto, forty miles to the northeast. It is now a Franciscan convent.)

Twenty miles south of Rolling Rock on Route 381, beyond Mill Run, stands Frank Lloyd Wright's world-famous **Fallingwater.** (The house is seventy-one miles from Pittsburgh via the Pennsylvania Turnpike; maintained by the Western Pennsylvania Conservancy, it is open daily except Monday from mid-

April to mid-November. Reserve by calling 288–2777 in Pittsburgh, or 329–8501 at Fallingwater.) Probably the most influential house of the twentieth century, Fallingwater was designed by Wright for Edgar and Liliane Kaufmann in 1936–37 on a 1,500-acre estate on Bear Run that was originally an excursion spot for employees of Kaufmann's Department Store. Three miles farther south on Route 381, at Ohiopyle, the Youghiogheny River rushes through a narrow gorge that provides excellent white-water rafting, then meanders northwest to join the Monongahela River at McKeesport.

From Uniontown, the nearby seat of Fayette County, the road back to Pittsburgh features two more homes of special interest. The **Isaac Meason House** (1802; private but accessible) stands off of Route 119 at Mt. Braddock, about eight miles north of Uniontown. It is a lavish building, and the best remaining monument to the planting of late Georgian culture in western Pennsylvania. A cut-stone tripartite home with symmetrical outbuildings, the Meason house could easily pass for an English manor house in the age of Christopher Wren. Its owner was a pioneer ironmaster who specially imported the English architect Adam Wilson to design his showplace.

About ten miles north of Mt. Braddock, Route 119 passes through the depleted coalfields around Connellsville and forks left to the town of Scottdale. In the hamlet of West Overton, on Route 819 between Scottdale and Mt. Pleasant, lies the Abraham Overholt homestead, with the birthplace of **Henry Clay Frick.** Overholt, a Mennonite farmer made rich by his Old Overholt

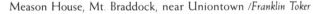

Meason House, Mt. Braddock, near Uniontown /*Franklin Toker*

Henry Clay Frick's birthplace (*right*) on the Abraham Overholt homestead, West Overton /*Franklin Toker*

whiskey, built an elaborate brick house here in 1838 and a large gristmill in 1859. Both still stand, as museums, together with the rustic stone dairy house in which his grandson Henry was born in 1849. A reconstructed coke oven recalls the thousands of ovens that Frick later built in the vicinity. The settlement is an affecting sight, not least because the shabby interior of the dairy house strikingly resembles the cramped home in which Frick's archrival Carnegie had been born a decade earlier, halfway around the world in Scotland.

South and West

The southwestern segment of the Pittsburgh periphery developed along two lines of communication: the Monongahela River and the National Road, or Pike. Route 837 parallels much of the Monongahela as it cuts through Pittsburgh's South Side and the steel towns of Homestead, Duquesne, and Clairton. The highway crosses the Monongahela at **Elizabeth,** a small but densely built-up village that flourished in the 1770s with the construction of flatboats. South of Elizabeth, the local road that hugs the east bank of the Monongahela is so little used that a visitor may think it is the trace of some forgotten Roman *via*. The route is nonetheless a lively mix of old river towns such as Belle Vernon and Monongahela (on the opposite shore) with the newer industrial towns of Donora, Monessen, and Charleroi. The eighteenth century reasserts itself at **Brownsville,** a fort and trading post laid out as a town in 1785. Brownsville was an important Monongahela River port as well as a main stop on the National Pike. It declined with the coming of the railroad, but its transitory wealth is still apparent in three remarkable structures: a cast-iron bridge of 1839, the rugged Gothic Revival St. Peter's Catholic Church of 1845, and the curious Nemacolin's or Bowman's Castle, an eccentric remake of a trading post of the 1790s. Twenty miles south of Brownsville on Route 166, still on the Monongahela River, lies **New Geneva,** where Albert Gallatin, Secretary of the Treasury under Jefferson and Madison, established an early glassworks and gun factory. These declined, but Gallatin's elaborate home at Friendship Hill (1789) survives.

The twenty-four miles on Route 40 from Brownsville to **Washington,** the seat of Washington County, covers a well-preserved stretch of the National Pike. Ordered by Congress in 1806 and completed within Pennsylvania by 1818, the Pike eventually stretched from Baltimore almost to St. Louis. Washington, laid out in 1781 (nine years before Washington, D.C.), is a distinctive hill town full of Greek Revival and Shingle Style homes. The main building of Washington and Jefferson College dates from 1793, while Frederick Osterling added the effusive Washington County Courthouse in the middle of town in 1900.

North and West

Less industrialized than the southern and eastern quadrants, the northern and western districts of the Pittsburgh region keep alive the pioneer phase of western Pennsylvania. At **Avella,** forty-seven miles southwest of Pittsburgh on Route 50, several dozen pioneer buildings have been imaginatively reassembled at Meadowcroft Village. The pioneer spirit is manifest also in the Amish country around **New Wilmington** in Lawrence County, an hour's drive northwest of Pittsburgh on routes I–79 and 208. Neighboring Butler County features two more pioneer settlements: **Zelienople,** laid out by a German baron in 1802, and **Harmony,** where a cemetery and a cluster of brick and log houses remain from the extensive Harmonist colony of 1805 (both on Route 68, west of the I–79 exit).

Like its farm colonies, the industrial colonies north and west of Pittsburgh have a pioneer quality about them, too. The most interesting in Butler County is John Augustus Roebling's **Saxonburg** (routes 8 and 387 from Pittsburgh), where Roebling's original wire rope manufactory of 1840 still stands. Beaver County, to the west, preserves another cluster of early industrial installations near the confluence of the Ohio and Beaver rivers at **Beaver Falls** and **New Brighton,** in addition to the Harmonist workshops at Ambridge, discussed earlier. The whole district between the Allegheny and Ohio rivers proved especially fertile to industry. A few miles from Beaver Falls, at **Shippingport,** the world's first nuclear-fueled electric power plant for commercial use started up in 1957, while an hour and a half to the northeast lies **Titusville,** where Edwin Drake ushered in the oil age in 1859. The Pittsburgh periphery is altogether a remarkable region, rich in inventiveness as well as in natural riches, and the perfect foil to a remarkable city.

Good Friday in Allentown (Mt. Washington) /*Courtesy* Pittsburgh Post-Gazette (*Tony Tye*)

A Pittsburgh Calendar

Pittsburgh has a thousand rituals that give every resident and visitor the chance to participate in its social life. Some of those civic ceremonies and events are listed here.

January

1 ▪ New Year's Day; the Sewickley Hunt Club holds a morning fox hunt amid the estates of Sewickley Heights.

7 ▪ Julian calendar Christmas, a major event in Pittsburgh; impressive Christmas mass with full choir at Holy Trinity Serbian Orthodox Church, Whitehall.

13 ▪ Stephen Foster died in 1864; commemorative service at the Temple of Memories, Allegheny Cemetery, Lawrenceville.

February

Lent ▪ North America's only indigenous passion play, *Veronica's Veil*, presented throughout Lent at St. Michael's Church, South Side.

March

(For Easter events, see April)

17 ▪ St. Patrick's Day; parade on Fifth Avenue, Golden Triangle.

April

Palm Sunday ▪ Gorgeously painted *pysanka* eggs are sold at Sts. Peter and Paul Ukrainian Orthodox Church in Carnegie.

Good Friday ▪ Calvary procession on Mt. Washington from St. George's Church, Allentown.

Easter Sunday ▪ The doors to the Mellon tombs are opened; East Liberty Presbyterian Church, East Liberty.

Third Friday ▪ Spring Carnival at CMU, with traditional buggy race on Frew Street, Schenley Park.

10 ▪ The Great Fire broke out in 1845; old city-hall fire bell is rung at the Historical Society of Western Pennsylvania, Oakland.

23 ▪ Shakespeare's birthday; CMU drama students garland his statue at Carnegie Institute, Oakland.

May

Late May ▪ Greek Food Festival at St. Nicholas Greek Orthodox Cathedral, Oakland.

Memorial Day ▪ Band and parade to veterans' graves at Voeghtly Cemetery on Troy Hill.

Memorial Day weekend ▪ Pittsburgh Folk Festival of ethnic dancing, folklore, and food at Lawrence Convention Center.

June

First weekend ▪ Smoky City Folk Festival (traditional American folk music and dance); Flagstaff Hill in Schenley Park.

Mid-month ▪ Three Rivers Arts Festival at Point State Park, Gateway Center, Market Square, PPG Place, and elsewhere downtown.

13 ▪ Feast of St. Anthony of Padua at his miracle-working shrine on Troy Hill.

16 ▪ Bloomsday; James Joyce celebration at the Irish Room, Cathedral of Learning, Oakland.

July

4 ▪ Fireworks at The Point and in Arsenal Park, Lawrenceville.

August

First weekend ▪ The Pittsburgh Three Rivers Regatta; steamboat races and aquatics at The Point, Station Square, and North Shore.

Mid-month ▪ Antique car races in Schenley Park, Oakland.

23 ▪ Feast of St. Roch; St. Michael's Church celebrates "Cholera Day" for cessation of plague on the South Side in 1849 and 1854.

September

Labor Day ▪ Parade and evening jazz concert at The Point.

First or second week ▪ Open house at Allegheny Observatory in Riverview Park, Perry Hilltop.

Last Sunday ▪ Great Race for joggers, Frick Park to The Point.

October
Steeler Sundays ▪ Tailgate parties at Three Rivers Stadium, North Side.

First half ▪ Jewish festival of Sukkoth brings out hundreds of wooden booths on porches and yards in Squirrel Hill.

Mid-month ▪ Haunted Pumpkin Patch and Mummy Catacombs transform Phipps Conservatory, Oakland.

November
Mid-month ▪ Light-up Night in the Golden Triangle, with sensational views from Mt. Washington, Perry Hilltop, Fineview, and the West End.

December
First week ▪ Christmas trees on Pittsburgh themes and Sarah Mellon Scaife's dollhouse go on view at Carnegie Institute, Oakland.

Mid-month ▪ Allegheny West Candlelight House Tour, North Side.

7 ▪ Willa Cather born in 1873; birthday dinner (by invitation) in her Pittsburgh home on Murray Hill Avenue, Squirrel Hill.

25 ▪ Christmas mass with Croatian hymns at the richly frescoed St. Nicholas Church, Millvale.

31 ▪ New Year's Eve celebration with Duquesne University's Tamburitzans dance troupe at Heinz Hall.

Pittsburgh in a Day

Pittsburgh is a small big city, and it is so well defined that it is possible to tour the whole of it by car or to sample significant parts of it on foot in a few days. A tourist or businessperson who is still more hard-pressed for time can even grasp the essential structure of the city in a day. Visitors with several days available should devote a full day to a walking tour of the Golden Triangle and of Oakland, following the first two chapters of this book. The succeeding four chapters on the main urban neighborhoods (the South and North sides and the Penn Avenue and Fifth Avenue clusters) require about half a day each by car. The itineraries outside the city demand a minimum of half a day each.

Pittsburgh can be viewed quite effectively by bus. Bus 54C rambles through the North Side, part of the Penn Avenue district, and much of central Oakland and the South Side. Bus 61C begins in the Golden Triangle, passes The Hill and The Bluff, cuts through Oakland and Squirrel Hill, then visits a number of steel towns in the Monongahela Valley. (Call PAT information, 412/231–5707, for schedules on these and other routes.)

Finally, Pittsburgh can be seen in a single day. The day should begin on foot in the Golden Triangle. Two hours will suffice—without dawdling—to view Fort Pitt, PPG Place, Fourth Avenue, Mellon Square, and Grant Street. Two more hours by car will cover the following itinerary: Fort Duquesne Bridge over the Allegheny River to Allegheny Avenue in Manchester, circle back through Manchester to Allegheny West, then through the Mexican War Streets in Old Allegheny to the Ninth Street Bridge and back to the Golden Triangle. Next, drive through The Strip on Penn Avenue and Railroad Street (AVRR), switch from Liberty Avenue to Polish Hill at Twenty-eighth Street, cross through The Hill on Herron Avenue into the University of Pittsburgh campus in Oakland. Here a tour of the Cathedral of Learning and Carnegie Institute will require two hours, plus lunch. To explore Squirrel Hill, drive west on Fifth Avenue, past Rodef Shalom Temple, to Woodland Road. Return on Fifth Avenue to the Birmingham Bridge and cross the Monongahela River to the South Side. Drive east on E. Carson Street, take the McArdle Roadway to Grandview Avenue on top of Mt. Washington, and return via E. Sycamore Street and the Smithfield Street Bridge to the Golden Triangle. The trip will take about nine hours.

Pittsburgh Resources

Museums, Galleries, and Libraries

Blatant Image Gallery, 431–1810 ▪ Carnegie Institute (Fine Arts & Natural History), 622–3172 ▪ Carnegie Library of Pittsburgh, 622–3131 ▪ Carnegie-Mellon University Art Gallery, 268–3110 ▪ Circle Gallery, 687–1336 ▪ Clay Place, 441–3799 ▪ Concept Art Gallery, 242–9200 ▪ Frick Art Museum,371–0600 ▪ Gallery G, 562–0912 ▪ Hillman Library, University of Pittsburgh, 624–4437 ▪ Historical Society of Western Pennsylvania, 681–5533 ▪ Hunt Library, Carnegie-Mellon University, 268–2444 ▪ The Mattress Factory,231–3169 ▪ Mendelson Gallery, 621–0159 ▪ Pittsburgh Center for the Arts, 361–0873 ▪ Society for Art in Craft, 828–6121 ▪ University Art Gallery, Frick Fine Arts Building, University of Pittsburgh, 624–4121 ▪ Westmoreland Museum of Art, 837–1500 ▪ Wiebe & Bonwell Gallery, 765–3444.

Lectures and Readings

Carlow College, 578–6089 ▪ Carnegie-Mellon University, 268–2900 ▪ Chatham College, 365–1140 ▪ Community College of Allegheny County, 237–3060 ▪ Duquesne University, 434–6124 ▪ Hemingway's Café, 621–4100 ▪ International Poetry Forum, 621–9893 ▪ Pitt's Informal Programs, 624–6829 ▪ Pittsburgh Council for International Visitors, 682–6151 ▪ University of Pittsburgh, 624–4147 ▪ World Affairs Council of Pittsburgh, 281–7970.

Music and Dance

American Wind Symphony, 681–8866 ▪ American Dance Emsemble, 391–4100 ▪ Bach Choir, 941–1459 ▪ Calliope House, 322–6359 ▪ Carnegie-Mellon University Music, 268–2372 ▪ Carnegie Music Hall, 622–3131 ▪ Duquesne

University Taburitzans, 434–5185 ▪ Civic Light Opera, 281–3973 ▪ Frick Art Museum concerts, 371–0600 ▪ Gateway to Music, 421–2251 ▪ Hartwood Acres, 767–9966 ▪ Heinz Hall for the Performing Arts, 281–5000 ▪ Mendelssohn Choir of Pittsburgh, 561–3353 ▪ Music in Pittsburgh, 682–1746 ▪ Performing Arts for Children, 344–1813 ▪ Pittsburgh Ballet Theater, 281–0360 ▪ Pittsburgh Chamber Music Society, 624–4129 ▪ Pittsburgh Dance Alloy, 361–4414 ▪ Pittsburgh Dance Council, 355–0330 ▪ Pittsburgh New Music Ensemble, 244–9996 ▪ Pittsburgh Opera, 392–4900 ▪ Pittsburgh Oratorio Society, 422–7464 ▪ Pittsburgh Savoyards, 361–0873 ▪ Pittsburgh Symphony, 392–4800 ▪ Pittsburgh Youth Symphony, 392–4872 ▪ Renaissance and Baroque Society, 682–7262 ▪ Renaissance City Ballet, 363–4217 ▪ Renaissance City Woodwind Quintet, 421–2183 ▪ River City Brass Band, 322–7222 ▪ Syria Mosque, 621–8700 ▪ University of Pittsburgh Music, 624–4126 ▪ Y Music Society, 521–8010.

Theater and Film

American Ibsen Theater, 363–4565 ▪ Museum of Art, Carnegie Institute, Section of Film and Video, 622–3212 ▪ Carnegie-Mellon University Drama Department, 268–2407 ▪ The Famous Rider, 681–1476 ▪ New Group Theater, 682–3990 ▪ Pittsburgh Filmmakers, 681–5449 ▪ Pittsburgh Playhouse, 621–4445 ▪ Pittsburgh Public Theater, 321–9800 ▪ TIX, 391–8368 ▪ University of Pittsburgh Theater Department (City Theatre, Studio Theatre, Stephen Foster, Three Rivers Shakespeare), 624–4101.

Family Outings

Allegheny County Parks, 392–8455 ▪ Allegheny Jail tour, 255–2946 ▪ Allegheny Observatory, 321–2400 ▪ American Youth Hostels, 362–8181 ▪ Arden Trolley Museum, 734–5780 ▪ Beechwood Farms, 963–6100 ▪ Buhl Science Center, 321–4300 ▪ Duquesne Incline, 381–1665 ▪ Expo Mart, 856–8100 ▪ Fallingwater, 288–2777 ▪ Fort Pitt Museum, 281–9284 ▪ Gateway Clipper, 355–7980 ▪ Kennywood Park, 461–0500 ▪ Lawrence Convention Center, 565–6000 ▪ Meadowcroft Village, 587–3412 ▪ Nationality Rooms, Cathedral of Learning, 624–6000 ▪ Old Economy Village, 266–4500 ▪ Phipps Conservatory, 622–6915 ▪ Pittsburgh Aviary, 323–7234 ▪ Pittsburgh Brewery tour, 682–4441 ▪ Pittsburgh Children's Museum, 322–5058 ▪ Pittsburgh City Parks, 255–2676 ▪ Pittsburgh History & Landmarks Foundation, 471–5808 ▪ *Pittsburgh Press* and *Post-Gazette* tour, 263–1421 ▪ Pittsburgh Toy Lending Library,

682–4430 ▪ Pittsburgh Zoo, 665–3640 ▪ Round Hill Farm, 384–4701 ▪ Station Square, 471–5808 ▪ Tour-Ed Mine, 339–9947 ▪ Western Pennsylvania Conservancy, 288–2777.

Spectator Sports

Civic Arena, 642–1800 ▪ Duquesne Dukes, 434–6564 ▪ The Meadows Racetrack, 563–1224 ▪ Penguins, 642–1800 ▪ Pirates, 323–5000 ▪ Pitt Panthers, 624–4601 ▪ Robert Morris Colonials, 262–8296 ▪ Spirit, 642–1800 ▪ Steelers, 323–1200 ▪ Three Rivers Stadium, 321–0650.

Nightlife

Crawford Grill, 471–1565 ▪ The Decade, 687–7655 ▪ The Electric Banana, 682–8296 ▪ Graffiti, 682–4210 ▪ Harper's, 391–1494 ▪ Mancini's, 771–1166 ▪ Mirage, 281–0349.

Restaurants

African: Born Free, 362–1645 ▪ *All-night:* Brandy's, 566–1000 ▪ Primanti Bros., 263–2142 ▪ Ritter's, 682–4852 ▪ *American:* Century Inn, 945–6600 ▪ The Colony, 561–2060 ▪ *Atmosphere:* Angel's Corner, 682–1879 ▪ The Redwood, 379–6540 ▪ *Breakfast:* La Plume, 553–5065 ▪ Ruddy Duck, 281–5800 ▪ *Cajun:* Roland's, 261–3401 ▪ *Chinese:* Anna Kao's, 782–3010 ▪ Peking Royal Kitchen, 421–1920 ▪ Sichuan House, 563–5252 ▪ *In the country:* Brass Duck, 593–7440 ▪ 1844 Restaurant, 845–7771 ▪ Hyeholde, 264–3116 ▪ La Tache, 586–9340 ▪ Ligonier Country Inn, 238–3651 ▪ *Downtown dependable:* The Common Plea, 281–5140 ▪ Promenade and Stirling's, 391–4600 ▪ Tambellini-Woods, 281–9956 ▪ *Downtown quick but not fast:* Colonnade Cafeteria, 281–3420 ▪ Palmer's, 471–5366 ▪ *Drinks:* Brady Street Bridge Café, 488–1818 ▪ Chiodo's Tavern, 461–9307 ▪ Top of the Triangle, 471–4100 ▪ Upstairs at Brendan's, 683–5661 ▪ *East European:* Sarah's, 431–9307 ▪ *Elegant:* The Carlton, 391–4099 ▪ The Terrace Room, 553–5235 ▪ The Wine Restaurant, 288–9463 ▪ *Family:* Del's, 683–1148 ▪ Eat'n Park, 923–1000 ▪ Gullifty's, 521–8222 ▪ Red Bull Inn, 276–5200 ▪ Sodini's, 521–0581 ▪ Siciliano's, 221–6370 ▪ *Fish and seafood:* Benkovitz, 263–3016 ▪ Klein's, 232–3311 ▪ Poli's, 521–6400 ▪ Wholey's, 261–3693 ▪ *French:* Le Bistro and La Normande, 621–0744 ▪ Le Pommier, 431–1901 ▪

Simply French, 687–8424 ▪ *Greek:* Suzie's, 261–6443 ▪ *Ice cream:* Dave and Andy's Homemade, 681–9906 ▪ Pace's, 683–2780 ▪ The Real Scoop, 828–0770 ▪ *Indian:* India Palace, 563–7575 ▪ *Irish:* The Blarney Stone, 781–1666 ▪ *Italian:* Emilia Romagna, 765–3598 ▪ Pasta Piatto, 621–5547 ▪ Piccolo Piccolo, 261–7234 ▪ Un Poco di Roma, 833–9009 ▪ *Japanese:* Kabuki, 823–0750 ▪ Kiku, 765–3200 ▪ *Lunch:* Café Azure, 681–3533 ▪ Carnegie Institute Café, 622–3131 ▪ Dingbats, 392–0350 ▪ Tramp's, 261–1990 ▪ Vincent's, 621–2700 ▪ *Mesquite:* Hot Licks, 683–2583 ▪ *Mexican:* Casa Lupita, 835–4200 ▪ Tequila Junction, 261–3265 ▪ *Middle Eastern:* Ali Baba, 682–2829 ▪ *Mt. Washington view:* Christopher's, 381–4500 ▪ Cliffside, 431–6996 ▪ LeMont, 431–3100 ▪ *Natural foods:* Galioto's, 391–0472 ▪ The Upper Crust, 281–1600 ▪ *Shadyside chic:* The Balcony, 657–0110 ▪ Le Petit Café, 621–9000 ▪ *Sunday brunch:* The Grand Concourse, 261–1717 ▪ Hugo's Rotisserie, 288–9326 ▪ Nemacolin Woodlands Inn, 329–8555 ▪ *Vietnamese:* Kim's, 362–7019 ▪ Le Vieux Saigon, 621–7733 ▪ Wok Inn, 621–6400 ▪ *Waterside:* Figgins, 321–9000 ▪ Gateway Clipper ships, 355–7980 ▪ *Yuppie:* Chauncy's, 232–0601 ▪ Froggy's, 471–3764 ▪ Hoolihan's, 232–0302 ▪ Papillon, 343–1000.

Selected Hotels

The Bigelow, 281–5800 ▪ Hyatt Pittsburgh, 471–1234 ▪ Pittsburgh Hilton Hotel and Towers, 391–4600 ▪ Pittsburgh Marriott/Green Tree, 922–8400 ▪ Pittsburgh Marriott/Monroeville, 373–7300 ▪ Sheraton at Station Square, 261–2000 ▪ Viking Motor Inn, 531–8900 ▪ Vista International, 281–3700 ▪ Westin William Penn Hotel, 281–7100.

Bibliography

The following studies on the social and urban history of Pittsburgh were used in the writing of this book. Not listed here, but at least as important, were several hundred oral interviews with the architects, planners, patrons, and users of Pittsburgh's built environment. Among important written but unpublished sources were the Allegheny County Survey (see below) and the ephemera (clippings, atlases, photographs) at Carnegie Library and the Historical Society of Western Pennsylvania. On the methodology and resources for the study of Pittsburgh, see Toker and Wilson, *The Roots of Architecture in Pittsburgh and Allegheny County*, cited below.

Alberts, Robert. *The Good Provider: H. J. Heinz and His 57 Varieties*. Boston, 1973.
————. *The Shaping of the Point*. Pittsburgh, 1980.
"Allegheny County Survey," unpublished manuscript, 1979–1984, Pittsburgh History & Landmarks Foundation (copy at the Pennsylvania Historical and Museum Commission, Harrisburg; synopsis in Kidney, *Landmark Architecture*, 1985).
Baldwin, Leland. *Pittsburgh: The Story of a City, 1750–1865*. Pittsburgh, 1937.
Barnett, Jonathan. "Designing Downtown Pittsburgh," *Architectural Record*, January 1982, 90–107.
Bodnar, John; Roger Simon; and Michael Weber. *Lives of Their Own: Blacks, Italians, and Poles in Pittsburgh, 1900–1960*. Urbana, IL, 1982.
Boucher, John N., ed. *A Century and a Half of Pittsburg and Her People*. 4 vols. New York, 1908. A genealogy and history of 850 leading families.
Buck, Solon and Elizabeth. *The Planting of Civilization in Western Pennsylvania*. Pittsburgh, 1939.
Buvinger, Bruce. *The Origin, Development and Persistence of Street Patterns in Pittsburgh, Pennsylvania*. Pittsburgh, 1972.
Carnegie, Andrew. *The Autobiography of Andrew Carnegie*. Boston, 1920.
Collins, John. *"Stringtown on the Pike": Tales and History of East Liberty*. Ann Arbor, MI, 1966.
Couvares, Francis. *The Remaking of Pittsburgh: Class and Culture in an Industrializing City, 1877–1919*. Albany, 1984.
Demarest, David, Jr., ed. *From These Hills, From These Valleys: Selected Fiction about Western Pennsylvania*. Pittsburgh, 1976.
Engineering Society of Western Pennsylvania. *Pittsburgh*. Pittsburgh, 1930.
Fleming, George. *Pittsburgh: How to See It*. Pittsburgh, 1916.
Gay, Vernon, and Marilyn Evert. *Discovering Pittsburgh's Sculpture*. Pittsburgh, 1983.

Hessen, Robert. *Steel Titan: The Life of Charles M. Schwab*. New York, 1975.

Hoffmann, Donald. *Frank Lloyd Wright's Fallingwater*. New York, 1978.

Hopkins, G. M. & Co. *Atlas of the Cities of Pittsburgh, Allegheny, and the Adjoining Boroughs*. Philadelphia, 1872.

Ingham, John N. *The Iron Barons: A Social Analysis of an American Urban Elite, 1874–1965*. Westport, CT, 1978.

Jucha, Robert. "The Anatomy of a Streetcar Suburb: A Development History of Shadyside." *Western Pennsylvania Historical Magazine* 62 (1979): 301–19.

Kelly, J. M. *Handbook of Greater Pittsburg*. Pittsburgh, 1895.

Kidney, Walter. *Landmark Architecture: Pittsburgh and Allegheny County*. Pittsburgh, 1985.

————, and Arthur Ziegler, Jr. *Allegheny*. Pittsburgh, 1975.

Killikelly, Sarah H. *The History of Pittsburgh, Its Rise and Progress*. Pittsburgh, 1906.

Klukas, Arnold. "H. H. Richardson's Designs for the Emmanuel Episcopal Church, Pittsburgh." *American Art Review* 2/4 (July-August 1975): 64–76.

Long, Haniel. *Pittsburgh Memoranda*. Pittsburgh, 1935.

Lorant, Stefan. *Pittsburgh: The Story of an American City*. Garden City, NY, 1964, and rev. eds.

Lubove, Roy. *Twentieth Century Pittsburgh*. New York, 1969.

————. *Pittsburgh*. New York, 1976.

McLean, Robert, III. *Countdown to Renaissance II: The New Way Corporate America Builds*. Pittsburgh, 1984.

Miller, Donald, and Aaron Sheon. *Organic Vision: The Architecture of Peter Berendtson*. Pittsburgh, 1980.

Palmer, Robert. *Palmer's Pictorial Pittsburgh*. Pittsburgh, 1905.

Parton, James. "Pittsburg." *Atlantic Monthly* 21 (January 1868): 17–36.

Pennsylvania: A Guide to the Keystone State (Writers' Program, Work Projects Administration). New York, 1940.

Russell Sage Foundation. *The Pittsburgh Survey*. 6 vols. New York, 1909–14.

Schuyler, Montgomery. "The Buildings of Pittsburgh." *Architectural Record* 30 (September 1911): 204–82.

Spencer, Ethel. *The Spencers of Amberson Avenue*. Edited by Michael Weber and Peter Stearns. Pittsburgh, 1983.

Stotz, Charles. *The Early Architecture of Western Pennsylvania*. New York, 1936. Reissued as *The Architectural Heritage of Early Western Pennsylvania*. Pittsburgh, 1966.

Stryker, Roy, and Mel Seidenberg. *A Pittsburgh Album, 1758–1958*. Pittsburgh, 1959.

Swetnam, George, and Helene Smith. *A Guidebook to Historic Western Pennsylvania*. Pittsburgh, 1976.

Tarr, Joel. *Transportation Innovation and Changing Spatial Patterns in Pittsburgh, 1850–1934*. Chicago, 1978.

Thomas, Clarke. *They Came to Pittsburgh*. Pittsburgh, 1983.

Toker, Franklin. "Richardson *en concours*: The Pittsburgh Courthouse." *Carnegie Magazine* 51/9 (November 1977): 13–29.

————. "In the Grand Manner: The P&LE Station in Pittsburgh." *Carnegie Magazine* 53/3 (March 1979): 4–21.

————. "Philip Johnson and PPG: A Date with History." *Progressive Architecture* 60 (July 1979): 60–61.

————. "Reversing an Urban Image: New Architecture in Pittsburgh, 1890–1980." In

Sister Cities: Pittsburgh and Sheffield. Pittsburgh: Carnegie-Mellon University, 1986.

————, and Helen Wilson. *The Roots of Architecture in Pittsburgh and Allegheny County: A Guide to Research Sources.* Pittsburgh: Historical Society of Western Pennsylvania, 1979.

Urban Design Associates. *The Olden Triangle: A Sequence of Forgotten History.* Pittsburgh, 1977.

Urban Design International 5/1 (Spring 1984). Issue devoted to the urban design of Pittsburgh; papers by Jonathan Barnett, David Lewis, Robert Lurcott, and Franklin Toker.

Van Trump, James. *An American Palace of Culture: The Carnegie Institute and Carnegie Library of Pittsburgh.* Pittsburgh, 1970.

————. *Life and Architecture in Pittsburgh.* Pittsburgh, 1983. Contains numerous articles on Pittsburgh buildings.

————, and Arthur Ziegler, Jr. *Landmark Architecture of Allegheny County, Pennsylvania.* Pittsburgh, 1967.

Vexler, Robert. *Pittsburgh: A Chronological and Documentary History, 1682–1976.* Dobbs Ferry, NY, 1977.

Wall, Joseph. *Andrew Carnegie.* New York, 1970.

Warner, A., ed. *History of Allegheny County, Pennsylvania.* 2 vols. Chicago, 1889.

Wilson, Erasmus. *Standard History of Pittsburgh.* Chicago, 1898.

Works of F. J. Osterling, Architect, Pittsburg. Compiled by J. Franklin Nelson. Pittsburgh, 1904.

Index

Architects who have worked in Pittsburgh (including builders, engineers, landscape architects, and professional planners) and architectural styles are grouped collectively under those respective headings. The neighborhoods and ethnic communities of Pittsburgh are grouped under Pittsburgh. Page numbers in *italics* refer to illustrations.